Borderland Blacks

ANTISLAVERY, ABOLITION, AND THE ATLANTIC WORLD

R. J. M. Blackett and Edward Rugemer, Series Editors
James Brewer Stewart, Editor Emeritus

Borderland Blacks

Two Cities in the **NIAGARA REGION** during
the Final Decades of Slavery

dann j. Broyld

LOUISIANA STATE UNIVERSITY PRESS BATON ROUGE

Published by Louisiana State University Press
lsupress.org

Manufactured in the United States of America
First printing

DESIGNER: Michelle A. Neustrom
TYPEFACE: Minion Pro
PRINTER AND BINDER: Sheridan Books, Inc.

JACKET PHOTOGRAPH: Two young Black women posing in front of a faux backdrop featuring Niagara Falls. Rick Bell Family Fonds, RG 63, Archives & Special Collections, Brock University Library.

Portions of chapter 2 first appeared, in somewhat different form, in dann j. Broyld, "Rochester, New York: A Transnational Community for Blacks Prior to the Civil War," *Rochester History* 72.2 2 (Fall 2010): 1–23.

LIBRARY OF CONGRESS CATALOGING-IN-PUBLICATION DATA

Names: Broyld, dann j, author.
Title: Borderland blacks : two cities in the Niagara Region during the final decades of slavery / dann j. Broyld.
Description: Baton Rouge : Louisiana State University Press, [2022] | Series: Antislavery, abolition, and the Atlantic world | Includes bibliographical references and index.
Identifiers: LCCN 2021053992 (print) | LCCN 2021053993 (ebook) | ISBN 978-0-8071-7706-8 (cloth) | ISBN 978-0-8071-7768-6 (pdf) | ISBN 978-0-8071-7767-9 (epub)
Subjects: LCSH: African Americans—New York (State)—Rochester—Social conditions—19th century. | Blacks—Ontario—St. Catharines—Social conditions—19th century. | Borderlands—Niagara Falls Region (N.Y. and Ont.)—History—19th century. | Transnationalism—History—19th century. | Rochester (N.Y.)—Emigration and immigration—History—19th century. | St. Catharines (Ont.)—Emigration and immigration—History—19th century. | Rochester (N.Y.)—Social conditions—19th century. | St. Catharines (Ont.)—Social conditions—19th century. | Rochester (N.Y.)—Race relations. | St. Catharines (Ont.)—Race relations.
Classification: LCC F129.R79 B53 2022 (print) | LCC F129.R79 (ebook) | DDC 305.8009747/89—dc23/eng/20211220
LC record available at https://lccn.loc.gov/2021053992
LC ebook record available at https://lccn.loc.gov/2021053993

To the Creator, Elders, and Ancestors (especially Aunt Lois Jacobs Cole)
and for

Albertha Washington Broyld and Dennis J. Broyld Sr.

Contents

Illustrations

Acknowledgments

S cholarship is a collective effort—professional and personal. Therefore, I have relied on many people, institutions, and inspirations in order to construct *Borderland Blacks*. Rochester, New York, and the transnational lifestyle it provides, was a primary inspiration. Thank you very much to those from Howard University who first toiled with me to craft this study, including Dr. Eden Greene Medford. I have learned from your tenacity, professionalism, and attention to detail. Thanks also to Dr. Jeffrey R. Kerr-Ritchie, Dr. Emory J. Tolbert, Dr. John Walton Cotman, and Dr. Harvey A. Whitfield, a dynamic team of intellectuals who have directly advised and guided me.

I am also deeply indebted to Dennis Gannon. I genuinely could not have written this book without Dennis, Paul Hutchinson, Brian K. Narhi, Harvey Strum, Benjamin Talton, and Alison M. Parker. I am fortunate to have the very best of personal editors, Lisa Middendorf and Bill Hoelzel, and likewise for cartographer Mary L. Eggart. The Special Collections and Archives were indeed helpful at Howard University, Brock University (David Sharron and Edie Williams), University of Rochester, York University, University of Toronto, St. Catharines Museum, Rochester Public Library (Christine L. Ridarsky and Michelle Finn), St. Catharines Public Library, and the Toronto Public Library. The skilled staff helped me find documents I was seeking and introduced me to those I did not know existed. Louisiana State University Press, Rand Dotson, and AAAS Editors R. J. M. Blackett, Edward Rugemer, and James Brewer Stewart all made my dream come true.

To Katherine K. Reist and Paul D. Newman in the University of Pittsburgh–Johnstown's History Department: Thanks for giving me my first professional professor gig. To Fulbright Canada and Brock University's Marian Bredin, Ronald Cummings, Natalee Caple, and Elaine Aldridge-Low: My time at Brock, was special, I will sincerely never forget it. To my colleagues in New Britain, Connecticut, special thanks to Audrey Riggins, Ivan Small, Kathy Hermes, Juan Coronado, Matthew Warshauer, Gloria Emeagwali, Kate McGrath, and Robert Wolff. Central Connecticut State University Africana Center family Janet Woodruff, Evelyn Phillips, William Fothergill, Sherinatu Fafunwa-Ndibe, and Wangari Gichiru were a wonderful support to me throughout the writing of this book. And to my new colleagues at the University of Massachusetts Lowell: Chad Montrie, Chris Carlsmith, Robert Forrant, Lisa M. Edwards, and Michael Pierson. I look forward to interacting with the other members of the Department of History.

Also, I am grateful to the BME Church of St. Catharines—Salem Chapel's Rochelle Bush and the congregation as well as the Church of Love Faith Center—for guiding me on matters of the soul, teaching me to be a passionate member of the Rochester community, and providing me with so many extended family members I continue to rely on. My dear friends Aidah, Shadia, John Fossitt, Kareem J. Hayes, Brandon Williams, Chaun Horton, Cahlil Cherubin, Ka'Mal A. McClarin, Zakia Henderson-Brown, Oronde London, Darren Sands, and A. Canada Rollins have informed and grounded me. To my dearest Nicole R. Manuel, you are my love, light, letters, and lyrics.

The most important acknowledgments go to my family: siblings Dennis J. Broyld Jr., Quiana D. Broyld, Vashon J. Broyld Sr., as well as James B. Murray, Francis J. Clement, and Sha Brathwaite. My two nieces Kaylee and Valon and four nephews Vashon Jr., Dennis J. III, Konnor, and Donovan: You all are bright, beautiful, Afrofuturists who inspire me to write the best history I possibly can. I am blessed by godmother Linda Freeman and goddaughter Shaniyah Hicks. Mark Anthony Broyld and Tina Whittington: I know if no one else in the entire world ever reads this book, the two of you would. Special thanks to Wanda and Brittany Jacobs, Maria Rosa, Freedom, RaHa, Jenny, Tony and Tory Broyld, and Kelley Broyld; uncles William Earl, Gary L., and Lorenzo; aunts Bernice, Virginia, Patricia, Mary, Dorothy, Linda Sue, and Marnetta; and likewise to all the Broylds, Reeses, Washingtons, and Gillons too numerous to name. To the greatest parents I could ever want, I remain grateful for your correction, care, and love.

Borderland Blacks

Introduction

The underground railroad had many branches, but that one with which I was connected had its main stations in Baltimore, Wilmington, Philadelphia, New York, Albany, Syracuse, Rochester, [and] St. Catharines (Canada) . . . J. P. Morris and myself received and dispatched passengers from Rochester to Canada, where they were received by Rev. Hiram Wilson. When a party arrived in Rochester it was the business of Mr. Morris and myself to raise funds with which to pay their passage to St. Catharines.

   —FREDERICK DOUGLASS, *The Life and Times of Frederick*
     Douglass (Dover, 2003), 190–91

Written primarily from the office of his Cedar Hill home in Washington, DC, Frederick Douglass's final autobiography includes reflections on his work in Rochester, New York, during the mid-1800s. It was there that Douglass and local barber Jacob P. Morris helped hundreds of Blacks escape to British Canada. Once fugitive slaves reached St. Catharines, Canada West, the abolitionist and missionary Rev. Hiram Wilson helped them establish themselves on foreign soil.[1] These two cities, Rochester and St. Catharines, located at the end of the Niagara branch of the Underground Railroad, developed cross-national relations that benefited those on both sides of the border. This book will investigate the local dynamics and transnational connections of each city between 1800 and 1865, with a particular focus on the 1850s when the movement of Blacks was at its peak.

Borderland Blacks will also illuminate the social and geopolitical climate of Rochester and St. Catharines by analyzing each town within the larger context of the Niagara international region. This study reconstructs the lives of Black Borderlanders as they struggled to achieve greater rights and reconcile their common African heritage in transnational settings.[2] Historically, the Niagara district has been defined as the Niagara Peninsula on the Canadian side and

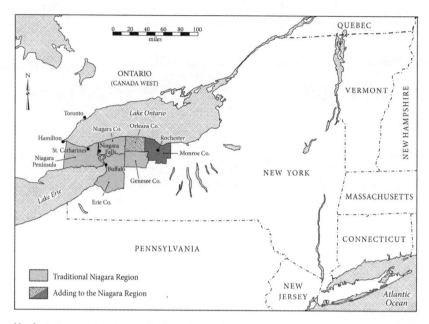

Map 1. The historical and expanded boundaries of the Niagara region. Map by Mary Lee Eggart.

Erie, Niagara, and Genesee Counties on the American side. This book argues for expanding the boundaries of the region to include the city of Rochester and the surrounding Monroe County (see map 1).[3] This choice is not based on the geography alone but more so on the human connections the two cities built over time and space. This approach rests on the idea that regions can be constructed, destroyed, and reconstructed, depending on the contextual circumstances. In the Niagara zone, Black commoners and abolitionists alike were familiar with the antislavery activists, institutions, and publications on each side of the border. The national divide did little to hamper the shared culture and interests in the area, and canals and railroads in the 1800s reduced distance and facilitated greater interaction. Blacks made use of differences in the territorial jurisdictions to achieve their personal and political objectives.

A COMPREHENSIVE FRAMEWORK FOR BORDERLANDS

In the past, historians have viewed Rochester and St. Catharines as singular local entities rather than recognizing the comprehensive borderland framework.[4] This study argues that Black inhabitants of each city possessed transnational

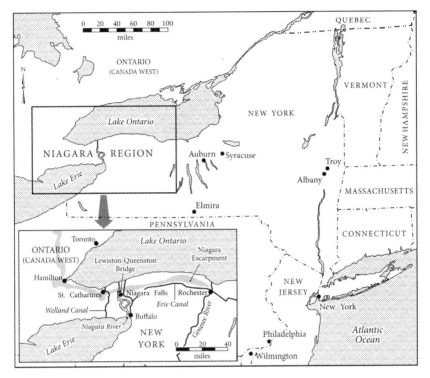

Map 2. Rochester and St. Catharines, connected via the Niagara Escarpment and Lake Ontario. Map by Mary Lee Eggart.

identities and strategically positioned themselves near the American-Canadian partition where immigration, movement, and interaction occurred.[5] It avoids a state-centered approach and embraces the ideas of scholars Pekka Hämäläinen and Samuel Truett that "borderlands history is far more than the sum of its local parts. In the end, it gives us a new way to navigate the past."[6] Some Blacks traveled across the international lines, while others were content to live in close proximity. Each side of the border presented unique social problems. Blacks in St. Catharines had clear legal advantages over Blacks in Rochester, but each city gave them options and opportunities that people in other places away from the border did not have. They lived within the fluid frontier intersection of the Niagara region where they could negotiate the contours of the United States and the British Empire.[7] These borderland Blacks did not isolate themselves from one another, nor were they burdened by one-sided state loyalty. Instead, they embraced a common struggle that transcended location and nationality.

As the last stops on the Niagara branch of the Underground Railroad, Rochester and St. Catharines handled substantial fugitive traffic in the early 1800s and were logical destinations for settling. They were regarded as progressive urban centers that addressed the social issues of their day—the abolition of slavery, women's rights, and temperance. Moreover, they were home to sizable free Black communities that were active and enterprising entities. Rochester and St. Catharines are physically affected by the Niagara Escarpment, connected via Lake Ontario, and separated by some 100 miles (160 kilometers) of land (see map 2).[8] Rochester benefited from the Erie Canal and St. Catharines from the Welland Canal that ran directly through them.[9] The canals brought in business and industry that vastly increased the size of the blossoming "Flower City" (Rochester) and "Garden City" (St. Catharines).[10] They moved passengers faster and more inexpensively. A trip on the Erie Canal, for instance, reduced a two-week stagecoach journey from Albany to Buffalo to five days and a trip from New York City to Buffalo went from $150 to as economical as one cent per mile for some boats. The trip from Rochester to St. Catharines could be achieved in as little as a day and a half once the Erie Canal opened. The Niagara region railroads, like the New York Central Railroad system and the Great Western Railway of Canada, soon eclipsed the canals and reduced travel times even more in the borderlands.[11]

NEW BRIDGES CONNECTING THE REGION

Each "boomtown" was a center of regional significance to inhabitants and transients, and the transportation links between them were further strengthened by the Niagara Falls Suspension Bridge, which spanned the Niagara Gorge, a natural barrier that separated America and Canada.[12] In 1845, the Honorable William Hamilton Merritt of St. Catharines, who served in the British Parliament and was called "the Father of Canadian Transportation," partnered with civil engineer Charles B. Stuart, who worked out of Rochester, to promote the building of the bridge.[13] The two men worked to build support for the project on both sides of the border. By early 1846, the *American Railroad Journal* reported that the suspension bridge venture "seems to be gaining favor daily," and Stuart boasted that an overpass would help people "either in going, or in returning" to Canada.[14]

The St. Catharines–Rochester team of Merritt and Stuart toiled to establish charters in their respective countries, gathered public support, and facilitated government approval to get the project underway. The edifice, which opened in 1848, allowed for pedestrian and carriage traffic, and trains began crossing on an upper deck in 1855. Once the top level was completed, the *Buffalo Morning Express* called the Niagara Falls overpass "one of the grandest accomplishments of modern engineering skill."[15] By 1860, an average of fifty trains a day and well over 50,000 carriages per year passed between the countries via the bridge.[16] Blacks, fugitive and free, unquestionably benefited from the ease of movement the overpass provided for those in each nation.

In 1851, the Lewiston-Queenston Suspension Bridge opened so people on foot or those with horse and buggy could cross for the same toll as the Niagara Falls Suspension Bridge—25 cents per person and 50 cents per wagon or passenger carriage.[17] Gatekeepers, however, often let fugitives traverse for free. The structure was praised by newspapers in both Rochester and St. Catharines for joining the United States and Canada. The *Rochester Democrat* explained that the overpass was a "magnificent structure . . . cheap and safe," while the *St. Catharines Journal* described an opening celebration where "the flags of both nations floated on the bridge."[18] The transportation developments in the evolving Niagara area were designed to encourage commerce and industry but, as a by-product, they enabled Blacks to pass easily between the two countries.[19] These structures highlight how advanced the Niagara region was over the greater Detroit "fluid frontier," where there was no overpass across the Detroit River to directly connect to Windsor, Ontario, until the Ambassador Suspension Bridge was completed in 1929.[20] Plus, with the exception of Buxton, the other Black Detroit frontier settlements were declining as Rochester and St. Catharines were steadily ascending. The Niagara bridges, in the mid-nineteenth century, became a symbol of the cohesive internationalism of the region, and they gave Blacks and especially fugitives new avenues for mobility, interaction, and transnational efficiency.

This robust Niagara zone, with its "spirit of improvement" and connective roadways, waterways, and railways between Rochester and St. Catharines, along with relaxed border-control, created "time-space compression" that nurtured a regional consciousness and social intercourse.[21] Too often, a one-way flow of fugitives on the Underground Railroad from America to Canada is the pervasive narrative, with Rochester a "sending" community and St. Catharines a "receiving" town.[22] The relationship, however, was far more complex, because two-way movement and social collaborations were common in this dynamic international zone.[23] Blacks shared newspapers, religious organizations, annual celebrations, and personal relationships, which were reinforced by frequent border crossings. These formal and informal exchanges make this study neither uniquely an American story nor separately Canadian, but it unites the nations' histories in a comprehensive manner. The interconnected circumstances of Blacks in the American North and Canada throughout the early 1800s were not restricted by national boundaries. Although Canada offered greater legal rights, the social belief in Black innate inferiority was a transcending sentiment on each side of the border.

SOCIAL FORMATION ACROSS NATIONAL BOUNDARIES

Historians have largely disregarded the overlapping interests of Black people in the Niagara region and the colliding worlds of the United States, Canada, Great Britain, and the African Diaspora that took place within this intersection. The postmodern scholarship of Afua Cooper and Harvey Amani Whitfield in the Detroit region, Lower Canada/Canada East, and the Canadian Maritimes, for example, have forcefully moved away from local and national approaches to a transnational and international conversation.[24] *Borderland Blacks* follows the same path of transboundary social formation, but it focuses on a new area—the Niagara zone.[25]

The goal is to put Rochester and St. Catharines firmly within the discourse of the new transnational historical wave and to fit Blacks into a larger conversation beyond the conventional American-Canadian national frameworks. Nationally driven studies ignore the fundamental bonds that tie nations and peoples together. This book analyzes the multiple political forces that acted simultaneously in the Niagara zone, underscores the social alliances that formed across national margins, and thus pushes the scholarship ahead by emphasizing the flow of people, ideas, and associations beyond set national divisions.[26] Blacks in each town occupied and moved through zones of in-betweenness, carrying signifiers of more than one identity, while fully embodying none.[27] As Frederick Douglass admitted candidly on the eve of moving to Rochester, "We are strangers to Nationality."[28] In fact, most cosmopolitan Blacks in the Niagara region also traveled to England and Europe to share antislavery strategies and to give public lectures. These Atlantic travels and exchanges resulted in money being raised to fuel fugitive movement and they nurtured genuine friendships. This dynamic adds another element to the borders Blacks crossed in the Niagara zone.[29]

Rochester and St. Catharines are like other towns in close proximity to international lines in the United States, such as Detroit and Buffalo. These places produced transnational people who were not tied to a geographic space or location per se; the cities were hubs of movement, which attracted a diversity of cosmopolitan persons who could migrate from one place to another, depending on the political climate. In addition, the two Niagara towns were gathering places for foreign economic exchange; they could be sites of international conflict; and they were places where national laws were sometimes overlooked, loosely imposed, or not enforced at all. Moreover, Rochester and St. Catharines each possessed traits that were unique to borderland towns, regardless of the time, location, or nations involved. In other words, these cities, as scholars Michiel Baud and Willem Van Schendel explained, had a "paradoxical character" which both divided and connected.[30] Although power holders set the political and national lines to establish sovereignty over a given territory to effectively "divide," ordinary Blacks reshaped the borderlands of Niagara on their own terms, which were not intended or anticipated to "connect" them with their counterparts. As a result, Rochester and St. Catharines helped Blacks throughout the early 1800s to challenge notions of "statehood" and to avoid oppressive conditions when they deemed it necessary.[31]

THE CONTRAST BETWEEN THE TWO CITIES

St. Catharines was located in the "heartland" of the Niagara border where movement and social interaction across the international lines were a constant, but Rochester was in the "intermediate borderlands" where the impact of the national divide manifested in different intensities from faint to moderate.[32] For instance, when the Fugitive Slave Act of 1850 gave slaveholders greater legal power to reclaim their human property, Rochester was firmly entrenched in the American-Canadian border dynamics as a result of the greater mobility of Blacks within the city.[33] In this political environment, Rochester became a destination, given its proximity to Canada and its importance as a jumping-off point for those on the way there or back. From the perspective of Rochester, a hint of the border was always present, but during the decades before the Civil War, the significance of the international border became more pronounced to those residing in the area. The Niagara borderland was a venue of national variability where people could abuse and exploit the border to flee injustice. Blacks were privy to this reality and, understanding the advantage of their locale, they weighed their alternatives wherever they were positioned along the borderline.

This study prioritizes Rochester and St. Catharines as the key junctions for Blacks in the Niagara region which were nourished by their surrounding communities. Although Buffalo had a larger Black population than the "Flower City" by 1850, there is no question that Rochester and St. Catharines were the leading Black portals in the Niagara region.[34] Buffalo lacked the cultural intensity and abolitionist activities found in Rochester, and it was polluted by slave catchers seeking their last chance to capture fugitives in the "immediate borderlands" before they crossed into British territory. Rochester never had a fugitive captured, but Buffalo was a focal point for such conflicts.[35] In fact, William Watkins, an assistant editor of the *Frederick Douglass' Paper,* understood the differences between the cities when he complained that "The colored people of this city [Buffalo] are not, I think, what they should be. They are given too much to slumber. They do not realize the solemnity of the hour."[36] Social reform in Buffalo moved at a slower pace. For instance, Rochester public schools were integrated in 1857, whereas this did not materialize in Buffalo until 1881.[37] In addition, while William Wells Brown was a noted Black Buffalonian, the city's other community leaders, including Abner Francis, a wealthy merchant, and George Weir Jr., a clothier and grocer, were not as active or well-known as Black leaders in Rochester, such as Rev. Thomas James, Austin Steward, and Frederick Douglass.[38]

No other city in Western New York embodied the unique borderland identity of Rochester. Niagara Falls and Syracuse did not have the Black population, culture, or outright abolitionist productivity of Rochester.[39] Since Niagara Falls offered direct access to Canada, Blacks often settled on the British side of the Niagara River, fearing the threat of slave catchers.[40] Syracuse's lack of a direct connection to the Great Lakes, leading to Canada, or even a major tributary to the lakes, reduced its transnational relevance. While Syracuse's foremost activist Rev. Jermain W. Loguen called himself the "Underground Railroad King" and the city was referred to as "the Canada of the United States," it was Rochester that actually lived up to this description because of its antislavery networks and geographical posture, which commanded regional respect.[41] Plus Loguen himself, after escaping slavery in Tennessee, had lived in both St. Catharines and Rochester before settling in Syracuse. Essentially, Buffalo and Niagara Falls were too near the international border, and Syracuse was too far from Canada on the "outer borderlands" to act as dynamic mediators of American-Canadian interchange.[42] Rochester was ideally positioned, and its people were committed to stewarding a momentous relationship with Canada.

The radical abolitionists Harriet Tubman and John Brown recognized the importance of Rochester and St. Catharines as borderland towns with ideal access to the neighboring nation. In 1858, Brown spent three weeks in Rochester at the home of Frederick Douglass, where he plotted his marron attack on the American South and drafted the Provisional Constitution for the Appalachian Rebel State he envisioned. By the time he arrived in Rochester, Brown was already a fugitive for killing five proslavery supporters at the Pottawatomie Massacre, an 1856 episode in Bleeding Kansas. Later, he confiscated eleven enslaved persons in Missouri and led them on an eighty-two-day trek to Canada.[43] Brown knew Rochester was an exceptional town for fugitives, Black or white, who were avoiding authorities and needed an escape route to Britain's North American colony if problems materialized. After finishing the Provisional Constitution, Brown printed the document as a pamphlet in St. Catharines by employing publisher William Howard Day, who was in town seeking to build a *North Star*–like Black newspaper.[44] Brown also went there to recruit men for his insurrection and to meet Tubman, who lived in St. Catharines for some seven years and had long maintained social networks with activists in Rochester to bring and sustain fugitives in Canada. Tubman, Brown, and their antislavery contemporaries knew the Rochester–St. Catharines connection was a key point in the Niagara region for two-way movement and vital support.[45]

On the Canadian side, St. Catharines was plainly the destination favored by Blacks over other places like Fort Erie, Niagara-on-the-Lake, and Niagara Falls. St. Catharines demonstrated a cultural potency, commercial success, community transnational exchange, and a significant Black population unequaled in neighboring towns.[46] Boston abolitionist Benjamin Drew passed by other Niagara settlements in the 1850s and declared "Refuge and Rest! These are the first ideas which arise in my mind in connection with the town of St. Catharines."[47] There, the August First Emancipation Day celebrations were lively, the "Colored Village," a section of town Blacks constructed, was robust with social organizations and bustling businesses. Indisputably Rochester and St. Catharines were the principal anchors of the Niagara region in terms of Black transnational activities and fugitive aid. They built a meaningful network of interaction with the help of the surrounding transitional hubs and the support of contemporary infrastructure, which were vital to Black movement and liberation in the early 1800s American-Canadian contested grounds.

Borderland Blacks is thus a narrative of social interaction on the Niagara border between Rochester and St. Catharines and the institutional, political, economic, and cultural issues in the two neighboring nations and Niagara towns. This study looks inward at Rochester and St. Catharines through community sketches that have elements of the classic social histories, and it looks outward at the border which shaped the experience and consciousness of Blacks.[48] In doing so, the book draws valuable inspiration from the internationalization of Black freedom struggles that has emerged in African Diaspora and Atlantic World scholarship.[49] These dual objectives and historical approaches reveal the situation Blacks faced in their immediate communities while simultaneously demonstrating the power and options the adjacent border gave to those in its vicinity.[50] The American-Canadian border did not have a singular meaning to Blacks; it was a pluralistic entity, actively moving between relevance (it divided two nations, legal bodies, and Blacks who reached Canada could not be recaptured without difficulty) and triviality (Blacks ignored and transcended the border by means of social organizations, annual celebrations, and regular crossings to connect with others of common cause).[51] Blacks in the Niagara zone did not fit neatly into a simple understanding of the border or the constraints of nationalism.

SOURCES, METHODOLOGY, AND HISTORIOGRAPHY

This book weaves together a multitude of sources, including slave narratives, autobiographies, and newly discovered and underutilized texts, to tell the story of Blacks on the American-Canadian border.[52] Its most important sources are the newspapers of the day. That choice was partly methodological and partly a matter of the materials available to investigate transient people in the Niagara district. Many times the movements of fugitive slaves and interactions across borders were documented only by a single blurb in a daily paper. The periodicals provide nuance to the dominant national narratives and are a window into "bottom-up history." Blacks who were not celebrated abolitionists and many who were unable to read or write sought to regain some control over their lives by crossing the international border or simply living in the borderlands.[53] The Rochester and St. Catharines newspapers, in particular, allow a closer understanding of the everyday circumstances faced by those moving through and living in the region. The reports they published reinforce the Niagara zone's importance and its shared sense of identity.

The historiography of the Niagara Underground Railroad trail has been highlighted in many studies, but it has not received the in-depth attention that the related Black settlements of the Detroit frontier or the Canadian Maritimes have received.[54] This book seeks to elevate the Niagara zone as an equally important place of transnational interface and to fill a needed gap in the borderland historical treatments. It works from historian Larry Gara's school of thought that the Underground Railroad had an overall fragmented character, which makes it challenging to draw direct lines of interaction between Rochester and St. Catharines. Fugitives needed secrecy to survive, and Frederick Douglass warned of making an *"Upperground Railroad"* by releasing too much intelligence about the means of fugitive movement. He explained, "Let us render the tyrant no aid."[55] At times, the Rochester–St. Catharines connections are clear-cut, but most of the times the linkage was loose and strategically underground.

In the past, historical treatments of Rochester, beginning with Whitney R. Cross's classic 1950 publication *The Burned-Over District: The Social and Intellectual History of Enthusiastic Religion in Western New York, 1800–1850,* have associated the city with the geographic space west of the Catskill and Adirondack mountains and the religious revivals of the Second Great Awakening.[56] This American-based treatment does not take into consideration its connections to neighboring British Canada or the relationships built by local Blacks with their nearby counterparts. Other studies, like Milton C. Sernett's *North Star Country: Upstate New York and the Crusade for African American Freedom,* are by and large a continuum of the scholarship created decades earlier by Cross. They position Rochester within the central and western section of the Empire State and do not deal with the city as a transnational space. *Borderland Blacks* asserts that the liberal thinking of the "Burned-Over District" was not as important to Blacks as having access to Canada. It moves away from American-centered studies that fail to look over the Canadian border to forge significant connections.[57]

Eric Foner's *Gateway to Freedom: The Hidden History of the Underground Railroad* adds to the historiography of the Niagara Underground Railroad trail. It underscores the journey of freedom-seekers and their supporters who moved through New York City.[58] His chief focus is on the newly discovered *Record of Fugitives* by Sydney Howard Gay, editor of the *National Anti-Slavery Standard* newspaper, which highlights his efforts to aid runaways going north from the

Empire City with the help of his closest associate, Louis Napoleon, a free Black man. This jewel of a primary document held at Columbia University provides an account of over 200 fugitives for a two-year period in the mid-1850s. It connects New York City intimately to the upstate cities of Albany and Syracuse, where Gay directed many runaways on the Niagara route.[59] Foner's work has skillfully brought the secretly kept register of Gay into the wider historical lens, but it leaves a major gap between Syracuse and the initial landing locations in Canada. Of those places, the most significant were Rochester and St. Catharines.

Borderland Blacks is a continuation of the Niagara trail historical narrative into its penultimate stages. Its major value lies in the fact that Sydney Howard Gay omitted Frederick Douglass and other key "Flower City" agents in the *Record of Fugitives,* "nor is there any mention of Rochester."[60] Gay was at odds with Douglass, mainly because he rejected the William Lloyd Garrison ideological brand of abolitionism, which was anti-Constitution and dismissive of the political processes, and because Douglass took fund-raising dollars, supporters, and subscribers away from the Garrisonians. This serious disagreement unfortunately appeared in his *Record.*[61] Gay furthermore did not grasp in his account the intricacies of the formidable network that ushered Blacks from Rochester to Canada, the circumstances they endured in the British colony, or the fundamental importance of St. Catharines. This book will not only emphasize how the odyssey ended for Blacks on the Niagara branch of the Underground Railroad, it will also discuss the new beginnings of life in the American-Canadian borderlands, the reverse migration, and the host of interactions that occurred across the international border.

HOW THIS BOOK IS ORGANIZED

The first chapter of this study examines the travel of Blacks through the Niagara zone and explains why some decided to stay in Western New York and others chose to go onward to Canada. The chapter highlights the federal and regional political dynamics that impacted each Niagara zone town.[62] The overarching legal structure and the social climate had serious implications at the local levels and must be placed into historical context before any meaningful transnational discussion of Rochester and St. Catharines can occur. The times and terms of emancipation, influential articles of legislation, and social reactions of Blacks are among the topics addressed.

The chapter asserts that throughout the early 1800s Blacks learned that British Canada was a more favorable environment for their rights, liberties, and immunities than the United States.[63] As a result, they sought to reach Canadian soil and reveled in the borderlands, which provided access to and interaction with the British territory and an abundance of progressive thinking. It affirms that Blacks in Canada lived "in a state of paradox," not a "promised land," as Barrington Walker suggested, "caught between formal legal equality and deeply entrenched societal and economic inequality."[64] The latter portion of the chapter highlights the two-way flow of transportation and transnational movement in the Niagara region and demonstrates that unpredictable circumstances characterized the lives of Black Borderlanders.

The second and third chapters are the core sections of the study. They address the transnational Black communities of Rochester and St. Catharines from 1800 to 1860. Both chapters follow the same pattern. Accordingly, chapter 2 covers the ways in which Black people formed churches, established social organizations, sought integrated institutions, battled for political inclusion, and advocated abolitionism in Rochester. Unfortunately, for all their efforts, the harsh outcome was a marginal status and a fragmented Black community. Despite disappointments, Black Rochesterians maintained an awareness of the larger world of the Niagara region and the accessible Canadian border—a critical factor that shaped their lives. They understood the possibilities that were available not far from their homes. It is no surprise that Rochester Blacks annually celebrated the August First British Emancipation Day holiday that freed Blacks in the Empire in 1834 instead of the contradictory July Fourth Independence Day, which they dubbed the "mockery of mockeries."[65] The chapter considers the more familiar transnational figures such as Austin Steward and Frederick Douglass, as well as like-minded common folks who were equally fluid in their orientation of the international border.[66]

Chapter 3 investigates mutual relief organizations, access to education, job opportunities, and political redress for Black grievances in St. Catharines. The tactics they used and the results they achieved were quite different than what transpired in Rochester. Blacks in St. Catharines managed to build a meaningful space that came to be known as the "Colored Village" where they could support each other's businesses and escape some of the prejudice and discrimination around them. Blacks generally had the same legal rights as whites, but their social dealings occurred in separated spheres. In St. Catharines, Blacks tried to integrate but were forced largely into exclusive spaces, which they promptly embraced as arenas of Blackness and a means of empowerment.[67] Located just twelve miles (nineteen kilometers) from the international border, St. Catharines possessed a sizable Black population, more than half of whom originated from the United States, which shaped its transnational culture. Blacks did not forget the *old country* once they stepped onto Canadian soil. In fact, they developed a vigorous cohesiveness with their counterparts independent of the border that divided them. Richard "Captain Dick" Pierpoint, Harriet Tubman, Anthony Burns, and hundreds of fugitives, as well as Hiram Wilson, called the city home and celebrated the legal protections of British-Canadian law while engaging the border.[68]

The concluding chapter highlights both the borderland social markers and the critical local distinctions of Rochester and St. Catharines. The comparative analysis reveals key similarities and stark contrasts between the towns. The most important was that Black Rochesterians insisted on being integrated into the white mainstream, while Blacks in St. Catharines preferred the separation and safety of their own established community.[69] This chapter demonstrates how in towns some 100 miles (258 kilometers) away, employment opportunities and living conditions had the potential to deteriorate, vastly improve, or be negotiated via the border. The chapter closes by discussing how the Civil War in the borderlands fully realized the transnational commitment of the Niagara region, as many Blacks returned to the South to aid in the liberation of their people. They actively followed the Union advancements and celebrated the downfall of the "peculiar institution."[70] The epilogue reinforces the notion that the Rochester–St. Catharines zone existed as a junction of movement and cross-pollination. The international border near Rochester and St. Catharines gave Blacks options to shift "allegiances," which many others in North America did not have the opportunity to experience. The borderlands empowered Blacks to go beyond the political status quo.[71]

In sum, *Borderland Blacks* is not another one-way flow "Underground Railroad" study, nor does it fall into the Canadian "Promised Land" discourse.[72] It offers an alternative approach to state-centered studies and their inherent limitations. As scholars Michiel Baud and Willem Van Schendel explained, "No matter how clearly borders are drawn on official maps ... people will ignore borders whenever it suits them."[73] This was certainly the case for Blacks in the Niagara region. By disregarding the American-Canadian border as a line of division, they transformed borders intended to be restrictive into flexible borderlands, which paved the way for increased self-agency and autonomy in shaping the trajectory of their own lives. Whether Blacks crossed the border or simply lived near the international line, it helped them to craft lifestyles quite different from their counterparts more inland. Thus, the Rochester–St. Catharines region represented a transnational conduit that was both significant and dynamic.

1

Setting the Stage for the Journey
UNDERSTANDING THE NIAGARA REGION AS A FLUID FRONTIER

If imperial and national histories are about larger-scale conquests, borderlands
histories are about smaller-scale accommodations or pockets of resistance. If
imperial and national histories fill the continent, borderlands history seeps into the
cracks in between those studies.

—PEKKA HÄMÄLÄINEN AND SAMUEL TRUETT,
   "On Borderlands," 351

No section of the American Continent has been watched with so much interest,
both by the oppressor, the oppressed, and the friends of freedom and civilization,
as the Canadas.

—WILLIAM WELLS BROWN, "The People of Canada,"
   Pine and Palm, 1861

In the early 1800s, the lives of Blacks in Rochester and St. Catharines were
strongly affected by federal laws, state and provincial laws, and the prejudice
they experienced throughout the Niagara region. Before one can understand
the local, yet transnational, dynamics of the towns in the region, it is important
to review the historical context of those times to grasp the social and political
climate. This chapter outlines the times and terms of emancipation in the borderlands, and it assesses the legal rights that Blacks had on each side of the border before the Civil War. What Blacks in both nations learned prior to 1860 was
that the British Empire gave them rights and protections that the United States
restricted or actively denied.

As the nineteenth century began, Black people saw the two nations on the
Niagara frontier as very different—an America that they loathed for its support
of slavery and a British Canada for which they felt a keen appreciation. This per-

ception materialized and was circulated via the "Black grapevine" in the wake of the American Revolutionary War and the War of 1812, which displayed the conflicting cultural attitudes and differences in national legislation.[1] For example, Jermain W. Loguen and Josiah Henson—each of whom entered and exited Canada via the Niagara region—shared this sentiment about Canada. "The excellent and most gracious Queen of England and the Canadas," said Henson, provided conditions "vastly superior to that of most of the free people of color in the Northern States."[2] And Loguen declared, "I am sorry to say that the only power that gives freedom in North America, is in England."[3] Blacks grasped the benefits of reaching British Canada and comprehended the value of living even in its borderlands. In spaces like Western New York, they knew that proximity and access to the American-Canadian border gave them ways to negotiate change, to communicate with like-minded people, and to share resources and ideas.

At the same time, this chapter will examine the means of transportation and the movement of Blacks in the Niagara district and explain how and why many elected to venture farther north to Canada throughout the early 1800s. Who were these individuals seeking refuge in Western New York and in Canada? Why did the North prove to be an inadequate refuge for some runaways? Why did a score of Blacks return to the United States once they reached the British colony? And why did others go back-and-forth between the two nations, depending upon the political climate or the economy?

Understanding how Blacks made the transition from the South to the North and to Canada has been clouded by the misconceptions about the Underground Railroad and about Canada as the "Promised Land." The historiography has progressively improved in this regard, but a fresh perspective is needed, one that focuses on the two-way flow of Blacks who made use of the Rochester–St. Catharines corridor prior to the Civil War. During this period, Blacks, particularly in the Niagara district, led lives of uncertainty and flux that prompted movement and migration. They relocated in search of social equality, political rights, and the legal protections they expected as free people. Whenever Blacks were denied these rights, or feared these rights would be seized, they moved within the Niagara borderlands in an effort to survive and prosper as their neighbors did. They preferred a more settled existence, but enhanced autonomy too often demanded mobility.

*   *   *

PATHS OF EMANCIPATION IN NORTH AMERICA

The United States and Canada took different paths in respect to slavery and emancipation. The neighboring nations evolved in separate ways partly because differences in climate affected the overall demand for manual labor. In the American South, cash crops produced by Blacks and Northern goods produced in mills became the foundation of the economy, but Canada's financial health was based primarily on fur and fish, and these industries did not require a wealth of enslaved labor. As a result, Canada evolved as a "society with slaves" and not a "slave society," meaning that Black bondage was an element of its economy but not a chief component.[4]

The largest influx of slaves to Canada came when white "Empire Loyalists" moved north following the American Revolutionary War and brought enslaved Blacks with them. They were allowed to import bound Blacks tax-free and the rights of slaveholders were protected. At the same time, over 3,000 free "Black Loyalists," who had fought or sided with the British, settled in Canada.[5] By 1784, more than 4,000 Blacks inhabited the British colony, and 40 percent of them were held as legal property.[6] In its historical memory, Canada has made slavery its "best-kept secret," as historian Afua Cooper asserts, "locked within the national closet."[7] This "secret" was largely overlooked because the overall character and number of people enslaved in Canada simply did not rival those in the Caribbean and in the United States.

However, there are significant American-Canadian similarities. For instance, New York State and Upper Canada/Canada West in the 1790s both enacted gradual emancipation laws that significantly decreased the number of enslaved Blacks in the early 1800s. Before such laws were passed, Blacks enslaved in America and in Canada sought the nation on the other side of the border as an alternative. Blacks in Canada looked to enter the New England states, New York, or Michigan, while those held in American bondage sought the doorway of Upper Canada/Canada West, Lower Canada/Canada East, and the Canadian Maritimes. The charismatic governors on each side of the border—John Graves Simcoe of Upper Canada and Daniel D. Tompkins of New York—both made the emancipation of Blacks a personal priority, and each oversaw the enactment of vital legislation that aided in the decline of slavery.

John Graves Simcoe, a veteran of the American Revolutionary War, was named the first Lieutenant Governor of Upper Canada and was responsible for shaping much of the foundational and forward-thinking public policy in the province.[8] Simcoe believed that slavery was both unlawful and a violation of his Protestant faith.[9] From the time Simcoe arrived in Canada, he also encouraged nonsegregated Black settlement. In the year before the passage of the 1793 Act Against Slavery, Simcoe tried to eliminate slavery altogether in Upper Canada. He was motivated by the story of Chloe Cooley, a female Black slave taken forcibly across the Niagara River from Canada by her master, William Vrooman of Queenston. She screamed and resisted violently but was overpowered and sold to an American owner. Afterward, Simcoe was determined to get emancipation legislation passed.[10] The 1793 Act Against Slavery protected the property of all existing slaveholders but forbade the further importation of slaves into Canada. The act freed children who were born after the passage of the law when they reached the age of twenty-five and limited the terms of indentured servitude to nine years.[11] Upper Canada was the first province to make advancements toward eradicating slavery; the others followed. By the early 1800s, the British colony had a heightened reputation as a "haven" for American runaways.

It was not until July 4, 1799, that New York passed its first emancipation law. Nonetheless, the gradual emancipation law of 1799 set in motion a nearly thirty-year-long process before universal emancipation was achieved in the state. The 1799 law freed no adult slaves but permitted freedom for all their children after they served a lengthy indentured term. Males had to serve their mothers' owners until age twenty-eight, while females had to work until the age of twenty-five. These "apprenticeships" for eventual freedom were supposed to "prepare" Blacks for emancipation, but they were really established to compensate slaveholders for their human property losses. To protect Blacks from being cheated out of their freedom, the Act also outlawed the exportation of slaves from the State.[12] After the enactment of the 1799 law, a score of enslaved Blacks engineered indenture contracts with their owners for freedom. Not all Blacks were able to obtain liberty by way of negotiation and tact; therefore, further legal means were needed to open the doors of emancipation to the masses.

In 1817, Governor Daniel D. Tompkins of New York, who was soon to be vice president serving President James Monroe, was determined to end slavery in the state before his term concluded. In his last session, Tompkins persuaded the New York State Legislature to end the painfully slow emancipation process which had begun in 1799. Although the lawmakers agreed to eradicate slavery, they adopted the longest time frame suggested by Tompkins to do so—one decade. The new 1817 law provided freedom to slaves by granting all Blacks born before July 4, 1799, their freedom on July 4, 1827.[13] Word of jubilee echoed in Canada. Margaret H. Hall wrote back to England on Independence Day from Niagara Falls, "To-day, all the remaining Slaves in the State of New York become free, but they have fixed upon to-morrow for their celebration, there is to be a great Assemblage of them at Rochester."[14] In the aftermath of this act, a number of Blacks remained enslaved on technicalities or abuses of the law. In fact, a decade following emancipation, a New York committee of Blacks declared "it is a very prevalent error that there are no slaves in this state."[15] Despite loopholes, the 1817 act greatly weakened the institution in the Empire State, and the 1827 act ignited a debate over Black suffrage and equality, though there was still formidable opposition.[16]

By the 1820s, slavery in Canada had been reduced by a combination of legislative action and judicial rulings to the point that it barely existed.[17] The word spread to the United States by way of abolitionists like David Walker, who understood that the British were leading the fight to end slavery. As he explained in his 1829 *Appeal,* "The English are the best friends the coloured people have upon earth . . . notwithstanding they have treated us a little cruel."[18] Still, Blacks in Canada did not officially obtain freedom until the passage of the Imperial Act of 1833, which took effect on August 1, 1834. Canada was not formally mentioned in the act, but the British colony shared in the legal outcome. The British government did not name Canada because it figured that slavery had all but ceased there.[19] Only some fifty of the approximately 800,000 slaves freed by the act were found in the Canadas. British authorities also did not compensate Canadian owners for their property losses as they did slave owners in the Caribbean and the Cape of Good Hope. In those areas, reimbursements were granted by way of set "apprenticeship" labor terms for Blacks.[20] This was viewed as unnecessary in Canada because there were so few slaves. The act gave Blacks in Canada an elevated social status and the ability to pursue legal action in court. Blacks could testify before a jury and vote in elections, but they still held a position of being "not slaves, but not equal."[21] These rights and social standing nevertheless gave them hope for a better future and signaled to Blacks in America to come north.

As a result of the Imperial Act, August First was a day of celebration throughout the African Diaspora.[22] The Canadian provinces hosted festivities that attracted Blacks from Rochester and other American cities. Blacks in the United States even held their own commemorations to demonstrate their common identity and shared political desires with those in British Canada. Scholar Nele Sawallisch explained the "day had become the symbolic anti-Fourth-of-July and the day of celebrating freedom" which was borderless in its appeal.[23] Whether on American or Canadian soil, these gatherings memorialized the freedom won by Africans in the British Empire and acknowledged the ongoing struggles in the United States and Caribbean islands. During the celebrations, people expressed loyalty to Britain for granting civil liberties, remembered the past, renewed the continuing fight for complete equality, and offered gratitude to Canada for protecting American fugitives.[24] Even before August First, Canada was regarded as an "asylum," and this perception grew. The Canadian promise of freedom, land ownership, and political rights was attractive. As Blacks fled north, however, slaveholders challenged British-Canadian courts by seeking to force the return of Black escapees to the United States.

THE FIGHT TO RECAPTURE BLACKS IN BRITISH CANADA

Between 1833 and 1842, American slaveholders seeking to reclaim their human property tested the freedom that British Canada gave to fugitives.[25] In 1833, runaways Thorton and Rutha Blackburn, who were making their way to Canada from Louisville, Kentucky, were arrested in Detroit under the 1793 Fugitive Slave Act. They were rescued by enthusiastic supporters and sent across the border to British Canada.[26] Their owner and Michigan's territorial governor petitioned to get them extradited, but the Canadian courts held firm. This set the stage for future diplomatic discussions and decisions that defined the British-Canadian legal disposition. Escapees to Canada could be returned to America by way of the Fugitive Offenders Act only if they committed a crime that called for hard labor, corporal punishment, or death.[27] However, the Canadian act gave vast leeway to the courts, governors, and council to decide whether a fugitive should be returned to the United States. American slaveholders saw this as an opportunity to contest the liberty of Black escapees.[28] The public sentiment in St. Catharines warned otherwise, explaining that "they need not take any farther trouble in the matter; for neither the British Government, nor the people of Upper Canada, would ever consent to give up those who have escaped from American 'chains and slavery.'"[29]

Canada's position was tested again by the court case of fugitive Solomon Mosley (or Molesby). He escaped from Kentucky to Canada on his master's horse. His owner David Castleman attempted to return him to bondage via ex-tradition. Mosley's defense was so poorly handled in court that the judge recom-mended he be sent back to the United States. Nonetheless, the "court of public opinion" was determined to free him. A three-week protest, from late August to September of 1837, was held around the Niagara jail, and a petition was circu-lated to lobby for Mosley's release. In response to the protest, the *St. Catharines Journal* editorialized about the eroding of "the very foundation of social order" and about the threat of Black "mobocracy."[30] On the day Mosley was to be trans-ferred to America under the supervision of a deputy sheriff and military guard, a multiracial crowd of men and women, led by mulatto pastor and teacher Her-bert Holmes, incited a riot that gave Mosley the opportunity to escape.[31] In the melee, Holmes was killed, and others were wounded, but the residents of the Niagara zone wanted to ensure runaway slaves were safe on British soil.[32] Cana-dian citizens appeared unwilling to be used as instruments to facilitate United States recapture.

Nonetheless, in 1842 Nelson Hackett became the first enslaved Black sent back to the United States. Hackett, a runaway from Arkansas, escaped to Canada by stealing the horse, saddle coat, and gold watch from owner Alfred Wallace. There was a dispute as to what should be done with Hackett. Although Attorney General William Henry Draper argued the court case in favor of Hackett, Sir Charles Bagot ordered his removal from the Queen's soil. Once back in the cus-tody of his master, he was beaten in public and sold to Texas. Hackett's story em-barrassed the British Canadian government, got the attention of abolitionists, and increased a general concern for recurring cases of this nature.[33] As a result of the Hackett case, the 1842 Webster-Ashburton Treaty was enacted, settling the dispute over the freedom of Blacks who entered Canada by declaring them vir-tually safe.[34] The treaty defined seven crimes subject to extradition in Article 10, including "Murder, or assault with intent to commit murder, or piracy, or arson, or robbery, or forgery, or the utterance of forged paper."[35] With foundational public policy in place by way of the litigation and regulations of 1833 and 1842, fugitives had sound reasons to cross the border, and the word spread.[36]

THE TWO-WAY FLOW IN THE NIAGARA BORDERLANDS

In the borderlands, the political winds could blow in either direction, shifting people from one side of the international divide to the other. The life of Jermain W.

Loguen is an example of this phenomenon. In 1834, Loguen fled Tennessee and entered Canada via the Detroit frontier in the same year the Imperial Act took effect. Throughout his journey in the American North, Loguen was directed to British soil, and upon arrival he "knew not a soul." He found work in Hamilton, Canada West, and then obtained education and 200 acres of land in St. Catharines.[37] However, in 1837, under strains of political unrest, he left the British colony and found employment at the fashionable downtown Rochester House Hotel. Back in the United States, he stayed in the borderlands near to what many deemed "the only asylum for African freedom in North America"—Canada.[38] Loguen's life was representative of the two-way flow in the Niagara zone and is a lens into the political and regional dynamics experienced by Black Borderlanders. He shifted from Canada to America in response to the Rebellions of 1837–38, and from America to Canada as a result of the 1850 Fugitive Slave Act, and then back to the United States.

When the Rebellions of 1837–38 or the "Canadian Rebellion" broke out in Lower and Upper Canada, led chiefly by William Lyon Mackenzie and Louis-Joseph Papineau, Jermain Loguen chose to flee.[39] The Rebellion(s) were precipitated by the desire for political reform, issues of ethnic conflict, and land grievances, all of which had been brewing for a long time. The Lower Canada conflict was primarily an ethnic and cultural battle between the English ruling class and the French Canadian nationalists, while the Upper Canada revolt was a matter of elite monarchical and republican ideologies clashing violently.[40] In the wake of the American Revolution, England became increasingly sensitive and responded more diplomatically to unrest in colonies with substantial English populations. In this case, they pressed seriously to lessen their firm political grip on their North American colony.

The Rebellion(s) heightened transnational movement. Loguen moved to Rochester just before the Patriot War, an episode in the larger conflict, but he crossed back into Canada during the war to "dispose of his house and lot" in St. Catharines, which was no longer profitable to him.[41] Crossing the border during the war was a dangerous proposition because the American-Canadian troops in rebellion knew that Blacks were largely "loyal" to the British. This made them a target; as printer Thomas Jefferson Sutherland warned, "for God's sake look out for the negroes."[42] Fortunately for Loguen, when he reached the international line, "though the forces were still under arms, the back bone of the invasion was fairly broken."[43] The Canadian outbreak did not deter Loguen's reverence for

Britain, though a prestigious job opportunity drew him to Rochester. Loguen decided to attend the racially integrated Oneida Institute, a school just miles from Utica, New York. But during breaks from school, his work at the Rochester House Hotel sustained him economically.[44]

By 1840, Loguen married his wife Carolina and moved to Syracuse, where he was an African Methodist Episcopal Zion (AMEZ) minister. He took positions in Utica, Bath, and Ithaca, New York, serving the AMEZ Church and as a teacher before settling down in Syracuse. There, he continued to educate, became active in New York State political conventions, and supported the abolitionist movement as a noted "conductor" on the Underground Railroad. He led people to greater freedom through his old stomping grounds of Rochester and St. Catharines. Loguen lectured and was selected president of several British August First celebrations in the Niagara region. On British or American soil, he expressed his gratitude every August for the abolition of Black bondage in the British Empire. Loguen shared stages with his Rochester counterparts Frederick Douglass and Austin Steward to applaud England and to push the United States towards the same objective.[45]

When the Fugitive Slave Act of 1850 passed, under President Millard Fillmore who was a Niagara District son, Rev. Loguen refused to leave the United States.[46] He took a firm stance against the 1850 Act when he declared, "I don't respect this law—I don't fear it—I won't obey it! It outlaws me, and I outlaw it."[47] In a note to Douglass, Loguen explained that the Fugitive Bill "had a good effect in making the people willing to hear on the subject, and I hope it will drive them to action, as action is what we need at present."[48] He was determined not to be driven out of the country. But after his involvement in the October 1851 rescue of William "Jerry" Henry, which broke him out of a Syracuse jail and sent him to Canada via Lake Ontario, Loguen found it difficult to remain in the United States.[49] Jerry was arrested at his workplace by federal marshals under the Fugitive Slave Act of 1850 while a Liberty Party convention, known antislavery advocates, was meeting a short distance away. Loguen's friends and family, fearing for his safety, convinced him to leave for British soil.[50] The danger he faced was real; more than twenty people were arrested for their involvement in Jerry's rescue.[51]

Loguen went back to St. Catharines by way of Rochester for seven months hoping to sidestep the snares of the American 1850 law. "The cheeks of every American," the *Syracuse Daily Standard* declared, "should burn with shame that such a man is compelled to fly to a monarchial government to preserve his liberty."[52] In December 1851, his wife and children joined him at the home of his "old friend" Hiram Wilson, and Loguen sent a letter to New York Governor Washington Hunt, among others, explaining that his crime was being "in favor of freedom."[53] He busied himself in exile by teaching literature to locals in St. Catharines and by lecturing.[54] In the spring of 1852, after things quieted down around the "Jerry" rescue, he returned to Syracuse with a message of resistance but still in danger of indictment.[55] The Fugitive Slave Act, which nationalized slavery, directly affected even the law's most staunch opponents.[56]

Back in Syracuse, Loguen and his wife helped some 1,500 fugitives reach Canada throughout the 1850s, many by way of Rochester and St. Catharines.[57] "Mrs. Loguen," the *Syracuse Standard* explained, "is often aroused from her bed to attend to the pressing wants of those flying for Liberty."[58] In 1856 alone, Jermain reported to the Syracuse Fugitive Aid Society that 186 fugitives had taken flight to Canada.[59] Loguen's Underground Railroad exploits in the latter 1850s received funds from the Ladies Aid Societies in English towns like Halifax, Liverpool, Coventry, Birmingham, and Berwick-On-Tweed. They were "kindly procured and sent to us," Loguen explained, "by our true and vigilant friend, Miss Julia Griffiths." She had helped to edit the *North Star* of Frederick Douglass, and she supported the movement of fugitives in the Niagara region.[60] Loguen also received money and assistance from the Rochester Ladies Anti-Slavery Society, and he depended heavily on other women's groups that did everything from benefit concerts, bake sales to bazaars and donation drives of food and clothing on his behalf. Their efforts were critical: the new Fugitive Slave Act brought more Blacks to Canada than ever before. The number of Blacks that fled to Canada before the Civil War was once estimated to be as high as 60,000 to 100,000, but modern scholars have reduced it to approximately 30,000 to 35,000. The current projections are more plausible and sober the notions of an outright "mass exodus."[61]

The Crown's soil had a decisive progressive edge over America by the turbulent 1850s. Blacks in the United States had long looked favorably on Great Britain because the British had rewarded Black "loyalty" in past wars and passed legislation ending slavery. This sentiment persisted as American laws reinforced Southern enslavement.[62] In Canada, universal emancipation, citizenship, and the ability to vote were possible for Black fugitives seeking shelter from American subjugation. These Canadian-specific advances, however, can be misleading. Racial tensions and institutional bigotry were just as present and oppressive on British soil as they were in America. While the British Empire was not faultless, Loguen's Niagara region comrade Frederick Douglass wisely noted that "England has steadily persisted in its abolition policy" as America moved in the opposite direction, and if left to its own devices, the United States would "fasten the terrible curse of human bondage upon every quarter of this [American] continent."[63]

The benefits of Canada were known and appreciated by the fugitive and the free. By and large, Blacks preferred the "Mane of the British Lion" and "Monarchial Liberty" to the "Rapacious Eagle" and "Republican Slavery."[64] One Black remarked simply that "we [Americans] are . . . in rear of old England and our neighbors across the lakes."[65] Henry W. Johnson, a onetime Rochester resident, inquired laconically, "Can it be that the despotic governments of the old world are in advance of us? Are they such apt scholars that they have learned our lessons of republicanism better than we know ourselves?"[66] Loguen also attempted to appeal to republican ideology by asking Blacks "to stand their ground and contend for their rights as did the Fathers of this country," though he himself had to flee under bleak circumstances.[67]

The contrast between the United States and British Canada left Blacks to weigh unequal halves in North America. The harsh truth was, as Douglass declared, that "the American government refuses to shelter the Negro under its protecting wing," and "wherever the star-spangled banner waves, there men hold men as slaves."[68] Because Blacks had limited access to conventional political means, they were forced to maneuver between the power structures of the United States and Canada in order to create spaces for their own agendas. In the process, they learned that England, as abolitionist David Walker suggested, offered them more "friendship" than America.[69] As the nations trended in two different directions, Blacks recognized the power of British soil and the shadow of protection it cast into the borderlands.

THREATS AND HARDSHIPS IN THE NORTHERN UNKNOWN

Once fugitives reached the American North, it was not simple to step out of their past and into a future of freedom.[70] Blacks quickly discovered a new set of challenges awaited them. When Harriet Tubman first crossed the Mason-Dixon line, she explained, "There was such a glory over everything; the sun came like gold through the trees and over the fields, and I felt like I was in Heaven."[71] These joyous feelings swiftly faded as the sobering reality set in that she had no friends or family to welcome her to the North. "I was a stranger in a strange land," Tubman realized.[72] She found herself in the northern unknown. Anthony Burns, who fled by hiding aboard a ship from Richmond to Boston, did not know the exact moment he entered Northern latitudes, but he had an idea he was in free territory when his feet were frozen inside his boots. Within a year of arriving in Boston, Burns was discovered by slave catchers, arrested, and sent back to the South from one of the most "progressive" Northern cities of his day.[73] Like other Blacks, it did not take Burns long to understand that his birthright of freedom was not secure in the American North. He quickly realized the perils of life in the North and later made St. Catharines his home.

Former slave Thomas Smallwood was disappointed and annoyed that American abolitionists advised fugitives to stay in the Northern states when Canada offered greater civil liberties. In his *Narrative,* he explained that before the Compromise of 1850, possibly thousands of fugitives were induced to stay in the North at the urging of abolitionists, "whereas, if they had been encouraged, or even let alone, they would have gone to Canada at first, and be now secure in their persons and property as British subjects."[74] Smallwood disliked the blind hope that many placed on fugitives to stay in America. "Come to Canada," he instructed, "and you will get freedom, yea British freedom!"[75] Henry Bibb and Samuel R. Ward also "encouraged Blacks to exile themselves" to avoid being captured, but Frederick Douglass fought against Black mass emigration outside the United States and told Blacks that America was their "rightful home."[76] While Douglass urged Blacks to see themselves as "Americans" instead of "Aliens" and preferred them to stay in the country to help destroy the institution of slavery, he understood that this was not always possible and therefore regularly helped pass runaways onward to Canada. Douglass described sending fugitives abroad as similar to attempting "to bail out the ocean with a teaspoon," yet he took pleasure in the thought of "one less slave and one more freedman."[77]

The American North could be a dangerous place for Blacks. The fugitive and free had to be mindful of their surroundings and cautious of suspicious and scheming individuals. Charles Nalle embodied the fears of all Northern "free" people.[78] In October of 1858, Nalle, enslaved in Virginia by owner Blucher W. Hansbrough, escaped on a pass to visit his free wife Kitty, who was reportedly ill in Washington, DC. Fleeing on board a vessel en route to Philadelphia, he met William Still and was sent further north to Troy, New York. Nalle found work as a coachman and settled comfortably into the community, yet Hansbrough maintained a strong desire to recapture him. He employed two experienced slave catchers who traced Nalle to Troy. On the morning of April 27, 1860, Nalle was running an errand to a local bakery when he was overtaken and handcuffed. A deputy US marshal, who accompanied the catchers, proclaimed, "Charles Nalle, I hereby arrest you in the name of the United States of America."[79] He was dragged off to a nearby federal law office where paperwork was completed to send him back to Virginia.

In the interim, local abolitionists, vigilance committee members, and concerned citizens swung into action, determined to liberate Nalle. Among the masses of his supporters, front and center was Harriet Tubman. Nalle was successfully rescued. He subsequently took the Erie Canal westbound toward Canada but decided to get off some forty miles away in Amsterdam, New York. For nearly a month, he hid from authorities while the citizens of Troy gathered $650 to purchase his freedom. Perhaps in an effort to throw off the catchers, the *Douglass' Monthly* reported that Nalle had "Arrived safely at St. Catharines."[80] Although cases like Nalle's were rare, the possibility of recapture was always present in the North. This caused many to ask the question that Austin Steward of Rochester did: "Is the poor, flying fugitive from the house of bondage, safe one moment within your borders?"[81]

Even in the American-Canadian borderlands, many dangers lay between bondage and freedom. No guarantees of safety or success could be assumed. In 1854, Isaac D. Williams knew that the borderlands between Rochester and St. Catharines were dangerous. Traveling from Jermain Loguen's house in Syracuse, Williams and his fellow fugitives Henry Banks and Christopher Nicholas were placed on a train with conductors and instructed to "look out for danger." After reaching Rochester, Williams was eager to get to British soil. He explained, "We were coming to the dividing line, where so many slaves had been captured. Just when the cup of liberty was raised to their lips."[82] On Christmas Day of 1854, Williams and his partners entered Canada by crossing the Niagara Falls Suspension Bridge on a horse-drawn carriage. Not knowing what to expect, runaways remained on edge even in the borderlands. William C. Nell reported from Rochester to *The Liberator* that fugitives gave "no rest to their feet nor slumber to their eyelids, until the protecting aegis of Queen Victoria makes them welcome freemen on Canada's shore."[83]

In 1858, four fugitives were boarded onto a mail train in Rochester by Frederick Douglass en route to the British side of the Niagara Falls Suspension Bridge, where they planned to take refuge. However, unsure of their surroundings, "They were very suspicious of certain railroad officials who eyed them closely."[84] This was a legitimate concern, for the group's liberty could be contested at any time. Loguen explained that "white loafers and villains . . . have poisoned and ruined the border towns and cities on the lines and Railroad" to Canada.[85] And Douglass added, "For it was not in the interior of the State, but on its borders, that these human hounds were most vigilant and active. The border lines between slavery and freedom were the dangerous ones for the fugitive."[86]

Regardless of where Blacks lived in the United States, they could be subject to slavery as long as it existed within the country. For this reason, many Northern Blacks had a profound conviction to help others reach freedom and to participate in the abolitionist movement.[87] This cause was their cause, and their fate was interlocked with their brothers and sisters in bondage.[88] Enslaved in North Carolina, John S. Jacobs fled on his owner's honeymoon trip to New York. Jacobs, later a Rochester resident, best explained the sentiment amongst Blacks when he stated, "I will not forget those that are slaves. What I would have done for my liberty I am willing to do for theirs."[89] Indeed, Blacks acted as the moral conscience and lead strategists of the struggle. Although physical bondage had been largely eradicated in the North by the 1840s, Blacks there still remained largely disenfranchised, segregated, and economically repressed in a social climate of white supremacy.[90] The majority struggled to build stable lives in the North, and whites wrongly attributed the conditions of Black life as evidence of their inabilities.[91]

Even in the face of systematic oppression, there were several reasons why Blacks elected to stay in the American North. First, some never intended or desired to go to Canada; they found adequate homes and work in the North. Others could not physically press on after battling to reach a "free state." Fugitives arrived in the North destitute and weary from their long journey. Many did not have the money or the connections to make the trip to Canada. Some Blacks felt a level of safety because of communities, associations known as "mutual protection organizations," or individuals who safeguarded them from recapture.[92] Places like Boston and Rochester, in particular, were considered "safe cities," since they were centers of the abolitionist movement. The most admirable reason why Blacks remained in America was because they felt a sense of duty. Douglass believed he was ordained to stay and struggle on behalf of Blacks.[93] He had opportunities to live comfortably in Europe and Canada, yet he forfeited these attractive offers to struggle for change in America. Once, when he was well received at a hotel in the Niagara Falls, Canada West area, Douglass wrote that "Were it not cowardly, and perhaps selfish, I could wish to leave the United States and become a resident in Canada."[94]

By the time most fugitives reached British soil, they were a long distance from where they had started. In the South, some Blacks had heard of Canada and originally set out to reach it; others learned of the British colony on their journey north. As John A. Hunter explained, "A great many slaves know nothing of Canada." Dan Josiah Lockhart ventured to St. Catharines despite being told that rice was the lone crop grown there and that all of the country's goods were imported.[95] A number of slaveholders deliberately misinformed their slaves about Canada, telling them that it was nothing but frozen terrain with bad soil and wild beasts and geese that would poke their eyes out.[96] Deacon Allen Sidney, who worked aboard his owner's ship, formed an unfavorable opinion because he was told that only "black-eyed peas could be raised there."[97] Slaves also heard that the Queen would demand half of their wages.[98] Owners told lies to deter their slaves from seeking refuge above the 49th Parallel and to detect any disloyalty. This plan often backfired, for slaves came to understand that what their masters disliked were the things that were negative for the institution of slavery but beneficial for them.[99] Slaveholders, Samuel R. Ward asserted, hated Canada more than any other nation in the world. No matter how runaways learned about Canada, they were pleased to know it existed and that greater freedom lay within its borders. In fact, the majority of the Black population in Canada before the Civil War had roots in America.[100]

Fugitives who arrived through the Detroit and Niagara zones entered into the province of Upper Canada/Canada West, where Blacks found people much like their American counterparts—people who spoke English and were Protestants. Blacks were chiefly found in Canada West's towns and cities around Lake Ontario or Lake Erie. There were advantages to entering Canada West instead of Lower Canada/Canada East.[101] The population in Canada East was predominantly French-speaking, Roman Catholics outnumbered Protestants, the weather was colder, and there was less of a Black community. One Black refugee who reached Canada East wrote to Henry Bibb that he was disappointed to find that the *Voice of the Fugitive* was unknown in Montreal. This was likely the result of the language differences that existed between the provinces.[102]

Although Lower Canada/Canada East was billed as a harder transition for Blacks than Upper Canada/Canada West, there were still individuals such as

Shadrach Minkins and Israel Lewis who made Canada East home. Minkins of Virginia came to Montreal after being rescued from a Boston jail, where he had been arrested under the Fugitive Slave Act of 1850.[103] Israel Lewis, an agent of the Wilberforce Colony who had mishandled the settlement's money, came to Rochester in the 1830s to raise funds, and then spent his last days in Montreal.[104] John W. Lewis, a traveling agent for the *Frederick Douglass' Paper,* wrote that the "difference is not so great" between Canada West and Canada East. On a February 1855 tour to enlist subscribers, he explained, "People have a wrong idea about Canada [East]. Some imagine it to be a cold, bleak, out-of-the-way part of the world, solitary, and uninviting. This is a mistake."[105] Lewis also championed the Montreal-Portland railroad, billed as the world's first international railway when it was chartered in 1845 to allow year-round American-Canadian travel. This train line was not only good for business, but it helped fugitive Blacks as well.[106] A decade later, in 1855, a railroad that traversed the Niagara River in the borderland region was built.

MEANS OF MOVEMENT IN THE NIAGARA ZONE

In the Niagara region, the main arteries of movement for fugitives were the Niagara Falls Suspension Bridge and the Lewiston-Queenston Suspension Bridge, as well as ships on Lake Ontario. These transportation conduits tied together two diverging realities, and they became goals for many who were fleeing slavery. Rochester and St. Catharines benefited from these channels as a result of being along their paths. The international overpasses of rope and wood for fugitives became well-known means of liberation. In the summer of 1856, James H. Forman, for instance, left Norfolk, Virginia, passed through Rochester, and reached Niagara Falls, New York, where he awaited his "sweet-heart," Miss Mariah Moore. From a room he rented at the International Hotel, he wrote to William Still of Philadelphia to plan for Moore's arrival at the Niagara Falls Suspension Bridge. In late June, when Moore disembarked in Niagara Falls, Forman reported, "I was down to the cars to receive her." They soon married at an Anglican Church in Canada.[107] Like other fugitives who crossed the bridges in the Niagara area, they revered those viaducts as immaculate edifices with as much symbolic value as structural power. Tubman used the Niagara overpass so often that she "knew by the rise of the center of the bridge, and the descent immediately after, the line of danger was passed."[108]

Black runaways in the Niagara region often discovered sympathetic gate-keepers at the tollgates of the international bridges. Samuel R. Ward told of an escaped slave who came face to face with his owner on the American side of the Niagara River. "In an instant," Ward explained, "he ran—almost flew—from the margin of the river, to gain the suspension bridge close at hand." The owner gave chase, but the fugitive, a few lengths ahead, reached the Niagara Falls Suspension Bridge first. Passage cost twenty-five cents, but the tollgate keeper elected not to collect the fee and cheered the freedom-seeker to reach the Canadian end of the overpass. On British soil, the winded fugitive looked the slaver in the eye and calmly smiled.[109] By virtue of the bridge and the Crown's soil, the two men stood on equal terms. It became commonplace in the Niagara zone to rely on the bridges. As the treasurer of Syracuse's Fugitive Aid Society, William E. Abbott, wrote to Maria G. Porter of Rochester, "It has been our custom to forward all directly on to the [Niagara Falls Suspension] Bridge."[110]

Fugitives could also employ ships in Rochester over Lake Ontario to connect to trail and rail to St. Catharines, such as the *Princess Royal, The Traveler,* and the *Chief Justice Robinson,* amongst many others.[111] These boats, which frequently left from Kelsey's Landing, were just as symbolic of liberty as the towering bridges over the Niagara River gorge. They were generally staffed with gracious captains, crews, and Black Jacks who were willing to grant a ride across the lake for little or no payment. Thomas Smallwood, traveling through the Niagara zone with others fleeing bondage and short on cash, explained that Captain Hugh Richardson of the steamer *Transit* "according to his usual benevolence reduced the fare for us."[112] And William Wells Brown asserted "friends of the slaves, knowing that I would transport them without charge, never failed to have a delegation when the boat arrived."[113] Sometimes runaways performed tasks aboard watercraft in exchange for the voyage. Many fugitives embarked on British and Canadian boats; their crews were viewed as more open-minded by virtue of their Empire affiliation. American shippers were also a viable option because the maritime subculture lent itself to freer thinking. One exception was Captain Robert Kerr of the steamer *Admiral,* which traveled Lake Ontario between Rochester and Toronto; he frequently did not allow Blacks to acquire passage aboard his boat. When he did permit Blacks to travel, Kerr wanted them to ride on the deck and not in the cabin, even in the winter months.[114]

Samuel R. Ward bore witness to the liberal gatekeepers on the waterways in the borderlands. On the bitterly cold day of January 11, 1853, while crossing the

Niagara River with Rev. Hiram Wilson at Youngstown, New York, Ward met a fugitive in the ferry office who was awaiting passage. The Irish ferryman let the Black runaway cross the river for less than half the fare. As the Irishman explained to Ward in no uncertain terms, "When a darky comes to this ferry from slavery, I guess he'll get across, shilling or no shilling, money or no money."[115] He, like many shippers on the Niagara River, Lake Ontario, and Lake Erie, understood the poverty of most fugitives, and he harbored a level of compassion. The Irishman told Ward that a score of fugitive Blacks had given him extra shillings for their voyage to freedom, which he used to subsidize the trips for others. In one case, a runaway insisted that the ferryman take twenty-four times the regular fare for the modest ride to liberty in Canada. When the shipper refused, the runaway firmly declared, "Keep it, then, as a fund to pay the ferriage of fugitives who cannot pay for themselves."[116]

Josiah Henson, an escapee from Kentucky who ran away with his family, made it from Sandusky, Ohio, to Buffalo on Lake Erie by working for a generous captain. In Ohio, Henson spotted a schooner and got work helping the mixed-race crew load bags of corn aboard the vessel. For his toil, he was able to get to Buffalo, where freedom was just on the opposite shore. "I want to see you go and be a freeman," the noble captain explained, but "I'm poor myself, and have nothing to give you; I only sail the boat for wages; but I'll see you across." He paid a ferryman three shillings for Henson and his family to cross the Niagara River to Canada.[117] When another Kentucky runaway, Francis Frederick, also landed in Sandusky looking for passage to Canada, friends bargained with a steamer captain to get him across the lake. "Have you only one?" the open-minded captain asked. "I wish you had one hundred, I would gladly take them over." Frederick was able to traverse both Lake Erie and Lake Ontario with the help of crews and willing captains, one of whom he deemed "a noble generous hearted man," until he reached Toronto.[118]

Escapee Isaac Mason benefited from the good graces of charitable captains as well. Once a personal servant in Kent County, Maryland, Mason settled in Worcester, Massachusetts, but he left his wife there to seek employment in Montreal and Toronto. "I went to the steamboat pier every day at four o'clock," Mason stated in Canada West, "and became familiar with the faces of the different boats that plied between Toronto and Rochester, N.Y." In 1851, after receiving a letter in Toronto that his spouse was ill, he explained, "I sought the captain of the boat that left Saturday evening, and asked him to allow me to work my way to

Rochester." Mason emphasized gratefully, "The letter with my pleadings moved his sympathy towards me." Nonetheless, the captain told Mason that "I could go but that I should have to work every hour of the time . . . I had to pay by hard work and no sleep."

All night, the ship stopped at different locations along Lake Ontario where Mason loaded and unloaded freight and assisted passengers. Eight o'clock Sunday morning, he arrived in Rochester exhausted and still facing the obstacle of getting to Worcester. After lodging and eating for a night, Mason was out of money. He decided to begin walking east toward Massachusetts and soon found work-for-passage on an Erie Canal boat, which vastly increased his pace of travel. Ironically, aboard the vessel, he spotted his former owner. Mason quickly disembarked and found other means to reunite with his wife and family. He was twice able to toil-for-transportation in the greater Niagara zone.[119]

Black sailors, whom historian Jeffrey Bolster called "angels of liberty," were trusted allies for escapees.[120] For example, Benjamin Pollard Holmes, once enslaved in King and Queen County, Virginia, worked on Lake Ontario vessels such as the *City of Toronto*, the *Chief Justice*, and the *Peerless*.[121] Holmes devised a plan that freed him, his wife Ann Eliza, and their young son Benjamin Alexander, but their masters insisted they go to Liberia, West Africa, as part of the manumission agreement. On August 3, 1840, the family left from Norfolk to go to Liberia abroad the American Colonization Society–backed *Saluda*. When a storm badly damaged the ship, the captain sought repairs in Philadelphia.[122]

There, Holmes was convinced to abandon plans to reach Africa, and he and his family instead set out for Canada via the Niagara route. They passed through Rochester for a few days, then took a steamer to Toronto, where they were greeted by Grandison Boyd, who had escaped bondage in Virginia and became a grocer in Rochester. The family was placed in the care of Rev. Hiram Wilson, who later moved to St. Catharines.[123] Holmes settled in Toronto and worked as a waiter on Lake Ontario ships which made regular scheduled day trips to the Niagara zone, and he frequented Rochester. Benjamin assisted countless Black fugitives aboard vessels bound for Canada. Holmes and his wife had another son, James Thomas, but Ann Eliza died in 1845. Benjamin, nonetheless, continued to work on Lake Ontario as a conduit of Black transnational interaction.[124]

Though people in the Niagara zone were willing to help, some Black runaways mistrusted their motives. Reportedly and according to family lore, Adam Nicholson of Virginia swam the Niagara River in the mid-1800s and settled in the outskirts of St. Catharines, and runaway Ben Hockley crafted a wooden raft made from a gate in an effort to reach Canada.[125] Of course, it was best to swim or row the Niagara River beyond the woes of Niagara Falls and its whirlpools, but even the "lower river" was very dangerous. Nicholson, described as "dark, rugged & sensible," was owned by Aaron Myers, "a hard man." The brutality of slavery was scarred on Nicholson's back, and he had only one eye, the other taken from an incident in bondage. As an escapee, he traveled under an alias, which further revealed his distrust of others in the unknown surroundings.[126] Hence, his alleged swimming of the Niagara River. On British soil, Nicholson toiled in a variety of agricultural pursuits.[127] In 1853, Hockley, a Tennessee escapee over the age of fifty, the *Niagara Mail* explained, "came to Lewiston but was afraid to go on the steamer to cross and tried to cross the river on the gate but the current being strong he was drifted out into the lake [Ontario]." Luckily, he was spotted and rescued by the *Chief Justice Robinson* and he gratefully exclaimed, "Thank the Lord, Massa, I am a freeman now."[128] Hockley learned the hard way that the Niagara region had people eager to bestow a hand.

Many of those in charge of transportation and tollgates in the Niagara region were more concerned with the passage of fugitives in need than with payment and profit. They acted with a faith that their good deeds would bring heavenly rewards to them personally and to the institutions they oversaw. Some knew that helping escapees was not going to put their employer out of business, but others, particularly on boats, demanded labor for passage. The Lake Ontario area sailors were part of a larger community of maritime workers—worldly, well-traveled, and conversant in a variety of languages.[129] Categorically, sailors encountered a diversity of people and had wide-ranging experiences, thus yielding a greater racial tolerance and a broader world view that ultimately benefited the fugitive.[130]

As technology evolved and railroad travel increased, Niagara region enterprisers harnessed the new means of transportation for American-Canadian international exchange.[131] The Niagara Falls Suspension Bridge added a deck for trains in 1855, putting the region light-years ahead of the Detroit frontier, which relied solely on water vessels. With time, more railroad ventures developed in the borderlands of Niagara, thus binding the already solid network of towns more closely together. "Our railroad facilities," boasted the *Niagara Falls Gazette* of the regional system, "must be deemed quite respectable, 'if not more so.'"[132] Although Rochester and St. Catharines were key to the composition of the region, other small towns such as Batavia and Lockport on the Erie Canal were

pivotal agents of movement between the two urban centers and the two nations. The Niagara region was fed escapees by many different people, including
John W. Jones of Elmira, New York; Gerrit Smith of Peterboro, New York; Sydney Howard Gay of New York City; and Stephen Myers of Albany, New York,
among others.[133] Fugitives were excited to find bands of active people and tangi-
ble systems of travel to navigate the unknowns of the Niagara zone.

Nonetheless, no matter where fugitives entered British North America,
they did not find a "Promised Land" or "sanctuary." The interconnected circumstances of Blacks in the American North and Canada throughout the early 1800s
were not restricted by national boundaries. Although Canada offered Blacks
greater legal rights, the belief in Black innate inferiority was a transcending sentiment in the Niagara region. Blacks arriving in Canada soon found that legal
privileges did not feed, clothe, or employ them. The work of building a new
life began right away. Neither the provincial government nor the local authorities made substantial arrangements to aid the newcomers. In fact, the question
that was continually asked of Blacks in the early 1800s was simple: Could they
fend for themselves? The fugitives who made it to Canada helped to answer
this query. Blacks, particularly in St. Catharines, demonstrated the ability to live
independently. The newcomers persistently proved that they were not slothful
or lazy; they possessed the ability to be "respectable" and useful inhabitants.[134]
The major problem that confronted Blacks was the attitudes of unsympathetic
whites. When Blacks pressed for equality, they stopped being the "interesting
negroes" and became the troublesome "niggers."[135]

CONSTANT BLACK MOVEMENT AND TRANSNATIONALISM

Once in Canada, Blacks sought greater rights and ways to be productive members of a community. Many fugitives did not stay where they first landed. When
Rev. Alexander Hemsley took the last leg of his trip out of America from Rochester aboard a British vessel, he disembarked in Toronto, a city that did not suit
his farming skills. In just a matter of days, he departed southward for the more
open frontier of St. Catharines.[136] Fugitive Isaac Riley and his wife crossed into
Canada at Windsor and had a tough time establishing themselves in the French
area of "Potico." They moved to St. Catharines, where they had better luck, yet
the Rileys eventually made their home in Rev. William King's Buxton settlement.
There, Riley helped survey the land, and he acquired one hundred acres.[137] As

Hiram Wilson in St. Catharines explained, "We have so many coming to us [that] we think it best for some of them to pass on to other places."[138] This is why historian Donald G. Simpson called St. Catharines an important "distribution center for many of the fugitives."[139] They were encouraged to find a community favorable to them, and movement and migration became part of the life of many antebellum Blacks. Alfred T. Jones explained, "I stopped a month at St. Catharines, then came to London [Canada West], and have remained here ever since."[140]

Mary Ann Shadd, for example, moved around Canada, spending time in several towns. But even before crossing the border, she had danced around America. Born in Wilmington, Delaware, she was raised in West Chester, Pennsylvania, and she taught in Black schools in Wilmington; Norristown, Pennsylvania; Trenton, New Jersey; and New York City. In 1849, Frederick Douglass published a letter from Shadd in which she added her voice to the "racial uplift" conversation of Northern Blacks. It crystalized her in ink for the first time on a major platform in the Rochester-based *North Star*.[141]

After the passage of the Fugitive Slave Act of 1850, Shadd joined a wave of emigration to Canada. By this time, she was used to moving around. Initially, Shadd landed in Windsor, Canada West, and she founded a school partly funded by the American Missionary Association, which provided provisions for fugitives. Shadd's passion to teach merged with her desire to edit and publish. In March 1853, she started the *Provincial Freeman* in Windsor, coedited with Samuel Ringgold Ward. The periodical later moved to Toronto and Chatham—as did she. On January 3, 1856, Shadd married Thomas F. Cary in St. Catharines at the home of her sister Amelia and husband David T. Williamson. At times, she traveled, using the "Garden City" as a stopping-point for trips between America and Canada.[142] It was the American Civil War that ultimately prompted Shadd Cary to return to the United States to become a recruitment officer and enlist Blacks in the Union Army.[143] Her constant movement in the early nineteenth century was the reality many Blacks experienced, especially those in a position to drive racial transformation.[144]

The two-way flow throughout this international zone was evident in the lives of people like Jermain Loguen, who reused his Rochester–St. Catharines connections to secure safety in Canada on several occasions. Horace H. Hawkins of Kentucky followed this strategy as well. In 1835, Hawkins first escaped to Malden, Upper Canada, by wagon, foot, and steamer, along with fourteen others. There, in the British colony, he worked in a tobacco factory before moving to

Rochester, as early as 1845, to preach the Gospel to Blacks at the Third Street Baptist Church. Fearing recapture, Hawkins retreated to British soil when the 1850 Fugitive Slave Act passed, but he later explained that "I didn't like to be pent up in Canada." After debating whether to return to America, he explained finally, "I just went back to my friends in Rochester . . . and soon raised the necessary money to purchase my free papers—$300."[145] Stories like these contravene the narrative of one-way migration from America to Canada that is commonly told; the borderlands were, in fact, a fluid frontier.

Cecelia Jane Reynolds, the second wife of Lake Ontario sailor Benjamin Pollard Holmes, witnessed and participated in the back-and-forth movement of people in the Niagara region. Cecelia was owned by attorney Charles M. Thruston of Louisville, Kentucky, and worked as the body servant to his daughter, Frances Ann. When the Thruston family decided to take an 1846 summer trip to Niagara Falls, New York, to stay at the luxurious Cataract House Hotel, Cecelia, only a teen, fled to the Canadian side of the cascades. She was likely helped by Black headwaiter at the Cataract, John Morrison, an agent for fugitives who, in the off-season, worked in Rochester as a waiter, butler, and barber.[146] She was then ushered from the Canada borderlands by Benjamin Holmes aboard the *City of Toronto* to its namesake. In Toronto, she worked in domestic pursuits to earn money and took care of Benjamin's boys, Benjamin Alexander and James. The two married, just five months after Cecelia arrived.[147]

The Holmes family traveled around Lake Ontario at the courtesy of the ships on which Benjamin toiled, visiting the Boyds, the Francis, and the Cleggett families in Rochester and other lake-bordering towns like St. Catharines.[148] Although they lived modestly, Cecelia longed to reunite with her mother, Mary, back in Kentucky, but she had no money to purchase her freedom. Faced with economic woes in the 1850s and the popularity of Niagara region railroads that reduced travel on ships, the couple decided to take a risk. They set out together for the gold fields of Australia via England, but the two returned separately without riches.

In March 1854, Cecelia came back to Canada to give birth to a daughter named Mary, who was not the child of her husband; the baby was affectionately called Mamie, after her grandmother. Benjamin returned in 1856 but was deathly ill, having been prescribed a lethal dose of mercury by an amateur physician when he was a steward on the ocean steamer *Black Eagle*. Back in Toronto, he declined rapidly but managed to work again for his former employer, Captain Thomas Dick on the *Chief Justice Robinson,* which often transported fugitives in the American-Canadian borderlands. Finally, his poor health forced him from lake to land as a common "labourer." He died on August 26, 1859, after which Cecelia moved to Rochester.[149]

The American-Canadian border swung open in both directions and was an ongoing reality. Tubman, Douglass, Loguen, Hawkins, the Holmes, and countless other Blacks all used the border as a liberation and networking tool for different reasons. William Henry Larrison, like his Niagara counterparts, reversed course. He fled New Castle County, Delaware, to reach Thomas Garrett's home in Wilmington and used all of the key means of the Niagara Underground Railroad network to move northward, including Philadelphia's William Still and New York City's Sydney Howard Gay. He reached the borderlands of Western New York and then traveled on to Canada, where he was deemed an "American-born, poor, Methodist." He settled briefly in Toronto but was driven to Rochester as a result of the 1857 Ontario financial recession. Larrison's fortunes changed when he found work farming at the home of William and Siba Slocomb on the outskirts of the city's East End. He soon fell in love and married widow Cecelia Jane Holmes.[150] In order to help support the family, Cecelia recrossed the American-Canadian border to see her stepchildren and to manage the house she inherited from her deceased first husband, Benjamin Pollard Holmes.[151] Samuel R. Ward explained it best: "There is a vast amount of intercourse . . . Canadians travel extensively in the States, as do the people of the States in Canada."[152]

* * *

In all, Blacks of the early and mid-1800s were a people of movement and migration in search of political agency to secure their freedom. Neither America nor Canada delivered Blacks from the flux of their erratic lives. Their journeys from the South to Canada challenged fugitives to be resourceful and also required a measure of good fortune. Successful runaways fit no one prototype. What freed one fugitive recaptured another. The journey to find favorable laws, better circumstances, and a basic livelihood took fugitives through many places, dangers, and changes. All the perils of escaping were worth it for those who made it to the North or to Canada. Although escaping bondage was a great achievement, arriving in the Northern states and the Canadian provinces gave way to new struggles and motivation for movement. Blacks often recrossed the borders of

America and Canada to interact with those of common cause. It is this dual-flow reality and the availability of transportation in the Niagara district that is so frequently overlooked. The movement from one location to another came at a great cost and with little guarantee. On the journey northward and many times back, a portion of fugitives passed through or settled in Rochester and St. Catharines, where they hoped to better their lives in the Northern unknown.

2

Rochester, New York
"RIGHT OVER THE WAY"

I was on the southern border of Lake Ontario and the Queen's dominions were right over the way.

> —FREDERICK DOUGLASS, *Life and Times of Frederick Douglass*
> (Park, 1881), 271

... my father's home in Rochester being the last Station on that road before reaching Canada the goal of the fleeing slaves ambition.

> —CHARLES REMOND DOUGLASS, "Some Incidents of the Home
> Life of Frederick Douglass," in Celeste-Marie Bernier and
> Andrew Taylor, eds., *If I Survive,* 672

Since Rochester's formation, Blacks have struggled in the city to achieve social mobility and to make use of the political processes as recourse for grievances. They faced issues of racial discrimination and unstable employment that limited their success in building churches, schools, institutes, and businesses important to their community. Most Blacks lived in the city's Third Ward, worked in service and travel-based industries, and were unable to break into the skilled labor class. Despite resistance from local power holders, Blacks made modest advances in areas such as education, where they were able to achieve their overarching goal of integration. Blacks also utilized Rochester's Niagara borderland frontier to their benefit, and antislavery activists constructed a network of interaction with Canadian towns such as St. Catharines. By focusing on the dynamic transnational location of Rochester, this chapter demonstrates how the Black community endured the decades before the American Civil War and used the city as an entry and exit point to Canada.[1]

EARLY BLACK CONNECTIONS TO CANADA

Long before the 1850s, Blacks inhabited the Rochester area and explored the alternative of life in nearby Canada. In fact, three of the city's best-known Black pioneers all ventured across the international lines at one point. Arriving in 1795, Asa Dunbar is credited with being the first Black to live in the Rochester region. In the 1790s, he joined a wave of "transplanted Yankee" New Englanders who settled in the Genesee Valley away from the Atlantic Coast.[2] Dunbar came from Massachusetts with his family of six and established a home in Irondequoit Bay. There, he cultivated fruit and sold salt gathered from a nearby deposit. In 1797, he relocated further south along the Irondequoit Creek where a new frontier was being settled—in what became Rochesterville, later Rochester.[3] The move offered greater opportunity: Dunbar found employment as manager of a large store, and through hard work, he earned the respect of his fellow citizens. He was so well respected in the community that he was once chosen to be the "city attorney."[4] When the town failed to prosper, Dunbar uprooted his family and headed for British Canada.[5] The move demonstrated that Rochester was a transnational junction, and it foreshadowed the back-and-forth migration of Blacks which yielded more nuanced social exchanges in the decades to come.

American Revolution veteran Nathaniel Rochester, the founder of the city, placed the settlement on a footing to flourish and introduced more Blacks to the area in the early 1800s. He and cofounders Charles Carroll and William Fitzhugh Jr. came to Western New York from Hagerstown, Maryland, on November 8, 1803, and they purchased 100 acres along the Genesee River.[6] Their property on the upper Genesee was located near waterfalls, a great potential source of power. Upper Falls and Lower Falls run through downtown Rochester, flowing northward and emptying into Lake Ontario opposite Canada.[7] In 1811, the land was surveyed, streets were built, and the population began to increase. However, development was delayed by the War of 1812 as militiamen defended the Genesee River and the Charlotte area from British Canadian invasion.[8] Carroll explained that Americans "should never sheathe the sword until we drive them [the British] from North America."[9] Many Blacks did not share this sentiment and looked to the British as a source of greater freedom. In 1817, after the conflict ended, the area's Southern landowners—Rochester, Carroll, and Fitzhugh—who had all owned slaves, combined their holdings, and Rochesterville was incorporated as an official village.[10] Colonel Rochester, who brought enslaved Blacks with him from the South, emancipated them when he first settled in Dansville, New York. Those formerly enslaved people, with the help of Mr. Rochester, moved to the new village in 1818 and, with others, formed the nucleus of a blooming community.[11]

Arriving a year before the village was incorporated, Austin Steward watched the town develop as he rose to prominence as its first Black business owner. Captain William Helm of Virginia had owned Steward. When Helm relocated to Sodus Bay, New York, and later to Bath, New York, Steward was forced to come with him, and he toiled as a hired-out enslaved laborer. He escaped from bondage around 1813, but Helm found him in Canandaigua, New York, some fifty miles away. Steward avoided recapture by seeking help from the New York Manumission Society, which cleverly used a legal technicality in the state's 1799 Gradual Emancipation Law to liberate him.[12] He also noticed that people in the region were "making every improvement in their power" and "flourishing villages were springing up as if by magic."[13] Steward wanted to get in on the action.

With his freedom secured, Steward started out in Rochesterville peddling cheese, meat, poultry, and other commodities, but he aspired to do more. In September 1817, instead of managing a store like Asa Dunbar, Steward opened his own meat market, centrally located on bustling Buffalo Street.[14] He attracted a substantial white clientele. His success made him a target for other local butchers. Steward's advertising signs were torn down and painted black. He demanded that the police launch an investigation, and he personally offered a $5 reward for information. His efforts were not in vain; law enforcement took one white offender into custody. The arrest sent a firm message throughout the village. The vandalism ceased, and Steward's social and economic stratification continued.[15]

By 1818, Austin Steward expanded his business by buying a new allotment of land on Buffalo Street for $500. He erected a two-story structure on the property, which served as his general grocery store and his home. In the summer of that year, Steward helped schoolmaster Zenas Freeman open a local Sabbath School to accommodate the growing Black population. A number of children were taught to read and write, including one of the community's future leaders, Reverend James Thomas, who later became a cornerstone of the Spring Street African Methodist Episcopal Zion Church. Unfortunately, the school failed due to the lack of funding and Black community support. Despite this setback, Steward's wealth and influence in Rochesterville grew.[16] He owned property in Brighton and Canandaigua, and he played a role in the early forms of the Canada-bound Underground Railroad that ran through the city.[17]

In the 1820s, Rochesterville started to grow rapidly. By 1823, the village expanded in landmass, the population reached 2,500 residents, and the settlement's name was shortened to Rochester. At the same time, the Erie Canal began operating in the area. When the canal officially opened on October 26, 1825, Rochester blossomed into the most thriving "boomtown" along its path.[18] Since the canal passed through the heart of downtown, it firmly established Rochester as a hub for commerce and industry above regional rivals such as Canandaigua and Batavia.[19] The Welland Canal later did the same thing for St. Catharines.

More advancements for Blacks in Rochester also occurred within the decade. The New York Emancipation Act took effect on July 4, 1827, freeing the remaining enslaved people in the Empire State. A celebration was hosted at Johnson Square (now Washington Square) by the small Black Rochester community, which featured the reading of the newly legislated act, music and dinner at a local hotel, and a keynote speech by the articulate Austin Steward.[20] In the following year, however, the emancipation-day festivities were called off. As signers of the cancellation notice explained, "we are poor, and it requires all the cash we can spare to pay our debts." They agreed that it was better to "stay at home and attend our business."[21]

By 1830, Monroe County had 475 Blacks, 263 of whom lived in Rochester where the general population was 5,000.[22] Most Blacks lived in the Third Ward and they worked as domestic servants or laborers for the city's elite.[23] Few were able to obtain work in skilled professions. In fact, there was only one Black mason, carpenter, and grocer in the entire town and two Black blacksmiths and teachers. Austin Steward, the grocer, was becoming well known within national abolitionist circles as a result of his activism. He was appointed vice president at the first Black national convention in Philadelphia, which discussed migration to Haiti, Mexico, Canada, and other locations. The delegates declared Canada "acceptable."[24] After returning to Rochester, Israel Lewis, an agent and fundraiser of the recently established Wilberforce Colony in Canada West, convinced Steward to relocate to Canada. "Some of my friends thought I had better remain in the States and direct emigrants to Wilberforce," Steward explained, "while others were certain I could benefit them more by going myself at once,—the latter I had determined to do."[25]

In 1831, Steward, the community's wealthiest Black citizen, sold his property, gathered six wagons packed with his possessions, and moved with his wife and five children to the Wilberforce Colony.[26] "I concluded to go to Canada,"

Steward asserted, "and try to do some good; to be some little service in the great cause of humanity."[27] However humble Steward's claims, he took a "principal" leadership role at the settlement and had the hope of gaining a seat in the British Parliament.[28] When he arrived, the Wilberforce settlement was 800 undeveloped acres in "the wilds of Canada," which was just the situation Steward desired. He believed that the "rough" rural environments, not crowded towns like Rochester or St. Catharines, were ideal places for Blacks to live independently and practice self-sufficiency.[29] Although the move seemed impractical, more Blacks in Rochester considered migration to Canada.

Reverend Thomas James filled the void that Steward left. Born a slave in Montgomery County, New York, James too had gone to Canada for asylum. As a teen, he escaped across the border to St. Catharines after his brutal owner, George H. Hess, set out to whip him. James explained, "I arose in the night, and taking the then newly staked line of the Erie Canal for my route, traveled along it westward" into the Niagara region where "a colored man showed me the way to the Canadian border." "Once on free soil," he expounded, "I began to look about for work, and found it . . . on the Welland Canal, which they were then digging. I found the laborers a rough lot and soon had a mind to leave them. After three months had passed, I supposed it safe to return to the American side, and acting on the idea I recrossed the [Niagara] river."[30] Despite facing the possibility of recapture, James journeyed back to the United States and settled in Rochester, demonstrating again that fugitives moved in both directions on the Niagara frontier, depending on their prospects for social mobility.

In 1823, James could not read or write and had never set foot in a church. Yet, eager to learn, he attended the Black Sabbath School on Buffalo Street, where Steward had once taught. At the freight warehouse along the Erie Canal where James worked, he wisely utilized the long winter and spring months, when the canal was closed or traffic was slow, to study.[31] Understanding the transformative nature of education, he opened his own school for "colored children" on Favor Street in 1828. The new school acted as a way station for runaways awaiting passage to Canada and as a place for religious gatherings. James also began formal training to preach the Gospel, and by 1830, he purchased property where the African Methodist Episcopal Zion Church was later constructed under his guidance. In the years that followed, James was officially ordained a minister and launched an abolitionist biweekly newspaper, *The Rights of Man,* with William C. Bloss and other progressive-minded Rochesterians. In 1835, James left to establish churches in Syracuse and Ithaca, on Long Island, New York, and in New Bedford, Massachusetts.[32]

After some six years away, Austin Steward returned to Rochester from the Wilberforce Colony in 1837 having spent his entire fortune on the collapsed Canadian settlement.[33] Reentering the city "penniless," he contemplated: "What would my Rochester friends think of my conduct?" However, a group of esteemed businessmen welcomed him back and helped him reestablish his business.[34] "Their frown and displeasure, I was better prepared to meet than this considerate act of Christian sympathy, which I am not ashamed to say melted me to tears, and I resolved to show my appreciation of their kindness by an industry and diligence in business."[35] Other Blacks were not as fortunate; only a small number of them listed in the City Directory of 1838 were employed. Of the fifty-nine heads of households documented, only eighteen were listed as having a skilled or semiskilled occupation. While the Rochester Common Council provided some relief for immigrants, Blacks often relied on the scarce resources of churches and sympathizers.[36]

In the early 1840s, Rochester developed into the top flour-producing city in the nation. The waterpower of Upper Falls drove the city's mills, and Rochester was dubbed the "Flour City" and "the Young Lion of the West."[37] The success was transitory because the center of the wheat processing industry shifted farther to the American West, where new frontier was being settled.[38] Consequently, Rochester was forced to rely on other industries to generate revenue. The area's nursery businesses, located primarily on the green outskirts of town, thrived, and they earned Rochester a new nickname, the "Flower City."[39] Harriet Jacobs explained that the city was "very pretty the trees are in full Bloom and the earth seems covered with a green mantle."[40] In the coming decade, over half of the state's nursery professionals were in greater Rochester, and more than 1,000 people were employed in nurseries.[41] Blacks like John Boston and William Anderson worked as gardeners and George James was a yardman at the Rochester House Hotel.[42] The Black population in Monroe County swelled to 655 people. Blacks came to town seeking jobs in the growing economy, and they valued the city's proximity and connections to Canada, but they fared little better than those of past decades.

By 1841, the Canada Mission Committee (CMC) was based in Rochester, and it sent missionaries, teachers, and funds to the British colony to aid fugitive slaves. Led by Hiram Wilson and other Oberlin College students working to support runaways in Canada, they partnered with Rochester businessman George A. Avery, Samuel D. Porter, Lindley M. Moore, and regional philanthropist Gerrit Smith.[43] The CMC was the beginning of more lasting connections that Wilson maintained with Rochester for years to come. In its tenure, the Canada Mission was able to supply over a dozen teachers to fifteen towns, including Toronto, Amherstburg, Chatham, Queens Bush, Sandwich, Dawn, the Wilberforce Colony, and St. Catharines. It poured some $9,000 into Canada West along with packages of clothing and books. Wilson declared the goal was "to cultivate the *entire being,* and elicit the fairest and fullest possible developments of the physical, intellectual and moral powers" of Blacks.[44]

The downside of the Canada Mission was that it let each entity act autonomously and unified the partners only through reports at annual meetings.[45] This management style prompted scholars to incorrectly proclaim that the CMC was nothing more than "a paper organization," "a loose federation" that "lacked any systematic plan." They also criticized its modest financial output.[46] A compounding issue was that some viewed Hiram Wilson with suspicion. He had been working in Canada since the winter of 1836 but was removed as an agent from the American Anti-Slavery Society in 1838 and was a part of the failed Dawn Settlement in Canada West.[47]

Nonetheless, the Canada Mission, despite criticism of its point man and its administration, was firm evidence of strategic efforts in Rochester to work in a transnational way and offer benevolence to fugitives fleeing into British territory. Moreover, out of this goodwill effort in Rochester, the American Missionary Association (AMA) was born in 1848. Better organized than its predecessor, the AMA provided more provisions to Blacks across the Canadian border, including a school in St. Catharines.[48] As Wilson explained, the "Committee is obviously superseded by the Am. Miss. Asso. which I think aught [*sic*] to adopt the missions in Canada, . . . & sustain them."[49] The AMA agreed, and gave Wilson a salary and resources to aid fugitives.[50] Unquestionably, the CMC and AMA fit the socially progressive mindset growing in Western New York.

Throughout the late 1840s, Rochester saw the three major social movements in full swing—abolition, women's rights, and temperance. The New England approach to abolitionism shunned the US Constitution and the political process as a means for ending slavery, but Western New York embraced them. When Reverend Thomas James relocated to New England, he met the emerging abolitionist Frederick Douglass in New Bedford, Massachusetts, and he told Douglass that Rochester was fertile ground for a newspaper. Quakers like pharmacist Isaac Post and his wife Amy—ambassadors for social change—made the atmosphere in the city ripe for activism. The Posts hosted a number of public figures in their home, including William Lloyd Garrison, Sojourner Truth, and Douglass on his first trip to town.[51] Heeding the advice of Reverend James, Douglass moved to Rochester, and he became a pillar of the community.[52] He continued the growing transnational interaction with Canada. At the time Douglass settled in Rochester, an experienced community of people worked across the border and plenty of fugitives used the city as a way station on their journey to Canada. The antislavery activism in the latter stages of the 1840s in Rochester foreshadowed the thriving movement of the 1850s.

Douglass established the *North Star* in Rochester on December 3, 1847, and carried on the legacy of Canadian relations. He initially opened an office in the damp basement of the AME Zion Church, which Reverend James, his former minister and newspaperman, had launched, but later Douglass relocated his headquarters to 25 Buffalo Street (now 25 East Main Street) in the center of downtown.[53] In a newspaper report about the new Black periodical, the *Daily Advertiser* declared, "Its mechanical appearance is exceedingly neat and its leading article indicates a high order of talent. Mr. Douglass, it will be not denied, is a man of much more than ordinary share of intellect." The *Advertiser* urged the public to "sustain Mr. Douglass' paper."[54]

From the outset, the periodicals of Douglass highlighted important Canadian events and maintained financial backers and circulation in the British colony. His papers covered many Canada-related topics, including the status of Black immigrants, Detroit frontier settlements such as Buxton, population calculations, and even the fair price of postage to the Queen's dominion.[55] "It is a source of no small satisfaction to me," a writer from Canada told the *North Star* in June 1848, "to learn that a press has been established with yourself [Douglass] at its head . . . it is just the thing we need."[56] In August 1848, Douglass also focused on the transnational overpass of the Niagara Falls Suspension Bridge, recognizing the vital role it would play in the lives of Black fugitives on each side of the border.[57] Engineer Charles Stuart praised the overpass for its ability to transport "merchandise, coal and iron, to and from the Great West and Canada," but it was also key in moving Blacks between nations in the borderlands.[58]

In August 1848, the Rochester community celebrated the British Emancipation Day holiday of August First, affirming again its transnational orientation.

The city's commemoration that year attracted between 1,500 and 2,000 people. A *North Star* advertisement urged, "Come out and devote one day to honor holy freedom and do what he may towards advancing the cause of Emancipation in our own land."[59] Some arrived from neighboring villages, while others journeyed from Canada and distant places abroad. The crowd included Black and white participants. "The occasion is not one of color," Douglass declared, "but of universal man."[60] Those from the Women Rights' Movement like Julia Wilbur and Abigail Bush supported the cause; they helped to organize and attended Emancipation Day celebrations.[61]

The 1848 festivities consisted of a procession with bands and banners with remarks such as "Ethiopia stretches forth her hands to God," and "Knowledge is power," and another bearing a Holy Cross proclaimed, "With this we overcome."[62] A parade marched from the Colored Church on Ford Street to Washington Square, where Douglass delivered the keynote speech. Blacks had several ways to end the day, including a grand ball at Irving Hall or a fair at Minerva Hall. The entire affair, local newspapers reported, was done in a gratifying manner.[63] Rochester celebrated the British Emancipation Day throughout the 1850s and early 1860s. A score of Blacks ventured to Canada to join in their gatherings as well. Though the emancipation law that the British Parliament passed in 1833 had no power on American soil, Rochester Blacks affirmed their common identity and celebrated the freedom of their counterparts, regardless of borders.[64]

BLACKS IN THE 1850S: FUNCTION AND FRICTION

By the 1850s, Rochester was a hub for Black fugitives and transients seeking Canada. They were a growing reality during the decade, and the local newspapers were dotted with their stories. It was common to hear reports like, "We learn that five runaway slaves left in this morning's Boat for Canada," or "A very valuable fugitive . . . passed thro' this city to Canada on Wednesday night."[65] And *Frederick Douglass' Paper* often described instances like how three families arrived in the neighboring British colony from Rochester, adding "Thanks unto a merciful God they are now safe in Canada!"[66] Rochester and the greater borderlands also featured a countercurrent of those reentering the United States from Canada like Thomas James and Jermain Loguen, both of whom once resided in St. Catharines.

In 1853 alone, there was an abundance of activity. In October, the *Rochester*

Daily Union reported that three runaways had found refuge in the city. One was a twenty-two-year resident of Philadelphia who was forced to flee after receiving word that a claimant was in town attempting to take him back South. The other two travelers, a married couple en route to the Queen's soil, were runaways from North Carolina, who took flight to the "City of Brotherly Love" aboard a vessel and reached Rochester with help from "friends" along the way. "They are by this time," the article cheerfully explained, "safe in Canada."[67] In the same year a Rochester newspaper reported that some ten "hearty" fugitives from Virginia had reached the borderland city. One was a youngster who was set to be sold South for $1,400 the day before he fled, and another had paid $120 toward his own emancipation. The newspaper noted Rochester's increase in foot traffic by explaining that "More fine negroes are finding their way into the Canadian province than ever before," and that Blacks "preferred to live on beechnuts in Canada, and own themselves, rather than be any man's chattels."[68]

Even the harsh winters of Rochester did not deter Black runaways from coming. On November 30, 1853, "Three stout colored fellows" passed through Rochester amidst a "threatening" storm of strong winds and rain. The weather created icy conditions and kept the *Princess Royal*, a ship that ran between Rochester and the British colony, on the Canadian side of Lake Ontario. The storm even hampered movement on the Erie Canal. Still, the determined Black trio eventually reached the warmth of the British Lion's mane.[69]

Runaways demonstrated the contingency and messiness of life in the Niagara borderlands. In 1858, a fugitive Black couple from Greenbrier County, Virginia, showed up in Rochester and had to wait a day until money could be raised for their passage to Canada. That evening, the woman got "beastly drunk, and made considerable disturbance." Things became so unmanageable that the police were called to restore peace. These escapees were clearly supposed to be sent back to the South under the 1850 Fugitive Act, but at the man's request, they were "locked up" by authorities until morning, when they "were discharged and sent off by the Underground Railroad to Canada."[70] Rochester maintained traits unique to borderland places, including the fact that federal law could be blurred or simply not enforced at all. Its proximity to British soil clearly provided power and options.

Some local Blacks of Rochester created problems for escapees by pretending to be fugitives for monetary gain. Henry Johnson and Charles Reed represented themselves as slave deserters from the South. "It is a favorite game of vagrant colored people to pretend to be fugitives and are often successful among the benevolent," the *Rochester Daily Union* explained. Fortunately, in this instance, Johnson and Reed were exposed and arrested.[71] Local abolitionists were warned about people performing such shameful tricks. Still, a few years later, Edward and Elizabeth Raising attempted to pull the same stunt. Justice Butler Bardwell sentenced the fugitive pair to three months in the Work House. The "friends of freedom" were asked to intervene, but no one stepped forward to help.[72] The reason why was revealed the next day when William James Watkins, an active Underground Railroad agent, wrote to the editor of the *Rochester Union and Advertiser,* exposing the Raisings. He explained that the *"happy"* couple, who often drank "Irish whiskey," had lived in Rochester for two or three years, having come to town from the Livingston County Poorhouse. The Raisings were not fugitives, Watkins explained; they were "drunken Black vagrants, without a home."[73] These crimes diverted resources from real fugitives. But such distractions did not keep Rochester from playing its role as a two-way gateway to and from Canada throughout the decade.

Enslaved coachman John Roberts, who served Richard C. Stockton for some twenty years, escaped to Canada on June 28, 1837, while in Western New York. He got help from abolitionist Gerrit Smith, but he returned to the United States in the 1850s. Stockton ran an advertisement in the *Rochester Daily Democrat,* on of all days the Fourth of July in 1837, requesting Roberts' return and stating that he would be "kindly received" if he were to do so. In the Toronto *Christian Guardian,* Roberts responded to his former owner in disbelief and outright rejection. "Can you think," he asked, "that I would voluntarily relinquish Freedom, fully secured to me by the British Government, to return to American Slavery . . . ?" Roberts candidly explained, "I cannot again become a Slave . . . no never. To ask it is an insult to the spirit of Liberty, to the Dignity of human nature, to that Heaven born religion you profess." Roberts thought Stockton had bought into the mythology of Black ignorance. "How has the habit of oppression" he asserted, "warped your judgment and dulled your sensibilities." Among his last words, Roberts declared, "I have been delivered." In the 1850s, Roberts corresponded with *Frederick Douglass' Paper* to encourage abolitionist unity and electoral support for antislavery candidates. He also resettled in the American borderlands, close enough to take advantage of the Canadian border again.[74]

In the mid-1850s, Isaac D. Williams returned to the American side of the Niagara zone to visit Syracuse for a needed hand surgery; he had been shot while escaping and "could hardly work" due to the pain. Williams explained, "I stopped at Rochester before going back and interviewed the great Fred. Douglas, and from there I went back to St. Catharines, after having a most eventful journey." Williams knew he "was running a great risk, though my new-made friends assured me they would stand by and protect me from my persecutors if they appeared."[75] On the British side of the border and in better health, he started working for the Great Western Railway of Canada the year its tracks opened on the Niagara Falls Suspension Bridge, which accelerated transnational travel.

In the 1850s, the general population of Rochester continued to grow, though not at the rate of the Erie Canal boom in decades past. Census records reveal that the city reached a total population of 36,403, making it slightly larger than Toronto. Black residents in Monroe County numbered 699 in 1850; 549 of them lived in the urban center.[76] The overwhelming majority of Blacks, 68 percent, were from Northern states, while 22 percent hailed from the American South. Others came to the city from Canada and from the Caribbean islands of Jamaica, St. Thomas, and Antigua. For a score of Blacks, the "place of birth" was listed as "unknown," and there were slightly more Black females than males.[77]

These population numbers should be tempered with the understanding of Rochester's borderland location, which made people exceedingly mobile. "I am now a Citizen of Rochester," Samuel Porter explained, "or rather I may say a Citizen of the World for my locomotive faculties have been so many times put in practice . . . that I am hardly entitled to call myself a citizen of any particular place."[78] For decades, life in Rochester was celebrated for its means of transience. A British visitor once noted, "every thing in this bustling place appeared to be in motion."[79] Of those recorded in directories during 1855, about 53 percent had died or moved before the decade concluded.[80] Many whites grew restless in the area and went farther West to the nation's new frontier. The Black population fluctuated as a result of the 1850 Fugitive Slave Act and the limited opportunities available to them in Rochester.

Early on, Douglass's experiences in Rochester caused him to assert that an "unrighteous spirit of *caste* . . . prevails in this community," and he complained of "Black-phobia."[81] "Our white fellow citizens" Douglass explained, "for the most part, whatever may be their private feelings on the subject of equality or negro inferiority, are generally sufficiently mindful of the characteristics of gentlemen and ladies, to treat us with perfect civility when they meet us in the street." However, he continued, "But there are others, (by no means the best looking part of our white community) who have adopted the custom of making their mouths about as ugly as their hearts, the moment they see us."[82] The prejudice that "ran rampant" in Rochester initially made Anna Douglass "distrustful" of her surroundings.[83] In fact, this "spirit of *caste*" was not only apparent to Blacks in passing jesters on the street, but in more concrete matters. Most Blacks lived in the Third Ward, they rented rooms or apartments, and their personal property did not exceed 100 dollars in value. This economic barrier or "*caste*" was virtually impossible to overcome, though a select few managed to do so.

THE THIRD WARD AND SURROUNDING AREAS

As they had in the past, most Blacks lived in the Third Ward throughout the 1850s. Of the 4,779 people who dwelled there at the beginning of the decade, 172 were Black.[84] The number continued to increase, and by 1860, 207 Blacks resided in the area.[85] Blacks in the Third Ward lived primarily on six streets: Washington, Clay, Ford, Spring, Troup, and Sophia. This extraordinary Third Ward neighborhood housed wealthy professionals, middle-class residents, and the working-class people who served them. Blacks stayed nearby because they worked in the mansions of the city's social elite. However, the elegant brick homes, elaborate carriages, stylish clothing, and the general aristocratic Victorian era behavior must have annoyed poor Blacks. After all, some snobbish citizens thought of themselves more as "Third Warders" than Rochesterians. Blinded by the tree-lined streets, the Greek revival architecture of their mansions and engulfed in European art and furniture, genteel folk many times did not acknowledge other city wards or the suffering in their midst. They flaunted their wealth through valuable merchandise and adornments that most Blacks simply could not afford, in part because their success was limited by white racist practices and attitudes.[86] Nonetheless, the Third Ward, or the "Ruffled Shirt" ward, provided Blacks with the greatest opportunities to improve their standard of living.[87]

Not all Blacks lived in the Third Ward. Others were scattered throughout various sections of Rochester. The First, Fifth, and Eighth Wards all averaged about sixty Black people at the beginning of 1850.[88] Ralph and Margaret Francis were quite typical of Blacks in Rochester. They moved a number of times after arriving in the city. When Ralph first came to town from New Jersey, he lived in the First Ward on Trowbridge Street. Years later, he and his family stayed at 71 Adams Street, and in 1847 they relocated to 20 Clay Street. Finally, the

Francis family settled on Greig Street, in the Kelsey's Landing area, which connected to Lake Ontario.[89] People shuffled about this way because of job losses or the need for closer proximity to work, but it was rarely done willingly. Stability of residency was difficult to maintain; the lowly economic circumstances of many allowed them little control over their living conditions. But no matter how downtrodden Blacks were, they were nonetheless aware of Rochester's heightened interconnectivity to neighboring Canada, given the constant movement in the city that was impossible to miss or dismiss. For example, the Francis family left America for Canada; they moved to Port Hope, Canada West, in 1856, and by 1859 to Peterborough, Canada West.[90] This consciousness of the British colony gave Blacks a transnational identity that differentiated them from others in the country.

The homes of leading abolitionist Frederick Douglass were not in the Third Ward where the majority of Blacks lived; they were located across town in the Seventh Ward and on South Avenue. In April 1848, Douglass purchased the first home for his family. Newspaper publisher Joseph Marsh, who maintained an office on the Talman Block not far from the *North Star* headquarters, engineered the sale. Douglass's home at 4 Alexander Street, near the corner of East Avenue, was a nine-room, two-story brick house, located in a growing neighborhood in the city.[91] It had a porch, home office, and space for a small garden in the backyard for Anna Murray Douglass.[92] The house had room for children Rosetta, Frederick, Charles, and Lewis to spread out.[93] Anne, the fifth and final child, was added to the family in this home on Alexander. In addition, a relative of Mrs. Douglass, Charlotte Murray, and the assistant editor of the *North Star,* Julia Griffiths, also lived with the family for a time.[94]

The Douglass family remained on Alexander Street for four years before moving south of the city to a hillside farm on a road which became South Avenue. Although they relocated, Douglass kept the Alexander home as a real-estate investment. The new South Avenue home was a "neighborless place" with a hilltop view of the city as well as space for Douglass to garden and plant fruit trees.[95] Charles Douglass simply called the homestead "a beautiful spot" and a local newspaper called it "an ornament to our city."[96] It was a valuable and fashionable property for a Black man in the 1850s.[97] Moreover, the move further outside of Rochester was timely and strategic. It came shortly after the 1850 Fugitive Slave Act passed, and it gave Douglass a private roadway leading to his door and access to the city via a southeast dirt road. Isolating his home from the main streets of Rochester gave Douglass tranquility, and it also helped to better facilitate the movement of Southern fugitives to Canada.

Although Douglass did not live in the Third Ward, he stayed connected with the local Black community as much as possible for a man with his lecture and travel schedule.[98] On average, Douglass spent five months of the year in Rochester.[99] When in town, he spoke at the local Black churches, was active at abolitionist gatherings, and befriended members of the community. Even when he was touring the country or abroad, he could recall the activities and issues confronting the Black population in Rochester. It did not take long for Douglass to make his home "among strangers" a place of familiar faces and to join in the city's social and political affairs.[100] The distance of Douglass's homes from the Black community did not weaken his firm connection with his people. He worked tirelessly to advance Blacks and never lost the support of his local contemporaries. Douglass even boasted that "colored travelers told me that they felt the influence of my labors when they came within fifty miles" of the "Flower City."[101]

Small pockets of Blacks lived outside of Rochester in lush rural communities. The town of Webster had thirty-seven Blacks; Sweden had thirty-four; Brighton, twenty-one; and eighteen lived in Greece.[102] Some lived more isolated in towns like Gates and Rush, and others dwelled in surrounding counties. After Austin Reed's father Burrell died and he got into trouble in Rochester, his mother Maria was worried that "the city will surely spoil that boy," so she sent him to work for Herman Ladd in Avon in Livingston County.[103] Charles Douglass explained, "I went to work of my own choosing" on the farm of English immigrant Thomas Pierson "20 miles from Niagara Falls."[104] These individuals, who commonly worked as field hands and laborers, grew crops and raised livestock that supported markets in Rochester. Scores of Blacks who originated in the South preferred agricultural work as a means to earn money. Like their urban counterparts, Blacks who lived on the outskirts of the city were landless and heavily dependent on white employers. Still, the center of Black life in the Rochester area was unquestionably the Third Ward. Blacks living outside its borders commonly ventured into the Third Ward to shop, worship, and to visit their friends and family. Austin Reed, for example, returned "Home" every three months.[105]

Whites and Blacks in many sections of Rochester lived in close proximity. Interracial relationships resulted, but they were considered taboo and intolerable. In 1840, at least four of the forty-five households headed by Blacks likely involved interracial marriages.[106] The numbers are difficult to track by way of city records since couples had a strong interest in hiding their private lives from the disapproving public.

Look, for example, at the friendship of Douglass and Julia Griffiths of Britain, which was harshly condemned. Julia arrived in Rochester with her sister Eliza in 1848 to help Douglass with his newspaper. Douglass and his daughter Rosetta took their guests sightseeing around the city, and rumors began. They intensified when Douglass was spotted walking arm-in-arm with the English woman. When people heard that the unmarried and attractive Julia was living at the Douglass residence, conservative townsmen and local abolitionists alike reacted with shock. There were reports of how endearing the two acted toward each other, and Julia's habits of doing things like her reading to Douglass at night drew much attention.[107] Even though Douglass denied the "scandalous reports" to local abolitionist Samuel D. Porter in early 1852, people still believed the friendship was suspiciously close. Douglass's close friends, Amy and Isaac Post, remained neutral in the midst of the Rochester gossip; they believed Douglass was a devoted husband. But the criticism continued.[108]

Julia moved out of the residence after claims of being a "home-wrecking Jezebel," but she remained a part of the local newspaper team until 1855.[109] The backlash against the friendship of Julia and Douglass was partly because he was married but even more so because she was white. Such public scrutiny was the reason why interracial relationships were not openly pursued, and interracial couples remained low-key in their communal dealings. Blacks and whites interacted in public, but they did so carefully.[110] For instance, during an 1850 antislavery fair, organizers invited "at least two hundred persons of both sexes, and all colors and classes" to dine together at one table. Amy Post believed that people sitting down to break bread together would help to "kill prejudice."[111] It was an honorable effort by a forward-thinking group, but the fact that gatherings like this did not happen regularly showed the deep-seated racial antipathy Blacks faced in the borderland city.

BORDERLAND RELIGIOUS, BENEVOLENT, AND ANTISLAVERY INSTITUTIONS

To escape from racism and prejudice, Blacks often retreated to places of worship. From the beginning, Black churches in Rochester were not stable entities in the community, and this situation continued into the 1850s. Due largely to lack of finances, churches had a hard time surviving as strong institutions. Several houses of worship closed only to reopen at a later date. Some lacked permanent locations and used temporary sites that varied each Sunday. Others simply could not survive because the operational costs were outweighed by the overwhelming financial needs of the membership.

The fragile nature and unclear life spans of Black churches in Rochester have generated some confusion among historians. What is certain is the African Methodist Episcopal Zion Church, founded in the 1820s, was the first of its kind in the city. Others would follow: the Abyssinian Baptist Church, the Bethel (African) Church, the First African Methodist Church, and the Third Street Baptist Church. All these churches were small in size and struggled to stay afloat. They occasionally filled their seats when there were guest speakers or for holiday services.

The African Methodist Episcopal (Zion) Society, established in 1823 on Ely Street, is a great example of church instability in Rochester. The religious society evolved into an established church within three years, and members initially worshipped in a modest brick building. But it was auctioned off in June of 1830 after the young congregation defaulted on the mortgage.[112] Shortly thereafter, Reverend Thomas James purchased another site, and the congregation rallied to erect a new brick building at Favor and Spring Streets.[113] It cost over $2,500 to construct, and it could seat 150 people. The edifice was made possible by $572 in subscriptions from the local Black population and contributions totaling $1,441 from the white community. One of the largest single Black pledges was made by barber Burrell Reed of $25, but he died before the temple was finished.[114] On October 7, 1828, the church opened with a dedication service.[115] In the 1830s, membership at Spring Street AME Zion fluctuated around fifty people.

With each decade, steady maturity and financial security eluded the church. By 1850, Spring Street AME Zion became a focal point of controversy for permitting a segregated public school to hold classes in their basement. Douglass attacked the church's leadership in his newspaper and organized a successful boycott against the school.[116] The church was also overly dependent on Reverend James, who spent periods of time on the road preaching and establishing other congregations. The Zion Church wavered or ceased to operate when he was absent. In fact, James had to revitalize the church when he came back to Rochester from New England in 1856.[117] The church not only battled internal hardships, but it also dealt with the reality that white Methodists did not worship with their Black denominational associates. The AME Zion Church on Spring Street constantly faced financial challenges, but it was the best the Black community could do in the early 1800s. Zion sheltered fugitives until they could find passage to Canada, it hosted public festivals that brought the Black community together, and the city's first female antislavery society was started at the church.[118] But for all the fine work done at Zion, there were still instances, such as the event in 1857, when ill-mannered attendees disrupted the worship service.[119]

Without strong churches, the Black community did not have a solid cornerstone. During this era, churches acted as more than spiritual centers. They were sites of community solidarity and offered mutual assistance sorely needed by fugitive slaves and newcomers. The churches cared for the sick, fed the hungry, clothed those in need, befriended widows, and provided guardians for orphans. They also ran literary societies, Sabbath schools, and the sanctuaries often served as meeting halls for social change. Everything from public celebrations to funerals were facilitated through the churches. Leaders expected members to conduct their affairs with dignity, and they preached a gospel of "upright" deportment. Within their congregations, Blacks could escape from the racist culture and institutions that surrounded them, and the Rochesterian clergy, such as Reverend Noah C. W. Cannon and minister David Green, were not marred in scandals as were their counterparts in St. Catharines.[120] The most important role served by "Flower City" churches, after saving souls, was helping fugitives. Nevertheless, they simply could not meet all of the social welfare needs of the community and its transients.

Local antislavery and mutual relief organizations played a major role in providing for Blacks where the churches fell short. The all-male Rochester Anti-Slavery Society and the Rochester Female Anti-Slavery Society predated the Western New York Anti-Slavery Society (WNYASS) formed in 1842 and the Rochester Ladies Anti-Slavery Society (RLASS) formed in 1848, which all helped to sustain the Black community.[121] The membership of each group was interracial, and its well-connected and internationally known leaders worked with ordinary people. Both groups found diverse ways to assist Blacks with food, housing, and other necessities. The WNYASS sold textiles and crafts, in America and Canada, at annual festivals called bazaars, commonly timed for holiday gift giving, to support fleeing fugitives.

The RLASS was started because of "the utter coldness in the community on the slavery subject." It hosted events similar to those of the WNYASS, held a lecture series, and invested hundreds of dollars a year to help fugitives get to Canada. The society reported in 1855 that it assisted fifty-eight Blacks further North and did so with "heartfelt satisfaction." Many Black runaways came to them and "asked for nothing, but for 'aid to CANADA!'"[122] A year later, they spent $130.42 toward train and boat rides for fugitives going to the Queen's soil.[123] In 1858, the Rochester women continued their generous ways by raising $530, and they helped some 150 people who approached them for aid, and they did the same for 129 in 1859.[124] Their Constitution stated simply that "its object shall be, to raise funds for Anti-Slavery purposes" and "slavery is an evil that ought not to exist, and is a violation of the inalienable rights of man."[125] The RLASS established a relationship with Harriet Tubman, and large sums of money went to supporting the newspapers of Douglass.

There were few abolitionists in Rochester compared to the general population, and some individuals, such as Quaker Julia Wilbur, an acquaintance of Douglass and Susan B. Anthony, held memberships in both antislavery groups. As a secretary of the WNYASS, Wilbur was deemed "a most efficient and ever faithful worker." In the RLASS, she had family and friends such as Charlotte Wilbur, who periodically hosted the group's biweekly meetings and owned a wig and ornamental hair business, and Anna Barnes, the niece of famous freedom fighter Lucretia Mott. Julia Wilbur noted "I can sympathize with *both*."[126] Rochester's abolitionist activities clearly surpassed those of Buffalo and Syracuse. Nonetheless, Charles Douglass explained, "The white people of Rochester while in the main were opposed to Slavery, they did not encourage to any marked degree Anti-Slavery agitation. They would aid an escaping slave in his flight to Canada but they did not care to have their names mentioned. They were afraid of being held to account under the infamous fugitive slave law."[127]

WORK IN THE BORDERLAND

Help from mutual relief organizations was a stopgap for Blacks; their real goal was employment and financial independence. Nonetheless, Blacks in Rochester, as the *Daily Democrat* reported, were "shut out from our [white] stores, offices and mechanic shops" and "consigned to the occupations of cooks, waiters, whitewashers, and bootblacks, with here and there a barber or a dealer in old clothes. This was the field of their efforts, or starvation."[128] To make matters worse, "Negro work" in the late 1840s and throughout the 1850s was threatened by European immigrants to the city. Local employers gave preference to white

Irish and German newcomers over Black laborers. With fresh competition in town, Blacks found it increasingly difficult to get work. Frederick Douglass and other community leaders, aware of the barriers, struggled to create new jobs in the community.

Throughout the 1850s, Douglass was one of the most prosperous Blacks in town. His newspaper shop on Buffalo Street was opposite Reynold's Arcade and just a short distance from Corinthian Hall.[129] The site was a real symbol of his status. The Reynold's Arcade—the central business center in Rochester—contained eighty-six rooms and fourteen basement stores. Among the tenants were the executive headquarters of Hiram Sibley's Western Union Company and John Jacob Bausch's optical business.[130] The Arcade also housed factories, artist studios, dentists, barbers, jewelers, tailors, and a post office, from which Douglass mailed his newspapers.[131] Corinthian Hall was the largest and most prestigious auditorium in the city, and it hosted concerts, plays, balls, fairs, and lectures. It was also the site of many abolitionist activities. On July 5, 1852, it played host to Douglass's "What to the Slave Is the Fourth of July?" speech, which was delivered before an audience of some 600 people.[132]

Black businesses opened and closed on busy Buffalo Street, but Douglass remained there for some fifteen years. Even so, he never made much money from the sale of his newspapers. In fact, after publishing for just five months, the paper faced financial embarrassment. The editors released a statement explaining that the *North Star* needed "more than the bare subscription list" if it was going to stay afloat throughout its first year; it needed donations in "liberal amounts."[133] Douglass had to mortgage his house and spent $12,000 of his own funds to finance the operating expenses for the new paper.[134] At the same time, the editorial staffs at his competitors, the *Liberator* and the *Standard,* attempted to stifle his success from the start. Presbyterian minister and abolitionist James Miller McKim, writing to Sydney Howard Gay, explained, "I don't like the establishment of the 'North Star' at Rochester. It will cripple the *Standard* sorely. What can be done to prevent this?"[135] Though some believed that Douglass was doing well financially, he faced the same debt and fear of going out of business as his fellow abolitionist editors. "To maintain" the *North Star,* Douglass's son explained, "every effort was put forth by every member of the family to keep it alive."[136]

In 1848, Julia Griffiths, the daughter of an English printer and publisher, came from Great Britain to help Douglass with his newspaper.[137] During her time in Rochester, she acted as the financial manager and coeditor. One of her first goals was to separate the newspaper's finances from the personal income of Douglass. Julia also instituted money-making projects that boosted earnings, including annual antislavery bazaars, subscription drives, and soliciting letters. In 1853, she alone coordinated a $10 gift campaign which brought in $1,000, and she produced the book *Autographs for Freedom,* which was a select collection of abolitionists' literature. Julia managed to get Horace Greeley, Gerrit Smith, and Henry Ward Beecher to contribute to the book, and she promoted it in local Rochester newspapers.[138] In addition, she used her position as secretary with the Rochester Ladies Anti-Slavery Society to generate even more revenue. Of all the people who helped Douglass sustain his newspapers, he was most indebted to Griffiths. In one year, she increased the Canadian and general circulation of the paper from 2,000 to 4,000 copies and eliminated his debt and home mortgage. "She seemed to rise with every emergency," Douglass explained, "and her resources appeared inexhaustible."[139]

Douglass was a skillful fundraiser as well. He lectured and published pamphlets of his talks for profit. In fact, Sydney Howard Gay, fearing his competition, believed he "would be more useful as a lecturer, than as an editor."[140] A seminal abolitionist, Douglass maintained supportive relationships with antislavery organizations and managed to get generous donations. Douglass also raised such large amounts of money in Canada for his papers that in 1854 he angered editor Mary Ann Shadd of the financially strapped *Provincial Freeman.* Shadd lashed out at Douglass in a series of editorial attacks, and she particularly took issue with Miss Julia Griffiths hosting bazaars in Toronto to sell English and Irish goods on behalf of Douglass and his American-based paper.[141] "We would rather the great Frederick Douglass," Shadd mockingly explained, "would stay out of our sunlight."[142]

Douglass refused to limit where he could raise funds, and his lifestyle was a constant battle against arbitrary social barriers. Despite the pushback from Shadd, Douglass persistently built business contacts on the Canadian side of the border and benefited from the vibrant "sunlight" of British soil.[143] When the *North Star* was renamed the *Frederick Douglass' Paper,* Henry Bibb, the editor of Canada's first Black newspaper, the *Voice of the Fugitive,* explained, "Much as we regret to see the *North Star* cease to shine . . . we wish our friends success, and hope that the cause may prosper under the new change."[144] By 1859, Shadd's paper and Bibb's *Voice of the Fugitive* failed, and it was the periodicals of Douglass that continued to highlight the news of Black Canada.[145]

Each of Douglass's newspaper endeavors between 1847 and 1863 were lead-ing messengers for the abolitionist cause and enjoyed relative success. Copies of his journals were distributed not only throughout the United States and nearby Canada but also to the distant lands of Mexico, Australia, and Europe. His big-gest foreign investors and supporters were in Canada and the British Empire. The subscribers were predominantly white, since Black purchasing power was low and some of them were reluctant to support abolition publicly.[146] Doug-lass used his papers to showcase Black poets, essayists, and rising journalists. He hired local Blacks, such as Nathaniel H. Moore, to help with the papers and others, such as William C. Nell, came to town to aid Douglass.[147] His publica-tions were largely free of poor grammar and orthographical missteps, and his periodicals never missed an issue.[148] Even Gay once admitted that the *North Star* was "well written," "neatly printed with handsome type," and was a "credit to the taste, the skill, and ability of its proprietor and editor." It was frankly, he added, "all that its best friends could wish it to be."[149] Although Douglass man-aged to keep his newspapers afloat, it was a sacrifice and a financial strain, and they brought him little wealth. The base of Douglass's financial strength was his income-producing properties. He was resourceful and learned to make his land-holdings bring him prosperity.[150]

Most Blacks in the city had more conventional ways of earning a living. Barbering was a popular occupation among Black men in Rochester. Barbers earned decent money and were conduits of news. Early in the 1800s Burrell Reed owned a barbershop on Carol Street and was able to support a family of five and buy a home with his earnings.[151] In 1851 alone, there were more than twenty bar-bers competing for the town's interracial clientele. Some Blacks managed their own shops, but they generally had trouble staying in business. Of all the Black barbers in Rochester, Jacob P. Morris and Ralph Francis were the most distin-guished. By 1850, Morris owned a barber saloon valued at $200; he was Douglass's Underground Railroad colleague and an executive committee member of the WNYASS. In addition, he acted as a spokesperson for local Blacks at state and national conventions and championed the cause of Black voting rights. Morris owned several shops in the downtown area before opening one in the Blossom Hotel at 37 Main Street. In January 1854, a fire broke out at the Blossom, and his shop was one of the many businesses destroyed.[152] Nearly a month later he was robbed of $15.[153] Disappointed by his misfortune, the intelligent and well-known master barber left for California. As the *Daily Democrat* said, "We wish him the success that industry and good conduct deserves."[154] Morris tried his luck in the Gold Rush but later returned to Rochester with empty pockets. He remained in the city until his death on September 5, 1866.[155]

Ralph Francis was also an esteemed barber in town. After Austin Steward and Frederick Douglass, Francis was one of the most recognizable and prominent Blacks in the community. He moved to Rochester in its Erie Canal boomtown days, and by 1840 he was working at the Rochester House Hotel alongside barber William F. Myers.[156] Four years later, Francis was listed as a "hairdresser," indicating that he had expanded his services to accommodate both men and women. In 1847, Francis had done so well that he was able to become a coowner in the Genesee Bathing House while still barbering in the basement of the Eagle Hotel.[157] In 1851, Francis joined forces with another barber to create the Francis and Clegget barbershop at 13 Reynold's Arcade, opposite the post office. The partnership gave Francis the time to establish the Steam Boat Hotel at Kelsey's Landing, where many fugitives departed for Canada and "Boatman" would frequent, such as Amos Williams and Charles Thurrell. Francis eventually left for Canada himself and there opened the British Restaurant and later ran the North American Hotel in transnational fashion.[158]

Rochester allowed Blacks little social mobility. Former Virginia slave John Jenkins achieved the greatest rise in occupational status. In the 1844 City Directory, Jenkins was listed as a "grocer," but just three years later, he was a "physician." He even had a medical understudy, William Cowles. By 1851, Doctor Jenkins opened an office on 39 Buffalo Street, where he offered bloodletting and herbology, which were relatively common in this period before professional medicine.[159] Business was good in Rochester, yet after spending sixteen years in the city, he elected to go to Canada after the passage of the 1850 Fugitive Slave Act. Jenkins was also troubled by the fact that his two daughters were still in bondage in the American South, and he actively searched for his children. Upon reconnecting with his long-lost brother, Jenkins discovered that his youngest daughter was in Richmond, Virginia. He paid a man to rescue her from slavery, but it was in vain. Jenkins later discovered that slaveholder Allen Y. Stokes owned her, and he wanted $850 to release her from bondage. When Jenkins gave Stokes the money, his youngest daughter and her free husband joined Jenkins on the Queen's soil. A year later, his older daughter was found to be the property of Florida's former territorial governor, Richard K. Call. She was purchased for $400 and reunited with her family on November 4, 1858, in Hamilton, Canada

West.[160] Although Jenkins was a physician, he could not be confident that his freedom would be preserved in Rochester.

In 1849, John S. Jacobs took over the Antislavery Office and Reading Room on the floor above Frederick Douglass's *North Star* office at 25 Buffalo Street.[161] The Reading Room featured the latest publications and leading works on slavery and other social issues. Harriet Jacobs assisted her brother with the endeavor, opening the office door at 9:00 a.m. on weekdays and closing at 6:00 p.m.[162] The Reading Room initially enjoyed some success. Every Thursday, a circle of abolitionists gathered there "to sew, knit, read" and, most importantly, "talk for the cause."[163] When Douglass and Griffiths dropped by to inspect the new business venture, they were pleased with what they found.[164] It had "desks," "a good supply of newspapers," and was "conveniently arranged."[165] Nevertheless, the Reading Room was short-lived because of sluggish business. Harriet explained, "We tried it, but it was not successful. We found warm anti-slavery friends there, but the feeling was not general enough to support such an establishment."[166] Unfortunately for John S. Jacobs, the Reading Room closed by the summer of 1849. He rebounded and opened "a spacious oyster saloon" in the Waverly buildings on State Street, but the restaurant did not stay open long either.[167]

The hotel industry and the occupations of porter and cartmen that Black males held in Rochester could provide a decent living and signified the dynamic movement which occurred in the Niagara region. The Rochester House, Clifton, Blossom, North American, National, United States, Eagle, Irving, and the Exchange hotels and taverns all employed Blacks. Some, such as James B. Wilson and William M. Perhamus, were elevated to "head cook," while others, like Simeon Schooner and George Sampson, waited tables, and people like George James toiled as the "Yardman." Perhamus was able to support a wife and several children with his salary.[168] And women like Julia Foot and Miss Phebe Bradley were able to forge their way into cooking at hotels.[169] A Clifton House ad explained "the charges are reasonable, and accommodations good" and "an omnibus leaves this House twice every day for Lake Ontario Steam-Boat Landing." The omnibus was good for guests and even better for fugitives. The Irving Hotel promised to "at all times endeavor to consult the pleasure and gratification of those who may favor him with their patronage."[170] A few Blacks owned their own places that surely housed runaways. Ralph Francis was a Black hotel proprietor, and James W. Clarkson, born in Canada, owned a boarding house on Buffalo Street.[171]

The porter and cartmen jobs were lucrative as well, but city regulations on these transportation jobs were so discriminatory that they led to a decline of Blacks in each trade. Porters, who worked for themselves or at local hotels in the area, hauled boxes, trunks, luggage, and goods for their employers. In 1837, when Jermain W. Loguen moved to Rochester from St. Catharines, he worked as a porter and confidential servant at the Rochester House Hotel. Loguen was "about twenty-four years of age," and "of gigantic strength" when he arrived; "being economical in his receipts, he laid up from three to five and six dollars a day, and at the end of two years became possessed of a small estate."[172] Porter Archibald Gaul Jr. used his work to move up the social and economic ladder; his father had been a day laborer.[173] Yet despite his efforts, city regulations limited Archibald's ability to excel. Rochester authorities required porters to pay a $2 fee to be licensed in the vocation, and the Common Council dictated the prices of their services. The rates hampered the ability of porters to maximize their earnings.[174]

Cartmen had similar restrictions placed on their profession. They did the same work as porters, but on a larger scale and for greater pay. The principal difference was that cartmen employed wagons, carts, or horses to transport industrial goods and household items. They were generally called when objects were too big to carry by hand. Their fees began at twenty-five cents for luggage and increased with the weight to be hauled. John H. Brown earned enough money as a cartmen to own $1,200 in real estate.[175] The trade also enabled wagon-maker James N. Hall to prosper; he possessed property valued at $900. But his revenue depended partly upon the success of his fellow laborers.[176] Although the compensation was good for cartmen, most Blacks could not take advantage of the opportunity. Cartmen needed a license that cost $250 to perform their duties. The fees and terms of this rule were a calculated measure to limit the number of Blacks in the profession. Throughout most of the 1830s, there was only one local Black cartman, but by 1848, the number increased to five. In the early 1850s, Blacks slowly started to lose ground in the trade because of the arrival of competing groups from Europe.

Isaac C. Gibbs was familiar with both the porter and cartman trades. In 1841, he met the requirements to become a porter, and he hauled freight for three years before becoming a cartman. His new position was less strenuous and more lucrative. As a cartman, Gibbs flourished and even had time to be a delegate to the 1843 Black state convention. By 1850, he owned $1,800 worth of real estate and supported a large family.[177] The industrious Gibbs disappeared from the City Directory after 1856. It is possible that he could have been forced out of the cartman profession to make room for more "desirable" whites. Gibbs resurfaced in 1860, but did not reenter the workforce as a cartman, where he had been skilled and successful.[178]

A number of Black men and women supported themselves in the clothing industry as secondhand clothes dealers, clothes cleaners, washerwomen, and seamstresses. Paul Robert and William Moore sold used clothing on Exchange Street.[179] Their merchandise was not the most fashionable, but they had a market within the Black community, particularly with new runaways from the American South. Shields "Emperor" Green pressed and cleaned garments out of his modest establishment at 2 Spring Street.[180] One ad explained that "he is prepared to do clothes cleaning in a manner to suit the most fastidious, and on cheaper terms than any one else." Green added: "I make no promises that I am unable to perform."[181] In 1856, Green had passed through Rochester en route to St. Catharines; he returned to the city in the spring of 1859 and opened his business, competing with Black washerwomen for work. These women normally cleaned the clothing of the wealthy in their homes, so their services were more convenient and desirable.

Most Blacks worked as domestic laborers in the Third Ward. Employment in affluent white households took on three different forms: "live-in" domestic servants; day-worker domestics who stayed in their own homes; and delivery or crafts people such as whitewashers and carpenters who performed tasks for cash. Seventy-year-old Francis Gibbs was a "live-in" domestic for the Alexander Kelsey family while Miss Clarissa Eason appeared to be living and working in the home of merchant Martian F. Reynolds at 36 South Sophia Street.[182] Their responsibilities included cooking, caring for children, doing laundry, shopping for food, and running household errands. Gibbs and Eason happened to be exceptions; there were few "live-in" laborers in Rochester. Most Blacks, like Melinda Jones, worked at the homes of the rich but lived with their own families. Jones resided with her husband and three children on Spring Alley, and even after her husband died, she maintained her independence. Literate and religious Maria Reed earned a living after her husband Burrell died doing laundry and piecework to keep her home on Hunter Street.[183]

The Black workforce of Rochester in the 1850s was marginalized, and the financial disparity among members of the community was apparent. A handful of

Blacks flourished, but most struggled to support themselves and their families. Blacks found it difficult to move up and do better. Most Blacks lived in homes they did not own. They commonly rented rooms from other, more established Blacks, or they lived on the premises of their white employers. With limited job opportunities and inadequate wages, all family members, including children, had to find ways to earn money or to aid their households. "My brothers and sister," Charles Douglass once explained, "were taken from school one day in each week to attend to folding and mailing of the [*North Star*] paper."[184] Moreover, the majority of Blacks did not attend school, missed church on Sundays, and had little time to gather in solidarity because working and finding work made heavy demands on them.[185]

THE TRANSNATIONAL UNDERGROUND RAILROAD NETWORK AND ACTIVISM

From the outset of the 1850s, Blacks in Rochester had reason to be concerned about their liberty. After the passage of the Fugitive Slave Law in September, it did not take the city long to get into the act of preserving Black freedom.[186] When three fugitive slaves—William Parker, Noah Buley, and Nelson Ford—killed Maryland slave owner Edward Gorsuch for attempting to recapture them on September 11, 1851, in Christiana, Pennsylvania, they made their way to the home of Frederick Douglass. His objective was to get them to Canada fast. He explained that the situation was a "delicate one" because the Christiana men were not only considered fugitives but also murderers by the officers actively in pursuit. The circumstances were intensified by telegraphs narrating the events, which New York newspapers picked up.[187] Fortunately for the three men and Douglass, the "manstealers" were always a step behind. The officers searched the mountains of Pennsylvania, but the fugitives, determined and armed, had eluded them by taking a train to Rochester. Once the men reached the home of Douglass, he acknowledged that their time there included "hours of anxiety as well as activity."[188]

Douglass sent Julia Griffiths to see if a steamer was leaving from the Genesee River to Canada anytime soon. He remained on guard at his home while the men slept, having traveled continuously for two days and nights. Griffiths returned with good news: a steamer was leaving that night for Canada.[189] The distance between Douglass's home and the harbor area itself presented the greatest danger. Under the dark of night, the men were loaded into a "Democratic carriage" and hurried to the Genesee port.[190] Once there, they waited at least fifteen minutes for the ship to arrive. Douglass boarded the vessel and remained with the fugitives until the steamer was set to depart.[191] From Rochester, the three men went to St. Catharines, where Hiram Wilson explained, "I have favored them what I could."[192] Fortunately, William Parker was able to reunite with his wife and children, and they eventually settled in Buxton on a fifty-acre lot.[193]

Blacks who were living in Rochester also felt pressure to leave. Fugitive slave Harriet Jacobs moved to town in March 1849 and remained until September 1850, when she was compelled to depart to New York City after the new fugitive law passed. Harriet had come to Rochester to spend time with her younger brother, John S. Jacobs, who was an abolitionist lecturer and organizer. John's oratorical skills were deemed second only to Frederick Douglass's, and Harriet told Amy Post that she was known as "John Jacobs' sister."[194] As the *North Star* explained, "He is eminently deserving large and generous audiences."[195] John was outright frustrated with the new Fugitive Slave Law.

Like Douglass and other Blacks in Rochester, John Jacobs believed in armed defiance to combat the new legislation. He agreed with Douglass that the best way to eradicate the act was "to make a dozen or more dead kidnappers."[196] John also sided with fellow antislavery lecturer and one-time Rochester resident William Watkins, who said "we believe in peaceably rescuing fugitive slaves if it can be . . . but if it cannot, we believe in rescuing them forcibly; we should certainly kill the man who would dare lay hands on us."[197] Even with this conviction, John Jacobs was afraid of losing his freedom. He proposed the organization of "a registry" to keep endangered fugitives from being recaptured, but he did not stay to see it through. He joined the rush to California and Australia to pan for gold.[198] On the night before he left, Harriet explained that she had never "seen him manifest such bitterness of spirit, such stern hostility to our oppressor."[199] Douglass remained in Rochester and withstood criticism by some Niagara region opponents for his opposition to the new fugitive bill. For instance, the *Buffalo Commercial Advertiser* called Douglass "an ignorant and bad tempered negro . . . [who] is working great injury to his race by recommending them to resist the laws, and take life, rather than be restored to slavery."[200]

To prevent a further exodus, Rochester's Black community worked to undermine the enforcement of the new legislation in the city. On the evening of October 13, 1851, a large meeting convened at the Zion Church to stop "the hunting of men in the valley of Genesee." Barber J. P. Morris chaired the meeting, and *North Star* printer William C. Nell was appointed secretary. Black community members such as cartman Isaac C. Gibbs and general store worker Lloyd Scott were in attendance.[201] Every colored man, woman, and child was told to be careful while walking the streets of the city, especially at night. If apprehended, people were told to call out so "that all within hearing may know and witness the deed over which angels weep and demons exult." To help keep a watch over the community, the group passed a resolution to establish a Vigilance Committee to alert citizens of slave agents. Black Rochesterians understood the importance of condemning the law, which denied trial by jury and habeas corpus. The group declared that "God made all men free," and they were determined that "God's will be done."[202]

Despite the vigilance of the Rochester community after the passage of the Fugitive Slave Act, a number of apprehensive Blacks moved out of Rochester for nearby Canada or other "safe" communities. Overall, as Douglass explained, the law was an "utter failure" in regard to recapture. He asserted that "its chief effect was to produce alarm and terror."[203] This was certainly the case in Rochester. Slave catchers did not frequently roam the streets of the city looking for runaways. Agents came to Rochester seeking specific individuals wanted for a crime or those sought after by their aggressive owners. This hunt for specific people drove the entire Black public into a state of uneasiness. "I was broken up in Rochester, N.Y.," Francis Henderson explained, "by the fugitive slave bill." He was an escapee from Washington, DC, who in 1849 had established a home and grocery store on Rochester's Main Street.[204] Henderson was not particularly at risk to be seized, but Canada was a better option at this point for Black Borderlanders. "Free Blacks" clearly understood that their fate was directly connected with those who were captured and taken back into bondage.

Escapee Grandison Boyd was affected by the Act of 1850 as well. He embodied the free movement possible in the Niagara region, which Blacks so dearly cherished. In 1833, he fled from slavery in Virginia and landed in Toronto. Boyd married Mary Ann Ross in Canada and purchased property. In 1845, he established a grocery store in Rochester, which was also his home, on South Fitzhugh Street. But he did not forfeit his ties to the English colony.[205] In fact, Boyd moved back and forth between Rochester and Toronto via Lake Ontario and took advantage of what each metropolis had to offer. He subscribed to the *North Star,* became a treasured friend to Douglass, and was named a trustee of Rochester's Third Street Baptist Church.[206] In the wake of the Fugitive Slave Law of 1850, however, Boyd decided it was "prudent to leave the country." In 1853, his pursuit of freedom led him to Liverpool, England, and then to the gold mines of Australia. Rochester newspapers reported that he earned "a handsome fortune" of $8,000 before returning to England. Thereafter, Boyd wished to resettle in Rochester, but he was unwilling to pay $1,500 to obtain "a title for himself" on the principle that his autonomy was "unalienable."[207] "Such a man," the *Rochester Democrat* asserted, should have "the privilege of living where he pleases."[208] The industrious Boyd settled in Chatham, Canada West, and became a respected businessman.[209]

A team of Rochester residents helped to transport fugitives on the Underground Railroad to nearby Canada. Frederick Douglass, a central point man in town, opened his office to runaways, who sometimes waited outside the door for his arrival to work in the mornings; they showed up at his home, as well.[210] He was responsible for assisting some eight runaways per month to flee the country.[211] His wife Anna was deemed the "general manager of the home," and she and their children played a significant role in helping Douglass move Blacks to Canada.[212] The standard procedure, as Douglass explained in 1860, was that fugitives "usually tarry with us only during the night, and are forwarded to Canada by the morning train. We give them supper, lodging, and breakfast; pay their expenses, and give them a half dollar over."[213] Unfortunately, due to Sydney Howard Gay's extreme dislike of Frederick Douglass, he did not mention Rochester in his *Record of Fugitives*. As a result, a score of escapees on the Niagara Underground Railroad dispatched to the city from Syracuse remain unrecorded in Gay's account. However, it is safe to conclude that Rochester was an important way station along the journey for many of those who fled bondage and whom Gay documents as making it to "Canada."[214] Often, Rev. Hiram Wilson and St. Catharines was the targeted destination for fugitives in Rochester, but the overall goal was to get runaways to British soil by any means.

Douglass's local coconspirators included J. P. Morris, Isaac and Amy Post, Samuel and Susan Porter, and Edward C. Williams, among others. Black barber Morris, who worked on Main Street, was instrumental in raising money for fugitives to complete their journey. Depending on the situation, Morris used his own earnings or solicited help from others to usher Blacks farther north.[215] Isaac and Amy Post hosted escapees at their 36 Sophia Street home and backyard barn. In one instance, Douglass wrote Amy, "Please shelter this Sister from the house of bondage till five o'clock-this afternoon—She will then be sent on to the land of freedom."[216] In another example, Amy explained, "One Saturday night, after all our household were asleep there came a tiny tap at the door, and the door was opened to fifteen tired and hungry men and women who were escaping from the land of slavery." She added, "They seemed to know that Canada, their home of rest, was near."[217] The group eventually boarded a Canadian steamer with a British flag and headed to the other side of Lake Ontario. The Posts, committed abolitionists, made the passage through Rochester as easy as possible for fugitives. Edward C. Williams did the same from his ship equipment business at 16 Buffalo Street. He hid fugitives in his sail loft, unbeknownst to his customers.

At 62 South Fitzhugh Street, machinist Samuel Porter and wife Susan frequently opened their doors to fugitives throughout the 1850s.[218] They lent their support to the Rochester Orphan Society and the Home of the Friendless, but they were deeply invested in assisting Black fugitives. Samuel was the first president of the WNYASS, and his wife was a member of the RLASS from its inception. The local authorities kept an eye on the Porter residence but never confronted the couple. As a precaution, the Porters sometimes asked Samuel's sisters, Maria and Elmira Porter, for help concealing fugitives. Maria, in particular, was useful because she ran a boarding house on the Erie Canal.[219] Even when Samuel and Susan did not have runaways under their roof, they gathered funds and coordinated transportation for freedom seekers. For example, Douglass wrote Susan in October 1857 to say that fugitive William Osborne "came to us last night from slavery. He looks fully able to take care of himself, but being destitute, he needs for the present, a little assistance to get him to Canada. $2.50 will be quite sufficient."[220] The Porters often answered such requests.

Once in Rochester, a number of fugitives were taken north of the Lower Falls to Kelsey's Landing or to Charlotte to ride the waves of Lake Ontario to Canada. Others were sent on foot or by rail west of the city toward Buffalo to cross the Niagara Falls Suspension Bridge or the Lewiston-Queenston Suspension Bridge to Canada's Niagara Peninsula.[221] Lake Ontario was the safest way to travel. Once aboard a vessel, fugitives had a virtually trouble-free ride to freedom. There were dangers involved in taking a train, and though walking was the cheapest way to Canada, the borderlands of Western New York could present problems since slave agents congregated in great numbers in Buffalo and Niagara Falls to recapture human property as fugitives entered or left the British territory.[222]

Perhaps no one made better use of Rochester's location than Harriet Tubman as she moved Blacks from the slaveholding South to Canada. In 1851, after fleeing to St. Catharines from Philadelphia, she made yearly spring and fall trips to Maryland's Eastern Shore until 1857. In Rochester, Douglass, the RLASS, and the AME Zion Church supported Tubman in her attack on Southern bondage. Douglass occasionally paid her passage over the Niagara Falls Suspension Bridge, and he once housed eleven fugitives in his home on her behalf.[223] As he explained, Tubman "made several returns at great risk" to get "others from the house of bondage."[224] The RLASS helped the esteemed leader by hosting antislavery fairs and gathering food and clothing at her request.[225] The AME Church congregation lent its pews and basement to fugitives waiting to go to British Canada. Abolitionists in the Rochester area knew their Niagara locale was a vital asset that helped freedom seekers brought in by Tubman as "a professional smuggler of slaves."[226]

Douglass supported individual fugitives fleeing to Canada, but not in mass emigration. At the National Negro Convention in Rochester on July 6, 1853, at Corinthian Hall, he addressed emigration and turned discussion and debate into resources and action.[227] The assembly, which drew some 170 Black delegates from cities around the nation and the globe, promoted Black unity among abolitionists, which had been wavering. Blacks in Rochester eagerly anticipated the national convention and many met at the Baptist Church on Ford Street to appoint three delegates to represent the city. The locals were not going to allow a convention of this magnitude to take place in town without their voices being heard.[228]

The idea of colonization outside of the United States was hotly contested among Blacks during the 1850s, and it came up at the 1853 Rochester Convention. Many Blacks around the country favored the idea of finding land where they could relocate—in Canada, the Caribbean, South America, or Africa. The majority of Blacks in Rochester stood firmly against leaving the United States for Africa but supported colonization endeavors to Canada. Blacks started to rethink their ideas after the 1830s failure of Austin Steward at Wilberforce and began to advocate for equal rights within the United States. In fact, when Black Rochesterians met in 1852, they declared that "any man who lends his hand to the colonization scheme is a traitor."[229] Ultimately, Douglass, a constant opponent of emigration, influenced the convention to stand against mass departure of Blacks from America.

His tactic worked at the convention, but the debate over resettlement did not end. The assembly in Rochester was principally little different from the other

Black conventions held between 1830 and 1864.[230] Competition, tactical differences, and distrust among the leading Black abolitionists stifled their unity. Years later in Cleveland, Martin Delany organized another convention of Blacks that explored the prospect of emigration to Haiti, Central America, or Africa.[231] After the convention in Rochester, there were lingering talks over emigration. Blacks started to reconsider the option of relocating to other areas. Individuals in Rochester such as Lloyd Scott moved to Haiti, and Barbara Ann Steward thought about leaving for Liberia; even Douglass was growing tired of fighting debates over emigration by 1860.[232]

CRAFTING INTEGRATED SCHOOLS

A top goal of those who stayed in Rochester was to provide education for themselves and for their children. However, being educated and going to a quality school that was competitive with white Common Schools and academies was nearly impossible. Throughout the late 1830s, Blacks relied on unstable Sabbath Schools at struggling local churches for their education. In 1841, the Board of Education, led by Levi A. Ward, approved the opening of "one or more" Black segregated schools. Only one school materialized from this measure, and it was located on the west side of the city in the Third Ward. It was organized by Austin Steward, who returned from Canandaigua, New York, after his Spring Alley store was lost in a fire. Teachers stayed at the school for brief periods, and the lack of localized schools caused the community to grow dissatisfied. Black parents on the east side of Rochester complained because their children had to make the journey west of the Genesee River in order to go to school. White teacher Lucy N. Colman, who once worked at the segregated Black school as an unpaid instructor, explained that "no matter what the distance from the homes, this was the place."[233] Blacks wanted a second school so that each side of the city had an institution to call its own.[234]

Frederick Douglass enrolled his oldest child, Rosetta, in the prestigious Seward Seminary for girls, run by principal Julia F. Tracy, near his home on Alexander Street.[235] Even in this academic environment, Rosetta could not escape discrimination. Though Douglass registered his daughter at Tracy's Seminary without any problem, Rosetta told her father several weeks later that she was being isolated at the new school. She was prohibited from interacting with her peers and kept in a room alone where she was neither seen nor heard. After

Douglass learned this, he explained, "I confess that I was shocked, grieved, and indignant."[236] He wanted answers, and went directly to the school to get them.

Douglass confronted Miss Tracy for not being frank with him about how Rosetta was going to be taught at the school. He challenged Tracy to ask the young students if they objected to having a Black classmate. The response was definitive: not one girl objected. But Tracy insisted that the academy could not be integrated without the approval of all the students' parents. Only one parent—newspaper editor Horatio G. Warner—had the audacity to reject the admission of Rosetta. Douglass, upset by the outcome, wrote an open letter to Warner in the *North Star.* "We differ in color, it is true (and not much in that respect)," he explained, "but who is to decide which color is most pleasing to God, or most honorable among men?" Douglass wisely dismissed Warner's objection and explained, "I do not wish to waste words or argument on one whom I take to be as destitute of honorable feeling, as he has shown himself full of pride and prejudice."[237] Teacher Julia Wilbur ironically explained "the beauty of it is" that regardless of their parents thoughts, schoolhouses were "so near" to each other in Rochester that "both white & colored during play hours" gathered together in glee.[238]

Despite the fact that Douglass paid local taxes, the Board of Education did not allow his youngsters to attend School No. 15, which was nearest to their home. The only option left in the city was an inferior Colored School located across town on North Washington Street.[239] Douglass refused to send his children there. He explained, "I was not prepared to submit tamely to this proscription."[240] Douglass arranged for his children to be home-schooled by a Quaker, Miss Phebe Thayer, and he prepared to take on the Rochester Board of Education, knowing that other Blacks were dissatisfied with the Colored School and with paying taxes in wards where their children could not attend school. He set up a hearing and organized a team of people who wanted to dismantle the system of public-school segregation, which included abolitionist William Bloss, spiritualist teacher Lucy N. Colman, and colonizationist Everard Peck. His friend Samuel D. Porter, a member of the Board, was also a great help.

In December of 1849, a meeting was held at the Court House to protest separate schools in Rochester. Porter called the actions of the city's policy "illegal, unjust, anti-republican, and unchristian."[241] The group put together a series of resolutions to outline their grievances. Blacks were being taught in inferior schools; they were prohibited from receiving instruction in district schools; and the policy was a clear violation of equity in public expenditures, since Blacks paid taxes in areas where their children could not attend school.[242] "No man of liberal mind," Porter asserted, "of dignity of soul, and of established position in society, objects to the extension to others of the privileges which he himself enjoys."[243] The opponents of segregated schools argued that power-holders were unreasonably inflicting a wound on the "least protected" people in Rochester. Blacks worked hard to pay their taxes, and they wanted the benefits of their contributions.

"The people of Rochester," a later resolution proclaimed, "may justly share the reproach of slavery in South Carolina if they give countenance to this wrong."[244] The protesters saw that a change in latitude had not meant a change in attitudes, and injustice needed to be met with resistance. Before dispersing, the group decided to publish the meeting's proceedings so that the whole community could see clearly what the Rochester Board of Education was doing. Lucy Colman also agreed that the Colored School "should die," and she "persuaded the parents in the different districts to send the more advanced children to the schools in their own districts."[245]

In the shadows of the 1850s, the walls of racial inequality around Rochester public schools began to collapse at the demand of activists. The Board of Education allowed Blacks to attend white public institutions in 1850, but the Board still maintained a separate Black school in the basement of the Zion Church and did not officially endorse a policy of desegregation. In March of 1850, however, there were twenty-four Black students enrolled in five different city schools. With pressure mounting, officials hoped that School No. 13 on the east side of Rochester would keep Black parents there quiet.[246] Douglass sent his younger children there for a time, but a greater breakthrough was needed. Charles Douglass explained, "The taunts of the school children whose parents were proslavery made the further attendance at No. 13 school of my youngest sister Annie and myself intolerable."[247] Finally, in the spring of 1856, when the trustees at the Zion Church raised the rent on the room where the poorly attended Black school was housed, the Board quietly withdrew support. As a result, the segregated Black school shut down, since "there was neither scholars nor school-house."[248] There was no mention of it in the Rochester newspapers, but by 1857, Blacks could attend Common Schools in their districts alongside white children.[249] Moving toward educational equality was a step in the right direction, but there were still many battles to fight.

POLITICAL RIGHTS

One battle still waiting to be fought was over the political rights of Blacks in Rochester, which were narrowly restricted. Although many in Western New York argued that the political process could propel social change, Blacks were limited in their ability to use the vote because New York State imposed a $250 property requirement and a three-year residency rule to vote. In 1845, there were 499 Blacks in Monroe County, but only thirty-five of them met the qualifications to take part in an election. Twenty individuals in Rochester cast ballots, while fifteen other Blacks voted in neighboring towns. Blacks protested the issue so strongly that the Constitution Reform Convention placed their suffrage on the ballot in the election for governor in November 1846. The results in Rochester were satisfactory; 1,433 voted to grant suffrage, whereas 1,258 voted against Black electoral inclusion. The outcome in Monroe County was the opposite; 3,942 voted in favor of suffrage, while 4,444 voted against it. The trend was followed throughout New York State. It took over twenty years to overturn the discriminatory state laws that kept the vast majority of Blacks from the polls.[250]

In the meantime, Blacks tackled smaller injustices and continued to use the border as a political tool. Between 1838 and 1852, Blacks were listed in a separate section of Rochester's Directories. In 1847, for example, when Frederick Douglass first moved to New York, his name was published in a section of the *Rochester* City *Directory* reserved for Blacks. By 1852, Douglass and the Black community succeeded in integrating the index of local residents and businesses. Also, from 1847 to 1850, they began the process of reforming the Rochester Public Schools. It took another several years to achieve full desegregation, but progress was being achieved.

By 1860, Blacks in New York succeeded in putting Black enfranchisement back on the state ballot as a referendum. Rochester voted 2,026 for suffrage and 3,655 in opposition. Monroe County voted 4,386 in favor and 6,950 against.[251] The support for the Black vote over time had only diminished. A local Rochester committee was formed to help launch yet another campaign for suffrage in 1869. Blacks worked long hours urging people to support the referendum. The proposal lost. Equal suffrage was finally won in New York, only when the Fifteenth Amendment was ratified in 1870.[252] Nonetheless, Blacks had lost ground between 1850 and 1860 in their struggle because people's attitudes were hardening. And the fight against Southern slavery and discrimination in Rochester only intensified in this period.

As the vocal agitation of antislavery activists grew, their meetings were met with more anger and resistance. To some, the local abolitionists were rabble-rousers seeking only to destroy the Union by bringing on civil war. The opponents used any opportunity to fuel controversy. One editor believed activists were traitors who "injure the reputation of our city by contributing to the fire which is consuming the nation" and asserted that they had "preference for the government of Great Britain."[253] In October 1858, a gathering arranged by Frederick Douglass and Susan B. Anthony ended in mob violence. When Anthony attempted to call the meeting to order, some in the crowd objected to a woman speaking publicly. There were antagonists among the abolitionists that day. The *Union and Advertiser* even suggested that the event organizers had welcomed the violence as a publicity stunt.[254]

In a letter to the editor, Douglass rebutted this claim as unjust. He explained "I am an humble citizen, a tax payer and a legal voter, and have, in common with others, a little stake in the welfare, safety and happiness of the people of Rochester." Miss Anthony, he said, did not consent to the "mobocratic spirit" either. Her speaking was not an invitation for disorder. "Mobs always have apologists," Douglass explained, "they are never without excuses. They usually find them in the character and conduct of their victims. The present instance is no exception." Abolitionists were blamed for the trouble to mask the wrongdoing of their opponents. The *Union and Advertiser* caught on to the real "agitators." Douglass stated that he had lived in Rochester for eleven years and had spoken on many occasions but was never met with resistance of this kind. He considered himself a peaceable man and thought he should be one of the last people suspected in backing violent demonstrations.[255] Even so, a storm was brewing, and his relationship with John Brown was growing during this time.

DOUGLASS AND JOHN BROWN IN THE AMERICAN BORDERLANDS

John Brown visited Rochester on several occasions to meet with fellow abolitionists. He befriended Douglass and Susan B. Anthony, as well as her brothers Merritt and Daniel, who were active in "Bleeding Kansas."[256] On January 28, 1858, Brown stopped in Rochester for a three-week stay at the home of Douglass. There he drafted his Provisional Constitution for the intended Appalachian Rebel State, which he wanted to establish once his slave insurrection was successful. It was not by chance that Brown selected borderland Rochester as the place for formulating his plan. Similar to "self-stolen" Blacks, Brown was a fugitive; he had led a band of abolitionists in the killing of five proslavery supporters at the Pottawatomie Creek Massacre in Kansas.[257] Thereafter, vigilantes, bounty hunters, and federal marshals were all on watch for him. Like fugitive slaves, the radical abolitionist felt both caution and comfort in Rochester and valued the city for its relatively seamless British-Canadian access. "While at our home," Charles Remond Douglass explained, "I became his errand boy. I went twice a day to the post office two miles away to receive his mail which was sent to my father's box addressed to N. Hawkins, the assumed name John Brown."[258] Brown wisely used an alias but also took some calculated risks. He once gave a talk at the Rochester City Hall "to vindicate the cause pursued by himself and his friends during the late troubles in Southern Kansas."[259] From Rochester, Brown departed to meet Harriet Tubman in St. Catharines and to print his Provisional Constitution. It was later ratified at a convention in Chatham, Canada West.[260] Unquestionably, Brown knew the value of Rochester's "right over the way" location.

At the home of Douglass in 1858, Brown insisted on paying a modest board for taking up workspace and living space. He hoped to enlist Douglass as an ally in his budding revolutionary scheme. It was in Rochester that Brown planned his original attack on Southern slavery.[261] To complete his mission, he needed money and men. For over a year, Brown worked to obtain them. He recruited Shields "Emperor" Green from Rochester, "who called himself by different names," to join him in his attack on Harpers Ferry, Virginia.[262]

Green, anywhere from twenty-five years old to his mid thirties, was "a full blooded negro" fugitive from Charleston, South Carolina, and had spent time in St. Catharines.[263] He met "Old Brown" at the home of Douglass. Green was described as being a dignified man of few "broken" words to "a perfect rattlebrain in talk," who was accustomed to adversity and danger.[264] Others had conflicting views of Green—one interviewer stated that he was of "a good countenance and a sharp, intelligent look" and was "not much inferior to Fred. Douglass in mind or education"; while another claimed he had "no evidence of either education or intelligence."[265] Nonetheless, Douglass explained that John Brown liked the "stuff" Green "was made of" and was eager to find men of his stature. Green needed little convincing to join in the insurrection. On a walk leaving the home of Douglass, Lucy N. Colman asked Green, "do you know that by going with Captain Brown into a Southern State, you expose yourself to the gallows?" And "that if you are taken you will surely be executed?" Green answered, "Yes; I shall probably lose my life, but if my death will help to free my race, I am willing to die."[266] Green pledged his devotion to Brown, and when the time came to act, he delivered.

At Brown's request, Douglass escorted Green to Chambersburg, Pennsylvania, in August of 1859 where "distinguished persons, convened for consultation."[267] It was there that Brown pleaded with Douglass for some two days to participate in his assault on the South. The strategy was to seize the federal arsenal at Harpers Ferry and to enlist the local slave population to help him establish a rebel state. Brown believed that his attack would induce "the bees" of Southern resistance to swarm, and he wanted Douglass to help "hive" Blacks into his new state.[268] He explained "Come with me, Douglass; I will defend you with my life. I want you for my special purpose."[269] Douglass rejected the invitation, and told Brown that he was walking into a "perfect steel trap" from which he would not escape alive. Before Douglass left Chambersburg, he asked Green about his plans. He replied calmly, "I b'leve I'll go wid de ole man."[270]

Shields "Emperor" Green was "brought up in the city," and having spent time in Rochester and St. Catharines, he "was not used to being in the woods." As Green ventured further into the American South to meet John Brown "in the woods, being unused to it" he started "looking as gloomy as ever" and explained "O, what a poor fool I am! I had got away out of slavery, and here got back into the eagle's claw again." He was a genuine Borderland Black who understood lines of demarcation and the dangers that accompanied them. Green even stated "I wouldn't have gone into this for all the wealth in Rochester."[271] Yet the worth of freedom outweighed the cost of slavery.

Despite Frederick Douglass's warning, Brown and his men forged ahead. Before the rebellion, the enlistees met at the late Doctor Robert Kennedy's farm in Virginia. There, Green was a "happier man" and biracial Osborne P. Anderson, who was born free in Pennsylvania but later moved to Canada, transnationally explained that "men from widely different parts of the continent met and united into one company."[272] On October 16, 1859, the raid began, but Brown's men soon ran into major problems. Green of Rochester, Anderson of Chatham, and others had been sent out to enlist the help of area Blacks.[273] When they tried to rejoin Brown, he was surrounded at a fire engine house by the Virginia militia, who foiled the attack. Anderson retreated to the mountains and urged Green to escape with him, but he refused and headed to the arsenal. As a result of his deep commitment, Green was captured, and Anderson left the United States by way of Rochester; he "eagerly flew through the city" because "the U.S. Deputy Marshal . . . was cautiously endeavoring to arrest him."[274] Green was one of Brown's most disciplined and brave soldiers, and he would have held a significant position in the planned government of the new state. As Anderson later said of Shields Green, "a braver man never lived."[275]

Douglass first learned of the insurrection at National Hall in Philadelphia, where he was scheduled to speak before a large audience. The following days brought more alarming news. When federal troops detained Brown and searched his belongings, they discovered papers in his carpetbag that implicated Douglass.[276] The leading abolitionist was in danger of being arrested, and a trial in Virginia was sure to result in his death. As scholar John Stauffer explained, "Suddenly, Douglass was the most wanted man in America."[277] Douglass left for Rochester quickly. On his journey north, he grew uneasy because letters and a copy of Brown's Provisional Constitution were locked in the desk of his home office. Douglass dispatched a message to Rochester telegram operator Burton F. Blackall to give to his oldest son, Lewis. He told him to secure the important documents in his high desk.[278] This gave Douglass some relief, but he was still anxious to reach Rochester.

After the raid, Douglass believed he would be safe if he got back to his adopted hometown. He explained, "I felt sure that, once in the city, I could not be easily taken from there." Douglass thought he would have the right to demand a preliminary hearing and that popular opinion could help his cause. But when Douglass arrived in Rochester and talked with friends, he quickly realized that his security was highly doubtful. "The efforts to get him," Charles Douglass explained, were "becoming hotter and hotter."[279] In order to avoid being surrendered to Governor Henry A. Wise of Virginia, Douglass was advised to "quit the country."[280] He was forced to enter Canada in the same fashion as the fugitives fleeing from Southern bondage he had once helped. Luckily, Charles highlighted, "the telegraph operator kept my father advised so that he knew what moves were being made to arrest him before the Marshal did."[281] Douglass's departure from Rochester was timed well. Within six hours of his leaving, federal marshals were in town searching for him.[282] "I am about convinced," Douglass said from Canada, "that nothing is to be feared at this point . . . I cannot be convicted unless I am tried, I cannot be arrested unless caught." He emphasized that British soil allowed him to "keep out of the way" of danger.[283]

John Brown's raid on Harpers Ferry had imposed a huge cost on the two Blacks from Rochester closely connected to the rebellion. "Insurrectionist" Green was captured along with Brown and hanged for what a local newspaper called "his folly."[284] Lucy Colman called him a "brave and good man!" And she explained of Green, "no amount of persuasion, or threat, could draw from . . . him on that fatal mission."[285] William C. Nell wrote glowingly of Green, proclaiming that he was "an uncommonly brave man, knowing no fear but possessed with all the properties of a hero."[286] Douglass was forced to live in exile. When he left town, there was much talk about his whereabouts.[287] He first spent time in the Niagara Falls and St. Catharines area before journeying further north to the port of Quebec.[288] He met with Osborne P. Anderson, artfully referring to him in the *Douglass' Monthly* as an "eyewitness, and a prominent actor in the transactions at Harpers Ferry, now at my side."[289] Douglass stayed in close communication with his Rochester friends throughout his time away. The banished abolitionist understood, as he told Amy Post, that it was going to take months to clear his name.[290] Determined to lead an active exile, in November 1859 Douglass boarded the Royal Mail steamer *Nova Scotian*, going to Liverpool, England. He had been planning a speaking tour of Europe, but the raid at Harpers Ferry caused him to leave sooner.[291] "The friends of the slave in Canada," the *Toronto Globe* explained, "will wish him God['s] speed wherever he goes."[292] There is no question that the outcome of the raid left the Rochester Black community at a disadvantage: Frederick Douglass, its leading advocate, was lost for six months.

To make matters worse, while Douglass was away, his youngest child, Annie Douglass, died, and he could not attend the funeral. Annie, the nine-year-old "pet" of her father, succumbed to "congestion of the brain." The *Douglass' Monthly* reported that, before Annie expired, "She was sadly distressed by the dreadful termination of the 'Harpers Ferry Tragedy,' and feared greatly for the safety of her father."[293] Charles Remond Douglass explained, "The execution of Capt. John Brown was a heavy blow to my youngest sister Annie, he had become very fond of her, and she of him, and to think of his being hung appalled her."[294] Just months before the raid, Annie had often sat upon the knee of the martyred "Old Man."[295] The prophetic words of Brown became a reality: indeed, it took blood to wash away the crimes of slavery.[296] Julia Wilbur called John Brown a "noble old man" who "will not die in vain!" And she ultimately understood, as he did, that "Bloodshed must ensue or Slavery will triumph."[297]

SUSTAINED MOVEMENT

In the late 1850s and early 1860s, Black runaways were still using Rochester as an entry and exit point to Canada. The *Rochester Evening Express* in October of 1859 reported that in one day "not less than fifteen thousand dollars worth of 'property' passed through this city, on the 'underground'" in the form of "a dozen smart, intelligent, young and middle-aged men and women."[298] In June 1860, Frederick Douglass returned to Rochester via Canada, after John Brown's raid at Harpers Ferry forced him to set out on a European tour. Seeing the persistent northward travel of fugitives through his adopted hometown, he explained, "I have never known the slaves to be escaping from slavery more rapidly than during the several weeks I have been at home." Douglass expounded: "Ten have found food, shelter, counsel and comfort under my roof since I came home, and have been duly forwarded where they are beyond the reach of the slave-hunter."[299] Douglass returned to sending runaways to Rev. Hiram Wilson in St. Catharines.[300]

In July of 1860, nine escapees from Franklin County, Virginia, utilized the city "right over the way." They were a unique collection of folks, including "a woman, a boy of eighteen, a small boy, and six girls, from six to sixteen years old." Permitted by her owner to make a simple "visit" of some sort, the woman and her companions extended the journey into Pennsylvania, where the "assistance of friends" helped them reach Rochester. They left the city with the "prospect of being free from pursuit in three hours" by means of the Niagara Falls Suspension Bridge.[301]

Later in 1860, Owen Rigney, who purchased the Ramsdell Farm in Monroe County, discovered that the former owner had been active in lodging fugitives until they could move on to Canada. Once Rigney acquired the property, he became frustrated with Black fugitives regularly coming to his home looking for "Massa Ramsdell." Rigney explained that "the Depot has been removed from his farm," and he urged area "friends of the fugitives" to "send the darkeys elsewhere." The new owner said he bought the farm to cultivate the land and to raise livestock—not to "keep a hotel—especially a black one."[302] Clearly Rigney was not one of the "friendly white farmers who took many risks, and suffered many inconveniences in passing their charges along from one point to another," as Charles Douglass once wrote.[303]

Runaways Henry Minton and Mark Antony each used Rochester in 1860 as well. Minton was owned by innkeeper Thomas McDowell in Baltimore; out of spite, an enemy of McDowell assisted Minton in fleeing Maryland. He walked from Philadelphia to New York and, like many other escapees, employed Rochester as a gateway to Canada. A native of Africa, Mark Antony employed Rochester after being enslaved in the British West Indies and New Orleans. He escaped the Lower South via a vessel to Boston and later utilized the city "over the way" as a means to Canada.[304]

In the winter of 1860, John William Dungy, who was hired out to former Virginia Governor John Munford Gregory, escaped after learning that his absentee owners in Alabama were planning to send for him.[305] He had been preparing to take flight for five years and saved $68.15 to do so. Dungy told Gregory he was going to visit his mother, who lived miles away, for one week. However, he fled north on a ship to Philadelphia, and his lie bought him some valuable time. On the shoreline of "the City of Brotherly Love" in February of 1860, Dungy was overcome with emotion and shouted: "Thank God!" Shortly, he learned the importance of journeying farther to Canada in order to maintain his freedom. With the help of William Still, his trip to the British territory brought him briefly to Rochester. There, Dungy wrote to Governor Gregory "that he need put himself to no trouble in hunting him up, as he had made up his mind to visit Canada."[306] Rochester had provided a refuge for the runaway where he could freely express himself, knowing that he was on the edge of safety under British law.

* * *

By the early 1860s, the Black community in Rochester was marginal and fragmented. Early pioneers Asa Dunbar, Austin Steward, and Rev. Thomas James were by no means satisfied with their lives there and looked to Canada for refuge. Their sentiments were a recurring theme among Blacks in Rochester in subsequent decades. Thousands used the city as a transnational gateway to Canada and as a reentry point. Many things made the town unattractive—the struggling churches, the dependence on help from whites, and the poverty that Blacks experienced from lack of opportunity. Steward left Rochester first in the 1830s and then in the 1850s for opportunities elsewhere. James first went to St. Catharines to escape bondage, then came back to Rochester to work. Countless others used this Western New York space for the seamless movement it allowed. Without stable institutions to anchor the community, solidarity wavered, leaving Blacks even more vulnerable to the prejudice and discrimination of the white community and no better equipped to redress their political grievances with velocity. Even with the odds set against Blacks in Rochester, during the transformative mid-1800s, they found comfort there because the city offered proximity to British Canada.

Niagara Falls Suspension Bridge, lithograph by Charles Parson (1856). The bridge, which opened in 1848, allowed for pedestrian and carriage traffic, and trains began crossing on an upper deck in 1855. It helped to tie Canada and the United States together, and Blacks, fugitive and free, commonly used the overpass. Library of Congress Prints and Photographs Division.

Lower deck entrance of the Niagara Falls bridge, c. 1857. The trusses on each side of the bridge's doorway and the tollbooth can be seen in the stereograph. For fugitives, this could be a gateway to a new life and greater freedoms and a doorway that swung open in both directions. Miriam and Ira D. Wallach Division of Art, Prints and Photographs, New York Public Library.

The Lewiston-Queenston Suspension Bridge. Built in 1850 and formally opened in 1851, this bridge helped to facilitate the passage of fugitive slaves over the international border between the United States and Canada. It was blown down in 1864. Miriam and Ira D. Wallach Division of Art, Prints and Photographs, New York Public Library.

The Erie Canal aqueduct in downtown Rochester. The aqueduct carried the Erie Canal over the northward-flowing Genesee River in downtown Rochester. From the collection of the Rochester Public Library Local History & Genealogy Division.

Kelsey's Landing marker in Rochester's Rose Garden. Photograph by Ve Jay Broyld Sr.

AFRICAN CHURCH,
ROCHESTER, NY.

AME Zion Church in Rochester (1831–1879). Everything from public celebrations to ensuring a proper burial for the deceased took place at Zion. The congregation also lent its pews and basement to fugitives awaiting the means to reach British-Canadian soil and those returning from Canada. From the collection of the Rochester Public Library Local History & Genealogy Division.

Salem Chapel, the Black BME Church in St. Catharines. It acted as one of the main hubs for American escapees before the Civil War. Photograph by Dennis Gannon, retouched by Ve Jay Broyld Sr.

Austin Steward, the first Black business owner in Rochester. In the early 1830s, Steward moved to the Wilberforce Colony in Canada, but he eventually moved back to Rochester after the settlement collapsed, demonstrating the border's fluidity. Original drawing by James B. Murry, photographed by Ve Jay Broyld Sr.

Rev. Thomas James. James lived in both St. Catharines and Rochester and worked on the Welland and Erie Canals. In Rochester, he established the AME Zion Church and helped to launch an abolitionist biweekly newspaper, *The Rights of Man*. From the collection of the Rochester Public Library Local History & Genealogy Division.

Frederick Douglass. Douglass used the transnational junction of Rochester to move Black fugitives beyond the reach of American slave catchers. He also interacted with Blacks in St. Catharines such as Rev. Thomas James, Hiram Wilson, Harriet Tubman, and others. Drawing by James B. Murry, photographed by Ve Jay Broyld Sr.

Harriet Tubman. Between 1851 and 1858, Tubman lived in St. Catharines' "Colored Village," among others from the American South and her native Eastern Shore of Maryland. Tubman made seasonal trips to Maryland to help escapees reach Canada, employing Rochester along the way. Library of Congress Prints and Photographs Division.

Jermain Wesley Loguen. After escaping from Tennessee, Loguen lived in St. Catharines and Rochester before settling in Syracuse. There, he actively sent fugitives westward via the Niagara region cities he knew well. Photo courtesy of the Onondaga Historical Association, Syracuse, New York.

William Howard Day. Day printed John Brown's Provisional Constitution for his planned rebel state in St. Catharines. He moved to town to start a Douglass-like newspaper to bookend the Niagara region. Drawing by James B. Murry, photographed by Ve Jay Broyld Sr.

Formal portrait of a Black couple taken in the Niagara region from the Rick Bell Collection. In the 2010s, the collection was found in a St. Catharines attic and processed for preservation. Collectively, the images show the sophistication of borderland Blacks. Rick Bell Family Fonds, RG 63, Archives & Special Collections, Brock University Library.

Shields "Emperor" Green, by David H. Strother. Green lived in St. Catharines and Rochester working as a second-hand clothes dealer. At the home of Frederick Douglass, John Brown enlisted Green for his 1859 raid of Harpers Ferry, Virginia. He was executed alongside Brown for his involvement in the insurrection. From the Boyd B. Stutler Collection, courtesy of the West Virginia and Regional History Center, WVU Libraries.

3

St. Catharines, Canada West
"AN IMPORTANT PLACE FOR THE OPPRESSED"

Miles from the American side of the Niagara river, and the principal depot for
fugitive slaves who escape by way of New York . . . St. Catharine's has long been
an important place for the oppressed, and consequently has become the home of
many of these people.

>   —WILLIAM WELLS BROWN, *The Colored People of Canada,* quoted
>   in Jacqueline L. Tobin, *From Midnight to Dawn,* 163–64

In the Niagara District, of which this [St. Catharines] is the most important place,
fresh fugitives are numerous.

>   —REV. HIRAM WILSON, *The Liberator,* December 4, 1850

This chapter, which mirrors the previous one on Rochester, outlines the con-
figuration of the Black settlement in St. Catharines during the early and
mid-1800s. It looks at factors that inhibited the progress of the Black community, such as the geography of the Niagara region and racial discrimination by British Canadians. It also focuses on the cultural markers that signified
the advancement of the community, such as the August First celebrations, the
building of a "Black Village," the Colored Corps that policed workers during
the expansion of the Welland Canal, and the gains Blacks made in participating
in politics and exercising their rights as free people. During this decades-long
struggle, Blacks in St. Catharines moved steadily toward self-reliance, and that
was clearly an important social objective. Blacks worked to create all the elements that identified their community as distinct and self-sufficient—Black
churches, Black philanthropic organizations, and Black-owned businesses that
created jobs. These were different objectives than was true for their counterparts
in Rochester. By focusing on the unique transnational location of St. Catharines,

this chapter will demonstrate the multifaceted dynamics of a thriving border-land community with meaningful connections to neighbors on the other side of the border.

EARLY BLACK CONNECTIONS TO AMERICA

By 1800, Black pioneers envisioned a settlement within St. Catharines where they could establish their own social organizations and institutions independent of whites, but an actual "Black Village" did not become a reality until the 1830s. The settlement was not the result of any authorization from the British Canadian government. Instead, it began when fugitive slaves came to town, found others like themselves, and congregated in one part of town. Over time, this section of town matured, and by 1850, it was a vital neighborhood with a host of business establishments and mutual aid societies. The development of this Black community ran parallel to the growth of St. Catharines.

Before St. Catharines was formally established in 1845, the land was part of the unincorporated Township of Grantham; it was known interchangeably as "The Twelve," after Twelve Mile Creek, "Shipman's Corner," or "The Corners."[1] In early 1788, Grantham was surveyed to provide land for displaced British Loyalists who had served the Crown as soldiers in the American Revolutionary War. Grantham was one of the fourteen townships created on the Niagara Peninsula.[2] However, development on the Peninsula was slow because of the obstacles posed by the Niagara River and the Niagara Escarpment. Vessels were unable to navigate the river because of Niagara Falls, and the steep slopes of the Niagara Escarpment impeded the flow of ground traffic.[3] Consequently, substantial advancements did not occur in the region of what became St. Catharines until these geological obstacles were overcome.

In the early stages of St. Catharines' history, there were a significant number of Blacks who had served as British soldiers in the American Revolutionary War and fought in exchange for their freedom. After the British defeat, Black soldiers were granted land entitlements equal to those of other Loyalists in Upper Canada. Veteran Richard Pierpoint was one of the first Black settlers in St. Catharines. He was an African, born in Bundu, West Africa (or Bondou, now part of Senegal), and was a "warrior" in his native land.[4] Pierpoint was captured around the age of sixteen and brought across the Atlantic Ocean to the American colonies to be enslaved. When the American Revolution began, he seized the opportunity to run away but was captured and imprisoned in Sunbury, Pennsylvania, where ads were placed in an area newspaper seeking his hometown and owner.[5] Later, Benjamin Franklin's *Pennsylvania Gazette* ran an ad stating that if no one claimed Pierpoint soon, he would be sold as the law permitted.[6]

While the details are not clear about how Pierpoint was released from jail, by 1780 he had joined John Butler's Rangers of Britain, a group that gained a reputation for courageously fighting the American colonists. In the aftermath of war, Pierpoint emigrated to Canada as a United Empire Loyalist.[7] Settling in the St. Catharines area, he and eighteen other free Blacks petitioned Lieutenant Governor John Graves Simcoe in June of 1794 to establish an all-Colored community in the region out of their allotments. They wanted to give Blacks a space where they could live together, support each other, and block out some of the prejudice and discrimination in the larger community around them.

The threats to Black lives in the Niagara region were evident in the pages of the *Upper Canada Gazette*. A year before the petition of Pierpoint and his fellow Blacks, one slave owner posted an ad offering a "five dollars reward" for "a negro manservant named John." The subscriber added, "all persons are forbid harboring the said negro man at their peril."[8] These kinds of threats prompted the Black veteran's urgent request for a separate community. The last line of their 1794 appeal firmly proclaimed, "Your Petitioners hope their behaviour will be such as to shew [show] that Negroes are capable of being industrious, and in loyalty to the Crown they are not deficient."[9] Governor Simcoe, however, rejected the request because he wanted newcomers to live with other Canadian colonists in an integrated society.[10]

Despite Simcoe's denial, Richard Pierpoint, or "Captain Dick" as he was affectionately called in honor of his military service, was granted a land certificate for 200 acres in the heart of Grantham Township below the Niagara Escarpment and along a modest creek. By March 1804, he gained full ownership of the land, and he was such a well-known figure in the area that the stream on the border of his property was named Dick's Creek.[11] The area's first church, mill, and store were nearby, and the Iroquois Trail, the main route for east-west travel and the only bridge over the creek, made Pierpoint's district a prime intersection for traffic moving in the region.

However, in 1806, for reasons unknown, Pierpoint sold his landholdings in Grantham. He could have been discontented with his proximity to fellow Blacks, or he may have needed the revenue his property could yield.[12] The now elderly

African and American-Canadian transnational moved to the adjacent township of Louth. There he acquired 100 acres but soon lost that property as well. For the next six years, details about the Captain's life are unclear. It appears that he remained on the Niagara Peninsula, somewhere between Niagara, Louth, and Grantham. Pierpoint's idea of a Black community in St. Catharines did not die; it was simply deferred and realized later as the Black population grew.[13]

Captain Dick reemerged during the War of 1812. Now age 68, he enlisted in the militia and joined the fight against America on behalf of Britain. Pierpoint once more petitioned the British Crown; this time, he wanted the permission of Major General Isaac Brock to form an all-African military unit so that they "may stand and fight together."[14] Before 1812, Africans had been integrated into various British regiments; so, like Pierpoint's 1794 request, his new petition was dismissed. The aging Captain Dick's yearning to have a Black unit mirrored his previous desire to build a "colored" community in St. Catharines. He thought both endeavors could create Black solidarity, demonstrate British "loyalty," and overall prove Blacks to be autonomous and respectable.

Still, the negative response by British authorities to have a separate unit did not deter Pierpoint or other Niagara region Blacks from serving in the War of 1812. The conflict had a deeper meaning for Blacks in Canada since many were ex-slaves or descendants of those once held in bondage. American law deemed them runaways and property, and if they were captured or if Canada were conquered, they would have faced certain enslavement. Patriotism and loyalty to Britain were less of a concern to Blacks; they fought honorably more for their own self-interest than anything else. Shortly after the war ended in 1815, Pierpoint and his fellow soldiers received land for their military service, but this time the veterans did not ask to combine their allotments as they did before.[15]

In the following years, British Canada invested in transportation infrastructure in the Niagara district, making it easier to move goods and people in the region and creating work for new Black residents. Also, "The Twelve" became St. Catharines and the accepted name of the town. It was named after one or perhaps both wives of area pioneers—Colonel John Butler, who was commander of Butler's Rangers, and Robert Hamilton, a justice of the peace and land board member. Each had wedded a woman named Catharine, spelled at times with an "er" and in other instances with an "ar." "St." was added to suggest reverence and religious significance.[16]

During the 1820s, the small village began to grow as a result of the Welland Canal construction, which overcame the geological challenges Niagara Falls presented and connected the Great Lakes of Ontario and Erie. The chief promoter behind the canal endeavor was merchant and British official William Hamilton Merritt. He managed to get the financial backing and governmental support necessary to build the Welland Canal. A Niagara area newspaper, *The Mail,* oversimplified Merritt's power by reporting via an anecdote that he had once said to a group of no-progress men: "GENTLEMEN THAT CANAL MUST BE MADE! And it was made."[17] Though certainly an embellishment, the statement still alluded to the real authority Merritt possessed in the region. As a result of his diligent work, the Niagara Peninsula became a booming economic center, and the Welland Canal became as fundamental to the development of St. Catharines as the Erie Canal was to Rochester. It was also at this time that the present-day downtown St. Catharines started to take shape, and the population boomed to more than 1,100 people.[18] The *Colonial Advocate* highlighted the growth when it reported that "this village thrives well," and it said the fluid travel in the area meant "a noise of carriages on going all the time."[19] Moreover, it was during this period that Blacks flowed into the greater St. Catharines region, a development Merritt welcomed.

In the early 1820s, however, this new influx of Blacks did not have the numerical, social, or political strength to make Pierpoint's dream of an all-Black district a reality. Consequently, Captain Dick petitioned the government one last time. Now in his late seventies, he explained in a letter to Lieutenant Governor Peregrine Maitland of Upper Canada that he was "old and without property" and "finds it difficult to obtain a livelihood by his labour." Pierpoint expounded that, "Above all things desirous" he wanted "to return to his native Country" of Bundu.[20] As with his last two requests, he was denied, but in place of returning to his native Africa, he was granted land in the remote Garafraxa, Upper Canada, in the mid-1820s. Pierpoint, in his eighties and frequently in poor health, was in no condition to improve the newly acquired land.[21] While it appeared that Captain Dick was running out of options and on his last legs, St. Catharines over the next couple of decades continued to experience Black migration, and a blossoming "Colored Village" started to take shape.

By the 1830s, the growing Black community in St. Catharines had great reason for optimism. The Imperial Act that went into effect on August 1, 1834, freed Blacks from bondage in Canada. The Black community hosted their first Emancipation Day celebration in St. Catharines on August 20, 1835. The festivities were extensive. A parade proceeded down two main streets in the village featuring banners and music and ending with lectures at an overflowing "African church."[22] Attendees were given a pamphlet telling them to be "good citizens" and to take advantage of the freedoms "so liberally provided by the Crown." At a banquet where the menu included sheep, quarters of beef, vegetables, and pastries, people reportedly dressed in their finest garments. There were some fourteen toasts to the British Empire and the King, applauding their actions to end Black bondage.[23] In one salute, John W. Lindsay declared, "Our present gracious King, William the Fourth—May we all join with our brethren in the West India islands, in thanking him for his encouragement towards the abolition of slavery throughout his dominions."[24] The 1835 commemoration started what became an annual celebration in St. Catharines.[25] By the end of the decade, a "Colored Village" had finally emerged, as Richard Pierpoint had envisioned in 1794.

In the mid-1830s, the Black community demonstrated growing strength and self-awareness. In 1835, Bacon Tate, a slave-trader from Nashville, Tennessee, who was dispatched to Buffalo to recapture Southern property, orchestrated an audacious kidnapping in St. Catharines. He was commissioned to capture some twenty fugitives, and a family named the Stanfords were among the first targeted. With help from a "colored" female informant at the Eagle Tavern in Buffalo, Tate learned the whereabouts of the Stanford family on the Niagara Peninsula. On July 12, 1835, Tate sent a band of agents over the international border under the cover of night and successfully beat, gagged, and captured Mr. Stanford, his wife, and their six-week-old child.

When Blacks in St. Catharines discovered them missing at sunrise, a group of people from the city headed to Buffalo, where they joined forces with others to track down the kidnappers. The defenders of liberty, who included abolitionist and sailor William Wells Brown, located the Stanfords at a hotel in Hamburg, New York, twelve miles south of Buffalo. The rescue was prompt; the family was found in the corner of a guarded room, bound and dressed in bloody nightclothes. The rescue party fled northward on a coach with the kidnappers in pursuit. The news reached Tate, who was still in Buffalo, and he enlisted help from the Erie County sheriff and a posse of some sixty to seventy men.[26]

After the Stanfords arrived back in Buffalo, approximately fifty area Blacks gathered and armed themselves with clubs, knives, and pistols to escort the family to Canada. The two groups faced-off in "a hard-fought battle, of nearly two hours" before the Stanfords finally boarded the Niagara River's Black Rock Ferry, cheered on by the victors on the American side as they made the passage. Disembarking on British soil, Mrs. Stanford exclaimed, "I thank God that

I am again in Canada!" The family was soon en route to their adopted home of St. Catharines.

In the wake of this affair, some forty of the rescuers were arrested by the sheriff's posse and incarcerated for the night.[27] On Monday morning, the freedom fighters were brought before a justice and condemned for unlawful assembly and breaking the peace on the Sabbath. Twenty-five individuals involved in the Stanford affair were found guilty and fined between $5 and $50.[28] The rescue had been set in motion by the St. Catharines community's vigilance and the Colored Village of St. Catharines, which was looking more like Captain Dick's vision. Regrettably, in late 1837 or early 1838, Richard Pierpoint, an honorable soldier and St. Catharines pioneer, passed away with little notice. His aspirations for St. Catharines were not fully achieved, but great strides had been made.[29]

In the 1840s, more Blacks made St. Catharines home. Early in the decade, the Welland Canal changed from private ownership to management by the Canadian government. To accommodate larger ships, the government planned improvements to repair and widen the Canal's locks. These enhancements required hundreds of laborers. While it was Irish immigrants who did most of the manual labor, a Colored Corps was created to maintain the peace and order among the Canal workers. Hostility between the Irish Catholics and Irish Protestants, in particular, ran high. On several occasions, the Colored Corps was called to restore order.[30]

In July of 1840, the most serious incident occurred in a canal community dubbed "Slabtown" for the district sawmills there, which produced inexpensive wood slabs. The "Battle of Slabtown" began when some fifty Protestant Orangemen assembled at Duffin's Inn for a celebration over dinner. Outside the tavern, several hundred Catholic canal laborers encircled the hotel and directed gunshots into the building. The Orangemen fired back. When urgent calls for help rang out, twenty-five Black troopers arrived and suppressed the uprising, to the delight of the public and government officials. Nevertheless, the Irish workers complained that "it was the climax of humiliation to be kept within the bounds of law and good order by 'a naygur' in a red coat.'"[31] The Colored Corp's role in maintaining order played a key role in the successful construction of the Welland Canal and demonstrated not only the respect Blacks had achieved but also the outright bigotry they experienced in St. Catharines.[32] Many area Black troops remained in the following decades; as the *Provincial Freeman* later reported, "We frequently meet colored men who are pensioners."[33]

BLACK INHABITANTS IN THE 1850S

Before the mid-1800s, Blacks in St. Catharines had struggled to establish churches and mutual relief organizations. However, by 1850, the community started to resemble what Richard Pierpoint had envisioned, principally because the Fugitive Slave Act of 1850 ushered many Blacks to Canada's door. There were no reports of Pierpoint's death in the Niagara district until an article finally appeared in the *St. Catharines Journal* in July 1856 that highlighted Captain Dick's work and aspirations.[34] Black inhabitants in the 1850s began to recognize Pierpoint's vision as the very foundation of their community. Numerous Blacks made their way to St. Catharines via William Still of Philadelphia, Sydney Howard Gay of New York City, and Frederick Douglass of Rochester, but the Garrisonian divide clouded this reality.[35]

Nonetheless, as with the general population of British Canada in the 1850s, there were discrepancies in St. Catharines over the size of the town's Black population. This was the result of poor governmental and private recordkeeping, which included lost documents and miscalculations. There are no definitive numbers on Blacks in St. Catharines.[36] The trouble with tracking their population started immediately in 1851 when the town's census data was destroyed; another official Canadian census was not due until 1861. The ten-year gap produced more inconsistencies in projections of Blacks, ranging from 200 to 800.[37] Freedmen's Bureau commissioner Dr. Samuel G. Howe found that the 1861 census data was unreliable. Although the Black population of St. Catharines was approximately 700, the census only accounted for 472.[38]

In all, the reason why the number of Blacks fluctuated in St. Catharines, as in Rochester, was that its transnational location caused back-and-forth travel, which made recordkeeping difficult.[39] Standing at an ideal junction for land and water movement made it nearly impossible to count the number of Blacks in St. Catharines at any given time. The number could change considerably from month to month or even weekly. Nonetheless, some generalizations can be made with confidence. First, the population in St. Catharines between 1851 and 1858 hovered around 700. Second, the majority of Blacks were American fugitives. As Benjamin Drew explained, "Nearly all of the adult colored people have at some time been slaves."[40] Finally, the number of Blacks declined during the American Civil War and its aftermath, showing that St. Catharines had been a refuge from American slavery.[41]

THE SEPARATE "COLORED VILLAGE" AND SURROUNDING AREAS

Black Borderlanders in St. Catharines during the 1850s occupied specific sections of the town that included the following streets: North, St. Paul, Geneva, Concession, Queenston, Niagara, William, as well as Queen and Cherry.[42] The area was primarily called "The Black Town," or "The Colored Village."[43] However, some referred to it in derogatory terms, such as "Coontown" or simply "Africa."[44] At the time, the Colored Village was located on the outskirts of St. Catharines proper. It was there that the majority of new property owners bought adjacent lots on which they constructed frame or log houses. Others rented or stayed in boarding houses nestled in the area.

William Hamilton Merritt, the Welland Canal promoter and British-Canadian political figure, laid the groundwork for this settlement in the early 1840s when he gave land grants to the British Methodist Episcopal (BME) Church and the Zion Baptist Church. These congregations eventually established houses of worship near the corner of Geneva and North Streets. Just a block north of the British Methodist Episcopal Church was the Welland Railroad Station, one of two railway hubs that served the community. This made the Colored Village a critical crossroads for transportation and an ideal location to receive American fugitives.[45]

The majority of Blacks in the Village lived in the vicinity of Geneva, Welland, and North Streets. North Street, the residential center, and Geneva Street, more of a business hub, were the busiest roadways in the settlement. The Village had approximately one hundred houses with some forty on North Street alone.[46] Many Blacks from Maryland's Eastern Shore were found on and around North, as government records show.[47] These individuals, all living in a radius of several blocks, established an intimate community alongside other Blacks.[48] Between 1851 and 1858, at times when Harriet Tubman was not away on missions to free those in bondage, she stayed on North Street; both of her brothers, John and William Henry Stewart, resided in the immediate vicinity. William Wells Brown once heard a woman in the Village talking, and he asked, "You speak as if you came from the eastern shore of Maryland." She replied, "God love yer heart, honey, I jess is."[49]

Geneva Street was a busy thoroughfare in the Black Village as well. It was a mixed zone with commercial businesses, private homes, and the Black churches, which acted as social networking centers. John W. Lindsay owned a home attached to his grocery store at the corner of Geneva and Concession Streets. Another grocer, Joseph A. Wilson, had a store blocks away on the corner of Geneva and Centre Streets, and his home was listed at the same location. Millwright James S. Madden, blacksmith Lewis Cornwall, and laborer John Shepherd all had Geneva Street addresses at some point.[50] Skilled artisans and common laborers alike could be found living in this area, shopping at stores, or fellowshipping at churches. In addition to North and Geneva, St. Paul Street was a high traffic zone. In the mid-1850s, David T. Williamson, an in-law of Mary Ann Shadd, owned a watch and jewelry shop on St. Paul, while Thomas Powers Casey's popular barbershop was located there as well.[51] However, for Black residents, "Main Street" was not one street, but two—North and Geneva.

The "Black Village" was a respectable section of town. There, freeholder Blacks owned valuable property and could expect their landholdings to increase in value over time.[52] The average house was worth $500 and stood on a lot that was roughly a quarter of an acre. Black families owned modest frame houses with three to six rooms. No Black person in the Village owned a brick home or luxuries like a private carriage, and few of the residences were whitewashed or painted; most of them were wood-colored.[53] Nonetheless, most did have gardens and livestock, such as pigs, chickens, and ducks.[54] Benjamin Drew, who in the mid-1850s visited the homes of Blacks, commented that they were plain, yet neat and comfortable inside.[55] The purchase deeds show that Blacks generally bought property from 1848 to 1854, and in some cases the land remained in a family's possession until the 1870s. The deed index shows that Blacks profited when they sold their property, and their investments gave them social mobility and a better quality of life.

Not all Blacks lived in the "colored" section of town. For instance, laborer Henry Gray and his wife Catharina dwelled on Cherry Street, around the Yates Street district, while carpenter John Hamshire resided in west St. Catharines on Hainer Street, near the shipyards.[56] Blacks living outside the Village were chiefly servants, yet a score of them managed to achieve much more. Coachman Thomas Douglas drove four-horse carriages between the Niagara River and Hamilton. He maintained a comfortable lifestyle in St. Catharines and owned property on Lake Street. Although Douglas lived outside of the Black Village, he maintained ties to the community. His wife Lizania was a faithful member of the local Black Methodist Church, and they frequented the area to see friends and run errands.[57]

Others took advantage of the fertile rural outskirts of St. Catharines. "Scattered around," William Wells Brown highlighted, "and within five miles, are a large number of farmers, many of whom have become wealthy since escaping into Canada."[58] Grantham Township was quite popular for Black settlement. Many of those who landed there escaped enslavement in Maryland and Virginia. Eastern Shore escapees Daniel Stanley and his wife Caroline fled with six kids in tow, and Perry Trusty came from Maryland traumatized by his mother's murder by a slave master.[59] A few Blacks from Nova Scotia and England were also part of the population. In Grantham, Blacks worked in a variety of agricultural pursuits as laborers and field hands. Those trained in skilled trades, like American-born teamster John W. Taylor, were rare. However, a number of them were able to buy acres of their own with earnings from years of working the soil. Black families inhabited the modest hamlet of McNab Point, named after early settlers Colin and John McNab, on Eight Mile Creek, which was also called disparagingly "Nigger Point" or "Coontown." Others were clustered throughout the region.[60]

In 1861, William Henry Stewart's family owned six acres of property in the Grantham countryside. They were located near other Black families like the Anthonys, the Stanleys, and Thomas Elliott.[61] Years later, Adam Nicholson brought two acres of land in Grantham on Church Road, near Read Road, from Alonzo and Sarah Bissell for $100 and built a two-story house.[62] Adam, known in some circles as "Blinker" because he lost an eye in slavery, married Mary Ann Amos, who was born in Batavia, New York. Her father, John Amos, was a Maryland escapee, and her mother, Ann, was a New Yorker; the Amos family spent time in Buffalo before moving across the border.[63] The Nicholsons had six children, four of whom lived into adulthood—John, Nellie, Adam (Alexander), and Tempy (or Tempie).[64]

Some Blacks preferred a rural setting and lifestyle as an alternative to the urban living of the "Colored Village." The property was cheaper so they could buy more acreage on the outer edges of town. Plus, they still had easy access to the city to bring goods to market, meet with friends, and to worship on the Sabbath. Scores of Blacks recreated in their new homes of St. Catharines the agricultural life they knew in the American South.

The "Black Town" of St. Catharines included some white inhabitants. In fact, white abolitionist and missionary Hiram Wilson was one of its most famous residents. He was New Hampshire–born and an Oberlin College graduate who established himself in the greater Colored Village area of St. Catharines after the collapse of the Dawn Settlement in Western Ontario and having lived briefly in Toronto.[65] By the time Wilson landed on the Niagara Peninsula in 1850, he had already developed relationships in Rochester. He called St. Catharines an "Advantageous position upon . . . the Niagara frontier, where the refugees are numerous, and frequently crossing over."[66] For many Black runaways, Wilson's brick, two-story cottage on Queenston Street was their first stop when they arrived in town. Between 1850 and 1856 alone, Wilson hosted some 125 fugitives in his home and assisted many others with their transition to Canada.[67] Frederick Douglass and J. W. Loguen often sent Blacks to him. Wilson provided initial help to newcomers until they could steadily support themselves. Isaac D. Williams was one of those runaways. In his *Narrative,* he explained that after passing through Rochester, he was told to head to Hiram Wilson in St. Catharines. Wilson supplied him and his fellow fugitives with clothing, boots, an axe, and provisions they needed to promptly get to work and earn their own way.[68]

A great deal of controversy surrounded Wilson in St. Catharines. Initially, he was forced to address questions about the misappropriation of funds in the Dawn Settlement. There were also attacks made on his personal character and Christian values. Throughout all the accusations, Wilson maintained his innocence, attributing the criticism to ignorant and envious individuals seeking to build themselves up at any cost.[69] Other charges of corruption arose not because of where he lived in St. Catharines but because of how he lived. His house in the Village was a major source of conflict.[70] Mary Ann Shadd attacked Wilson for using missionary funds to construct an expensive home, arguing that the money could have been used toward the advancement of fugitives. Shadd stated that the "large brick mansion" situated "in the suburbs" with all its adornments would "cost several thousand dollars" when completed.[71]

Wilson's home sat on a valuable lot, and it was quite a fashionable dwelling for a missionary. "No missionary field is more profitable," Shadd added, "than that of the fugitive Negroes in Canada!"[72] Shadd was fed information about Wilson from her sister, Amelia Shadd Williamson, who lived in St. Catharines and wrote critically of him as well.[73] Wilson rejected the charges, but when the *Provincial Freeman* invited him to file a lawsuit to prove the newspaper wrong, he explained that "mingled feelings of mercy and compassion prevented me from doing so."[74] Despite Wilson's shortcomings, real or imagined, he enjoyed widespread support in the international community and with Blacks in the Village.

He was considered by scores of people to be "the fugitive's friend" and "a distinguished, self-denying philanthropist."[75]

Throughout the 1850s, Wilson was a reliable first line of temporary relief to fugitives and a promoter of their self-reliance. Like Douglass's home in Rochester, Wilson's home was often filled with runaways who arrived on his doorstep at all times of day and night. Furthermore, Wilson occasionally preached to the local Black congregations, and he held both an evening school and a Sabbath School to educate Blacks.[76] He explained "I am kept as busy as a bee."[77] In Hiram's absence from St. Catharines, his wife, Mary, who "warmly seconds his benevolent exertions," continued to make sure the needs of fugitives were met "with her words of kindness and her cheerful smile."[78] Hiram Wilson frequently traveled to the United States to obtain funds to support Blacks crossing the international border; Rochester was a common destination or go-between.[79] Wilson explained, "I cannot, WILL NOT FALTER, nor shrink from the faithful discharge of my duty, whether in the United States or Canada."[80] The Wilson couple often wrote letters for runaways addressed to family left behind in the United States. Many Blacks returned to the Wilsons to express gratitude and to inform them of how they had prospered in St. Catharines.[81] However, Wilson commonly complained that his resources were scant. He once told William Still of Philadelphia, after receiving two new fugitive arrivals, "I hope you are not moneyless, as I am," and he was habitually "under the necessity of asking for some money."[82]

Other whites were dotted throughout the Village, and a number of them were involved in interracial relationships. On January 3, 1855, Black barber Thomas Powers Casey married white Anne Eliza Adams at the prestigious St. George's Church in St. Catharines.[83] Reverend Richard R. Godfrey of Zion Baptist Church was married to a white woman and lived on North Street in the heart of the Village.[84] Nathan, a white soap peddler, was wedded to a Black woman and lived on St. Paul Street East. David Baxter, a Black laborer from the United States who owned property and livestock on Welland Avenue, was married to Margret, an Irishwoman; the pair had two "mulatto" children, Robert and John.[85]

Local residents were tolerant of interracial relationships, to a degree. They certainly did not want to see open public displays of affection between the races. Once, at an August First celebration, carriages paraded down the streets of St. Catharines to mark the anniversary of emancipation. The *Constitutional* reported that "a slight tendency towards miscegenation was observable in one or two of the vehicles—a few white women being where they ought not to be." The newspaper firmly warned that "such unseemly exhibitions in public should be avoided."[86]

SEPARATE "COLORED VILLAGE": FRICTION AND FUNCTION

Regardless of cohabitation, intermarriage, and a general white-Black tolerance, the reality of racial friction lay just beneath the surface in St. Catharines. The hostility revealed itself in the early 1850s. At an annual "Training Day" in June 1852, when military and fire companies demonstrated their skills, there was a race riot. Among the participants were colored companies, who put on an impressive display of service and "loyalty." One onlooker commented that if ever Canada were in need of the Colored Corps, they would "do good service in defence of the country."[87] Despite the admirable demonstrations on the parade grounds, some whites hurled insults, and a rumor spread through the crowd that a Black had killed a white fireman. In response to the verbal offenses and misinformation, Blacks retaliated. After a brick was thrown, the melee began. Whites descended upon the neighboring Black Village. Several individuals were seriously injured in the riot, and a number of arrests were made. Ultimately, the Colored Village was left in ruins.[88]

Reports of the race riot appeared in the *Hamilton Gazette,* the *Toronto Globe,* and the *Frederick Douglass' Paper.*[89] The local St. Catharines newspapers criticized the police magistrate and police force for not safeguarding life and property. As part of the local outcry, people demanded "that mutual good feeling be restored," and "that a subscription list be opened for the purpose of restoring the property of those innocent parties who were the sufferers."[90] The riot was precisely the reason why Blacks wanted their own "Colored Village." As Mrs. Susan Boggs told the Freedmen's Commission, "If it was not for the Queen's law, we would be mobbed here."[91] Nonetheless, the Village recovered rapidly. Just months later, on August 24, 1852, Frederick Douglass and J. W. Loguen visited St. Catharines to lecture at the town hall. The outspoken Douglass gave the impression that all was well and explained that "he saw no destitution, misery" or "starvation."[92] Furthermore, the City Council ultimately paid for the damages to the Colored Village. In 1853, the City Council passed a motion by William Hamilton Merritt Jr. to set aside funds to repair the damages inflicted on the settlement.[93] By the time abolitionist Samuel R. Ward journeyed to St. Catharines in the same year, he called the City Council decision "a just and honourable settlement" and was "pleasantly surprised" at the level of comfort in which Blacks lived.[94]

In 1852, another major event stunned the Black community in St. Catharines. Mary Elizabeth Green, a fourteen-year-old "Colored" girl, arrived in town by way of Chippawa, Canada West, after escaping from a New Orleans merchant in Buffalo.[95] A slave catcher, allegedly a "colored kidnapper," pursued Mary to St. Catharines.[96] There, Hiram Wilson took her into his home. He reported, "The girl is here in my family, cheerful and contented." Nonetheless, she received two visits from a suspicious Black woman, who was believed to be a kidnapper sent to entice the teenager back into bondage.[97] Once local Blacks heard the news, they organized and threatened to "administer lynch law" on any slave agents in St. Catharines. The activists refused to allow another kidnapping; they had already witnessed the seizure of the Stanford family in 1835. The suspicious woman was soon forced out of town by Blacks committed to maintaining the law of liberty on the Queen's soil.[98]

Mary E. Green remained with Wilson until April 1854, when she received a visit from two women claiming that Mary's mother wanted to reunite with her daughter in California, where she now lived. People were confused about who these visitors really were. One claimed she was an "Aunt," but Wilson and most Blacks were convinced that this was another "sham" to recapture Mary. The women on this trip, however, presented all the necessary documentation to prove they were messengers from Mary's mother. The mayor and magistrates were persuaded and accepted their legitimacy, gave them custody of the girl, yet the Black community was not satisfied with the claim.[99] Approximately 300 people surrounded the house where the young girl and her purported relatives were staying. The crowd broke windows and attempted to capture the women they believed to be kidnappers.

The conflict resulted in the arrest of eleven Black men. With the permission of the court, Mary E. Green left St. Catharines with her mother's associates. For a safe departure, they were placed in jail for protection and escorted to the railroad station. If not for town authorities, someone would have been lynched. The St. Catharines officials understood the Black population's desire to protect Mary, but they emphasized the importance of following the rule of law. Afterward, the local community was perplexed as to why Blacks turned so quickly to mob justice and why Blacks did not trust British Canadian law. As for the eleven arrested "ringleaders," they received sentences of hard labor because they were given poor legal advice.[100] This episode revealed that even in this "important" Canadian town, the nearby border—and slave catchers who could cross into Canada—created very real fears among Black people.

While these tragedies were part of St. Catharines, its intrinsic value still resonated in the Colored Village—a prime destination on the Underground Railroad. In the same year as the 1852 Riot and the beginning of the Mary E. Green episode, a very special occurrence captivated the borderland town and showed its unique stature as a place for Blacks seeking to escape oppression. The former enslaved Blacks of farmer Benjamin Dicken of Halifax, North Carolina, were brought to St. Catharines in compliance with his will, which instructed they be "freely and cheerfully" manumitted. The will also ordered that after the payment of Dicken's "debts, notes, bonds, money, judgments, accounts, &c.," the remainder of the assets of the estate should be given "unto my poor negroes, to be equally divided among them."[101] The executor of the estate, Joseph J. W. Powell, was directed to send the "negroes to some free State, say, 1st. Indiana, Illinois, or Ohio, or some Western State, or Middle or Eastern State, or St. Domingo, or the British West Indies." In the summer of 1852, however, Powell elected to send the twelve formerly enslaved Blacks of Dicken to St. Catharines, and the local *Journal* reported that each of them was bequeathed $1,000.[102]

The now-freed Blacks from Edgecombe County, North Carolina, of both sexes and of all ages, were placed under the care of missionary Hiram Wilson, who reported that "their prospects are encouraging."[103] Unfortunately, the two youngest in the group died shortly after arriving in St. Catharines. "One about 3 years old," Wilson explained, "the other a babe of 2 months." The rest of the group were said to be in "good health."[104] Wilson was appointed the legal guardian of Alavana Dicken, after her mother, Mariah, passed away before she could make the trip north. Mariah intended to come to Canada from North Carolina but was pregnant with a boy she named John.[105] To make matters worse, Alavana's sister Florence was one of the youngsters who expired shortly after reaching St. Catharines.

In 1853, Alavana bravely ventured back to North Carolina to sue executor Powell for the money her mother and siblings were ordered to receive from Benjamin Dicken's estate. The final judgment allowed the free Black woman to inherit the funds of her deceased mother and her sister Florence, but not those of her brother John, who was born outside the scope of the will.[106] Alavana was grateful for the comforts of St. Catharines and the benevolence of Hiram Wilson.

Despite rare problems like the 1852 Riot and the disturbance around Mary Green's departure, the Black Village of St. Catharines was a respectable community, not a slum riddled with crime.[107] The land that the Village inhabited was neither swampy nor infertile, not rural or isolated. The settlement was within a third of a mile from the city's main streets, and whites owned homes in the vicinity.[108] For abolitionist Samuel R. Ward, the Village exceeded his expectations. He thought the neighborhood was going to be a "Mud-hole," but it turned out to be thriving.[109] The settlement hosted a spectrum of Blacks from Loyalists of the American Revolution and veterans of the War of 1812 to recently arrived American fugitives; the Village was not homogeneous. Skilled artisans and common laborers lived side by side. People of all ages filled the area. "Entering North Street at the lower end," William Wells Brown highlighted, "I was struck with surprise at the great number of children in the street." Later he explained, "I met one old lady who escaped at the advanced age of eighty-five years—she is now *one hundred and four.*"[110] Throughout the 1850s, this section of town continued to attract displaced people. In 1857, ninety-four Black families dwelled in this district, and by 1861 the number grew to 117.[111] People kept coming to the Village for its economic opportunities and social climate.

It appears that the Colored Village was partly a matter of Blacks choosing to live with other Blacks rather than being forced to dwell in a specific neighborhood by restrictive laws. For example, the wealthiest Black in St. Catharines, John W. Lindsay, called this section of town home. In 1856, Lindsay owned property on Welland Avenue and Centre Streets, and in 1860 he purchased another plot of land nearby. By 1862, he owned five properties, and he added two more in 1869. At one point, this industrious businessman's real estate was assessed at $6,000.[112] His total worth was between $8,000 and $10,000.[113] Lindsay's properties earned him over $300 a month in rents, and made him an asset to the community as a landlord.[114] He rented to everyone from common laborers to skilled tradesmen to widows. His tenants included a molder, a carpenter, a mason, a sailor, and a teamster.[115] Occupation, age, and sex did not play a factor in choosing tenants for his properties. Single individuals and small families called his places home.

Throughout his tenure of renting, no one complained that Lindsay was a slumlord who unjustly evicted residents. He sought to properly manage and maintain his holdings as an honorable landlord. Although he rented the majority of his houses to Blacks in the North Street area, on occasions he hosted white tenants in other neighborhoods, such as Mary Hogle, a tenant on Duke Street.[116] Lindsay could have very well lived in any section of St. Catharines, yet he chose to stay close to his people. This settlement was the place to be for Blacks, regardless of their economic status, national origin, or political views. It was a transnational enclave, a place where Blacks lived, worked, and worshipped together.

RELIGIOUS, BENEVOLENT, AND ANTISLAVERY INSTITUTIONS
IN THE BORDERLAND REGION

A gemstone of the Black Village in the 1850s was the African Methodist Episcopal (AME) Church. With land granted to the church by William Hamilton Merritt and Oliver Phelps for the price of five pounds (roughly one dollar at the time), the congregation built its first house of worship on North Street in 1838. The modest church-house, made from crude logs and built for its seventy members, was named Bethel Chapel.[117] It remained in use for over a decade before being demolished to make room for the town's growing Black population.[118] The building of a new church, on the corner of North and Geneva Streets, got under way in October 1851 as a direct response to the enactment of the 1850 Fugitive Slave Act in the United States.[119] The trustees and congregation anticipated more Blacks would arrive in the borderland town.

Through much physical and financial toil, the church, also known as Salem Chapel, was completed in four years. Designed and constructed by Blacks, Salem Chapel measured 1,098 square meters (11,800 square feet) and from the outside it resembled a Southern Baptist or Methodist church.[120] The distinctive Southern-style architecture made it a unique edifice in Ontario.[121] It clearly reflected the origins of the newcomers who labored to erect the temple. The *Constitutional* praised the new church as "a fine frame structure, and very neatly finished."[122] The walnut timber, wrought iron pulpit, and rounded staircase leading to the church's gallery were stylistically sophisticated for the mid-1850s.[123]

Visiting Bishop Daniel A. Payne from Cincinnati, Ohio, dedicated the building on November 15, 1855, at a Sunday service.[124] The chapel was packed to capacity for its opening; many were unable to enter. An advertisement announcing the public dedication service said that a collection would be taken in order to aid the Building Fund.[125] The cost of constructing Salem Chapel was a major test for the developing Black congregation. The $2,000 expense strained the financial means of the membership. At the time, the church was 195 members strong, but a large number of them were newly arrived American refugees.[126] Understanding the extent of the Church's fiscal needs, the trustees explained that they would accept contributions "no matter how small the amount."[127]

A few years after Salem Chapel was dedicated, the church moved from the African Methodist Episcopal (AME) to the British Methodist Episcopal (BME) denomination. Fugitives from America played a large role in this change. They wanted to rid themselves of a portion of American "baggage," including the AME name.[128] Fugitive American Blacks and Canadian-born Blacks could not enter the United States for AME Conference fellowship and business without the threat of being captured. Moreover, it was an inconvenience to follow foreign bishops, administration, and church discipline when they could simply join a British denomination.[129] Despite the name change from African to British Methodist in 1856, the church and its members remained transnational. They continued to reach out to other congregations across international lines. Black American clergy still took the pulpit, and the church remained committed to building relationships with abolitionists outside of Canada and providing aid to their chief benefactors' fugitive newcomers. Life in the Black Village centered on the BME church.[130]

Zion Baptist Church was the other major place of worship in the Black community. Located near the BME chapel on Geneva Street, the Baptist church was founded by Virginia-born Elder Washington Christian, who had launched other congregations in Toronto and Hamilton.[131] In 1838, he established a Baptist Society in St. Catharines, and soon the group planned to build its own meetinghouse. After failing to find a suitable property among the landholdings of William Hamilton Merritt, who had recently helped the Black Methodists, the congregation acquired an allotment from Henry Mittleberger for $300 in early 1840. Zion agreed to pay installments of $50 annually. However, when the payments came due, the pledgers could not fulfill their promises. Zion needed help; they returned to Merritt, who first denied them only to later give the church two lots free of charge, provided that a chapel was erected within five years.[132]

In an open letter in the *St. Catharines Journal,* Henry Gray praised Merritt "as the poor man's benefactor, and the friend of the despised African." Gray, a longtime resident of St. Catharines and an Emancipation Day organizer, expressed the surprise the Black Baptist committee felt in response to Merritt's generosity, writing, "We could not have expected that he would have given us two lots." Gray also noted that Merritt quietly helped other Blacks in the community out of public view. Some fifteen people he knew, likely American fugitives, had been provided land by the statesman at a bargain rate, with no stress of repayment and eviction or interest on the purchase price. From the time that

Gray settled in St. Catharines, he had heard and seen the positive news about Merritt, and in his letter he asserted that "I have had no reason to change my opinion of him." "To the colored population," Gray affirmed confidently, "he has been very kind and lenient."[133]

By 1844, the construction of the Zion Baptist Church was finished on Geneva Street, and the congregation, under the leadership of Reverend John Anderson, was forty members strong. Merritt, as promised, granted the church a land deed for completing the sacred edifice in the prearranged five-year time frame. On average, only a quarter of Black churchgoers in St. Catharines attended Zion; the others worshipped at the BME church.[134] The *Journal* gave mixed reviews of the new Baptist building, stating initially that the church was a "rough-cast one" but reporting just weeks later that it was "a very respectable new structure."[135] Zion overall had simple features, including a choir loft, seating for sixty, a coal-fired stove for heat, and a baptismal pool.[136] In the church's first year, misfortune struck when the building caught fire from combustible materials. Nonetheless, it sustained only modest damages due to the quick response of the local fire company.[137]

In the 1850s, Zion faced major issues with its pastoral and ministerial leadership. In 1852, Pastor John Peterson was removed from the pulpit for being drunk and degenerate. Reverend Richard R. Godfrey replaced Peterson, but his time at Zion ended in 1859 when it was discovered he was a bigamist. Pastor Godfrey had a Black wife, Elizabeth Miller, in Lockport, New York, and he had married a second woman, who was white, in Canada.[138] When the congregation confirmed Godfrey's misdeeds, he was released from his duties. Godfrey was scheduled to appear at the St. Catharines Town Hall to defend himself against this accusation, but he did not show up. In the same year, formally ordained minister John Anderson, who was pastor in 1844, was found to be intoxicated on the Sabbath. He was summarily excommunicated from the church.[139]

Zion's financial troubles also continued into the 1850s. James R. Young, in December of 1855, was appointed as an agent to raise funds to pay off the church's debt. In June 1856, however, the trustee board saw that no progress was being made, and they reported that "Young is no longer our agent, or a member of our church."[140] Both the pastoral and fiscal challenges of the decade weighed heavily on Zion. Church membership declined, and the local community became concerned with the fate of the church. Individuals like Dr. Daniel Lawson warned the church not to trust preachers until members knew they were "duly qualified."[141] The Baptists followed this counsel and picked their next pastor wisely. It was the famous runaway Anthony Burns, who was arrested in Boston under the Fugitive Slave Act of 1850.[142]

Burns served as pastor of Zion beginning in early 1861 after he bravely recrossed into the United States to attend Oberlin College in Ohio. By the time he came to St. Catharines, the congregation had shrunk to thirty-five members. William Wells Brown stated simply that "His congregation is not large."[143] Still, in Burns, the church finally found a trusted spiritual leader.[144] However, his time was short; Burns died on July 27, 1862, at the age of twenty-eight after a long battle with inflammation of the lungs. His obituary mentioned the difficult situation he inherited at Zion and the progress made under his leadership.[145] In a short time, Burns had started to improve the affairs of the church, he was a model pastor, and he reduced the church's debt.[146] The remains of the epic figure were buried at the St. Catharines Cemetery, and the church was forced to move on.[147]

Like the BME Church, Zion Baptist provided a range of services and aid to the Black community. Unfortunately, the white local newspapers focused chiefly on the problems of the churches while overlooking their Biblical good works and outreach.[148] The churches fed the hungry, clothed those underdressed for the Canadian weather, and helped to nurse the sick and shut-in. The local press seemed fixated on their financial debt, ministerial shortcomings, and problems that reflected badly on the congregations. The newspapers concentrated more on the building of their temples than on the ways in which the churches attempted to build up their people. The positive contributions of the houses of worship, according to editors, did not make for interesting stories or top headlines. The Black Canadian papers, the *Voice of the Fugitive* and the *Provincial Freeman,* did modestly better in their portrayal of the Black community, but they covered only a small number of St. Catharines' stories, similar to the coverage of American papers with a transnational-orientation, like those of Frederick Douglass. Even though readers might not know it from the biased and scant reporting, the Methodist and Baptist churches were the centers for social life and activities in the Village; they each served their members and the wider transnational community.

In 1853, for instance, Hiram Wilson shared with Miss Hannah Gray of New Haven, Connecticut, the status of fugitives and of "a glorious revival of Religion" happening in the "Garden City," which mirrored the "Burnt-Over District." The churches in St. Catharines were crucial to the spiritual resurrection of American runaways. Wilson wrote to Gray that "Among the first fruit of the work was the hopeful conversion of Mary Elizabeth the girl you saw in my family but recently from New Orleans. (You are not ignorant of her history) Since she has been with us, she has been well instructed, has learned to read & write & what is best of all, has learned to sing the song of '*redeeming love*.'" The importance of these religious centers in providing essentials such as food and shelter and addressing matters of the heart and soul cannot be overstated. These churches did tremendous work to aid the "poor strangers from the prison house of slavery."[149]

In addition to local Black churches, newcomers benefited from organizations like St. Catharines Refugee Slaves' Friend Society. This interracial, philanthropic society, which was started in 1852, extended support to the increasing numbers of Black fugitives in town.[150] The more than seventy members in the society each paid a yearly fee of one dollar, and the proceeds went toward relief for Blacks.[151] Local giants were all society members, including Mayor Elias Adams; William Hamilton Merritt, the merchant and politician; James Lamb, the editor of the *St. Catharines Journal* and customs house officer; missionary Hiram Wilson; and abolitionist Harriet Tubman. The Blacks involved with the society inspired Wilson to proclaim that the "Colored people here are heart in hand in the cause."[152]

Together the group resolved to provide practical tools to help American refugees. They built networks of communication with American correspondents and distributed clothing, money, and books to the needy. Moreover, this respectable assembly of people showed that progress was a possibility in St. Catharines, and discrimination would not go unchecked. When some young whites attempted to disturb a meeting of the society on April 15, 1852, local editorials expressed their disgust.[153] The *Constitutional* recognized Blacks as an industrious and honest class of people who required only modest assistance to become ideal citizens. The newspaper wished St. Catharines Refugee Slaves' Friend Society well in their endeavors.[154]

In 1861, Tubman established the Fugitive Aid Society of St. Catharines, another interracial association. The *Liberator* proclaimed that it "may be relied on as worthy of confidence by those who wish to help the fugitives in Canada, many of whom are undoubtedly in need of such aid."[155] Fortunately, its existence was brief because the American Civil War started the year it began, and the migration of Blacks to Canada slowed.[156]

BORDERLAND WORK

Blacks were thankful for temporary relief efforts from the local churches and organizations, but they longed to be self-sufficient. Finding work was the first step to independence. "If furnished with employment," Hiram Wilson explained, "they can take care of themselves and make a comfortable living."[157] The Black workforce in St. Catharines was diverse, with more skilled and semiskilled laborers than other Niagara Peninsula towns, and they prospered in the travel-and-transportation-driven community. On the peninsula, St. Catharines was the center for industry and commerce, and this drew Blacks into its workforce.[158] Nonetheless, like most places in America and Canada during the 1850s, the majority of Blacks in St. Catharines worked as common laborers and servants. Typically, they were unskilled and picked up odd jobs to pay their rent and support themselves.

Most Blacks, as government records demonstrated, changed jobs a number of times once in town. They utilized every opportunity to improve upon their newfound freedoms and show their economic fortitude. In 1854, nineteen-year-old Thomas Douglas was listed on the assessment records as a laborer, but just a year later he was a teamster, and he went on to become an esteemed citizen and the "best horseman" in town.[159] John W. Lindsay arrived in St. Catharines "penniless," yet by his hard work over some four decades, "he hammered out quite a fortune."[160] The industrious Lindsay worked as a laborer, farmer, teacher, huckster, and blacksmith. On the 1856 assessment record, he was listed as a "gentleman," which signified that he was a substantial property owner.[161] Lindsay managed to have a few long-standing business ventures, none more lucrative than his dry goods and grocery store. Unfortunately, the majority of Blacks were unable to stay in any profession for very long.

Many Black residents of St. Catharines worked as crew members on ships, tour guides, and employees in the spa and hotel industries. Colonel Eleazer Williams Stephenson opened the first spa in St. Catharines, the Stephenson House, in 1855. A year later, the Welland House welcomed guests on the corner of King and Ontario streets. These businesses initially provided jobs in construction for Blacks and then more long-term work. The *St. Catharines Constitutional* reported that "a large number of Negro slaves, skilled artisans who had fled across the Niagara River to safety, were put to work building the Welland House Hotel."[162]

The spas were needed for urban development and bolstered the local economy.[163] "Hotel accommodation," an 1856 navigation guide explained, "until recently, has been very poor." The opening of the Stephenson House and Welland House were said to have "worked a great improvement in this respect," and St. Catharines was called the "Saratoga Springs of Canada."[164] At summer's peak, the town bustled with activity. A local newspaper noted that "Pleasant signs of prosperity are all about us. The tide of Southern travel has begun to flow in upon the metropolis."[165] In a *Toronto Globe* ad, E. W. Stephenson issued an invitation: "To all who have the ability and the will to come and make an effort at casting off disease or obtaining relaxation and repose—we say come!" He added, "Hasten to this spring of health and commit yourself to the hands of pleasure assisted by every auxiliary which a pleasing excursion brings into play, and rest assured that a short stay with us will terminate in sending you 'on your way rejoying' back to your former duties."[166]

In 1865, Dr. Theophilus Mack opened another spa on Yates Street, the Springbank Hotel. The spas of St. Catharines became a popular destination for Canadian and American tourists. Many wanted to come to drink its "pure" waters and to bathe in the "curative mineral waters" brought in from nearby springs of the Twelve Mile Creek, a tributary of the Niagara River and Niagara Falls. A large portion of the guests were Southerners seeking cooler weather in the hot summer months. The *Constitutional* noted, "The Southern States are largely represented."[167] One woman escaping the heat of Virginia in 1860 for the comfort of the Stephenson House was Agnes Lee, the aunt of Confederate General Robert E. Lee. Agnes Lee explained that she took shower-baths and drank wine twice a day in the spa.[168] This was quite typical of the average elite customer's experience. "The St. Catharines Baths," many asserted, "are refreshing and invigorating, leaving after them a delightful, soft and moist condition of the skin."[169] The spas were complete with medical physicians to oversee the healing and comfort of patients. They boasted that their clients "bear testimony to the beneficial effects of it [treatment] in Rheumatism, Fever and Ague, Indigestion, or disordered functions of the Stomach, Liver or Kidneys," among other things.[170]

The guests were served by a predominantly Black workforce.[171] In the spa and hotel businesses, they were able to find employment as waiters, porters, carriage drivers, and cooks. It reminded Southern patrons of the "comforts of home" when Blacks served them in St. Catharines. By the end of the decade, the spas gained an international reputation. The Stephenson House attracted so many people at peak season that it had to arrange cottages for overflow accommodations on its property.[172] This put Black workers in demand. They were paid a decent, livable wage for their work, but their occupations closely resembled those of the uncompensated slave laborers in America. Nonetheless, through hard work Blacks could advance. Two Black laborers, Mr. Morris at the St. Catharines House and Mr. Dyke of the American Hotel, were promoted to head-waiter positions.

Although Blacks found hospitality jobs in St. Catharines, their lives were burdened by certain restrictions. For instance, the very hotels in which they labored denied them guest services. In 1854, the St. Catharines House and the American Hotel began a policy that excluded Blacks from boarding the inn's coach shuttles. Complaints started immediately.[173] Two Black ministers visiting St. Catharines had their trips interrupted by this change in regulation. Disregarding this new discriminatory policy, Philadelphia's Reverend Paul Quinn, an old gentleman in feeble health, boarded a shuttle into town. Cincinnati's Reverend Daniel Payne and his wife were not as fortunate. On their way from Toronto, they encountered no trouble until they reached Port Dalhousie, a community near St. Catharines, which in the 1850s reported as a "local improvement" that no colored people inhabited the town.[174] There they were refused the services of an omnibus. Payne and his wife remained stuck at the port deep into the night. These occurrences, along with other reported incidents of racial discrimination, incited the Black community to speak out.[175]

When Black inn workers on August 4, 1854, protested the segregation at their jobs and threatened to boycott, local hotel and omnibus owners gave in to a portion of their demands. Local Blacks met at the BME Church on August 6, 1854, to organize around the issue. Mr. Dyke, headwaiter at the American Hotel, said he would quit if the hotel did not make the changes he demanded. Dyke explained that he "could stand it no longer" and urged others to follow his lead.[176] Mr. Morris, headwaiter at the St. Catharines House, told the crowd that he took the insults directed at his fellow Blacks personally. Morris viewed the prejudiced acts committed against others as an attack upon himself. He told the assembly "to respect themselves, and their rights as a people, and submit no longer to such degrading treatment."[177]

After the headwaiters spoke out, others were able to address their coworkers and residents concerned with the injustices at the hotels. The voices of the various speakers represented a unity in the community, and together the group put forth resolutions that appealed to the humanity of their employers. They resolved, "Man is man, without respect to the colour of his skin." Moreover, the workers made it apparent that they would not continue to work under oppressive and offensive conditions. In a brilliant tactical move, the group agreed to allow the meeting's proceedings to be published. This allowed the local community and the international community to learn what the innkeepers and owners were doing.[178] Newspapers like the *North Star* in Rochester picked up the story and highlighted the insulting treatment that Rev. Paul Quinn and Rev. Dr. Payne experienced.[179] The *Provincial Freeman* called the situation "disgraceful" and explained, "It is clear enough that coloured men need not accept service in hotels . . . as their only alternative."[180] Ultimately, the protesters obtained accommodations that allowed them to return to work, and this demonstrated that Blacks in St. Catharines had legitimate recourse for their grievances. It was a matter of using the right dose of organization, tact, and the press to achieve their goals.

Although the hotel industry provided scores of jobs for Blacks, there were many other occupations they could enter into in town. Barbering was popular among Black men in St. Catharines. At times, there could be six to eight major barbers and others competing for the town's multiracial clientele. Barbers in the St. Catharines market were extremely competitive. John Anderson, for example, reduced his rates to get an edge over his rivals.[181] The more prosperous barbers ran advertisements in the local newspapers to promote their establishments. T. P. Casey and Aaron Young were the two most popular and well-respected barbers in town. Casey frequently ran ads, using the art of charm by expressing deep gratitude toward his customers. In an 1851 ad, he thanked his "liberal patronage" for five years of business before plugging his new line of women's wigs.[182] Casey constantly expanded his business to offer new products and specialty services, such as dentistry and bleeding.[183] The ads were a fruitful vehicle; T. P. Casey remained a barber in St. Catharines until 1867, when he moved to Toronto and continued in the same line of work.[184]

Aaron Young owned a barbershop on Queenston Street in 1856, but two years later he moved to St. Paul Street. He advertised his new business in the local newspapers to remain competitive. One of his ads claimed that "Those patronizing his saloon will receive entire satisfaction" and "at low prices."[185] Young's shop lived up to the publicity and pulled in its fair share of local business. Like Casey, Young expanded his business beyond shaving, shampooing, and hairdressing. In 1861, he publicized that he could dry clean and refurbish clothing.[186] Although Young added new services, barbering remained his chief moneymaker. He kept the competition honest, too. Once, Young accused barber Jeff Anderson of working on Sunday, which violated the local Sabbath Day Act. Anderson had to pay a five-dollar penalty. Later that year, Young, who had begun working at the Stephenson House, was charged with the same crime. However, he was acquitted of the misdeed because the owner, Col. Stephenson, came to his defense.[187]

Several Blacks in other professions operated their own businesses as well. For example, Renix Johnston, Francis Scott, and Nelson Williams made livings as shoemakers. Daniel Williams, a watchmaker, and David T. Williamson, a jeweler, got into industries that Blacks only occasionally worked in throughout Canada.[188] Williamson, a former slave, opened a store on St. Paul Street in 1855, where he offered a full line of jewelry, including chains, bracelets, lockets, and earrings. He also repaired broken jewelry and watches. Williamson classified his business as "respectfully intimate" to patrons with "moderate charges."[189] The store got off to a strong start, but after it was robbed in September of 1855 for a large number of watches and valuables, Williamson never made a full recovery.[190] He posted a reward seeking information about the robbers and the recovery of his merchandise. The Black jeweler reported in the months following the burglary that he had replenished his stock and possessed jewelry equal to his competition.[191] Nonetheless, he could never rebuild his business to be as successful as before. In 1856, Thomas F. Cary and Mary Ann Shadd Cary were married at the St. Catharines home of Williamson, who was married to Mary Ann's sister, Amelia.[192] Later that year, following the birth of a daughter, Williamson informed customers to pick up their jewelry repairs and settle their accounts.[193] He held a public auction to sell off his merchandise and closed his doors. Years later he was a farmer in Kent, Canada West.[194] In all, Black men in St. Catharines had access to a variety of jobs besides simply being "labourers or servants."

The majority of Black women had to work to help support their families. Most of these women worked as servants and usually in gender-based occupations such as laundress, dressmaker, cook, or hairdresser.[195] Married women, in general, did not formally file their occupations in census reports, yet they found ways to earn income. Like several female children in this era, Amanda Hemsley worked as a laundress, as did her mother Elizabeth Hemsley.[196] Elizabeth showed her daughter the secrets of the trade, whether it was the removal of entrenched dirt and stains or properly drying garments. Elizabeth and her husband, Rev. Alexander Hemsley, who explained "our people all start poor, and have to struggle to support themselves," were able to accomplish much through hard work and multiple incomes. The Hemsley family lived in a frame house on North Street that sat on a quarter of an acre.[197] Women working outside set gender roles were rare, but Maria Notes managed to become a "green grocer."[198] And some Black women, like Mrs. LaBrush and Lane, transcended gender roles by owning property.[199]

Unfortunately, in a patriarchal society, the majority of woman without "bread-winning males" were financially vulnerable. Seamstress Elizabeth Wheaton Dunlop of Drummondville, for instance, was married to Elijah Barnett Dunlop, a native of Richmond, Virginia. He came to Toronto in the 1830s and eventually moved to St. Catharines after spending time at the Dawn Settlement and Oberlin College. The couple married on October 30, 1848, and the mobility-minded Elijah, an active antislavery advocate, traveled within Canada and across the border in Western New York. He attended meetings and shared spaces with Henry Bibb and Martin R. Delany in Toronto's St. Lawrence Hall. Once, at an 1851 St. Catharines August First celebration at City Hall, he spoke and sang to "a large crowd, mostly colored."[200]

Nonetheless, in short order, he got "gold fever" and left his wife and children in St. Catharines for the distant goldfields of Australia. To their dismay, he abandoned them. After Elijah's extensive absence, Elizabeth declared herself a "widow" and fought to raise her children in the Colored Village by learning to be a seamstress.[201] Elijah never returned to St. Catharines, never got rich in the outback as Grandison Boyd of Rochester did, and died decades later in an Australian poorhouse.[202] Perhaps Elijah would have done better by simply remaining in the transnational and financial center of Black Niagara, where his family struggled, primarily because he was not present.

Economically, Blacks were capable of doing reasonably well in St. Catharines. The *Provincial Freeman* reported in 1854 that "work is abundant and wages good."[203] Once Blacks overcame the challenge of settling in, most were able to attain a decent standard of living. As long as Blacks remained flexible and creative, they could earn good money in this urban, transnational environment. Many common laborers worked more than one job, and Black business owners provided a diversity of goods and services under one roof. Barbers Casey and Young were masters of this craft. John W. Lindsay owned a grocery store on Geneva Street and a small beer company.[204] Each business complemented the other. Remaining resourceful was essential. In the Village, Blacks grew gardens to subsidize their income and bartered for some transactions. Blacks may not have had job security or the luxury of holding a single occupation as whites did, but through skillful planning they could live on almost equal economic terms. Local Blacks celebrated their financial independence and felt humiliated when "beggars" went back to the United States asking for charitable contributions on their behalf.[205]

Blacks in St. Catharines were also well aware of the need to develop new businesses in the region. Seeing the 1853 National Negro Convention in Rochester, Blacks in St. Catharines the following year hosted a similar gathering to promote industry in coordination with their borderland counterparts. Fortunately, issues of emigration did not hamper this conference as they did in Rochester. The convention attracted Blacks from around the British colony, including Toronto, Hamilton, and Amherstburg. The participants had three main goals. First, they wanted to establish a formal coalition of Blacks in order to "better attain the object so desirable." Second, they aspired to create a Mechanical Institution so that their "sons may have the opportunity of becoming tradesmen." The committee wanted to provide the means to improve the "Minds, Morals, and Mechanical powers" of the race. Finally, the gathering sought to get English, American, and internal Canadian help for refugees escaping servitude. They concluded with the firm message: "awake to this all-important object."[206] The assembly allowed like-minded Black leaders to discuss their interest in transnational interaction and an industrial school to secure future economic viability. Though an official "Mechanical Institution" never materialized in St. Catharines, Blacks ran effective apprenticeships.[207] For instance, the top barbers all had understudies, and blacksmith Lindsay passed along his skills as well.[208]

On a basic level, hardworking Blacks in St. Catharines were able to own real estate and live relatively comfortably.[209] The living standard of many Blacks exceeded those of the Irish and Germans who arrived in the 1840s and 1850s. "Our people in St. Catharines," Samuel R. Ward explained, "are not the poorest in the town, by a good deal."[210] Frederick Douglass made a similar observation, stating that Blacks "compare, in their outward circumstances, with any class of emigrants we saw there."[211] In St. Catharines, Blacks also benefited from being a smaller minority group than the Irish or the Germans. They fit into the local social structure in a seamless fashion that did not directly threaten established power-holders. Blacks took advantage of their unique position in the job market. For example, in the 1840s, Blacks oversaw Irish laborers as police—the Colored Corps—during the expansion of the Welland Canal.[212] Years later, the 1864 Freedmen's Bureau report noted the elevated status of Blacks in relation to that of the Irish and Germans.[213]

CRAFTING A SEPARATE SCHOOL

One major goal of Blacks in St. Catharines was to provide education for themselves and for their children. Fugitive William Johnson from Virginia, like many newcomers, was excited to get his studies underway. Johnson explained, "I have been trying to learn to read since I came here, and I know a great many fugitives who are trying to learn."[214] Blacks saw the pursuit of education as a means to a better life. However, learning at a quality school with competent instructors was at times nearly impossible in St. Catharines. John W. Lindsay was infuriated by the deficient education Blacks received in St. Catharines. Without good education, he asked, "What are you going to do with the colored people? What will become of them? What kind of citizens will they make?" Lindsay concluded that power-holding whites "will only make paupers and culprits of them."[215]

The Black community voiced their concern and fought for quality education. "Although the British Constitution draws no distinction between the sons of Adam, of whatever complexion their skin," activists argued, "we are practically denied such blessings and advantages, by being excluded from the district and other schools, on account of colour, and denied the privilege of intermixing with our fellow creatures in the home of God." These people of transnational experiences and minds did not want to endure "the same unchristianlike treatment that our brethren are forced to submit to in the neighbouring Republic."[216] Still, they found themselves in similar circumstances. The 1843 Common School Act allowed public schools for all inhabitants funded by the government. Conversely, a quasi-formal 1850 act amended its predecessor to "authorise the establishment of one, or more, Separate schools for Protestants, Roman Catholics or Coloured People" if a dozen or more applied to a school. This set the stage for Blacks in St. Catharines to have schools that were separate but financed fairly.[217]

However, the private St. Paul Colored School, established in 1846, was the only place in town that Blacks could attend throughout the 1850s.[218] The segregated school was the target of many complaints. First, the colored school was not a government-run Common School, which meant that Blacks were not getting their fair share of tax revenue. Second, critics noted that the school was poorly managed and had inadequate teachers. The school ran "help wanted" ads for instructors "with testimonials of good moral character," but it attracted the contrary.[219] Mr. James Brown, for instance, was released as schoolmaster because of his "free use of liquor."[220] Lindsay complained that Brown had been "an old drunken teacher for several years" who killed time "half teaching the children" and "sometimes lying drunk in the school house" while the students played outside.[221] Brown's replacement, Mr. Oscar F. Wilkins, beat out "six proficient competitors" for his position.[222] However, Blacks still felt that the teachers and administrators were not up to par. The underfunded private school simply could not provide the facilities or the faculty capable of teaching approximately 250 children and an abundance of adults who desired to learn.[223]

The *Provincial Freeman* reported in 1854 that St. Catharines had "an inferior school, in consequence of a few negrohaters" who took "advantage of their ignorance and against the law . . . assigned to them an exclusive school."[224] The grievances over the private St. Paul Colored School reached a peak in 1855 when Attorney James F. Saxon addressed the school board on their refusal to admit Blacks into government-supported public schools.[225] The board sidestepped his indictment. The Black community was actively engaged over this issue and debated whether to have an integrated or a segregated school. Blacks eventually petitioned the school board to establish a separate Black school on the assumption that the board would properly fund their school's needs, but that never happened. The school board continued to avoid their legal and civic responsibilities to the St. Paul Colored School.

The status of the Colored School and Black education was alarming to Hiram Wilson. He had been responsible for recruiting teachers to Canada from Oberlin College since the late 1840s, when he had worked at the Dawn Settlement. He had been accountable for dispatching needed teachers to Amherstburg, Toronto, Chatham, the Wilberforce Settlement, and St. Catharines. In fact, Harriet E. Hunter of Cincinnati was sent to St. Catharines in 1839 through the efforts of Wilson.[226] Hunter, an activist and teacher, married John W. Lindsay and played an important role in his business success, later resigning from her teaching duties largely to attend to domestic affairs.[227]

When Hiram Wilson moved to St. Catharines, he and his wife tried to make up for deficiencies of the St. Paul Colored School by opening their own day and evening schools to help educate Black adults and children. Mary Wilson started a school for Black girls at their personal residence, and the endeavor enrolled more than eighty students.[228] However, most of the Black population was not fortunate enough to study with the Wilsons, so ensuring equality in education remained a major issue.

The Black community was stuck with the same deficient St. Paul Colored School until 1871. Blacks accepted the idea of a separate school before the 1860s, but the concept was undermined when the city did not support the school with tax dollars, which was the chief reason for the school's shortcomings. Long after his children had graduated, John W. Lindsay signed a petition to permit students to attend schools in their own lawful wards. "Here are our children," he explained, "that we think as much of as white people think of theirs, and want them elevated and educated; but, although I have been here thirty years, I have never seen a scholar made amongst the colored people."[229] The education of Blacks in St. Catharines had long been a source of discontent for Lindsay. Education, to him and to the community, was directly connected to social achievement and the building of a vital transplant culture.

Finally, in early 1871, laborer William Hutchinson filed a suit against the Common School for refusing to admit his son, Robert.[230] Afterward, community members signed a petition to permit individuals to attend schools in their own legitimate wards. Justice Curran Morrison ruled in *Hutchinson vs. St. Catharines* that the practices of the government-run institutions were unlawful. After a deferment due to "overcrowded" white schoolhouses and "lack of space," reasons totally fabricated to reject Blacks, Robert was finally admitted. Hutchinson's lawsuit effectively desegregated the local schools in St. Catharines.[231]

Illiteracy rates in the Black community were tremendously high in the 1850s and 1860s. Birthplace played a key factor in whether an individual could read or write. Those born in the United States generally could not read or write, while Blacks born in Canada were literate or at least functioned at a reasonable level.[232] Gender also played a role in literacy as well.[233] Most young Black boys did not attend school regularly because they worked to help earn money for their families. Government documents such as land deeds and wills provide insight into the educational backgrounds of Blacks. For instance, a number of men actually signed their full names on land deeds, signifying a degree of literacy, while others could mark only with an "X." Why was education and the access to formal instruction such a point of contention in St. Catharines? Other Canada West towns did not struggle over education as much, but those towns were largely not seeking to build separate institutions, which was an act of self-determination.

Despite educational discrimination, Blacks in St. Catharines had access to political recourse that enabled them to change their circumstances.

POLITICAL RIGHTS

Political rights were a key reason why many Blacks came to St. Catharines. It was here that American fugitives could exercise some of the same rights guaranteed in the US Constitution. For the first time, most Blacks found themselves living in a society where they had some form of legal recourse to address their grievances. Blacks enjoyed many of the same rights, liberties, and immunities as other law-abiding taxpayers. However, the unjust bigotry they faced in St. Catharines taught Blacks the democratic principles of how to assemble themselves and petition for change. These rights gave Blacks a confidence that all they had achieved and earned could not simply be swept away. The status and self-assurance this provided was transformative. Some Blacks went from not even owning themselves in the American South to being respectable real estate freeholders in St. Catharines.

As early as 1841, local politicians solicited Black voters during election campaigns and championed their rights in St. Catharines.[234] In the 1850s, the first mayor of the town, Elias S. Adams, was active in abolition and fugitive aid endeavors. *The Mail* reported that he did his "duty fearlessly and fully, whether the individual coming before him be a poor man or a mighty man."[235] Blacks found an ally in Adams; a political parallel of his status was not found in Rochester. Landowning Blacks and others in St. Catharines viewed the ballot as a compelling right and a civic responsibility. Fugitive William Grose from Harpers Ferry, Virginia, who vividly remembered being denied the right to vote in the South, was pleased to exercise the same electoral power as other British Canadians. In St. Catharines, he declared, "I have a vote every year as much as any other man." Grose felt like a stakeholder in the society. "Now I feel like a man," he explained, "And I wish to God that all my fellow-creatures could feel the same."[236]

Despite pervasive racism in Grantham's "Nigger Point" section of the township, Blacks utilized their right to vote. During election seasons, politicians clamored for the Black vote in "Nigger Point," and it became "a regular Mecca." Some candidates tried to influence voters with "a large jug of whiskey or a dollar bill," which was "always a factor in the proceedings." Candidates sought the Black vote through means foul or fair. If not led astray, the vast majority of Blacks in the greater St. Catharines area voted liberal for the Clear Grits, whose motto was "all sand and no dirt," instead of for the conservative, traditionalist Tory line. The Grits appealed to Ontario farmers, working-class people, and to those in the lower ranks of society. Black former slaves, along with an abolitionist contingency, felt commonality with the party, although their interests were not always directly represented. In Canada, however, Black political life and access to legal recourse in court, on equal terms with whites, plainly surpassed the civic powers of American Blacks.[237]

No matter how small the offense, Blacks could invoke their civil rights in St. Catharines. When butcher John Duher called gentleman John W. Lindsay "a black son of a gun," he was charged for the insult and was forced by the court to settle the grievance by paying a dollar fine.[238] Ann Jackson accused Sarah Hight of slander for using unorthodox language. Jackson's complaint was also resolved with a payment of one dollar.[239] American-born Black laborer Joseph Champ was detained for assaulting white carpenter Richard Tuite. Champ, who the *Evening Journal* called "One of the descendants of Ham," referring to the Hamitic myth, threatened to file a countersuit against Tuite for what apparently started the conflict: Tuite had allegedly called Champ a "nigger." In response, Champ exercised his legal right to redress the case to favor a better outcome for himself.[240] Blacks could not only protect their property and assets, but they could also safeguard their character and "honor."[241] British law clearly gave Blacks rights that were not available to them in the American North.[242]

Although Blacks valued these rights, the overwhelming majority of those in the Niagara borderlands did not apply for legal citizenship. This was true of St. Catharines as well. There were several reasons for this phenomenon. First, in the 1850s, fugitives had to have seven years residency in Upper Canada before they could become citizens.[243] Upon arrival, Blacks were focused on providing for themselves and their families, and the majority thought they would be in Canada only for a short time. However, months turned to years and most stayed for a long time, some even for life. Second, a significant number of newcomers thought citizenship was unnecessary. Blacks assumed many of the rights of natural-born British subjects without formal citizenship; therefore, they saw no need to pledge an oath to any country. They could play British Canada and the United States against one another for the best results.

The formal naturalization records in the Niagara Peninsula show that only five "colored men" became Canadian citizens—also called "British subjects."[244]

Three of them lived in St. Catharines. One was John Washington Linzy (Lindsay), a thirty-five-year-old blacksmith. The others were John Thomas, a thirty-year-old yeoman farmer, and John Bird, a thirty-year-old yeoman plasterer.[245] The other two people, both residents of Niagara Falls, were teamster Henry Garrett and laborer Charles Freeman. Lindsay distinguished himself by actually signing the naturalization paperwork with his first two initials and a rendition of his last name, "J. W. Linzy," on his naturalization paperwork, demonstrating a degree of literacy. Thomas and Bird, as well as many whites, could only mark with an "X." The citizenship papers of Lindsay, Thomas, and Bird were registered and signed in 1842, but their citizenship did not formally take effect until June 10, 1844.[246]

By going through the process of becoming British subjects, Lindsay, Thomas, and Bird gained no significant rights or privileges that the average Black on the Queen's soil did not have. Other transnationals did not see the value that these three men placed on becoming official Canadian stakeholders. Throughout the 1850s and as the Civil War neared, there was less emphasis placed on citizenship. As a consequence of their borderland location, national affiliation was trivial to Blacks. However, it is important to recognize that in Canada Blacks retained the option to become citizens, whereas in the United States the *Dred Scott* decision in 1857 foreclosed all hope of gaining citizen status. Only the ratification of the Fourteenth Amendment in 1868 made that possible. Most Blacks, on the Niagara Peninsula and in St. Catharines, realized citizenship did not matter, since they could recross the border at some point if the political climate changed in the United States.

HARRIET TUBMAN AND JOHN BROWN IN THE CANADIAN BORDERLANDS

In April of 1858, radical John Brown came to St. Catharines, accompanied by Jermain W. Loguen, who had lived in both Rochester and St. Catharines. Brown planned to visit with Harriet Tubman to discuss and recruit Blacks for his planned attack on Harpers Ferry, Virginia.[247] The two met on April 7, 1858, at Tubman's rented residence, on Lot 11 on North Street near Geneva in the heart of the Colored Village. Her house was in sight of the BME Church, where a modest group had assembled. The residence had previously been occupied by her brother William Henry Stewart and his family before they set out for the Grantham countryside.[248] By this time, Tubman had retired from her daring trips to the American South and refocused a portion of her energy into aiding local Blacks in St. Catharines. Specifically, she petitioned Western New York and Boston abolitionists to aid the local fugitives in town.[249] Tubman and Brown shared a common belief in direct action against the institution of slavery.[250] This approach to ending bondage made for vivid conversations. Brown wrote to his son afterward that Tubman "hooked on" to his team. He remained in St. Catharines for a few days, during which time Tubman and Brown offered support for each other's interests. While Tubman advocated on behalf of Brown, he understood her difficult financial situation and gave her $15.[251]

Besides meeting with Tubman, Brown had other business on his agenda. He had finished writing the Provisional Constitution for his intended Appalachian Rebel State in 1858 at the home of Frederick Douglass in Rochester, and he sent it to print in St. Catharines. Black abolitionist and publisher William Howard Day printed Brown's Constitutional pamphlet; the two men met on April 13, 1858, and Tubman coordinated the introduction.[252] Day was an Oberlin College graduate, a participant in Rochester's 1853 Black national convention, and a recent transplant to town. He was a skilled tradesman and a brilliant antislavery orator who shared his gift with the locals. Day came to St. Catharines hoping to start a Black newspaper; the city was an ideal market for one. He had published the *Aliened American* in Cleveland, but it collapsed because the subscription list was not robust.[253]

In St. Catharines, William H. Day sought to utilize his old newspaper benefactors and Gerrit Smith for financial support, just as Frederick Douglass of Rochester had done to back his new newspaper endeavors in the Niagara region. Plus, the failing *Provincial Freeman* created a void in the market and a need for a fresh voice in Canada. Much like Mary Ann Shadd Cary, Day clearly understood the "great need of a paper through which our mis-represented people can speak their sentiment."[254] And what better place for a newspaper than St. Catharines, the Niagara regional counterpart of Rochester? Unfortunately, Day could not marshal the startup funds needed to establish the periodical, but he did manage to help John Brown print his Constitution with a small hand press.[255]

As the *St. Catharines Journal* later reported, "In May or June, 1858, Captain John Brown, or 'Ossawatomie Brown,' was stopping at Gross' Saloon in this place, and was accompanied by a mulatoo [*sic*], who was a printer, and during this time they were engaged in printing a pamphlet."[256] Once William Howard Day completed printing Brown's "pamphlet," really his Constitution, the radical abolitionist set out from St. Catharines to meet in Ingersoll, Canada West, with

Harriet Tubman. However, travel mix-ups prevented them from meeting. From Canada, Brown went to Iowa and Chicago to reunite with a group of men he had previously recruited. Having gathered his band of men, Brown returned to Canada to hold the Chatham Convention, where on May 8, 1858, he ratified the new Constitution and enlisted his only Canadian comrade, Osborne P. Anderson.[257] Black entrepreneur and Underground Railroad supporter Mary Ellen Pleasant was also there and donated $30,000 to the cause. Historian Kellie Carter Jackson explained that Pleasant, Tubman, and Anna Murray Douglass—who cared for Brown in Rochester—were the women "silent and silenced black partners of Harpers Ferry."[258]

Later that year, on December 20, 1858, Tubman petitioned the St. Catharines City Council "stating that she had taken a child off the street and requested the council to make an appropriation for its maintenance." Following the Christmas holiday on December 30, 1858, the Council approved her request, writing in their notes, "H. Tubman one dollar per week for four weeks: for keeping child found in street, carried."[259] This is evidence that Tubman did not simply bring people to town but that she also cared for them once they reached St. Catharines. Tubman was a well-known figure, and the council was certainly aware of her enterprise of escorting fugitive slaves out of the United States and helping them settle in town. Tubman most likely told her brother, William Henry Stewart, how she sought and received money from the city to care for the needy, because he made a similar petition on March 15, 1859. His request explained that "he had taken a boy off the street, who was in a state of starvation." Nearly a month later, on April 11, 1859, the council declared that "one dollar weekly for ten weeks be granted."[260]

In the fall of 1859, John Brown was almost ready to launch his rebellion plot. Tubman believed in Brown's cause but was not directly involved with the raid, even though Brown dubbed her "General Tubman."[261] Other than their meeting in St. Catharines, there are no other confirmed encounters between the two. Both abolitionists spent time in Boston in late May of 1859, but they did not cross paths. Tubman was in New England to obtain funds to relocate her parents to America, while Brown was there to solicit additional capital for his insurrection.

With the two out of correspondence, Brown stayed on task with his plans. When the Harpers Ferry Raid occurred on October 16, 1859, Tubman was far from the action; apparently she was in New Bedford, Massachusetts, stricken by sickness.[262] William H. Day, the printer of the Provisional Constitution and one-time St. Catharines resident, was farther away in England on a fund-raising venture.[263] Douglass stated in exile, "England was nearly as much alive to what had happened at Harpers Ferry as the United States."[264] The raid plainly failed, but the news reverberated as the *St. Catharines Journal* declared "there can be no doubt but that thousands of refugees now in Canada would have proceeded to the scene of hostilities. Brown was too hasty, otherwise the insurrection would have been far more formidable than it was."[265] Demonstrating her profound admiration and respect for Brown, Tubman later told a close acquaintance that Brown had "done more in dying, than 100 men would in living."[266]

In 1859, when US Senator William H. Seward offered Harriet Tubman a home near Auburn, New York, she accepted his offer and moved away from St. Catharines.[267] During Tubman's stint in the "Garden City," she led a transnational dual-life, which kept her chiefly out of town but still intimately connected to the community. Despite her absences, Tubman's presence was felt by way of her charitable works and through the individuals she brought to town. In the greater Auburn area, there was a modest Black settlement called "New Guinea" that held a constituency of runaways and transplants from Maryland's Eastern Shore; it resembled the "Colored Village" of St. Catharines. Auburn was also on the edges of the "Burnt-Over District," a hotbed for social reform in Western New York, which gave Tubman a liberal space where others shared her in-depth spirituality and political thinking. She moved out of St. Catharines largely because her parents disliked the brisk weather of the Niagara Peninsula in their old age.[268]

In Auburn, as in St. Catharines, Tubman spent a great deal of time traveling, in part to raise money to pay her $1,200 mortgage.[269] However, in Central New York, the American-Canadian border hardly played a role in day-to-day life, though a hint of its presence always loomed, and Auburn gave the mobile-minded Tubman reasonable access to Canada. In fact, following John Brown's raid on Harpers Ferry, Tubman returned to St. Catharines to elude the American investigation commission charged with finding all the individuals involved with the insurrection.[270] Tubman still had family members and supporters in St. Catharines, and her decision to go back was wise, considering that marshals visited Auburn in January of 1860 and were conducting an investigation.[271] The spirit of "Old Brown" remained alive in St. Catharines long after his Virginia raid, and for years the town commemorated the anniversary of his death.[272]

In the early 1860s, the transnational-minded Harriet Tubman, no longer a resident of Canada, established the Fugitive Aid Society of St. Catharines, an interracial relief organization that gave support to lowly American escapees.[273]

Hiram Wilson explained that Tubman was "a remarkable colored heroine" and "unusually intelligent and fine appearing."[274] Yet, Tubman's new society blossomed as a manifestation of her frustration with Wilson, who was repeatedly accused of misappropriating funds meant to help Black newcomers. While Frederick Douglass and Jermain W. Loguen expressed faith in Wilson's handling of fugitives, Mary Ann Shadd and Tubman did not share the same confidence.[275] They did not believe Hiram Wilson's claim that he was doing "all that can reasonably be done in this section of Canada for the welfare of the Refugees."[276] Consequently, Tubman staffed the electoral board of the Fugitive Aid Society of St. Catharines with a core group of runaways from the Eastern Shore of Maryland, whom Tubman trusted.[277] Although the Society was short-lived because the Civil War began, it plainly demonstrated that Tubman divided duty between the United States and Canada—making her a true transnational. And her work with fugitives to manipulate regional and national borders proved she was, as John Brown had reportedly proclaimed, "one of the best and bravest persons on this continent."[278]

SUSTAINED TRANSNATIONALISM

Toward the end of the 1850s, the economy in St. Catharines became sluggish. The financial system had been strained by a massive influx of German and Irish immigrants and by the inflow of Black Americans, fugitive and free. The economy of the town was doing well at the beginning of the decade, but the rapid growth in population slowed things down. Blacks started to lose jobs or found they could not earn the money they did before. Hiram Wilson said the economic slump was "seriously felt," and noted that many had "lack of means with which to pay their honest debts."[279]

Despite the economic downturn, fugitive Blacks from America continued to arrive and depart. So many were coming that Wilson told William Still in late 1858 that St. Catharines' operatives thought it was best for some to settle in other places.[280] Wilson could quickly dispatch Blacks to other Canadian locations, and freedom seekers often used the town as a launching pad to go elsewhere. In 1858 alone, Ann Maria Jackson of Delaware and her son, James Henry Jackson, who had been sold away from his family, used St. Catharines in this way on separate occasions to reach Toronto.[281] Blacks who remained in the town were resilient in hard times. A clear indicator was the 1858 August First celebration in St. Catharines. The commemoration of freedom was the biggest date on the calendar for local Blacks and despite a "very shabby turnout" because of rain, "which descended in copious showers for some hours," a procession led by a brass band marched the city's streets.[282]

The August First celebration in 1859 drew a larger crowd, although a score of Blacks, particularly those in the hotel industry, had to miss the festivities because of work. The *St. Catharines Journal* outlined the events of the day and expressed mocking astonishment that guests from the American South were there to witness this celebration of freedom. The paper noted that "Many Southerners were present, and we feel sure it must have made their hearts pulsate with pleasure to see so many 'real, live, likely niggers,'—wh 'mout' [whose amount] be worth $1,000 apiece 'down South'—in the enjoyment of freedom and the 'inalienable rights' of humanity."[283]

In the following year's August festivities, Hiram Wilson delivered a prophetic poem that expressed the hope for jubilee over American slavery. The last two stanzas read:

> May Freedom shed her glorious light,
>   O'er lands where darkness reigns,
> To bless the slave with visions bright,
>   And burst his galling chains.
>
> May people all enjoy the boon
>   Of Freedoms peaceful sway;
> And Southern Slavery have its doom
>   And soon be swept away.[284]

While the economic downturn pressed heavily on Blacks, most did not want to leave St. Catharines because of the economy. Instead, it was the Civil War and the desire to reunite with family members in the United States that pulled them back across the border.

* * *

In the 1860s, the Black Village in St. Catharines had truly become what Richard Pierpoint and his fellow petitioners envisioned at the beginning of the nineteenth century. It was a thriving settlement within the city where Blacks could live together, worship together in their own churches, and support each other's businesses and interests. In the borderland Village, Blacks could shut out some of the prejudice and discrimination in the world surrounding them while allowing sincere whites into their fold. Blacks found in St. Catharines the protection of law, recourse for their grievances, and opportunity in the transportation hub and economic center of the Niagara Peninsula. Clearly Blacks embraced their new freedoms and opportunities in British North America, but they understood that the belief in their innate inferiority was a transcending sentiment not restricted to the United States.

Just because St. Catharines was "an important place for the oppressed" does not mean it was part of some "Promised Land" or "Glory Land." Blacks experienced intolerance and degradation just as they did in other nineteenth-century American and Canadian locations. Still, St. Catharines served as a key locale for American Blacks who were genuinely in need of refuge and opportunity. Its location on the border, and the flow of Blacks, back and forth, over the international border made it an "important" space in the decades before the Civil War.

4

A Border That Divides but Also Unites

The paradox of how borders simultaneously separate and unite is the direct consequence of the mental mapmaking. Borders divide people living on both sides, who may have had a long history of cultural and social contact, but at the same time it unites them in the experience of closeness to the border and (partial) dependence on it. The paradoxical character of borders can be considered a metaphor of the ambiguities of nation building.

—MICHIEL BAUD AND WILLEM VAN SCHENDEL, "Toward a Comparative History of Borderlands," *Journal of World History* 8 (Fall 1997): 242

"Let my people go!" . . . Its nationality is universal; its language everywhere understood by the haters of tyranny; and those that accept its mission, everywhere understand each other. There is an unbroken chain of sentiment and purpose.

—OSBORNE ANDERSON, *A Voice from Harpers Ferry*, 65–66

Positioned near the American-Canadian border, Blacks in Rochester and St. Catharines developed transnational identities and learned to negotiate the contours of the United States and the British Empire. By doing so, they transformed borders intended to be restrictive into flexible borderlands, which allowed for greater political agency. Each city's Black pioneers—Asa Dunbar and Richard Pierpoint—crossed the international line and signaled to future generations a viable alternative to nationalism. On both sides of the national divide, Blacks faced the same social and economic problems as a result of bigotry. However, the political environment gave Blacks in St. Catharines better life opportunities than their counterparts in Rochester.[1] Herein lies the decisive difference between the two cities that made them seem a world apart, instead of a matter of miles. As scholars Michiel Baud and Willem Van Schendel explained, borders have a "paradoxical character" which "divides" and "separates," but also "connects" and "unites."[2]

At first glance, Rochester and St. Catharines had sharp differences that divided them, but these local and national distinctions led to meaningful regional connections. Each town was located within the Niagara intersection and their regional proximity yielded constant social exchange, which connected the two. The "spirit of improvement" in the region that engineer Charles B. Stuart spoke of produced the "public conveniences" of canals, railroads, and bridges that stitched its communities together.[3] The area's leading abolitionists traveled in the same circles; they supported and disagreed with each other, but visited one another, and built a network of communication, interaction, and continuous cross-fertilization of ideas.

The links were not always clearly traceable, but sketches existed. Common folks were aware of the international border and the available means of transportation to cross the border. Those like Hiram Wilson and Austin Steward who tried living in Detroit frontier Black settlements ultimately found the modern amenities of the Niagara region more transnationally efficient.[4] Black women such as Anna Murray Douglass, Caroline Loguen, and Harriet Tubman, as well as ally Mary A. H. Wilson, were vital agents of information and movement in the North American international zone. Blacks in the Niagara zone engaged in employment related to transportation and travel at hotels and as cartmen, had common experiences and obstacles that blurred the meaning of the border, created a cross-national identity, and forged "ubiquitous connections."[5] Over time these relationships strengthened and weakened but then reached a climax in the 1850s. The Niagara region acted as a hybrid-gathering place for fugitives and a negotiating chip between American and British Canadian authorities. By challenging the notions of statehood, Blacks exposed the gap between border control rhetoric of complete sovereignty and the day-to-day reality of actual movement in the borderlands.[6]

On no other day was the transnationalism and shared consciousness of Blacks in the Niagara district put on display more plainly than at the British August First celebrations. Austin Steward characterized the celebrations best when he stated that it was "indeed, a glorious day for the coloured people generally."[7] Douglass, a critic of the American Independence Day and its hypocrisy, explained that "Great Britain bowing down, confessing, and forsaking her sins against the weak and despised—is a spectacle which nations present but seldom fulfill." He, and most Blacks in the Niagara region, honored England for "contributions to the world's progress," which was borderless in its appeal.[8] On the American side of the border, thousands of people gathered at these August First commemorations in places like Rochester, Niagara Falls, Buffalo, and Canandaigua. A celebration in Buffalo was so "grand" that it was said to be an "imposing spectacle." Steward once estimated that "not less than ten thousand people" had congregated in Canandaigua to hear the messages of Frederick Douglass, Henry Highland Garnet, and Samuel Ringgold Ward.[9] The volume of Black participation spoke to the relevance of the Emancipation Day in both countries. Ward explained, "They wrought and rejoiced on one side of the line; we did the same on the other side of the line. We were yokefellows, why should we not recognize each other as such? We did; we do yet. They attend our annual anti-slavery gatherings, we attend theirs."[10]

COMMUNITIES THAT INTEGRATE AND SEPARATE

A major difference in the Black populations of Rochester and St. Catharines was their approach to community building and political activism. Blacks in Rochester looked almost strictly toward challenging all-white institutions and spaces; whereas Blacks in St. Catharines, after failed attempts to integrate, focused strategically on maintaining their own "Colored Village" and building social institutions and business establishments separate from the white mainstream. Black Rochesterians continuously fought to integrate city directories, to enroll in institutions like the public schools, and to break down discriminatory barriers that prevented them from succeeding economically. In contrast, St. Catharines' Blacks largely avoided complaining about limited access to exclusive arenas of whiteness and set out to build a comparable school, commercial enterprises, and equivalent circumstances for themselves. There, Blacks employed racial self-reliance in a practical fashion that left them far less dependent than their Western New York counterparts.[11] "The 'Negro Village' of which so much has been said," Samuel R. Ward declared, "the site is good, the property valuable, the part of the town respectable, and whites live in the most immediate vicinity of it."[12]

For Blacks in St. Catharines, it was critically important to maintain their own institutions and section of town. The school system reflected their disposition of self-determination. In the mid-1850s, the Black community elected to have a separate school instead of integrating with whites. Unfortunately, the Council for Common Schools did not finance the endeavor with "a fair proportion of the taxes and monies" as it had promised, leaving the St. Paul Colored School deficient for years to come.[13] This form of separatism created a Black-run learning environment for children, and it instilled racial pride, but it also caused a backlash from those who did not quite understand this marron disposition to craft Black spaces.[14]

Outsiders like Mary Ann Shadd believed that "negrohaters" had manipulated an ignorant population in St. Catharines, and Samuel R. Ward called St. Catharines "the most Yankee town in Canada" for its exclusion of Blacks from common schools.[15] The *Douglass' Monthly* asked, "Why not let the negro children of Canada go into the same schools, the same institutions of learning, with the children of other people? They do so in this city [Rochester], and do so in the most enlightened and refined parts of this country." The article concluded, "No one here or elsewhere has been or can be injured by this association in schools."[16] The Blacks in St. Catharines disagreed, and despite the commentary swirling around the community's bold decision, they refused to send their children to integrated schools where they could be miseducated, mistreated, or even abused. Many Blacks were content with separate institutions of learning as long as they were funded equally by the government.

St. Catharines demonstrated that Blacks could develop significantly through their own efforts instead of by receiving overt philanthropic aid and institutional handouts. Rochester struggled to keep pace with the "Garden City." Rev. Jermain W. Loguen and Samuel R. Ward expressed this sentiment clearly. Loguen noted that while fugitives "may suffer some in Canada for the first year . . . after the first year they will take care of themselves."[17] The *Douglass' Monthly* legitimized the initial needs of Black newcomers in Canada. It explained that "the newly arrived fugitive, fresh from slavery, a perfect stranger, without money or friends, should upon his first entrance upon a life of freedom, need assistance." Yet it "must be obvious to all," the paper emphasized, that this, "implies no necessary incapacity on the part of the race to take care of themselves, and is therefore no discredit to any body."[18] After Loguen attended an abolitionist assembly in 1856, he remarked that "Not like the Anti-Slavery meetings of Syracuse and Rochester was this meeting at St. Catharines." He found the Blacks to be "noble exiles" capable of "detailing their wrongs, and commemorating their escape." Loguen expounded, "I never saw a stronger, braver, or more intelligent looking mass of men and women than that."[19] And Ward declared "Our people . . . have done all they ought to do, in St. Catharines towards their own elevation."[20]

Throughout the early 1800s, Blacks in Rochester and St. Catharines unques-tionably had the same aptitude to succeed. However, the difference was in their political environment and the tactics they used to facilitate social change that helped determine the level of achievement each town reached. Blacks concen-trated on "themselves" and "their own" in St. Catharines, and they were proud of the Black marron-like spaces they built.[21] At a Masonic Festival and Ball, which Blacks from Rochester attended, Black leaders of St. Catharines celebrated that "this affair was in every respect superior to many gathering[s] among 'white folks.'"[22] This gives validity to Samuel G. Howe's conclusion in his *Freedmen's Inquiry Commission* report that "the negro does best when let alone." He ex-pounded: "The white man has tried taking care of the negro, by slavery, by ap-prenticeship, by colonization, and has failed disastrously in all; now let the ne-gro try to take care of himself."[23] The stance that Blacks took in St. Catharines to care for themselves differentiated them from Blacks in Rochester; however, their common cause and borderless social connections gave both communities greater strength. Certainly, when Rochester is compared with national counter-parts such as Buffalo or Syracuse, it stands out as a dynamic space for Blacks, but when it is placed in a transnational context with St. Catharines, its glaring limitations are illuminated.

SETTLING IN CANADA

In Canada, some Blacks felt genuine patriotism toward the British Crown and planned to stay there the rest of their lives. Others did not think much of life on Canadian soil. Rev. Alexander Hemsley, who utilized Rochester on his way to British Canada and settled quite comfortably in St. Catharines explained, "I am a regular Britisher. My American blood has been scourged out of me. I have lost my American tastes."[24] He praised the country and never planned to depart. His "Garden City" counterpart Christopher Nichols agreed and stated, "I feel no inclination to go back—I don't want to cross the line."[25] But everyone did not share this sentiment. "I do not like Canada, or the Provinces," Thomas F. Page explained. "I have been to St. John, N.B., Lower Province, or Lower Canada, also St. Catharines, C.W., and all around the Canada side, and I do not like it at all. The people seem to be so queer."[26] Maryland-born George Williams, who spent a brief stint in Rochester, lamented his move north: "I dread the day that ever I left the States to come here [to Canada]." Parker Theophilus Smith said that after just a few months in Canada he was "home sick" and wished to reenter the United States at once, declaring *"in Canada I will not stay."*[27]

Still, other individuals like John William Dungy, who ventured through Rochester, had a favorable view of Canada. When asked, "How have you been getting along in Canada"? "Do you like the country"? Dungy replied it was "First-rate." "Have you had plenty of work," he was questioned, "made some money, and taken care of yourself?" Dungy responded simply, "Yes." However, he eventually recrossed the border.[28] Joseph Taper explained in St. Catharines that "Since I have been in the Queens dominions I have been . . . well contented for Sure, man is as God intended he should be. That is, all are born free & equal."[29]

Blacks who came to Canada in the pre–Civil War period were exiles seeking asylum from the enslavement and bigotry in America. If they had been given the same freedoms in the United States, Canada would never have seen an influx of fugitives. As Thomas L. Wood Knox explained, "I would rather have remained in my native country, among my friends, could I have had such treatment as I felt that I deserved. But that was not to be."[30] Isaac Williams of St. Catharines put it simply, "If slavery were abolished, I would rather live in a southern State."[31] Moreover, Blacks, as the Freedmen's Bureau reported, had never "taken firm root in Canada" because of their "love of home" and their desire for the "Old place."[32]

It is important to view Black fugitives through the lens of being exiles; returning to the United States was not necessarily evidence of Canadian mistreatment. Those who flee their home country usually still favor it to their host nation, and Blacks were no different. The lack of legal freedoms and political rights drove Blacks to Canada, but political change, opportunity, and family pulled them back to the United States, creating the flow and counterflow at the border. Borderland Blacks hoped that the long-awaited Civil War, which Jermain W. Loguen deemed "God's war with this guilty nation," could decrease the outright necessity of the border.[33] John W. Lindsay of St. Catharines stated: "I think that perhaps God means to bring good out of this great war," and Douglass was profoundly encouraged that the outcome of the Civil War could "determine the destiny not only of the American Republic, but that of the American Continent."[34]

CIVIL WAR IN THE NIAGARA BORDERLANDS

By 1861, Hiram Wilson was unsure of what the future of Blacks in Canada held, but he remained hopeful that his missionary work had prepared fugitives for the next steps in their lives.[35] Wilson envisioned decades earlier that "The majority would soon speed their way back to the embrace of their brethren and kindred at the south."[36] Writing from Rochester to the *Montreal Witness,* he said, "I believe the days of oppression and slavery are numbered, and that the time is not distant when the present Slave States of America will be open, as one of the most interesting and inviting Missionary fields on earth."[37] Wilson, a genuine transnational, did not argue against Blacks returning to the United States. In fact, he was confident that Blacks could return to America to become good soldiers "in a warfare for the cause of freedom, should an emergency arise."[38] Jermain Loguen agreed: "Should pro-slavery folly and persistence raise the spirit of the North . . . to the point that admits the African element in a war for freedom, the blacks of Canada will be found overleaping national boundaries; and . . . will imprint upon the soil of slavery as bloody a lesson as was ever written."[39] The words of Wilson and Loguen were prophetic.

Throughout the Civil War era, Blacks from Rochester and St. Catharines headed southward, demonstrating the kinship between people and place. At the beginning of the decade, the population of Monroe County was over 100,000, with Rochester hosting nearly half of those people. In the entire county, the Black population was officially listed as 567, of whom 410 dwelled in the urban center.[40] A similar decline occurred in the greater St. Catharines area. The Black population dwindled to some 574; the American-born remained high among them, with some 300 hailing from the United States.[41] The southward movement left those behind to cope with the fragmentation of their communities. Landless Blacks in each location were more likely to leave than landholders or business owners. Why did others join this reverse migration?[42] Several explanations have been offered, including the northern weather, the longing for relatives and friends, the dissatisfaction with their economic status, a determination to join the Union Army, and a desire to assist the newly emancipated.[43]

From the start of the Civil War, abolitionists in Rochester wanted Blacks to be able to join the fight. Yet many people in the city questioned whether Blacks were capable of becoming quality soldiers. Their apprehension and the federal ban on Black troops did not stop Douglass from trying to turn a war for the preservation of the Union into a struggle for emancipation. He urged Blacks to form militia companies, arguing they could "wield a sword, fire a gun, march and countermarch."[44] In July 1861, three Black regiments were offered to Governor Edwin D. Morgan of New York; however, he was unable to accept their services.[45] Disheartened, Douglass lamented that the "Government has resolved that no good shall come to the Negro from this war." He was convinced that only extreme pressure and dire necessity would give Blacks the opportunity to fight.[46] A local newspaper countered, "Whatever Fred. Douglass may say about this matter . . . we do not believe a regiment of negroes can be raised in New York State to go to the field."[47] Meanwhile, many Blacks were unsure of the hardships wartime would bring; therefore they continued to flee to Canada. Fearful that the war could pull England into the battlefield in support of the South and "King Cotton," Julia Griffiths Crofts, Douglass's former assistant, wrote to Douglass urging him, if trouble came, to "cross the frontier with all your household & edit your paper at Toronto."[48] The conflict left Borderlanders, as Douglass explained, "continually oscillated between the dim light of hope and the gloomy shadow of despair."[49]

When Blacks finally were authorized to fight after the Emancipation Proclamation on January 1, 1863, those in Canada saw it as a fundamental change in United States public policy. Borderland traffic started to move southward. In Rochester, Blacks sprung into action. Frederick Douglass urged local Blacks to join the Union forces: "Action! Action! . . . is the plain duty of this hour." He believed it was important for Blacks to play a role in the emancipation of Southern slaves. "Liberty won by white men," Douglass asserted, "would lack half its luster."[50] Eager to wage war, New York Blacks joined the 54th Massachusetts Regiment and other divisions in states that formed "Colored" units more rapidly. Douglass alone recruited some 100 soldiers from Upstate New York for the 54th Massachusetts Regiment. The first men he enlisted were his sons, Lewis and Charles, and Douglass traveled tirelessly to enlist more Black soldiers. "The iron gate of our prison stands half open," he told Blacks, and the time has come to "fling it wide open."[51]

After a nonstop sixteen-year publishing career, Douglass discontinued his *Monthly* in 1863 in order to recruit Black troops. As the *Union and Advertiser* explained, "It is not for any lack of patronage that he abandons the field of the journalist, but because duty calls him."[52] In the early newspaper career of Douglass, it was predicted that he "will probably swallow up several others," and he most certainly did.[53] Douglass published newspapers that outlasted and outsold his Canadian counterparts—the *Voice of the Fugitive* and the *Provincial Freeman*.[54] Moreover, after 1859, when both Black periodicals in Canada had shut down, the newspapers that Douglass published helped to fill the void for the cause of

Blacks on the other side of the border. As Charles Douglass explained, the sub-scribers "of our own race . . . they of course were scattered throughout the North, and Canada."[55] The St. Catharines *Evening Journal* reported, "Douglass retires from control of his journal which he had published for so many years," adding, "He is for the Abolitionist side of the war" and "is heading south where he can do more good."[56] Douglass felt that nothing was more essential than to dispatch Black troops to the South. "Words," he emphasized, "are now useful only as they stimulate to blows."[57]

Harriet Tubman helped the Union Army interchangeably as a nurse, spy, cook, and laundress, and she fought the ever-present outbreaks of disease in en-campments. She also helped to house and gather intelligence from "contraband" at Beaufort and Port Royal, South Carolina. Throughout the war, she passed along valuable information to Generals David Hunter, William T. Sherman, and Isaac Stevens. In June 1863, she scouted in Confederate territory and led an armed assault on plantations, alongside Colonel James Montgomery, to liber-ate some 700 slaves in the Combahee River Raid. Biographer Larson explained that "Tubman became the first woman to plan and execute an armed expedi-tion during the Civil War."[58] The raid in South Carolina added Black troops to the Union Army and signaled to other enslaved people to flee to Union lines.[59] In July 1863, Tubman was active with Colonel Robert Gould Shaw and the 54th Massachusetts at the Second Battle of Fort Wagner. She knew a number of the members of the 54th, like the two sons of Douglass, from her time in New En-gland and Western New York, and she got acquainted with other soldiers and with Colonel Shaw. In Fort Wagner's wake, she cared for the wounded and com-forted the dying.[60]

In the fall of 1863, Tubman took a much-needed leave from her military du-ties and made her way back home to family in Auburn. In November 1863, she traveled via Rochester to visit friends in St. Catharines and relatives in nearby Grantham, where her brother William Henry and his family resided. Tubman may have accompanied Samuel Gridley Howe on his trip to St. Catharines to conduct interviews with Black escapees of the United States for the American Freedmen's Inquiry Commission. Howe was interested in seeing how Blacks in Canada were living, understanding that their counterparts in the American South would soon be emancipated. Tubman could have introduced a score of fugitives to Howe. Nonetheless, she soon recrossed the border for Auburn, then went back to the South to help finish the Union cause, particularly at Fort Mon-roe in Hampton, Virginia, where her service was most desired.[61] Tubman was no stranger to hard-fought battles or crossing borders—South-North, American-Canadian, or Union-Confederate; she excelled in these realms. Like her fellow Black Borderlanders, Tubman hoped the Civil War, as the *Douglass' Monthly* explained, would result in "breaking the chains of every American slave, and placing America side by side with noble old England."[62]

Just the anticipation of the Civil War placed Canadians, and particularly Blacks, on guard. Canada was still part of the British Empire, and a large purchaser of the cotton coming from the American South, and there was concern that its connection to England and its wartime diplomatic stance might yield an attack and reenslave Blacks. Throughout the developing nation, cricket associations and curling clubs were transformed into rifle companies.[63] Blacks in St. Catharines organized themselves into a Colored Company of some eighty men strong and met twice a week to drill and prepare for potential conflict.[64] They were simply unwilling to surrender all they had gained in British Canada without a fight.

The troops shared the sentiment of the *Provincial Freeman* that "if the time should ever come when your Majesty might need our aid, our lives would be as they *are, at your service.*"[65] "In case of a rupture," Austin Steward once explained, Blacks would, "take up arms in defense of the government which has protected them and the country of their adoption. England could . . . very readily collect a regiment."[66] Although their services were never required, Blacks demonstrated "loyalty" to Canada and to the profound value they placed on their freedom. Blacks who remained in Canada throughout this period worked to protect the colony from possible outside forces and continued to help Black American fugitives. As one Black woman in St. Catharines explained, "De war makes good times now for our people, while de white folks is fightin', de colored people can run away. Heaps of 'em comes along now."[67]

As more Blacks settled in the "Colored Village" and the surrounding areas of St. Catharines, however, white anxiety steadily heightened regarding their presence. The concerns of St. Catharines residents about the "astonishing" numbers of Blacks "skedaddling" in "from the parental government of Uncle Samuel" alarmed them.[68] Fear rose that another race riot could transpire in town, as it did in 1852. People were distressed by the "deep-seated prejudice" "overheard on the streets daily" displayed by "certain portions" of the whites who "brought it [bigotry] out more prominently than it has been developed for the past ten years, the threats of violence being as frequent and as fervent as at that time." The *Evening Journal* explained that "those of us who were here then have no desire to see a repetition. One such disgraceful riot is enough in a century."[69] Reports of possible unrest came regularly. An article asserted: "The prejudice against the colored man always exists in the breast of the white, and he who says he entertains no prejudice on account of color is either a liar and a hypocrite or an anomaly, an exception to the rule."[70] A later *Evening Journal* piece proclaimed, "The two races have never lived together amicably in this town, and the feeling of antipathy has been increasing instead of the opposite . . . there is danger, great danger, of another riot."[71] St. Catharines was an "important place" for fleeing fugitives, but Canada was clearly no "promised land."

A number of Blacks opted to leave the "safety" of St. Catharines to fight in the American Civil War.[72] At the age of twenty-five, John Goosberry enlisted in America as a private for three years in the soon-to-be-famous 54th Massachusetts Infantry. He kept up morale by playing the fife in the regimental band and battled alongside Black Rochesterians.[73] Seaman C. W. Haxie served aboard the US Navy's *USS Midnight,* as Corporal Samuel Green signed on with the 45th US Colored Troops. In 1864, Private Hinton Griffin, twenty-seven, and Private Alfred Harris, nineteen, both from St. Catharines, joined the fight. Griffin served three years in the 6th US Colored Troops, while after twelve months of service, Harris was honorably discharged from the 23rd US Colored Troops. Private James Peak, born in St. Catharines, worked as a cook before enlisting at Mason's Island, Virginia, the island located on the Potomac River between Rosslyn, Virginia, and the Georgetown waterfront, which served as a training camp for the 1st United States Colored Troops. Peak joined the troops on June 17, 1863, for a three-year term, but he ran into problems during his service. On November 21, 1863, he was court-martialed for "riotous conduct," and sentenced to hard labor.[74] Private Joseph Thomson of St. Catharines, who enlisted in Syracuse, was more of a standard bearer; he served three years alongside his fellow soldiers in the 26th US Colored Troops.[75] Some locals suspected that Blacks were being recruited to fight for the Union directly within St. Catharines. The *Evening Journal* reported, "Quite a number of gentlemen of the African persuasion may be seen perambulating our streets almost daily dressed in Uncle Sam's uniform. What are they doing here? They may not be seeking recruits, but it looks very suspicious, and it is certainly in very bad taste."[76] People believed that St. Catharines had become "a centre of Civil War espionage." This was more a manifestation of greater vigilance over transnational travelers in the Niagara region because of the American North-South conflict than any real "espionage."[77]

In July 1863, racial tensions in St. Catharines made residents fearful that an outbreak like the New York City Draft Riots could occur in their town. The Draft Riots were fueled by inequities in conscription, and it resulted in the racially charged killing of over 100 Blacks, more than 2,000 injuries, and thousands in property damage.[78] The event sent shockwaves across the border and forced those in British Canada to examine their own race relations. When the Circus Royal came to St. Catharines to perform in July 1863, rumors of a riot spread. The *Evening Journal* reacted by stating, "Such conduct will not do. Order must be preserved, and we trust that any one who attempts unjustifiably to assault a colored man will be arrested and confined at once. We cannot afford to have the robberies and murders of New York repeated in this christianized land." It continued, "Those who would by force of numbers overpower and injure the colored man are scarcely fit men to call British subjects."[79] Despite "the rowdy element of the town" being "fully represented," at the circus, "the colored people very sensibly remained away, to which circumstance may in part be attributed the comparative peace maintained." However, when "a couple [of Blacks] did show themselves just before the performance commenced, and were met by all kinds of foul and opprobrious calls . . . no attention was paid."[80]

Scores of wealthy men in the Rochester area used immigrants and Blacks as substitutes to avoid fighting in the Civil War themselves. Reluctant to fight, Ayres' Hotel barkeeper and Seventh Ward resident Charles S. Skinner paid $300 to nineteen-year-old William H. Johnson to replace him.[81] On September 5, 1864, Johnson joined the Union Army for a period of three years and was assigned to the 8th US Colored Volunteer Infantry. Lawyer Francis J. Mather of the luxurious Third Ward sidestepped the battlefield by recruiting the underprivileged laborer James Wilson.[82] A Bermuda native, Wilson signed with a mark to enroll because he could not read or write. William W. Marsh of Pittsford paid barber William H. Brown $1,200 to take his place. When it was discovered that Brown was underage, his father gave consent for the enrollment of the young lad.[83]

Eager to find ways to help in the Civil War effort, the Rochester Ladies Anti-Slavery Society (RLASS) sent Julia Wilbur to the American South. Early on Wilbur explained that the "Disunion troubles do not disturb me," and as the North-South conflict got underway, she was on a family trip to Canada.[84] But duty and the RLASS called, and she spent several years in Union-military-occupied Alexandria, Virginia, aiding Blacks who escaped enslavement and hospitalized Union soldiers. After Douglass stopped publishing his newspapers, which consumed the majority of the society's funds, the RLASS looked at the war as "a new field of labor."[85] They paid Wilbur for her toil during the war, and sent clothing and other items for the newly freed Blacks.[86] Wilbur grew homesick and frustrated with teaching the "A.B.C. of Abolition" to young Northern white women who arrived in Alexandria to educate Blacks in "contraband" camps, but she found camaraderie with Harriet Jacobs. The two had met in Rochester's Anti-Slavery Reading Room, and Wilbur noted that Jacobs was "quite an interesting person."[87] In mid-December 1863, Amy Post of Rochester traveled to the war-torn Alexandria to see her friends and explained "I don't know how Julia & Harriet can stay their."[88] Nonetheless, they desired to improve conditions for freed Blacks, as emancipation was manifesting right before their eyes.

As the battle raged on in the American South, on April 16, 1864, Hiram Wilson, longtime friend of Frederick Douglass, was reported to be "very ill" and only "slight hopes are entertained of his recovery." He died later that day of inflammation of the lungs.[89] A casket and hearse were sent for the "Clerical Do-Gooder" Wilson, and his funeral took place at the American Presbyterian Church in St. Catharines on April 24, 1864.[90] Wilson's "cottage," which Mary Ann Shadd had highlighted was costly to construct, was put on sale in short order for "very reasonable terms."[91] Three of Hiram's children—Lydia Maria, Mary Ellen, and George Sturges—died shortly after he did.[92] His adopted Black daughter, Alavana Dicken, who joined the family in 1852, had returned to North Carolina. That left only John Joel Wilson to recall the times when American fugitives showed up to his father's home seeking assistance.[93]

Other progressives in St. Catharines got involved in the fight for Black freedom and rights. Irish immigrant Harper Wilson, who settled in St. Catharines as a young boy, served as a captain of the 23rd US Colored Troops in the Civil War. He came to the "Garden City" in 1852 at the height of Black movement in the borderlands and enlisted in New York as a private in May 1861. Eventually, he was promoted to captain and fought with the Army of the Potomac.[94] The 23rd recruited in Washington, DC, and in Baltimore, and they organized for combat at Camp Casey, Virginia. Wilson described the Black unit as "being quiet and orderly, and [they] never failed to gain the confidence of its various commanding Generals."[95] After the war, Wilson returned to St. Catharines and went into business as a grocer on St. Paul Street.[96] He, like Blacks, could have stayed comfortably in St. Catharines, but they made sacrifices to give others the freedoms they enjoyed in Canada.

Blacks in St. Catharines unquestionably supported Union troops in their efforts to put down the Southern rebellion. They closely followed the war and political developments. When President Abraham Lincoln announced his Emancipation Proclamation, the Black community celebrated at the BME Church as if the document held power on Canadian soil.[97] Local Blacks knew that their fate was in many ways linked with the fate of their brothers and sisters in American bondage. John W. Lindsay emphasized, "We feel the effects of slavery desperately in this country [Canada], slavery curses every man on the continent of America."[98] When President Lincoln was assassinated in 1865, Blacks gathered at their churches on both sides of the border to mourn. Days after his death, the BME Church in St. Catharines, reported the *Evening Journal,* was "appropriately draped in mourning . . . on account of the sad death of President Lincoln," and the Union Jack was displayed at half-mast over the house of worship.[99] Frederick Douglass came to the town hall of St. Catharines on August 23, 1865, to give an address on Lincoln's death and the recently emancipated Black population. Attendance was low, largely because Douglass had been expected to speak a week earlier. Nonetheless, his lecture was polished and he concentrated on critical issues.[100] He spoke on political injustices, on the immediate need for Blacks to be guaranteed citizenship and suffrage, and on his concerns with President Andrew Johnson's ability to oversee the new era of Reconstruction.[101]

In the wake of the Civil War, scores of Blacks and Southern Confederates chose to use the Canadian-American border for different reasons. Over half of Blacks in Canada elected to return "home," while Confederates and Southern sympathizers entered Canada to escape political prosecution. These people of opposing interests were passing each other as each sought the neighboring nation. As the number of Blacks decreased in Canada, the volume of Southern sympathizers increased, thereby making the environment less hospitable for Blacks who remained. The St. Catharines *Evening Journal* explained, "The result of the policy of the American Government in reference to the slaves of the South is proving highly beneficial to Canada." It expounded, "we feel pleased to note the fact that the negro population of Canada since the American rebellion is gradually lessening."[102] A large portion of the public in British Canada reacted happily to the exodus of Blacks and was frankly not too concerned about the types of American whites it received—they could be Confederates, former slaveholders, bigots, or criminals; the most important thing was their skin color.

*　*　*

REMEMBERING THE BONDS OF ROCHESTER AND ST. CATHARINES

It is impossible to tell a strictly "national" story of Blacks in Rochester and St. Catharines when their disposition and affairs were driven largely by proximity to each other and their understanding of the wider Atlantic world. Blacks knew that their lives were affected by the overlapping dynamics of the United States, Canada, Great Britain, and the African Diaspora, all of which collided in the Niagara region. Moreover, viewing these two cities through the lens of trans-nationalism better fits their histories and better reflects the experience of Borderland Blacks who lived there or simply chose to employ them as doorways. By underscoring the awareness and alliances across national margins, Blacks demonstrated how these borderland communities shared mutual interests that transcended the border itself. Blacks in Rochester and St. Catharines struggled in distinct ways to petition, organize, and agitate to create enduring political and social change. However, what united them was their overarching objective to end slavery in North America.

Overall, the connections between Rochester and St. Catharines were not fleeting; they lasted for decades, before the Civil War and after. Confirming the connection between these Niagara towns in the 1850s, John J. Wilson, the old-est son of missionary Hiram Wilson, wrote to Frederick Douglass years later in 1888 at his Cedar Hill home in Washington, DC, praising his courageous work in Western New York.[103] "My Dear Sir," he wrote "No doubt you remember well the Rev. Hiram Wilson, who before the war was at the Canada end of the under-ground railroad. I well remember the large number of fugitive slaves who having escaped from the south, making their way to Canada, came to my father's house with a letter from you or your son."[104] These transnational experiences were em-bedded into his mind, and time could not erase what the borderlands had so deeply engrained. As Frederick Douglass once said, "it is not well to forget the past. Memory was given to man for some wise purpose."[105]

* * *

Charles Remond Douglass, the youngest son of Douglass, explained that Roch-ester and the "old homestead" on South Avenue left a lasting impression on him. He highlighted that when fugitives arrived at the door in Rochester on their way to Canada, "Every member of the family had to lend a hand to this work and it was always cheerfully performed. We felt that we were doing a Christian and humane duty."[106] Rosetta Douglass Sprague, the older sibling of Charles, explained that "the dear old home of hallowed memories" was where "the panting fugitive, the weary traveler, the lonely emigrant of every clime, received food and shelter."[107] The relationship between the two Niagara frontier towns is indisputable, and it was people like Douglass and Wilson who helped to cement the bond across the American-Canadian border in the final decades of slavery.

Epilogue

Where the timeline of *Borderland Blacks* ends, Reconstruction in America and Confederation in Canada begins. Each nation sought to rebuild and define itself, as Blacks regardless of the border suffered in the "Nadir Era," meaning the "lowest point," of race relations in North America. The "Nadir Era" is a term coined by historian Rayford Logan and later applied to Canada by historian Robin W. Winks.[1] Throughout the nadir, Blacks in each nation lost many of the civil rights gains achieved. Anti-Black violence, lynching, segregation, racial discrimination, and expressions of white supremacy increased. Logan aggressively asserted that Blacks were oppressed worse than in any period before or since. The broken promises of America and Canada left Blacks vulnerable to the Ku Klux Klan, Black Codes, de jure and de facto Jim Crow laws, and debt peonage until 1930.[2]

Frederick Douglass was disappointed that the nadir dimmed the hopes of Blacks, but he still manifested his transnational mindset well after he moved from Rochester to Washington, DC, in 1872.[3] He kept in contact with friends in the Niagara region and Canadian associates in the American South. During a honeymoon with his second white wife, Helen Pitts, in late 1884, they ventured to Niagara Falls and the Thousand Islands to relax in the American-Canadian international zone Douglass had once manipulated to aid freedom seekers. Throughout his life, Douglass navigated the power and politics of proximity, whether in the "border state" of Maryland, in the borderlands of Canada, or in the Capital City, a junction of North-South interface.[4] He also challenged racial lines by marrying Helen Pitts at the height of the nadir when Black men were lynched for mere suspicion of interacting with white women. The *Washington Grit* declared the marriage "a national calamity," but Douglass asserted biblically that God "made of one blood all nations of men."[5] His personal life and disposition were driven by the crossing of societal borders and insisting on outright freedom.

Toward the end of Douglass's life, a new generation of Black leaders emerged, including Booker T. Washington, Ida B. Wells, W. E. B. Du Bois, and Marcus Garvey. They struggled for racial uplift and to obtain "equal protection under the law." A new genre of music—the Blues—expressed the woes of the nadir. In 1892, when Wells and Washington met Douglass, they each shared a passion for the Blues, and sought his advice on how to proceed. Douglass built a strong friendship with the antilynching crusader Wells; he thought she was ideal to guide Blacks into a new era of freedom.[6] However, Washington, the president of Tuskegee Institute, was the most popular of his contemporaries, and Douglass spoke at the Institute's 1892 commencement ceremony. On February 20, 1895, Douglass died, and was buried at Rochester's Mount Hope Cemetery not far from his old South Avenue homestead that Blacks employed to enter and exit Canada.[7] In September of 1895, Booker T. Washington delivered his "Atlanta Compromise" speech, which told Blacks to forgo enfranchisement, legal equality, and higher education for vocational and economic pursuits.[8] Douglass would have strongly disagreed with these concessions. Radical Blacks criticized Washington's "cast down your bucket where you are" approach, and change was brewing in the Niagara region—the same place Douglass employed to distance himself from the Garrisonians of New England.[9]

Historian Jacqueline M. Moore noted Rayford Logan's concept of the nadir was "certainly right," but she asserted that his analysis overlooked the "creative efforts" of Blacks during the period.[10] One of those "efforts" to address Black uplift was the Niagara Movement, a strategic board of Blacks designed to counter the Washingtonians and to break America's "Colored Line."[11] Its twenty-nine delegates met in Fort Erie, Ontario, at the Erie Beach Hotel in 1905, due to discriminatory and unfavorable accommodations in Buffalo that they refused to accept. The group, led by Du Bois and William Monroe Trotter, drew inspiration for its name from the nearby Niagara Falls, and the "mighty current" of the Niagara River that motivated them to mirror its action until racial injustice fell.[12]

The Niagara Movement continued in the tradition of borderland Blacks who assembled to discuss issues critical to their communities and worked across the American-Canadian border. Those in the new movement acknowledged the past Underground Railroad activity that occurred in the area, and they mirrored the Black conventions/conferences held in Buffalo, Rochester, and St. Catharines in 1843, 1853, and 1854.[13] The Niagara Movement opposed the moderate accommodationism approach of Booker T. Washington and sought to construct a radical alternative. At the Fort Erie meeting, the all-Black male delegates crafted a constitution, elected an executive board, established subcommittees, and wrote the "Declaration of Principles," also called the "Niagara Manifesto." It outlined their overarching demands for economic justice, educational equality, full suffrage, and the eradication of racial segregation.[14]

In the following years, the Niagara Movement held annual meetings, allowed women to join, and continued to attack the Tuskegee philosophy of Black political exclusion.[15] Its 1906 gathering, the first major meeting on American soil, was held at Storer College in Harpers Ferry, West Virginia, to honor John Brown. Of course, Brown knew the Niagara region well; he planned his attack on Virginia in Rochester and printed his Provisional Constitution in St. Catharines. Attendees to the 1906 Niagara Movement meeting visited John Brown's Fort. There, they chose to enter the Fort in silence and barefoot to show respect for this Holy Ground. "Niagarians" created a host of committees, including the Departments of Education, Economics, Health, Suffrage, and Suppression of Crime, as well as a Legal, Civil Rights, Junior, Student, Women's, Arts, and Pan-African Departments.[16] The Health and Junior committees, for instance, led campaigns to fight tuberculosis and targeted college students to join the group.[17] This inclusive political and cultural Niagara Movement countered the "bought" "Washingtonians" backed by Carnegie, Rockefeller, and George Eastman of Rochester, and it was better suited to address the "Negro Problem."[18]

Subsequent Niagara Movement meetings were held in Boston (1907), Oberlin, Ohio (1908), and Sea Isle City, New Jersey (1909).[19] Between 1905 and 1908, the Niagara Movement membership climbed from 29 to 450, and for several years the Niagarians ran their own monthly magazine the *Horizon*.[20] After a violent race riot in Springfield, Illinois, in 1908, Du Bois and a like-minded biracial group formed the National Association for the Advancement of Colored People (NAACP). In 1910, Du Bois convinced the remaining Niagara Movement members to join and fund the NAACP, thus disbanding the all-Black organization forged in the borderlands. The Niagara Movement–NAACP merger brought together the worlds of separatism, integration, and assimilation, which had been debated and lived out in Rochester and St. Catharines. Du Bois traded his post as editor-in-chief of the *Horizon* for the same position with the NAACP's *The Crisis*.[21] The key problems with the Niagara Movement were financial and philosophical. It did not keep pace with Booker T. Washington's high-powered Tuskegee Machine and the National Negro Business League (NNBL), which had over 550 chapters in more than thirty states.[22] Also, Trotter and Du Bois each struggled with the constraints of being "organizational men"; they conflicted over issues of policy, personnel, and tactics.[23]

Nonetheless, the Niagara Movement is deemed a "success" by many scholars because its legacy is the NAACP.[24] Unquestionably, it was a bridge from the so-called Negro Problem to the New Negro wave, and fed into the watershed Civil Rights Movement, which washed through North America and brought about legislation in America and Canada that led to greater rights. Like the Niagara Movement's Junior Department, the "Second Reconstruction" NAACP activists employed the youthful energy of the Congress of Racial Equality (CORE) and the Student Nonviolent Coordinating Committee (SNCC) to strengthen the call for change.[25] And the Niagara Legal Department gave way to a better coordinated NAACP effort to push "test cases," like *Brown v. Board of Education*, to kill Jim Crow.[26] The long fight against racial segregation in North America was advanced by women like Viola Desmond in Canada and Rosa Parks in the United States. In solidarity with Americans, Canadians produced groups such as the Friends of SNCC and the Nova Scotia Association for the Advancement of Coloured People.[27] Other groups like the Universal Negro Improvement Association (UNIA) and the Brotherhood of Sleeping Car Porters organized seamlessly on both sides of the border. North American, Black Power activists and university students in the Black Panther Party and Canada's Black United Front (BUF) exchanged ideas.[28]

This wave in Canada caused a retraction of its 1960s race-based immigration policy and ushered in a significant number of Blacks from African and Caribbean nations. They came in from Egypt, Somalia, Ghana, Jamaica, Trinidad-Tobago, Haiti, and many other countries to escape political repression, civil wars, and ethnic unrest, as well as economic conditions that pushed them to flee to Canada.[29] These individuals arrived in North America with a clear understanding of fighting national, racial, and sexual borders; many of the earliest arrivals were women working in the domestic realm. They demonstrated that the border was not simply binary but involved a multiplicity of elements. During the Vietnam War, African American draft-dodgers joined them. Each group added to the diversity and complexity of the borderlands considering that some 90 percent of Canadians live within 100 miles (160 kilometers) of the American border. The modern borderland Blacks, like the old ones, grasp the power of proximity.

The border is still a regular part of life in St. Catharines today. It is just nineteen kilometers (twelve miles) away. And there are multiple entry and exit points to the United States to choose from, including the Lewiston-Queenston Bridge, the Niagara Falls International Rainbow Bridge, the Peace Bridge, and the Whirlpool Rapids Bridge. The international travelers at Niagara Falls who go to see the dynamic cascades seep over into St. Catharines. Tourists to the Falls, like Frederick Douglass, can feel "it is impossible that the eye can weary in looking upon these rapids; they possess a charm which it is difficult to break." If they analyze their position more, as Douglass did, they will find it "astonishing that people living within a stone's throw of each other, should be so opposite in their tastes, feelings, and principles."[30] Margaret H. Hall once explained "so near the [Niagara] frontier . . . the Canadians are not slow to seize all opportunities to quiz their neighbours."[31]

The Niagara region is also a commercial hub where millions of dollars of imports and exports are exchanged. In St. Catharines, the Welland Canal, which was expanded in the 1840s by Irish and other immigrants under the watchful eyes of the Colored Corps, still transports ships from Lake Erie to Lake Ontario. The "Colored Village," now part of downtown St. Catharines, and Rochester's Third Ward, now the "Corn Hill" neighborhood, have fundamentally changed and their Black populations have dispersed throughout the region due to social mobility, suburbanization, and gentrification.[32] US dollars are accepted in the Canadian borderlands of St. Catharines today and well beyond; whether at a gas station in Hamilton or in a lively eatery in Toronto, employees know the foreign exchange rate and easily render change. Credit card users are reminded of a "hard border" when they view their bank statement for the exchange rate and international fees.

In Rochester, the principal indicators of the border are the frequent sight of Ontario license plates seen throughout the city, the circulation of Canadian coinage, and the day and weekend trips to Niagara Falls that residents often take. American and Canadian coins are used interchangeably to purchase goods and services. People take trips to Niagara Falls as weekend getaways and to entertain friends and family from the American South and other parts of the country. The Black borderland interactions enjoyed in Western New York are not experienced in other parts of the country farther away from the border. These things are a regular part of Black life in Rochester; they simply go unnoticed until Border-landers travel to other American locations and then do comprehend their significance. For some, interactions with Canada happen so frequently they feel it is an adopted home away from home.

Chief summer dates on the calendar for Rochester area Blacks are Toronto's annual Caribana Festival and the Montreal International Jazz Festival. Caribana is a carryover from August First commemorations, which celebrated the British government for ending slavery throughout the Empire in 1834. Rochesterians, since inception, hosted and attended these commemorations and the legacy has continued. Caribana in Toronto, one of the largest festivals of its kind held outside the Caribbean, is a vivid emancipation celebration that features a massive street parade with bands, banners, flags and costumes as well as numerous cultural events. For decades, in the bustling downtown of Montreal, a showcase of the Blues-infused, New Orleans–born art form of jazz has taken place. The more than weeklong festival features a host of gifted artists from around the world. Among the concerts and crowds, like the Caribana, are Rochester and St. Catharines folks.[33]

In the post–September 11th world, key changes were made to the American-Canadian border. A passport was required. No longer would a valid driver's license or birth certificate allow entry into the neighboring nation. This documentation was no longer a luxury item; even though the national authorities do not generally stamp the booklet, it is mandatory. The development of Enhanced Driver's Licenses issued by states and provinces, like New York, Ontario, Michigan, and British Columbia, ease the need for a passport. The NEXUS, Global Entry, FAST (Free and Secure Trade), and other "Trusted Traveler" programs speed travelers through the border but still complicate the passage. Passports and prerequisites take time to obtain and are too costly for the underprivileged. Also, 9/11 caused the international border to become more tightly controlled. There are more surveillance cameras at terminals and border control guards ask more probing questions in an attempt to stop the smuggling of drugs, firearms, and illegal "aliens"; the so-called longest undefended border in the world feels otherwise. The new border prerequisites hamper the international travel flow in both directions and disproportionately affect Blacks.[34]

If, and when, entry is made to America and Canada, the difference between the countries is more than just measuring distance in miles or kilometers, or having a president versus a prime minister, or using American spellings of words versus British spellings of the English language. The differences are concretely noticed when you compare health care, gun control, immigration, banking prac-

tices, and education. The history of these neighboring nations has unfolded with
"*striking contrast*" as Douglass noted.[35] Many times, the way Americans and Canadians define themselves is as the opposite of the other, and the overlap and
exchange, which is a constant phenomenon, does not easily fit into the compart-
ments of nationalism.

Blacks in the past, and now, do not simply shed their national attributes
because they land on foreign soil in North America. Look, for example, at the
BME Church, still today located on Geneva Street in St. Catharines. It stands
out among the storefronts and residential homes because it strongly resembles
a Southern Baptist Church, even though it is in the midst of Canada's Niagara
Peninsula. As a historian this piqued my curiosity. The church looks totally out
of place; it looks similar to churches in Maryland and Virginia. This distinctive
American Southern-style architecture is indeed a unique edifice to the building
scenery of Ontario. It plainly reflects the Black newcomers, fugitive and free,
who toiled to erect the temple in the early 1850s. This Black British Methodist
Church is considered so architecturally significant to the city of St. Catharines
that it bears a historical designation. It demonstrates that American fugitives
retained aspects of the *old* country on Canadian soil, even when it came to concepts of construction and design. The intermingling of identities and ideas could
not be more obvious.[36]

Nonetheless, nationalistic concepts continue to be imposed on borderland
Blacks who understood the importance of working across them. For example,
US Treasury Secretary Jack Lew in 2016 announced that the image of Harriet
Tubman would be placed on the front of the US $20 bill.[37] It is an unlikely place
for Tubman, an American-Canadian transnational, militant direct-action abolitionist, who struggled with finances for the majority of her life. Deeming Tubman, as many assert, an "American Hero" is unbefitting as well, and it is outright
dismissive of British Canada. The US government wants to project a rigid na-
tionalist message that Tubman was a Union Civil War spy and nurse; not that
she was an unpaid veteran who had to petition repeatedly for her rightful compensation. In 1899, nearly eighty years old, she received $12 per month for her
service as a nurse, and $8 as a widow's pension for her deceased Union husband
Nelson Davis. Ironically, the total was $20.[38] To Tubman and other freedom
seekers, Canada provided them with a portion of the rights, liberties, and immunities they were unable to obtain in America.

When Tubman decided to return to the United States in 1859, she settled in Auburn, New York, an ideal location on the edges of the "Burnt Over District." While the American-Canadian border hardly played a critical role in Central New York, it allowed reasonably swift access to Canada, in case of an emergency. Years later, after Queen Victoria read Tubman's narrative and was "pleased with it," she mailed her a silver medal, which memorialized Victoria's Diamond Jubilee in 1897. At Harriet Tubman's 1913 funeral in Auburn, the medal from the Queen was placed in her coffin, and an American flag was draped over her casket, suggesting dual national identities and Atlantic world sensibilities.[39] In the aftermath of her death, the *Toronto Globe* highlighted that "Throughout Ontario to-day there are hundreds of colored people whose ancestors were brought out of slavery by the strong arm and keen intellect of Harriet Tubman."[40]

Yet the transnationalism of Tubman, and Black Borderlanders, is not a convenient characteristic, and usually an avoided one, when attempting to tell an American-centered story of slavery and race. A broader conversation could take flight in the region, as Monroe County lawmakers in August 2020 voted to rename the area's airport the Frederick Douglass Greater Rochester International Airport. The official name change materialized on Valentine's Day of 2021 to commemorate his self-proclaimed birthday.[41] One hopes this will help people to understand Rochester's history of Blacks and the American-Canadian borderlands much better. The Flower City's "Fast Ferry" endeavor, established in September 2001, which linked Rochester and Toronto together via Lake Ontario, set out to do the same thing, but it came to a disappointing end in January 2006.[42] My goal in this book has been to move the narrative forward to demonstrate that the allegiances of Blacks in the Niagara region have never been distinctive to one nation. Rather, the Niagara borderlands has always existed as a fluid space where the beliefs, aspirations, and history of Black people have transcended nationality.

Appendix

"FIRST OF AUGUST," BY REV. HIRAM WILSON

From *St. Catharines Journal,* August 16, 1860, p. 1:

The following lines were written by the Rev. H. Wilson, and read by him at the celebration on the 1st inst. They have been handed to us with a request that we would publish them, and we comply with the request:—

FIRST OF AUGUST

Auspicious day! We hail thy dawn!
   So welcome to the free;
We fain would all unite as one,
   To keep this jubilee.

Emancipation is our theme.
   The king of kings we praise;
All glory to the Savior's name,
   Who did the lowly raise!

The adverse powers of darkness fell,
   And despotism fled!
When He that "doeth all things well,"
   Struck British slavery dead!

The light broke forth and shone abroad
   Upon the land and sea!
A nation's born—the power of God
   Has set the captive free,

Thanks, under God, to British power,
   And pure philanthropy;
Which hastened Freedoms prayed for hour,
   And brought forth victory.

May Freedom shed her glorious light
   O'er lands where darkness reigns,
To bless the slave with visions bright,
   And burst his galling chains.

May people all enjoy the boon
   Of Freedoms peaceful sway;
And Southern Slavery have its doom,
   And soon be swept away.

Notes

INTRODUCTION

1. Britt Rusert, *Fugitive Science: Empiricism and Freedom in Early African American Culture* (New York, NY: New York University Press, 2017); Damian Alan Pargas, *Fugitive Slaves and Spaces of Freedom in North America* (Gainesville, FL: University Press of Florida, 2018); Sheldon Wolin and Nicholas Xenos, eds., *Fugitive Democracy and Other Essays* (Princeton, NJ: Princeton University Press, 2016); Bradley Miller, *Borderline Crime: Fugitive Criminals and the Challenges of the Border, 1819–1914* (Toronto, ON: University of Toronto Press, 2016); Nele Sawallisch, *Fugitive Borders: Black Canadian Cross-Border Literature at Mid-Nineteenth Century* (New York, NY: Columbia University Press, Transcript Publishing, 2019). See also Kellie Carter Jackson, *Force and Freedom: Black Abolitionists and the Politics of Violence* (Philadelphia: University of Pennsylvania Press, 2019), chap. 2: "Fight, Flight, and Fugitives: The Fugitive Slave Law & Violence."

2. See the use of "borderlander" in Hastings Donnan and Thomas M. Wilson, eds., *Borderlands: Ethnographic Approaches to Security, Power, and Identity* (Lanham, MD: University Press of America, 2010).

3. Erie County is home to Buffalo, while Niagara County plays host to Niagara Falls, and Batavia is in Genesee County. Rochester is in Monroe County, and Orleans County helps to link all of them together. These counties directly or indirectly connect to the Niagara River and Lake Ontario. In the past, Rochester has not been considered part of the Niagara region, but this study plainly situates it in this international zone. See Janet Dorothy Larkin, *Overcoming Niagara: Canals, Commerce, and Tourism in the Niagara-Great Lakes Borderland Region, 1792–1837* (Albany: SUNY Press, 2018); Neil O'Donnell, *The Niagara Frontier's Unwritten History* (Kernersville, NC: Argus Enterprises International, 2012); William Wyckoff, *The Developer's Frontier: The Making of the Western New York Landscape* (New Haven, CT: Yale University Press, 1988); Kevin H. Siepel, *Joseph Bennett of Evans and the Growing of New York's Niagara Frontier* (Angola, NY: Spruce Tree Press, 2011); Janet Dorothy Baglier, "The Niagara Frontier: Society and Economy in Western New York and Upper Canada" (PhD diss., State University of Buffalo, 1993); and Max J. Andrucki and Jen Dickinson, "Reinking Centers and Margins in Geography: Bodies, Life Course, and the Performance of Transnational Space," *Annals of the Association of American Geographers* 105, no. 1 (Jan. 2015): 203–18.

4. Blake McKelvey, *Rochester*, 4 vols. (Cambridge, MA: Harvard University Press, 1945–61), vol. 4. See the following national histories: Blake McKelvey, *Rochester on the Genesee: The Growth of a City* (Syracuse, NY: Syracuse University Press, 1993); Paul E. Johnson, *A Shopkeeper's Millennium:*

Society and Revivals in Rochester, New York, 1815–1837 (New York, NY: Hill & Wang, 2004); Eugene E. Du Bois, *The City of Frederick Douglass: Rochester's African-American People and Places* (Rochester, NY: The Landmark Society of Western New York, 1994); Adelaide Elizabeth Dorn, "A History of the Antislavery Movement in Rochester and Vicinity" (MA thesis, University of Buffalo, 1932); John N. Jackson, *St. Catharines Ontario: Its Early Years* (Belleville, ON: Mika Publishing Company, 1976); John N. Jackson and Sheila M. Wilson, *St. Catharines: Canada's Canal City* (St. Catharines, ON: The St. Catharines Standard Limited, 1992).

5. Certainly "transnational" can be a very open-ended term. However, the phrase is carefully applied to Rochester and St. Catharines because their inhabitants and transients alike understood that the border between the United States and British Canada separated political sovereignties, but it could not mitigate social and cultural ties and a common cause to end bondage. See the "transnational" definition in Michael D. Behiels and Reginald C. Stuart, *Transnationalism: Canada–United States History into the Twenty-First Century* (Montreal: McGill-Queen's University Press, 2010). They explain simply that "'Transnational' accepts political sovereignties but argues that cultural, social, economic, and even many political themes transcend borders" (6). *Borderland Blacks* seeks to put Rochester and St. Catharines on course with the new historical wave to fit Blacks into a larger conversation beyond the conventional American and Canadian national framework. For examples, see Ifeoma Kiddoe Nwankwo, *Black Cosmopolitanism: Racial Consciousness and Transnational Identity in the Nineteenth-Century Americas* (Philadelphia: University of Pennsylvania Press, 2005); Elizabeth Stordeur Pryor, *Colored Travelers: Mobility and the Fight for Citizenship Before the Civil War* (Chapel Hill: University of North Carolina Press, 2016); Lisa Brock, Robin D. G. Kelley, and Karen Sotiropoulos, *Transnational Black Studies* (Durham, NC: Duke University Press, 2003); Manning Marable and Vanessa Agard-Jones, *Transnational Blackness: Navigating the Global Color Line* (New York, NY: Palgrave Macmillan, 2008).

6. Pekka Hamalainen and Samuel Truett, "On Borderlands," *Journal of American History* 98, no. 2 (2011): 361, and John Agnew, "The Territorial Trap: The Geographical Assumptions of International Relations Theory," *Review of International Political Economy* 1, no. 1 (1994): 76–77.

7. The term comes from Afua Cooper, "The Fluid Frontier: Blacks and the Detroit River Region—A Focus on Henry Bibb," *Canadian Review of American Studies* 30, no. 2 (2000): 129–49. I prefer to use the term "fluid frontier" rather than Nina Reid-Maroney's term "intellectual migration" as discussed in Boulou Ebanda de B'béri, Nina Reid-Maroney, and Handel Kashope Wright, eds., *The Promised Land: History and Historiography of the Black Experience in Chatham-Kent's Settlements and Beyond* (Toronto, ON: University of Toronto Press, 2014), 107.

8. William Gillard and Thomas Tooke, *Niagara Escarpment* (Toronto, ON: University of Toronto Press, 1975), and Hugh J. Gayler, *Niagara's Changing Landscapes* (Ottawa, ON: Carleton University Press, 1994), chap. 1.

9. See John N. Jackson, John Burtniak, and Gregory P. Stein, *The Mighty Niagara: One River—Two Frontiers* (Amherst, NY: Prometheus Books, 2003), chap. 3: "Two Canals Transform the Pioneer Landscape"; Carol Sheriff, *The Artificial River: The Erie Canal and the Paradox of Progress, 1817–1862* (New York, NY: Hill & Wang, 1996); Peter L. Bernstein, *Wedding of the Waters: The Erie Canal and the Making of a Great Nation* (New York, NY: W. W. Norton, 2006); Patrick McGreevy, *Stairway to Empire: Lockport, the Erie Canal and the Shaping of America* (Albany, NY: State University of New York Press, 2009); Jackson and Wilson, *St. Catharines: Canada's Canal City;* Roberta M. Styran and

Robert R. Taylor, *The Great National Object: Building the Nineteenth-Century Welland Canals* (Montreal: McGill-Queen's University Press, 2012); John Jackson, *The Welland Canals and Their Communities: Engineering, Industrial, and Urban Transformation* (Toronto, ON: University of Toronto Press, 1997); and Hugh G. J. Aitken, *The Welland Canal Company: A Study in Canadian Enterprise* (Cambridge, MA: Harvard University Press, 1954).

10. Rochester's nursery businesses, located primarily on the green outskirts of town, earned it the name "The Flower City" in the 1840s, and St. Catharines was called "The Garden City" because of its well-groomed trails, parks, and gardens. St. Catharines adopted its nickname between 1890 and 1900.

11. Frank Walker Stevens, *The Beginnings of the New York Central Railroad: A History* (New York, NY: G. P. Putnam, 1926); Edward Hungerford, "Early Railroads of New York," *New York History* 13, no. 1 (Jan. 1932): 75–89; Blake McKelvey, "Railroads in Rochester's History," *Rochester History* 30, no. 4 (Oct. 1968): 1–26; David R. P. Guay, *Great Western Railway of Canada: Southern Ontario's Pioneer Railway* (Toronto, ON: Dundurn Press, 2015); and Sheriff, *Artificial River,* chap. 3, "Reducing Distance and Time."

12. The Niagara Falls Suspension Bridge was the first working railway suspension overpass of its kind. It connected Niagara Falls, Ontario, to Niagara Falls, New York. A temporary bridge was opened on August 1, 1848, and the railway deck opened March 18, 1855. The bridge served the transnational region until 1897 (Donald Sayenga, "Wired Together," *Wire Journal International* 40, no. 10 [Oct. 2007]: 72–80).

13. *Rochester Democrat,* December 16, 1845; *St. Catharines Journal,* January 29, 1846; Commercial Advertiser (Buffalo, NY), November 20, 1845; Charles B. Stuart, *Report of Charles B. Stuart, Chief Engineer of the Lockport and Niagara Falls Rail-Road Company: to the Directors: Showing the Estimated Cost, and Probable Income of the Road, If Extended from Lockport to Rochester* (Rochester, NY: J. M. Patterson & Co., January 1, 1846); *Niagara Falls International Bridge Company* (Rochester, NY: Jerome & Brother, 1847).

14. Rosemary Sadlier, *Harriet Tubman: Freedom Seeker, Freedom Leader* (Toronto, ON: Dundurn Press, 2012), 100; *American Railroad Journal,* January 17, 1846; and Stuart, *Report of Charles B. Stuart,* 5.

15. "The Suspension Bridge," *Buffalo Morning Express,* March 24, 1855. See also "Progress at Niagara Falls," *Toronto Global,* November 15, 1855, and "Sounding the Niagara Below the Suspension Bridge," *Toronto Global,* May 3, 1855.

16. Paul E. Lewis, *Niagara Gorge Bridges: Marvels of Engineering* (St. Catharines, ON: Looking Back Press, 2008), 26. D. B. Steinman, *Spanning Niagara: The Builders of the Bridge* (New York, NY: Arno Press, 1972), 33.

17. These rates would increase over time. Completed on March 20, 1851, the Lewiston-Queenston Suspension Bridge allowed for the crossing of horse, buggy, and pedestrian traffic at the same rate as the Niagara Falls overpass. In the winter of 1864 (some sources incorrectly cite 1854), a storm with strong winds caused the center span of the bridge to plummet into the river. In the absence of the bridge, ferryboat service shuttled people and materials between the two points (John J. Bukowczyk, Nora Faires, David R. Smith, Randy William Widdis, *Permeable Border: The Great Lakes Basin as Transnational Region, 1650–1990* [Pittsburgh, PA: University of Pittsburgh Press, 2005], 48, 62, 70).

18. "Lewiston Suspension Bridge," *Rochester Democrat,* March 24, 1851; "Queenston Suspension," *St. Catharines Journal,* March 27, 1851.

19. George Rogers Taylor, *The Transportation Revolution, 1815–1860* (New York, NY: Harper & Row, 1951); Harry N. Scheiber and Stephen Salsbury, "Reflections on George Rogers Taylor's 'The Transportation Revolution, 1815–1860': A Twenty-Five Year Retrospect," *Business History Review* 51, no. 1 (Spring 1977): 79–89; G. P. De T. Glazebrook, *A History of Transportation in Canada* (New Haven, CT: Yale University Press, 1938); and Berthold Herrendorf, James A. Schmitz Jr., and Arilton Teixeira, "The Role of Transportation in U.S. Economic Development: 1840–1860," *International Economic Review* 53, no. 3 (Aug. 2012): 693–715.

20. Tiya Miles, *The Dawn of Detroit: A Chronicle of Slavery and Freedom in the City of the Straits* (New York, NY: New Press, 2017); Karolyn Smardz Frost and Veta Smith Tucker, eds., *A Fluid Frontier: Slavery, Resistance, and the Underground Railroad in the Detroit River Borderland* (Detroit, MI: Wayne State University Press, 2016); Cooper, "The Fluid Frontier"; Herb Boyd, *Black Detroit: A People's History of Self-Determination* (New York, NY: HarperCollins, 2017); Irene Moore Davis, *Our Own Two Hands: A History of Black Lives in Windsor* (Windsor, ON: Biblioasis, 2019); Marsha R. Robinson, *Purgatory between Kentucky and Canada: African Americans in Ohio* (Newcastle upon Tyne, UK: Cambridge Scholars Publishing, 2013).

21. Stuart, *Report of Charles B. Stuart,* 3; David Harvey, *The Condition of Postmodernity: An Enquiry into the Origins of Cultural Change* (Oxford: Blackwell, 1989). British engineer Marcus Smith (1815–1904) made a map of Rochester in 1851 (copublished with B. Callan) and a map of St. Catharines in 1852. They both show the Third Ward and "Colored Village" where Blacks lived in the cities. Smith was born in Berwick-on-Tweed, England, and was trained as a civil engineer. Employed in the survey and construction of the early English railways, he eventually came to America in 1849, made maps for a number of towns and cities, and crossed the Canadian border to survey settlements. See Paul Hutchinson, *An Index to the Map of the Town of St. Catharines, Canada West: Surveyed, Drawn and Published by Marcus Smith, 1852* (St. Catharines, ON: Slabtown Press, ca. 1996), 1–32.

22. Alexander C. Diener and Joshua Hagen, *Borders: A Very Short Introduction* (New York, NY: Oxford University Press, 2012), 86.

23. Historian Nora Faires explains that "African Americans traversed the international border line in the opposite direction" but "scholars are only beginning to trace the migrations." Nora Faires, "Across the Border to Freedom: The International Underground Railroad Memorial and the Meanings of Migration," *Journal of American Ethnic History* 32, no. 2 (Winter 2013): 56.

24. Cooper, "The Fluid Frontier," and Harvey Amani Whitfield, *Blacks on the Border: The Black Refugees in British North America, 1815–1860* (Hanover, NH: University Press of New England, 2006). The first major studies focusing on Blacks in Canada came from Fred Landon of the University of Western Ontario during the 1920s in the *Journal of Negro History.* While most professional historians ignored African-Canadian history, Landon continued to write robustly on the topic into the 1950s. The social upheavals of the 1960s brought new attention and research to the subject of Blacks in Canada. In 1971, this materialized in the publication of Robin Winks's *The Blacks in Canada: A History,* which became a staple. It was so painstakingly researched that Winks employed only half of the materials accumulated in the book; the rest are held at the Schomburg Center. Nonetheless, *The Blacks in Canada* fell subject to viewing Blacks from the perspective of victims and subjects instead of as historical actors with agency. From Winks, the scholarship blossomed; the most popular of his

contemporaries who added to the conversation are James W. St. G. Walker, Jason H. Silverman, and Daniel G. Hill. Subsequently, a new generation of scholars produced a broad host of works that benefit and build on the foundational contributions. For more on the historiography, see David C. Este, "Black Canadian Historical Writing 1970–2006: An Assessment," *Journal of Black Studies* 38, no. 3; *Blacks in Canada: Retrospects, Introspects, Prospects* (Jan. 2008): 388–406; Leo W. Bertley, *Canada and Its People of African Descent* (Pierrefonds, QC: Bilongo, 1977).

25. "Transboundary social formation" is a term used by Lawrence A. Herzog to explain the political, cultural, and economic networks which overlie the borderlands (Lawrence A. Herzog, *Where North Meets South: Cities, Space, and Politics on the U.S.–Mexico Border* [Austin: University of Texas Press, 1990], 135).

26. The scholarship on borderlands history is immense. The works I have found most helpful include Michiel Baud and Willem Van Schendel, "Toward a Comparative History of Borderlands," *Journal of World History* 8 (Fall 1997): 211–42; Tony Freyer and Lyndsay Campbell, eds., *Freedom's Conditions in the U.S.–Canadian Borderlands in the Age of Emancipation* (Durham, NC: Carolina Academic Press, 2011); Robert Lecker, *Borderlands: Essays in Canadian-American Relations* (Toronto, ON: ECW Press, 1991); Jeremy Adelman and Stephen Aron, "From Borderlands to Borders: Empires, Nation-States, and the Peoples in Between in North American History," *American Historical Review* 104, no. 3 (June 1999): 814–41; Andrew Graybill and Benjamin Johnson, eds., "Introduction: Border and Their Historians in North America," in *Bridging National Borders in North America: Transnational and Comparative Histories* (Durham, NC: Duke University, 2010); Emmanuel Brunet-Jailly, *Borderlands: Comparing Border Security in North America and Europe* (Ottawa, QC: University of Ottawa Press, 2007); Michael Kearney, "Borders and Boundaries of State and Self at the End of Empire," *Journal of Historical Sociology* 4, no. 1 (March 1991): 52–74; Allen Buchanan and Margaret Moore, eds., *States, Nations, and Borders: The Ethics of Making Boundaries* (Cambridge, MA: Cambridge University Press, 2003); Joel S. Migdal, ed., *Boundaries and Belonging: States and Societies in the Struggle to Shape Identities and Local Practices* (Cambridge, MA: Cambridge University Press, 2004); Steven Hahn, *A Nation without Borders: The United States and Its World in an Age of Civil Wars, 1830–1910* (New York, NY: Viking, 2016); Matthew Salafia, *Slavery's Borderland: Freedom and Bondage along the Ohio River* (Philadelphia: University of Pennsylvania Press, 2019); and David Newman, "The Lines that Continue to Separate Us: Borders in Our 'Borderless' World," *Progress in Human Geography* 30, no. 2 (2006): 143–61. I found the borderlands history on the American-Mexican borderlands to be quite compelling as well. See Oscar J. Martinez, *Border People: Life and Society in the U.S.–Mexico Borderlands* (Tucson: University of Arizona Press, 1994); Andres Resendez, *Changing National Identities at the Frontier: Texas and New Mexico, 1800–1850* (New York, NY: Cambridge University Press, 2005); Samuel Truett, *Fugitive Landscapes: The Forgotten History of the U.S.–Mexico Borderlands* (New Haven, CT: Yale University Press, 2006).

27. Jeremy Adelman and Stephen Aron, 15; Gustavo Cano, "Organizing Immigrant Communities in American Cities: Is this Transnationalism, or What?" (Working Paper 103 Center for Comparative Immigration Studies University of California, San Diego, La Jolla, CA, August 2004); Jane Rhodes, "The Contestation over National Identity: Nineteenth-Century Black Americans in Canada," *Canadian Historical Review of American Studies* 30, no. 2 (2000): 174–86; Kim D. Butler, "Abolition and the Politics of Identity in the Afro-Atlantic Diaspora: Toward a Comparative Approach," in *Crossing Boundaries: Comparative History of Black People in Diaspora*, edited by Darlene Clark Hine

and Jacqueline A. McLeod, 121–33 (Bloomington: Indiana University Press, 1999); James W. St G. Walker and Patricia Thorvaldson, *Identity: The Black Experience in Canada* (Toronto: Ontario Educational Communications Authority and Gage Educational Publishing, 1979); James R. Barret and David Roediger, "Inbetween Peoples: Race, Nationality, and the 'New Immigrant' Working Class," *Journal of American Ethnic History* 16 (Spring 1997): 3–44.

28. *National Anti-Slavery Standard,* August 19, 1847. Russ Castronovo, "'As to Nation, I Belong to None': Ambivalence, Diaspora, and Frederick Douglass," *American Transcendental Quarterly* 9, no. 3 (Sept. 1995): 245–55. The historiography on Douglass before the Civil War has transitioned from a national disposition to a more international understanding of the lead Black abolitionist. See, for example, James A. Colaiaco, *Frederick Douglass and the Fourth of July* (New York, NY: Palgrave Macmillan, 2006); Bernard R. Boxill, "Frederick Douglass's Patriotism," *Journal of Ethics* 13, no. 4 (2009), 301–17; Alan J. Rice and Martin Crawford, eds., *Liberating Sojourn: Frederick Douglass and Transatlantic Reform* (Athens: University of Georgia Press, 1999); Fionnghuala Sweeney, *Frederick Douglass and the Atlantic World* (Liverpool: Liverpool University Press, 2007); David W. Blight, *Frederick Douglass: Prophet of Freedom* (New York, NY: Simon & Schuster, 2018); and D. H. Dilbeck, *Frederick Douglass: America's Prophet* (Chapel Hill: University of North Carolina Press, 2018).

29. See Rice and Crawford, eds., *Liberating Sojourn;* Nwankwo, *Black Cosmopolitanism;* Hannah-Rose Murray, *Advocates of Freedom: African American Transatlantic Abolitionism in the British Isles* (Cambridge, UK: Cambridge University Press, 2020); Alasdair Pettinger, *Frederick Douglass and Scotland, 1846: Living an Antislavery Life* (Edinburgh, UK: Edinburgh University Press, 2020); W. Caleb McDaniel, *The Problem of Democracy in the Age of Slavery: Garrisonian Abolitionists and Transatlantic Reform* (Baton Rouge: Louisiana State University Press, 2015); Edlie L. Wong, *Neither Fugitive nor Free: Atlantic Slavery, Freedom Suits, and the Legal Culture of Travel* (New York, NY: New York University Press, 2009); J. R. Oldfield, *The Ties that Bind: Transatlantic Abolitionism in the Age of Reform, c.1820–1866* (Liverpool, UK: Liverpool University Press, 2020).

30. Baud and Van Schendel, "Toward a Comparative History of Borderlands," 242.

31. Kearney, "Borders and Boundaries of State and Self at the End of Empire," 52–74. See also Alexander C. Diener and Joshua Hagen, eds., *Borderlines and Borderlands: Political Oddities at the Edge of the Nation-State* (New York, NY: Rowman & Littlefield Publishers, 2010).

32. Baud and Schendel, "Toward a Comparative History of Borderlands," 221–22.

33. R. J. M. Blackett, *The Captive's Quest for Freedom: Fugitive Slaves, the 1850 Fugitive Slave Law, and the Politics of Slavery* (New York, NY: Cambridge University Press, 2018); Andrew Delbanco, *The War Before the War: Fugitive Slaves and the Struggle for America's Soul from the Revolution to the Civil War* (New York, NY: Penguin Press, 2018); Steven Lubet, *Fugitive Justice: Runaways, Rescuers, and Slavery on Trial* (Cambridge, MA: Belknap Press, 2010); Stanley W. Campbell, *The Slave Catchers: Enforcement of the Fugitive Slave Law 1850–1860* (Chapel Hill: University of North Carolina Press, 1971); Scott J. Basinger, "Regulating Slavery: Deck-Stacking and Credible Commitment in the Fugitive Slave Act of 1850," *Journal of Law, Economics, and Organization* 19, no. 2 (Oct. 2003): 307–42; H. Robert Baker, "The Fugitive Slave Clause and the Antebellum Constitution," *Law and History Review* 30, no. 4 (Nov. 2012): 1133–74.

34. Buffalo and Erie County Black population—1830: 243, 1840: 608, 1850: 825, and 1860: 878. Compare that with the Black population in Rochester and Monroe County—1830: 465, 1840: 655, 1850: 699, and 1860: 567. Data derived from US Census. No counts are available between 1790 and 1820.

35. Fugitives Christopher Webb and Daniel Davis found out the dangers of being *too* close to

the border in Buffalo. In 1847, Webb, a local saloon waiter, had two Kentucky slave catchers draw a "six-shooter" gun on him and then declare he had to return to his "owner." Thanks to the "energetic action" of fellow Blacks, explained the *North Star,* he was able to elude his captors. In 1851, Davis, a cook on the steamer *Buckeye State,* was apprehended in Buffalo by catcher Benjamin Rust, who hit him over the head with a wooden stick. Before Davis and four companions could use the knives they pulled out to defend themselves, a marshal arrived and ended the conflict. Davis was jailed; when he was transported from the penitentiary to the federal courthouse, local Blacks attempted to rescue him. The plot did not work, but fortunately for Davis the legal system triumphed. He was released and went to Canada (*North Star,* March 3, 1848; *Buffalo Commercial Advertiser,* October 1, 1847, and October 5, 1847; *Buffalo Commercial Advertiser,* August 15, 1851; *Frederick Douglass' Paper,* August 21, 1851; *Buffalo Daily Courier,* August 20 and 30, 1851; The *Globe and Mail* (Toronto), August 19, 1851, and September 20, 1851).

36. "'Letter,' from Wm. J. Watkins," *Frederick Douglass' Paper,* March 24, 1854. See David A. Gerber, *The Making of an American Pluralism: Buffalo, New York, 1825–1860* (Champaign: University of Illinois Press, 1989); Lillian Serece Williams, *Strangers in the Land of Paradise: Creation of an African-American Community in Buffalo, New York, 1900–1940* (Bloomington: Indiana University Press, 2000), chap. 1: "The Early Years"; Mark Goldman, *High Hopes: The Rise and Decline of Buffalo, New York* (Albany: State University of New York Press, 1983); Ralph L. Pearson, "A Quantitative Approach to Buffalo's Black Population of 1860," *Afro-Americans in New York Life and History* 12 (July 1988): 19–34.

37. Arthur O. White, "The Black Movement against Jim Crow Education in Buffalo, New York, 1800–1900," *Phylon* 30, no. 4 (4th Qtr. 1969): 375–93; and William Wells Brown, *Narrative of William W. Brown, a Fugitive Slave. Written by Himself* (Boston: The Anti-Slavery Office, 1847). Brown published four American and five British editions of his *Narrative* before 1850.

38. Lillian Serece Williams, *Strangers,* 9–20. See also Ezra Greenspan, *William Wells Brown: An African American Life* (New York, NY: W. W. Norton, 2014) and William E. Farrisson, "William Wells Brown in Buffalo," *Journal of Negro History* 39, no. 4 (Oct. 1954): 298–314. Born in Trenton, New Jersey, Abner Francis settled in Buffalo circa 1835–36. He owned a clothing and drycleaning store and was one of Buffalo's main affluent Blacks until his business failed in 1851. Son of Rev. George Weir Sr., pastor of the Vine Street AME Church, George Weir Jr. was part of a select group of Black merchants in town. It was around 1835 when the Weir family arrived in Buffalo from North Carolina. William Watkins did note that George Weir Jr. was an exception to Buffalo's "slumber." In August 1849, Rev. Weir died; see Jean Richardson, "Buffalo's Antebellum African American Community and the Fugitive Slave Law of 1850," *Afro-Americans in New York Life and History* 27, no. 2 (July 2003): 29–45.

39. Niagara Falls, NY, and Niagara County Black population—1830: 102, 1840: 241, 1850: 371, and 1860: 517. Syracuse and Onondaga County 1830: 492, 1840: 477, 1850: 613, 1860: 555. Data derived from US Census. See also Milton C. Sernett, "'A Citizen of No Mean City': Jermain W. Loguen and the Antislavery Reputation of Syracuse," *Syracuse University Library Associates Courier* 22 (Fall 1987): 33–55; Milton C. Sernett, "On Freedom's Threshold: The African American Presence in Central New York, 1760–1940," *Afro-American in New York Life and History* 19 (Jan. 1995): 43–91, and Carol Hunter, *To Set the Captives Free: Reverend Jermain Wesley Loguen and the Struggle for Freedom in Central New York, 1835–1872* (New York: Garland, 1993).

40. Michelle Ann Kratts, *Melting Pot: Niagara's Rich Ethnic Heritage* (Scotts Valley, CA: CreateSpace Independent Publishing Platform, 2017), 21–68.

41. Eric Foner, *Gateway to Freedom: The Hidden History of the Underground Railroad* (New York, NY: W. W. Norton, 2015), 14; and Fergus M. Bordewich, *Bound for Canaan: The Epic Story of the Underground Railroad, America's First Civil Rights Movement* (New York, NY: Amistad, 2006), 412–13. Also see "To the Friends of the Fugitives From Slavery," National Anti-Slavery Standard, October 3, 1857, which explained that Loguen was the key person in Syracuse to help Blacks escaping bondage "having been a slave and a fugitive himself, [he] knows best how to provide for that class of sufferers, and to guard against imposition." And, Monique Patenaud, "Bound by Pride and Prejudice: Black Life in Frederick Douglass' New York" (PhD diss., University of Rochester, 2012). The Oswego Canal opened in 1828 and helped Central New York and Syracuse to connect to Lake Ontario (Janet Larkin, "The Oswego Canal: A Connecting Link Between the United States and Canada, 1819–1837," *Ontario History* 103 [Spring 2011]: 23–41).

42. Hence the anxiety in the "outer borderlands," which yielded a number of anti-1850 Fugitive Slave Act meetings in Central New York. There were seven meetings in Western New York, nearly double the number of meetings in Central New York because vulnerability depended upon proximity to the border (Baud and Schendel, "Toward a Comparative History of Borderlands," 222; Blackett, *Captive's Quest for Freedom,* see map on 16–17).

43. David S. Reynolds, *John Brown, Abolitionist: The Man Who Killed Slavery, Sparked the Civil War, and Seeded Civil Rights* (New York: Alfred A. Knopf, 2005), 138–78, 268–87. William S. Rasmussen and Robert S. Tilton, *The Portent: John Brown's Raid in American Memory* (Richmond: Virginia Historical Society, 2009), 20. Rasmussen and Tilton suggest that Brown's liberation of these slaves by Brown and his men was in retaliation for the killing of at least five, but possibly eleven, Free State settlers in the summer of 1858 by a man named Charles A. Hamilton. J. C. Furnas and David Potter considered the liberation of these slaves as "the only time Old Brown ever completed a thing according to plan." J. C. Furnas, *The Road to Harpers Ferry* (New York: William Sloane Associates, 1959), 25; David M. Potter and Don E. Fehrenbacher, eds., *The Impending Crisis, 1848–1861* (New York: Harper & Row, 1976), 369; H. W. Brands, *The Zealot and the Emancipator: John Brown, Abraham Lincoln, and the Struggle for American Freedom* (New York, NY: Doubleday, 2020), 75–101.

44. William Howard Day to Gerrit Smith, June 21, 1858, Gerrit Smith Papers, George Arents Research Library, Syracuse University; Jane Rhodes, *Mary Ann Shadd Cary,* 131–32; Donald G. Simpson and Paul E. Lovejoy, eds., *Under the North Star,* 94–96; and R. J. M. Blackett, *Beating against the Barriers: The Lives of Six Nineteenth-Century Afro-Americans* (Ithaca, NY: Cornell University Press, 1989), 312–13.

45. The historiography of John Brown is extensive. The works I have found the most useful are W. E. B. Du Bois, *John Brown* (Philadelphia, PA: George W. Jacobs & Co., 1909); Robert Penn Warren, *John Brown: The Making of a Martyr* (New York: Payson and Clarke, 1929; reprint, St. Clair Shores: Scholarly Press, 1970); Stephen B. Oates, *To Purge this Land with Blood: A Biography of John Brown* (New York: Harper & Row, 1970); Evan Carton, *Patriotic Treason: John Brown and the Soul of America* (New York: Free Press, 2006); Robert E. McGlone, *John Brown's War Against Slavery* (Cambridge: Cambridge University Press, 2009); Tony Horwitz, *Midnight Rising: John Brown and the Raid that Sparked the Civil War* (New York: Henry Holt and Company, 2011); Brian McGinty, *John Brown's Trial* (Cambridge, MA: Harvard University Press, 2009); Rasmussen and Tilton, *The Portent;* and R. Blakeslee Gilpin, *John Brown Still Lives! America's Long Reckoning with Violence, Equality and Change* (Chapel Hill: University of North Carolina Press, 2011).

46. For the Black population of the Niagara region, see the census data and statistical discourse of David P. Gagan, "Enumerator's Instruction for the Census of Canada 1852 and 1861," *Histoire Sociale/Social History* 8, no. 14 (Nov. 1974): 333–65, and Michael Wayne, "The Black Population of Canada West on the Eve of the American Civil War. A Reassessment Based on the Manuscript Census of 1861," *Histoire Sociale/Social History* 28, no. 56 (Nov. 1995): 465–81.

47. Benjamin Drew, *The Refugee: Or the Narratives of Fugitive Slaves in Canada* (New York, NY: John P. Jewett and Company, 1856), 11.

48. In the 1970s, "new social histories" came in vogue as historians explored the lives of ordinary people and their families, social institutions, and communities, in contrast with the earlier studies that were more nationally and elite-focused. These "history from the bottom up" treatments involved workers, slaves, immigrants, and the like who were involved in different activities and left different sorts of scarce records than was true for leading influential groups. New social histories strategically detailed localized endeavors and thereby have also been called "micro-histories" and "thick description" examinations. David E. Kyvig and Myron A. Marty, *Nearby History: Exploring the Past Around You, 3rd ed.* (Lanham, MD: AltaMira Press, 2010), 227–56. See the works of Eugene Genovese, John W. Blassingame, Stephan Thernstrom, Herbert Gutman, Charles Tilly, Oscar Handlin, and Bryan D. Palmer.

49. The African Diaspora and Atlantic World studies are not wedded to national histories but use a comparative method to analyze how different experiences of Black peoples unfolded in different places and times. In 1965, this field of study started at an international conference on African history at the University of Dar es Salaam in Tanzania. Thereafter, scholars studying Africans, Black Europeans, African Americans, Afro-Caribbeans, Afro-Latin Americans, and Black Canadians began to make transnational and international connections beyond set national and regional divisions. As Kim D. Butler explained of Atlantic World histories in chapter 1 of the Olaniyan and Sweet edited volume: "The methodological demands force scholars to probe the relationship between overarching meta-Diaspora constructs and locally lived experiences," Tejumola Olaniyan and James H. Sweet, eds., *The African Diaspora and the Disciplines* (Bloomington: Indiana University Press, 2010), 29. British Canada fits comfortably into the Atlantic World discourse due to its ties across national borders and back to the "Old World," though often enough Blacks in Canada are not covered with the same intensity as is true for Blacks in other parts of the Diaspora. See dann j. Broyld, "The 'Dark Sheep' of the Atlantic World: Following the Transnational Trail of Blacks to Canada," in *Black Subjects: Race and Research in Africa and the Atlantic World,* ed. Benjamin Talton and Quincy T. Mills (New York, NY: Palgrave MacMillan, 2011), chap. 7, 95–108. My work here in *Borderland Blacks* simply draws inspiration from the intriguing African Diaspora and Atlantic World studies to make meaningful connections, despite systems of oppression and structures of division.

50. See Freyer and Campbell, *Freedom's Conditions,* which states that the book explores "the legal experiences of those of African descent who lived in borderlands areas and oriented themselves toward the border between the United States and British North America in the middle of the nineteenth century. The period was characterized by intensive human and economic mobility across the border, but at the same time, by a considerable amount of tension as well" (3). The book looks at the border chiefly by way of the law, while *Borderland Blacks* examines specific local examples of the lives of Blacks in the shared borderlands.

51. Baud and Schendel, "Toward a Comparative History of Borderlands," 242.

52. Blight, *Frederick Douglass;* Dilbeck, *Frederick Douglass: America's Prophet.* My book also benefits from the newly discovered narrative of Austin Reed, entitled *The Life and the Adventures of a Haunted Convict,* which was acquired by Yale University's Beinecke Rare Book & Manuscript Library in 2009; the *Record of Fugitives* by Sydney Howard Gay in the Sydney Howard Gay Papers at Columbia University (highlighted in the book); and the private Walter O. Evans Collection of Savannah, Georgia. Reed was born to a prominent Black family in Rochester and provides a window into the community. The Evans Collection has documents on Frederick Douglass and his family members and their activities in the borderlands of Rochester. See Austin Reed and Caleb Smith, eds., *The Life and the Adventures of a Haunted Convict* (New York, NY: Random House, 2016); Sydney Howard Gay Papers, Rare Books and Manuscript Library, Columbia University, NY; and Celeste-Marie Bernier and Andrew Taylor, eds., *If I Survive: Frederick Douglass and Family in the Walter O. Evans Collection* (Edinburgh, Scotland: Edinburgh University Press, 2018).

53. See Raymond A. Bauer and Alice H. Bauer, "Day to Day Resistance to Slavery," *Journal of Negro History* 27, no. 4 (Oct. 1942): 388–419; Cynthia R. Nielsen, "Resistance Is Not Futile: Frederick Douglass on Panoptic Plantations and Un-making of Docile Bodies and Enslaved Souls," *Philosophy and Literature* 35, no. 2 (2011): 251–68; James C. Scott, *Weapons of the Weak: Everyday Forms of Peasant Resistance* (New Haven, CT: Yale University Press, 1985); James C. Scott, *Domination and the Arts of Resistance: Hidden Transcripts* (New Haven, CT: Yale University Press, 1990); and Robert L. Paquette, "Social History Update: Slave Resistance and Social History," *Journal of Social History* 24, no. 3 (Spring 1991): 681–85.

54. For insight on the Niagara Underground Railroad branch, the works I found most useful on Maryland and Delaware were those of Priscilla Thompson, Kate Clifford Larson, William J. Switala, Patience Essah, and James A. McGowan; on Philadelphia, see William Still, Robert Clemens Smedley, Nilgun Anadolu Okur, William C. Kashatus, Stephen G. Hill, and Richard Bell; on New York City, see Sydney Howard Gay, Graham Russell Gao Hodges, Erie Foner, Don Papson, and Tom Calarco; on Upstate and Western New York, see Judith Wellman, Milton C. Sernett, Musette S. Castle, Ena L. Farley, Elbert Cook Wixom.

55. Larry Gara, *The Liberty Line: The Legend of the Underground Railroad* (Lexington: University of Kentucky Press, 1961); Wilbur H. Siebert, *The Underground Railroad from Slavery to Freedom: A Comprehensive History* (New York, NY: Dover Publications, 2006); and Bordewich, *Bound for Canaan,* 238–39. The Underground Railroad was traditionally regarded as a well-organized network of devoted conductors with secret codes and symbols, as put forth by Wilbur H. Siebert between 1896 and 1951 in several volumes. That idea has given way to the modern understanding of the fragmented character of the Underground Railroad, a critique that started with Larry Gara in the 1960s. The Railroad was strongest in Northern areas like Cincinnati, Detroit, Philadelphia, Boston, and Rochester. It was the fugitives, not the abolitionists, who played the key role in engineering their own escape and risked the gravest repercussions. Due to the limited scope of the Underground Railroad, fugitives had to rely heavily on themselves and on Black communities for successful travel.

56. The "Burned-Over District" produced the Mormons of the Church of Jesus Christ Latter-day Saints, a church established by Joseph Smith; William Miller's Millerites, who believed the Second Coming was to occur on October 22, 1844; the Shakers, a religious sect that died out partly because its members were forbidden to have sex or marry; as well as the Fox sisters, who educated others on communicating with the dead; and the Oneida Community, where people engaged in

communal marriage, birth control, and eugenics. The district was fertile ground for the Quakers, Baptists, Methodists, Presbyterians, and Unitarians. In addition, the "Burned-Over District" was a hub for political causes like Abolition, Women's Suffrage, and the Temperance Movement.

57. Whitney R. Cross, *The Burned-Over District: The Social and Intellectual History of Enthusiastic Religion in Western New York, 1800–1850* (Ithaca, NY: Cornell University Press, 2006, reprint from 1950); Milton C. Sernett, *North Star Country: Upstate New York and the Crusade for African American Freedom* (Syracuse, NY: Syracuse University Press, 2002), 157; Linda K. Prichard, "The Burned-Over District Reconsidered: A Portent of Evolving Religious Pluralism in the United States," *Social Science History* 8 (Summer 1984): 243–65; and Judith Wellman, "Crossing Over Cross: Whitney Cross's *Burned-over District* as Social History," *Reviews in American History* 17 (March 1989): 159–57. See also Thomas Bender, "Historians, the Nation, and the Plenitude of Narratives," in *Rethinking American History in a Global Age,* ed. Thomas Bender (Berkeley: University of California Press, 2002), 1–22; and Thomas Bender, *A Nation Among Nations: America's Place in World History* (New York, NY: Hill & Wang, 2006).

58. Foner, *Gateway to Freedom.* See also Don Papson and Tom Calarco, *Secret Lives of the Underground Railroad in New York City: Sydney Howard Gay, Louis Napoleon and the Record of Fugitives* (Jefferson, NC: McFarland, 2015).

59. In 1855 and 1856, Sydney Howard Gay sent some thirty-seven fugitives to Albany and another eighty-one to Syracuse (Papson and Calarco, *Secret Lives,* 108–10).

60. Foner, *Gateway to Freedom,* 181; and Papson and Calarco, *Secret Lives,* 102.

61. Benjamin Quarles, "The Breach between Douglass and Garrison," *Journal of Negro History* 23, no. 2 (April 1938): 144–54; Tyrone Tillery, "The Inevitability of the Douglass-Garrison Conflict," *Phylon* 37, no. 2 (2nd Qtr. 1976): 137–49; Mark Voss-Hubbard, "The Political Culture of Emancipation: Morality, Politics, and the State in Garrisonian Abolitionism, 1854–1863," *Journal of American Studies* 29, no. 2 (Aug. 1995): 159–84; Nick Bromell, "A 'Voice from the Enslaved': The Origins of Frederick Douglass's Political Philosophy of Democracy," *American Literary History* 23, no. 4 (Winter 2011): 697–723; and Ronald Osborn, "William Lloyd Garrison and the United States Constitution: The Political Evolution of an American Radical," *Journal of Law and Religion* 24, no. 1 (2008/2009): 65–88.

62. Ontario was called Upper Canada from 1791 to 1841. It was later labeled Canada West from 1841 to 1867 before acquiring its current name of Ontario. Throughout this study, each of these names will be used interchangeably.

63. See Barrington Walker, *Race on Trial: Black Defendants in Ontario's Criminal Courts, 1858–1958* (Toronto, ON: University of Toronto Press, 2010); Barrington Walker, *The African Canadian Legal Odyssey* (Toronto, ON: University of Toronto Press, 2012); David F. Ericson, *Slavery and the American Republic: Developing the Federal Government, 1791–1861* (Lawrence: University of Kansas Press, 2011).

64. Walker, *Race on Trial,* 3.

65. Frederick Douglass, "What to the Slave, is the Fourth of July" (Rochester, NY, Corinthian Hall, July 5, 1852), in which Douglass emphasized: "your celebration is a sham; your boasted liberty, an unholy license; your national greatness, swelling vanity; your sounds of rejoicing are empty and heartless." The overarching was the "Fourth of July is *yours,* not *mine. You* may rejoice, I must mourn." W. Caleb McDaniel, "The Fourth and the First: Abolitionist Holidays, Respectability, and Radical Interracial Reform," *American Quarterly* 57, no. 1 (March 2005): 129–51, the quote is on page

133. See also Colaiaco, *Frederick Douglass and the Fourth of July;* William B. Gravely, "The Dialectic of Double-Consciousness in Black American Freedom Celebrations, 1808–1863," *Journal of Negro History* 67, no. 4 (Winter 1982): 302–17; "The ever-glorious Fourth," *North Star,* July 13, 1849; and "New York," *Voice of the Fugitive,* July 29, 1852, which stated: "The distinguished orator brought the burden of his argument to bear on the question of slavery—the truth being ably enunciated without fear or favor . . . it was done up in Frederick Douglass's best style."

66. Austin Steward, *Twenty-Two Years a Slave and Forty Years a Freeman* (1857; rpr. Syracuse, NY: Syracuse University Press, 2002); and Thomas James, *Life of Rev. Thomas James, by Himself* (Rochester, NY: Post Express Printing Company, 1886). Frederick Douglass left a wealth of resources for scholars to investigate, including three narratives, four newspapers, and a treasure trove of speeches and correspondence. His *Narrative of the Life of Frederick Douglass, an American Slave* was published in 1848; *My Bondage and My Freedom* in 1855, and *Life and Times of Frederick Douglass* in 1881 (revised in 1892). His newspapers—the *North Star* (1847–51), the *Frederick Douglass' Paper* (1851–60), and the *Douglass' Monthly* (1859–63)—are also used extensively in this study.

67. Historian James W. St. G. Walker was critical of Robin W. Winks's *The Blacks in Canada* for "'dangerously' suggesting that Blacks themselves, not White racism, were responsible for their unequal position in society." Walker explained that Black separation of social institutions, like churches, in Canada was initiated and the result of white bigotry (xvii). David C. Este, in "Black Canadian Historical Writing, 1970–2006: An Assessment," explained that "Walker maintains that Blacks attempted to integrate into Canadian society; however, they were subjected to racism and discrimination. As a result, members of the community turned inward and created institutions to help them deal with the realities of living in a society in which they were regarded as second-class citizens" (*Journal of Black Studies* 38, no. 3: 388–406, quote on 393). I assert that this same set of circumstances is applicable to the Blacks in St. Catharines.

68. Peter Meyler and David Meyler, *A Stolen Life: Searching for Richard Pierpoint* (Toronto, ON: Natural Heritage/ Natural History Incorporated, 1999); Charles Emery Stevens, *Anthony Burns: A History* (Boston: John P. Jewett and Company, 1856); Albert J. von Frank, *The Trials of Anthony Burns: Freedom and Slavery in Emerson's Boston* (Cambridge, MA: Harvard University Press, 1998); Earl M. Maltz, *Fugitive Slave on Trial: The Anthony Burns Case and Abolitionist Outrage* (Lawrence: University Press of Kansas, 2010). See also the long historiography on Harriet Tubman: Sarah H. Bradford, *Harriet Tubman, the Moses of Her People* (New York: Geo. R. Lockwood & Son, 1886); Earl Conrad, *General Harriet Tubman* (Washington, DC: Associated Publishers, 1943); Rosemary Sadlier, *Harriet Tubman and the Underground Railroad: Her Life in the United States and Canada* (Toronto: Umbrella Press, 1997); Jean M. Humez, *Harriet Tubman: The Life and the Life Stories* (Madison: University of Wisconsin Press, 2003); Kate Clifford Larson, *Bound for the Promised Land: Harriet Tubman, Portrait of An American Hero* (New York, NY: Ballantine Books, 2004); Catherine Clinton, *Harriet Tubman: The Road to Freedom* (New York, NY: Little, Brown and Company, 2004). In addition, see dann j. Broyld, "Harriet Tubman: Transnationalism and the Land of a Queen in the Late Antebellum" (*The Meridians: Feminism, Race, and Transnationalism* 12, no. 2 [Nov. 2014]: 78–98), which argues that Tubman was a transnational and not just an "American Hero." It also claims that the quest by Tubman and female fugitives from the United States to reach Canadian soil was twofold: they wanted to resist enslavement in America and to sidestep and stand against sexual exploitation and gender degradation on the "Queen's soil."

69. See Nicholas Guyatt, *Bind Us Apart: How Enlightened Americans Invented Racial Segregation* (New York, NY: Basic Books, 2016).

70. See Adam Arenson, "Experience Rather than Imagination: Researching the Return Migration of African North Americans during the American Civil War and Reconstruction," *Journal of American Ethnic History* 32, no. 2 (Winter 2013): 73–77. The classic works include Robin Winks, *The Civil War Years: Canada and the United States* (Montreal: McGill-Queen's University Press, 1999); John Boyko, *Blood and Daring: How Canada Fought the American Civil War and Forged a Nation* (Toronto, ON: Vintage Canada, 2013); Richard M. Reid, *African Canadians in Union Blue: Volunteering for the Cause in America's Civil War* (Kent, OH: Kent State University Press, 2014); and Bryan Prince, *My Brother's Keeper: African Canadians and the American Civil War* (Toronto, ON: Dundurn Press, 2015).

71. Michael Peter Smith and Luis Eduardo Guarnizo, eds., *Transnationalism from Below: Comparative Urban & Community Research, Vol. 6* (New Brunswick, NJ: Transaction Publishers, 1998).

72. See, e.g., Siebert, *The Underground Railroad from Slavery to Freedom;* and Bordewich, *Bound for Canaan.* Note also the key scholars in Underground Railroad studies: Charles Eric Lincoln, Wilbur H. Siebert, Larry Gara, Marion Wilson Starling, Rev. William M. Mitchell, Christopher Densmore, Charles Blockson, John Hope Franklin, Fergus Bordewich, Bryan Prince, Richard Newman, Charles Wesley, Bettye BeRamus, David Blight, Kate Clifford Larson, Carolyn Smardz Frost, and Cheryl Janifer LaRoche. The Canadian "Promised Land" discourse overemphasizes Black freedoms enjoyed in Canada before the Civil War and after. It casts the British colony as a "haven" and overlooks the transcending sentiment of racism that was present on both sides of the American-Canadian border. While there were legal differences that hampered bigotry in Canada, the social reality must not be taken out of context, as prejudice could be just as pervasive on the Crown's soil. The "Promised Land" historical literature treats Canada as if it were an ideal "heavenly" place floating above nineteenth- and twentieth-century intolerance and Black degradation. See Karolyn Smardz Frost, *I've Got a Home in Glory Land: A Lost Tale of the Underground Railroad* (New York, NY: Farrar, Straus and Giroux, 2007); Sharon A. Roger Hepburn, "Following the North Star: Canada as a Haven for Nineteenth-Century American Blacks," *Michigan Historical Review* 25, no. 2 (Fall 1999): 91–126; Sharon Hepburn, *Crossing the Border: A Free Black Community in Canada* (Champaign: University of Illinois Press, 2007); and Nancy Kang, "'As If I Had Entered a Paradise': Fugitive Slave Narratives and Cross-Border Literary History," *African American Review* 39, no. 3 (Fall 2005): 431–57. See also B'béri, Reid-Maroney, and Wright, *The Promised Land,* which explains that it is trying to "move beyond the boundaries of the term [Promised Land] itself" (4).

73. Baud and Schendel, "Toward a Comparative History of Borderlands," 211.

1. SETTING THE STAGE FOR THE JOURNEY

1. Booker T. Washington explained of his rural Virginian childhood: "The slaves throughout the South, completely ignorant as were the masses so far as books or newspapers were concerned, were able to keep themselves so accurately and completely informed about the great National questions that were agitating the country . . . by what was termed the 'grape-vine' telegraph" (Booker T. Washington, *Up from Slavery: An Autobiography* [Garden City, NJ: Doubleday, 1901], 8). The "Black grapevine" was historically referred to as the "Negro grapevine."

2. Josiah Henson, *Truth Stranger Than Fiction. Father Henson's Story of His Own Life* (Boston: John P. Jewett, 1858), 211.

3. Jermain Wesley Loguen, *The Rev. J. W. Loguen as a Slave and a Freeman: A Narrative of Real Life* (Syracuse, NY: J. G. K. Truair & Co., 1859), 304–5.

4. Ira Berlin makes the distinction that slave societies were those that slaves served as the fundamental base of the economy, whereas societies with slaves human bondage was an element of the economic system but it did not rely solely on the labor of those held in captivity. Ira Berlin, *Many Thousands Gone: The First Two Centuries of Slavery in North America* (Harvard University Press, 1998) and Afua Cooper, *The Hanging of Angelique: The Untold Story of Canadian Slavery and The Burning of Old Montreal* (Athens: University of Georgia, 2007), 68.

5. See John W. Pulis, ed., *Moving On: Black Loyalists in the Afro-Atlantic World* (New York, NY: Garland, 1999); Barry Cahill, "The Black Loyalist Myth in Atlantic Canada," *Acadiensis* 29, no. 1 (Autumn 1999): 76–87; and Harvey Amani Whitfield, "White Archives, Black Fragments: The Study of Enslaved Black People in the Maritimes," *Canadian Historical Review* 101, no. 3, (Sept. 2020): 323–45.

6. Jason A. Silverman, *Unwelcome Guests: Canada West's Response to American Fugitive Slaves* (Millwood, NY: Associated Faculty Press, 1985), 4; Clinton, *Harriet Tubman,* 99; and see the Imperial Act of 1790.

7. Cooper, *The Hanging of Angelique,* 68.

8. Winks, *Blacks in Canada,* 25, 96.

9. See Mary Beacock Fryer and Christopher Dracott, *John Graves Simcoe, 1752–1806: A Biography* (Toronto, ON: Dundurn Press, 1998).

10. Walker, *Race on Trial,* 28; Jacqueline Tobin, with Hettie Jones, *From Midnight to Dawn: The Last Tracks of the Underground Railroad* (New York, NY: Anchor Books, 2007), 152–53. Afua Cooper explained: "We know very little about Cooley. We do not know her age, her marital status, or even if she had children. She remains in the shadows, silenced. But in March 1793, as Vrooman threw the slave woman in the boat, she 'screamed violently and made resistance'" (Cooper, *The Hanging of Angelique,* 104). See also Adrienne Shadd, "Chloe Cooley and the 1793 Act to Limit Slavery in Upper Canada" (unpublished report to Ontario Heritage Trust, 2007).

11. J. R. Kerr-Ritchie, *Rites of August First: Emancipation in the Black Atlantic World* (Baton Rouge: Louisiana State University Press, 2007), 123.

12. Ira Berlin and Leslie M. Harris, eds., *Slavery in New York* (New York, NY: New Press, 2005), 113–33.

13. See David N. Gellman, *Emancipating New York: The Politics of Slavery and Freedom, 1777–1827* (Baton Rouge: Louisiana State University Press, 2006); "Abolition of Slavery," *Freedom's Journal,* July 6, 1827; *Farmers' Journal & Welland Canal Intelligencer* (St. Catharines), May 2, 1827; "Gov. Tompkin's Letter to the Legislation of New York," *Freedom's Journal,* July 13, 1827; *Farmers' Journal,* July 9, 1828.

14. "Papers of Margaret H. Hall," MMC 618, Manuscript Reading Room, Letter no. 5, Library of Congress, Washington, DC. Margaret was the wife of Captain Basil Hall and she accompanied her husband on a trip around North America in 1827–28. See Captain Basil Hall, *Travels in North America in the Years 1827 and 1828* (Edinburgh: Cadell and Co., 1829).

15. David Ruggles et al., "First Annual Report of the Committee of Vigilance for the Protection of People of Color" (1837) in Richard Newman, Patrick Rael, and Philip Lapsansky, eds., *Pamphlets*

of Protest: An Anthology of Early African-American Protest Literature, 1790–1860 (New York, NY: Routledge, 2000), 150; and *Farmers' Journal* (St. Catharines), July 18, 1827.

16. Berlin and Harris, *Slavery in New York,* 139; and Steward, *Twenty-Two Years a Slave,* 150–51.

17. Silverman, *Unwelcome Guests,* 12.

18. Peter P. Hinks, ed., *David Walker's Appeal to the Coloured Citizens of the World* (1829; rpr. University Park: Pennsylvania State University Press, 2000), 43. See Van Gosse, "As a Nation, the English Are Our Friends': The Emergence of African American Politics in the British Atlantic World, 1772–1861," *American Historical Review* (Oct. 2008): 1003–28. Also, the Lieutenant-Governor of Upper Canada Sir John Colborne (later Lord Seaton) encouraged Blacks "on your side of the line [in the United States]," to "come to us." This call was mainly directed to Blacks seeking settlement in the Detroit frontier, but a number of those in the Niagara region, like Austin Steward, heeded this favorable invitation. Winks explained the full quote: "Legend holds that Colborne replied" to a Negro colonization group, "Tell the Republicans on your side of the line that we do not know men by their color. If you come to us, you will be entitled to all the privileges of the rest of his Majesty's subjects" (Winks, *Blacks in Canada,* 155–56).

19. Michael Power and Nancy Butler, *Slavery and Freedom in Niagara* (Niagara-on-the-Lake, ON: Niagara Historical Society, 1993), 31. Also see Seymour Drescher, *The Mighty Experiment: Free Labor versus Slavery in British Emancipation* (New York, NY: Oxford University Press, 2004).

20. Power and Butler, *Slavery and Freedom in Niagara,* 31. "Apprenticeship" labor meant indentured servitude.

21. Matthew Mason, "The Battle of the Slaveholding Liberators: Great Britain, the United States, and Slavery in the Early Nineteenth Century," *William and Mary Quarterly* 59, no. 3 (July 2002): 665–96; and Joe Bassette Wilkins Jr., "Window on Freedom: The South's Response to the Emancipation of the Slaves in the British West Indies, 1833–1861" (PhD diss., University of South Carolina, 1977); Philip Girard, Jim Phillips, and Blake Brown, *A History in Law in Canada, Vol 1: Beginnings to 1866.* (Toronto, ON: University of Toronto Press, 2018), quote 633–68.

22. Kerr-Ritchie, *Rites of August First,* 1.

23. Sawallisch, *Fugitive Borders,* 53.

24. Natasha L. Henry, *Emancipation Day: Celebrating Freedom in Canada* (Toronto, ON: Dundurn Press, 2010), 26–27; Jason H. Silverman, "Monarchical Liberty and Republican Slavery: West Indies Emancipation Celebrations in Upstate New York and Canada West," *Afro-Americans in New York Life History* 10 (January): 7–18.

25. Miller, *Borderline Crime,* 114–52; and Girard, Phillips, and Brown, *A History in Law in Canada, Vol. 1,* 662–82.

26. Boyd, *Black Detroit,* 27–34; and *Detroit Journal and Advertiser,* July 19, 1833. See also Frost, *I've Got a Home in Glory Land.*

27. Power and Butler, *Slavery and Freedom in Niagara,* 49.

28. Gary Botting, *Extradition Between Canada and the United States* (Ardsley, NY: Transnational Publishers, Inc., 2005), 49–78. See also Arnett G. Lindsay, "Diplomatic Relations Between the United States and Great Britain Bearing on the Return of Negro Slaves," *Journal of Negro History* 5 (Oct. 1920): 391–419.

29. "Surrender of Runaway Slaves," *St. Catharines Journal,* February 27, 1840.

30. *Niagara Reporter,* September 21, 1837; *St. Catharines Journal,* September 21, 1837, and Sep-

tember 28, 1837. See also Janet Carnochan. "Slave Rescue in Niagara Sixty Years Ago." *Niagara Historical Society* 2 (1897), 8–18.

31. Frost, *I've Got a Home in Glory Land,* 239–46; David Murray, "Hands across the Border: The Abortive Extradition of Solomon Moesby," *Canadian Historical Review of American Studies* 30 (2000): 186–209; Roman J. Zorn, "Criminal Extradition Menaces the Canadian Haven for Fugitive Slaves, 1841–1861," *Canadian Historical Review* 38 (Dec. 1957): 284–94.

32. "Petition of African Canadians, Niagara," September 2, 1837, Canada National Archives, RG1, E1, 49.

33. Roman J. Zorn, "An Arkansas Fugitive Slave Incident and Its International Repercussions," *Arkansas Historical Quarterly* 16, no. 2 (Summer, 1957): 139–49; and S. Charles Bolton, *Fugitives from Injustice: Freedom-Seeking Slaves in Arkansas: Historic Resource Study* (Scotts Valley, CA: CreateSpace Independent Publishing Platform, 2013), 17–18, 65–66, 86. This is a National Park Service (NPS) and National Underground Railroad Network to Freedom work. See also "Another Family Are Free," *Voice of the Fugitive,* June 18, 1851.

34. Walker, *Race on Trial,* 34; Frost, *I've Got a Home,* 246–52; Botting, *Extradition Between Canada and the United States,* 78.

35. Webster-Ashburton Treaty, Article 10. See Howard Jones, *To the Webster-Ashburton Treaty: A Study in Anglo-American Relations, 1783–1843* (Chapel Hill: University of North Carolina Press, 1977); Francis M. Carroll, *A Good and Wise Measure: The Search for the Canadian-American Boundary, 1783–1842* (Toronto, ON: University of Toronto Press, 2001); and Jeffrey R. Kerr-Ritchie, *Rebellious Passage: The Creole Revolt and America's Coastal Slave Trade* (New York, NY: Cambridge University Press, 2019), 171–213.

36. Fred Landon, "The Anderson Fugitive Case," *Journal of Negro History* 7, no. 3 (July 1923): 233–42; and Patrick Brode, *The Odyssey of John Anderson* (Toronto, ON: University of Toronto Press, 1989).

37. Loguen, *The Rev. J. W. Loguen as a Slave and a Freeman,* 335–36; and *Douglass' Monthly,* May 1859.

38. Loguen, *The Rev. J. W. Loguen as a Slave and a Freeman,* 344.

39. Historian Allan Greer argued that the Rebellions of 1837–1838 had "internal diversities," but were a "single historical phenomenon," meaning it was a "Rebellion." Others like Michel Ducharme, Maxime Dagenais, and Julien Mauduit follow in this claim of the "Canadian Rebellion." Allan Greer, "1837–38: Rebellion Reconsidered," *Canadian Historical Review* 76, no 1 (1995), 8; Michel Ducharme, *The Idea during the Age of Atlantic Revolutions* (Montreal: McGill-Queen's University Press, 2014); and Maxime Dagenais and Julien Mauduit, eds., *Revolutions across Borders: Jacksonian American and the Canadian Rebellion* (Montreal: McGill-Queen's University Press, 2019).

40. Allan Greer, *The Patriots and the People: The Rebellion of 1837 in Rural Lower Canada* (Toronto, ON: University of Toronto Press, 1993); Greer, "1837–38: Rebellion Reconsidered," 1–18; Andrew Bonthius, "The Patriot War of 1837–1838: Locofocoism with a Gun?" *Labour/Le Travail* 52 (Fall 2003): 9–43; William Kilbourn, *The Firebrand: William Lyon Mackenzie and the Rebellion in Upper Canada* (Toronto, ON: Dundurn Press, 2008); Frank Murray Greenwood and Barry Wright, *Canadian State Trials: Rebellion and Invasion in the Canadas, 1837–1839, Vol. 2* (Toronto, ON: University of Toronto Press, 1990); Michel Ducharme, *Le concept de liberté au Canada à l'époque des Révolutions atlantiques 1776–1838.* (Montreal: McGill-Queens University Press, 2010); Christopher Raible, "'A Journey Undertaken Under Peculiar Circumstances': The Perilous Escape of William Lyon Mack-

enzie, December 7 to 11, 1837," *Ontario History* 108, no. 2 (Autumn 2016); 131–55; R. A. MacKay, "The Political Ideas of William Lyon Mackenzie," *Canadian Journal of Economics and Political Science* 3, no. 1 (Feb. 1937): 1–22; Dagenais and Mauduit, *Revolutions across Borders;* Stephen R. I. Smith, *Violence, Order, and Unrest: A History of British North America, 1749–1876* (Toronto, ON: University of Toronto Press, 2019).

41. The Patriot War, led by Scotland-born Mackenzie, involved some 150,000 men in an American-Canadian secret association who supported the initial wave of the rebellion. On December 13, 1837, they established a self-proclaimed government on Navy Island in the Niagara River just upstream from Niagara Falls. The Royal Navy attacked the island, forcing Mackenzie and coconspirators to withdraw to Buffalo for safety. Many found refuge in Western New York, while Mackenzie retreated to New York City. In January 1839, he moved to Rochester and for several months attempted to persuade Canadian exiles in the borderlands to launch a second invasion of Upper Canada. Eventually, Mackenzie left Rochester after being unable to galvanize backing for another attack (Lillan F. Gates, *After the Rebellion: The Later Years of William Lyon Mackenzie* [Toronto, ON: Dundurn Press, 1996]). Historian Thomas Richards Jr. explained the "Americans made up a majority of the patriot forces" and the "Americans and Canadians were most likely socially and culturally indistinguishable from one another, a result of the ubiquitous connections of the Great Lakes borderland" (Dagenais and Mauduit, *Revolutions across Borders,* 97).

42. Thomas Jefferson Sutherland to Van Rensselaer, December 1837 and January 1838, Mackenzie-Lindsey Fonds, Ontario Archives, Toronto, ON; Fred Landon, "Canadian Negroes and the Rebellion of 1837," *Journal of Negro History* 7, no. 4 (Oct. 1922): 377–79; Gerald Horne, *Negro Comrades of the Crown: African Americans and the British Empire Fight the U.S. Before Emancipation* (New York, NY: New York University Press, 2012), 114–19.

43. Loguen, *The Rev. J. W. Loguen as a Slave and a Freeman,* 345, and his full description of the Patriot War and aftermath on 343–46. See also these classic works: Landon, "Canadian Negroes and the Rebellion of 1837"; William P. Shortridge, "The Canadian-American Frontier during the Rebellions of 1837–1838," *Canadian Historical Review* 7 (March 1926): 13–26; Wayne Edward Kelly, "Canada's Black Defenders: Former Slaves Answered the Call to Arms," *Beaver* 77 (April–May 1997): 31–34; Orrin Edward Tiffany, "The Relations of the United States to the Rebellion of 1837–1838," *Buffalo Historical Society Publication* 8 (1905): 7–147, as well as T. P. Dunning, "The Canadian Rebellions of 1837–38: An Episode in Northern Borderland History," *Australasian Journal of American Studies* 14, no. 2 (Dec. 1995): 31–47; and Marc L. Harris, "The Meaning of Patriot: The Canadian Rebellion and American Republicanism, 1837–1839," *Michigan Historical Review* 23, no. 1 (Spring, 1997): 33–69.

44. Milton C. Sernett, *Abolition's Axe: Beriah Green, Oneida Institute and the Black Freedom Struggle* (Syracuse, NY: Syracuse University Press, 1986); Milton C. Sernett, "First Honor: Oneida Institute's Role in the Fight Against American Racism and Slavery," *New York History* 66, no. 2 (April 1985): 101–22; and Hunter, *To Set the Captives Free,* 54–57.

45. *Colored American,* May 15, 1841; and Hunter, *To Set the Captives Free,* 52–73.

46. See Delbanco, *The War Before the War,* 6, 204, 261; Manisha Sinha, *The Slave's Cause: A History of Abolition* (New Haven, CT: Yale University Press, 2016), 527, 542; Paul Finkelman, *Millard Fillmore: The American Presidents Series: The 13th President, 1850–1853* (New York, NY: Times Books, 2011); and "Good—growing out of Evil—Fillmorism," *Provincial Freeman,* October 14, 1854. Fillmore became president after Zachary Taylor died suddenly on July 9, 1850.

47. Loguen, *The Rev. J. W. Loguen, as a Slave and as a Freeman,* 341–45, 393–94; and Angela Murphy, "'It Outlaws Me, and I Outlaw It': Resistance to the Fugitive Slave Law in Syracuse, New York," *Afro-Americans in New York Life History* 28, no. 1 (January 2004).

48. *Frederick Douglass' Paper,* August 21, 1851.

49. See Jayme A. Sokolow, "The Jerry McHenry Rescue and the Growth of Northern Antislavery Sentiment during the 1850s," *Journal of American Studies* 16, no. 3 (Dec., 1982): 427–45; Monique Patenaude Roach, "The Rescue of William 'Jerry' Henry: Antislavery and Racism in the Burned-Over District," *New York History* 82, no. 2 (Spring 2001): 135–54; Angela F. Murphy, *The Jerry Rescue: The Fugitive Slave Law, Northern Rights, and the American Sectional Crisis* (New York, NY: Oxford University Press, 2014); Samuel Ringgold Ward, *Autobiography of a Fugitive Negro: His Anti-Slavery Labours in the United States, Canada, and England* (London: John Snow, 1855), where he stated of the rescue that it was ironic "A man in chains, [was] in Syracuse! . . . They say he is a slave. What a term to apply to an American! How does this sound beneath the pole of liberty and the flag of freedom" (122–25).

50. *Syracuse Standard,* September 24, 1850, and October 7, 1850; *Syracuse Daily Star,* October 4, 1851; *New York Daily Star,* October 2, 1851.

51. Roach, "The Rescue of William 'Jerry' Henry," 142.

52. *Syracuse Daily Standard,* October 6, 1851.

53. Hiram Wilson to George Whipple, November 5, 1851, and December 17, 1851, American Missionary Association Archives, Tulane University. Jermain Wesley Loguen to Washington Hunt, December 2, 1851, reprinted in *The Liberator* May 14, 1852. See also Jermain Wesley Loguen to Rev. Joseph R. Johnson, December 18, 1851, in *Frederick Douglass' Paper,* January 8, 1852, p. 2, cols. 2–3. Hunt was the seventeenth governor of New York and was in office from January 1, 1851, to December 31, 1852.

54. *Frederick Douglass' Paper,* January 8, 1852, and May 6, 1852; and *Syracuse Standard,* June 28, 1852, Loguen's friends held a fundraiser for him and his family at Market Hall in Syracuse.

55. Loguen, *The Rev. J. W. Loguen as a Slave and a Freeman,* 208–9; and Rev. Jermain Wesley Loguen to Henry Bibb, August 13, 1852, in *Voice of the Fugitive,* September 9, 1852. See also *Syracuse Standard,* October 2, 1851.

56. See the 1850 reaction of Hiram Wilson to President Fillmore and Attorney General Crittenden. Wilson explained they will "strengthen the fiendish purpose of slave-hunters and kidnappers; and in all the range of cities and towns which lie near the Northern frontier of slavery, the colored people, whether bond or free, will be unsafe. I would not sound a note of alarm without cause, but, in pro-slavery localities, I tremble for the colored people. May the Lord in mercy raise up a numerous and powerful army of Samaritans" (*The Liberator,* October 25, 1850).

57. Bordewich, *Bound for Canaan,* 410–11.

58. *Syracuse Standard,* January 3, 1855, and December 13, 1856.

59. *Syracuse Standard,* April 16, 1857, and September 30, 1857.

60. Loguen to Dear Friend, July 1859, AMA Archives; *Syracuse Standard,* April 20, 1859; and *Douglass' Monthly,* February, March, and July 1859.

61. James Oliver Horton and Lois E. Horton, *In Hope of Liberty: Culture, Community, and Protest Among Northern Free Blacks, 1700–1860* (New York, NY: Oxford University Press, 1997), 60. Wayne, "The Black Population of Canada West on the Eve of the American Civil War," 465–81. See

William Still, *The Underground Railroad* (Philadelphia, PA: Porter and Coates, 1872), 598; and *The Liberator,* December 13, 1850.

62. Vanessa D. Dickerson speaks of "Black America's romance with Victorian Britain" in *Dark Victorians* (Champaign: University of Illinois Press, 2008), 4. See also Gretchen Holbrook Gerzina, ed., *Black Victorians, Black Victoriana* (New Brunswick, NJ: Rutgers University Press, 2003). This work highlights how Blacks esteemed England over the United States in the nineteenth and early twentieth centuries.

63. *Douglass' Monthly,* September 1860.

64. *Frederick Douglass' Paper,* June 24, 1852, and February 4, 1853; Hepburn, *Crossing the Border,* 95. See Silverman, "Monarchial Liberty and Republican Slavery," 7–18.

65. *Douglass' Monthly,* September 1860; and Kerr-Ritchie, *Rebellious Passage,* chap. 1, "Eagle verse Lion."

66. *Frederick Douglass' Paper,* August 12, 1858. See also *Ontario Messenger,* January 19, 1842; "Celebration by the Colored People, *Daily Democrat* (Rochester), August 1, 1848; *North Star,* August 4, 1848; "Speech of H. W. Johnson," *Frederick Douglass' Paper,* April 15, 1852; and Preston E. Pierce, "Liberian Dreams, West African Nightmare, Part One," *Rochester History* no. 4 (Fall 2004): 1–24. It appears that Henry W. Johnson's son Henry G. Johnson, born in 1846, grew up to be a barber, eventually married, and had five children. However, he deserted his family and left for St. Catharines "with a white woman" (*Rochester Union and Advertiser,* August 15, 1885).

67. *Syracuse Standard,* June 2, 1860.

68. Philip S. Foner, ed., *The Life and Writings of Frederick Douglass, 5 vols.* (New York, NY: International Publishers, 1950–75), vol. 2, 95 (first quote); John W. Blassingame, ed., *The Frederick Douglass Papers, 5 vols.* (New Haven: Yale University Press, 1979–92), vol. 2, 417–18 (second quote).

69. See Gosse, "As a Nation, the English Are Our Friends," 1003–28; and Melvin L. Rogers, "David Walker and the Political Power of Appeal," *Political Theory* 43, no. 2 (April 2015): 208–33.

70. There is a wealth of resources on Blacks in the American North. The historiography includes the classic works of Arthur Zilversmit, Leon Litwack, James Oliver Horton and Lois E. Horton as well as Harry Reed, *Platform for Change: The Foundations of the Northern Free Black Community, 1775–1865* (East Lansing: Michigan State University Press, 1994); Leonard P. Curry, *The Free Black in Urban America, 1800–1850: The Shadow of the Dream* (Chicago: University of Chicago Press, 1981); and Patrick Rael, *Black Identity and Black Protest in the Antebellum North* (Chapel Hill: University of North Carolina Press, 2002).

71. Bordewich, *Bound for Canaan,* 350.

72. Sarah Bradford, *Scenes in the Life of Harriet Tubman* (Auburn, NY: W. J. Moses, 1869 and 1926), 18.

73. Stevens, *Anthony Burns: A History,* 179.

74. Thomas Smallwood, *A Narrative of Thomas Smallwood, (Coloured Man:) Giving an Account of His Birth—The Period He Was Held in Slavery—His Release—and Removal to Canada, etc. . . .* (Toronto: Smallwood; James Stephens, 1851), 45. See also Sawallisch, Fugitive Borders, 59–99.

75. Smallwood, *Narrative,* 44.

76. Colaiaco, *Frederick Douglass and the Fourth of July,* 115.

77. Frederick Douglass, *Life and Times of Frederick Douglass* (Mineola, NY: Dover Publications, 2003), 190; and Bernard R. Boxill, "Douglass against the Emigrationists," in Bill Lawson and Frank

Kirkland, eds., *Frederick Douglass: A Critical Reader* (Malden, MA: Blackwell Publishers, Inc., 1999), 21–49.

78. Solomon Northup explained, "I have been in Montreal and Kingston, and Queenston, and a great many places in Canada, and I have been in [New] York State, too—in Buffalo, and Rochester, and Albany," indicating his past fluid international and Western New York travels as a workman on the Champlain and Erie Canals. Solomon Northup, *Twelve Years a Slave: Narrative of Solomon Northup, a Citizen of New-York, Kidnapped in Washington City in 1841, and Rescued in 1853* (Auburn, NY: Derby and Miller, 1853), 269–70, 23. See also David A. Fiske, Clifford W. Brown, and Rachel Seligman, *Solomon Northup: The Complete Story of the Author of Twelve Years a Slave* (New York, NY: Praeger, 2013), chaps. "The Journey South" and "Rescue"; and *New York Times*, January 20, 1853. See also Richard Bell, *Stolen: Five Free Boys Kidnapped Into Slavery and Their Astonishing Odyssey Home* (New York, NY: Simon & Schuster, 2019).

79. Scott Christianson, *Freeing Charles: The Struggle to Free a Slave on the Eve of the Civil War* (Champaign: University of Illinois Press, 2010), 102.

80. Christianson, *Freeing Charles*, 74–112; and *Douglass' Monthly*, June 1860. The full article states: "Charles Nalle, the fugitive who was rescued twice from the official kidnappers at Troy has arrived safely at St. Catharines, C. W.—The friends of the fugitive in Troy have raised $1,000 to purchase his freedom." See also "A 'Jerry Rescue' in Troy," *Tory Daily Times*, April 27, 1859; *Tory Whig*, April 28, 1859; and *The Liberator*, May 4, 1860.

81. Steward, *Twenty-Two Years a Slave*, 325.

82. Isaac D. Williams and William F. Goldie, *Sunshine and Shadow of Slave Life, Reminiscences as told by Isaac D. Williams to "Tege"* (East Saginaw, MI: Evening News Printing and Binding House, 1885), 47–49.

83. William C. Nell to William Lloyd Garrison, February 19, 1852, and published in *The Liberator*, March 5, 1852.

84. "Underground," *Niagara Falls Gazette* (Niagara Falls, New York), September 22, 1858.

85. *Provincial Freeman*, May 24, 1856.

86. Frederick Douglass, "My Escape From Slavery," *Century Illustrated Magazine* 23, n.s. I (Nov. 1881): 127.

87. Sinha, *The Slave's Cause*.

88. See Benjamin Quarles, *Black Abolitionists* (New York, Oxford University Press, 1969). This book is one of the first treatments to outright claim that Blacks were the backbone of the abolitionist movement in the United States.

89. John S. Jacobs, *A True Tale of Slavery. From The Leisure Hour: A Family Journal of Instruction and Recreation*, February 7, 14, 21, 28, 1861 (London: Stevens and Co., 1861), 141.

90. See Wong, *Neither Fugitive nor Free*.

91. Steven Hahn, *The Political Worlds of Slavery and Freedom* (Cambridge, MA: Harvard University Press, 2009).

92. Blackett, *Captive's Quest for Freedom*, 357.

93. Colaiaco, *Frederick Douglass and the Fourth of July*, 115–16.

94. *North Star*, July 6, 1848; *The Liberator*, July 13, 1849; "New York," *Voice of the Fugitive*, July 1, 1852; and C. James Trotman, *Frederick Douglass: A Biography* (Santa Barbara, CA: Greenwood, 2011), 52–56.

95. Drew, *The Refugee,* 80 and 34.

96. Bordewich, *Bound for Canaan,* 113.

97. Siebert, *The Underground Railroad from Slavery to Freedom,* 197.

98. Samuel Gridley Howe, *The Refugees from Slavery in Canada West: Report to the Freedmen's Inquiry Commission* (Boston: Wright and Potter, 1864), 11.

99. dann j. Broyld, "Fannin' Flies and Tellin' Lies: Black Runaways and American Tales of Life in British Canada Before the Civil War," *American Review of Canadian Studies* 44, no. 2 (April 2014): 169–86.

100. Howe, *Refugees from Slavery,* 161, 17.

101. Lower Canada and/or Canada East were the southern half of modern-day Quebec and stretched along the St. Lawrence River to Newfoundland and Labrador.

102. "For the Voice of the Fugitive," *Voice of the Fugitive,* November 5, 1851. The writer made plans to move to Chatham and requested to be an agent to build the paper's subscriptions in Montreal.

103. Gary Collison, *Shadrach Minkins: From Fugitive to Citizen* (Cambridge: Harvard University Press, 1997). See also *Voice of the Fugitive,* February 26, 1851. Henry Bibb criticized the government's actions to recapture Shadrach Minkins and comments on the public response.

104. Frank Mackey, *Black Then: Blacks and Montreal 1780s–1880s* (Montreal: McGill-Queen's University Press, 2004), 120–26, and 139–47. See also Gary Collison, "'Loyal and Dutiful Subjects of Her Gracious Majesty, Queen Victoria' Fugitive Slaves in Montreal, 1850–1866," *Quebec Studies* 19 (1994–95): 59–70. For more on Israel Lewis in Rochester and his death in Montreal, see Steward, *Twenty-Two Years a Slave,* 176–78, and 283. See also Henry David Thoreau, *A Yankee on Canada* (1866; rpr. Portland, OR: WestWinds Press, 2016). In 1850, Thoreau wrote about his journey to the region of Montreal and Quebec City.

105. John W. Lewis (Stanstead, Canada East) to Frederick Douglass (Rochester, New York) on March 20, 1855, printed in the *Frederick Douglass' Paper,* April 27, 1855.

106. Glazebrook, *A History of Transportation in Canada,* 153, 161–64, 169.

107. Still, *The Underground Railroad* (London: Benediction Books, 2008), 269–70. Letters written from James H. Forman (Niagara Falls, New York) to William Still (Philadelphia), June 5 and July 24, 1856, in Still's *The Underground Railroad;* and 1861 Canada Census.

108. Bradford, *Scenes in the Life of Harriet Tubman,* 28.

109. Ward, *Autobiography,* 176–77.

110. William E. Abbott to Maria G. Porter, November 29, 1856, Rochester Ladies' Anti-Slavery Society Records, William L. Clements Library, University of Michigan, Ann Arbor.

111. Drew, *The Refugee,* 23; *Rochester Daily Union,* November 30, 1853; *The Globe* (Toronto) September 13, 1851. See also Karolyn Smardz Frost, *Steal Away Home: One Woman's Epic Flight to Freedom and Her Long Road Back to the South* (Toronto, ON: HarperCollins Publishers, 2017), 45.

112. Smallwood, *Narrative,* 43.

113. William Wells Brown, *Narrative,* 109.

114. *Frederick Douglass' Paper,* December 11, 1851; Rochester City Directory, 1849; C. Peter Ripley, ed., *The Black Abolitionist Papers, Vol. 2: Canada 1830–1865* (Chapel Hill: University of North Carolina Press, 1987), 224–32. Ironically, Captain Robert Kerr later became the captain of a ship named *America.*

115. Ward, *Autobiography*, 175–76. See also Jeffrey R. Kerr-Ritchie, *Freedom's Seekers: Essays on the Comparative Emancipation* (Baton Rouge: Louisiana State University Press, 2013), chap. 4, "Samuel Ward and the Making of an Imperial Subject," 87–100.

116. Ward, *Autobiography*, 175.

117. Henson, *Truth Stranger Than Fiction*, 120–27. Josiah Henson produced several different versions of his narrative, including two initial versions in 1849 and 1858, followed by 1876, 1877, and 1890 editions that appeared in England, in the United States in 1879, and in British Canada in 1881. While sections of the narrative are reprinted without alternations, other parts add more detail and dialogue to the core story.

118. Francis Frederick, *Autobiography of Rev. Francis Frederick, of Virginia* (Baltimore: J. W. Woods, Printer, 1869), 34–35.

119. Isaac Mason, *Life of Isaac Mason as a Slave* (Worcester, MA: s.n. 1893), 60–66.

120. W. Jeffrey Bolster, *Black Jacks: African American Seamen in the Age of Sail* (Cambridge: Harvard University Press, 1997), 190–91.

121. Frost, *Steal Away Home*, 47–50, 130.

122. For the request of Holmes to go to Liberia, see Charles Cummins to Samuel Wilkerson, July 8, 1840, American Colonization Society Papers, Incoming Correspondence, Reel 34, A78, pt.1, Library of Congress; and Hiram Wilson (Toronto) to Joshua Leavitt (New York), in *The Emancipator*, reprinted in *Colored American*, September 19, 1840. The entire manumission document is in *The Emancipator*, September 10, 1840. See also Marie Tyler-McGraw, *An African Republic: Black and White Virginians in the Making of Liberia* (Chapel Hill, NC: University of North Carolina Press, 2014); and Eric Burin, *Slavery and the Peculiar Solution: A History of the American Colonization Society* (Gainesville, FL: University of Florida, 2005).

123. Hiram Wilson to William Goodell, copied in *The Emancipator*, September 10, 1840.

124. *St. Catharines Journal*, April 27, 1842; and Frost, *Steal Away Home*, 42–46.

125. Still, *The Underground Railroad* (Philadelphia, PA: Porter and Coates, 1872), 228–29; *St. Catharines Standard*, June 9, 1989; Debra Ann Yeo, "Niagara's Freedom Trail," *What's Up Niagara Magazine* (Oct. 1993), 10–16. I personally talked with Donna M. Ford (St. Catharines) a descendent of Adam Nicholson on Thursday, October 5, 2017. Ford could neither confirm nor deny the family lore.

126. Still, *The Underground Railroad* (London: Benediction Books, 2008), 228–29. Please note that the entry on Adam Nicholson in William Still's published book is different from the original transcript held at the Pennsylvania Historical Society (Philadelphia's Library of American History, Philadelphia, PA). Nicholson was owned by Aaron Myers and not by "Alexander Hill, a drunkard, gambler, &c." Also, in the published account William Still wrongly attributed to Adam's fellow runaway, Reuben Bowles (alias Cunnigan), that "the sight of one of his eyes had been very much injured." It was Adam Nicholson who had the damaged eye, an injury that was still apparent in his appearance decades later when he was in the greater St. Catharines area. Fred Parnell, "The Colored Village," in *The Days of Long Ago*, 36; see the manuscript memoir as it was published as columns in the *St. Catharines Standard*, 1946–49 (St. Catharines Museum, Ontario).

127. St. Catharines Census, 1871.

128. *Niagara Mail*, August 10, 1853; "Remarkable Incident. Escape of a Slave," *Patriot* (Toronto) August 4, 1853; "A Desperate Venture for Liberty," *St. Catharines Journal*, August 11, 1853; and "Daring Attempt and Successful Escape of a Slave: Another Bold Stroke for Freedom," *National Anti-Slavery Standard*, August 20, 1853.

129. Bolster, *Black Jacks,* 190–91.

130. Captain Daniel Drayton of *The Pearl,* who tried to help over seventy slaves escape Washington, DC, in April of 1848, embodied much of the character of watermen when he explained, "I had found out, by intercourse with the negroes, that they had the same desires, wishes and hopes as myself," and that "God had made of one flesh all the nations of the earth." See Daniel Drayton, *Personal Memoir of Daniel Drayton, for Four Years and Four Months a Prisoner (for Charity's Sake) in Washington Jail, Including a Narrative of the Voyage and Capture of the Schooner Pearl* (Boston: B. Marsh, 1854); *Daily Union* (Washington, DC), April 19, 1848; Josephine F. Pacheco, *The Pearl: A Failed Slave Escape on the Potomac* (Chapel Hill: University of North Carolina Press, 2005); and Mary Kay Ricks, "Escape on The Pearl," *Washington Post,* August 12, 1998, H1, H4–5.

131. See Taylor, *Transportation Revolution;* and dann j. Broyld, "The Underground Railroad as Afrofuturism: Enslaved Blacks Who Imagined a Future and Used Technology to Reach the 'Outer Spaces of Slavery,'" *Journal of Ethnic and Cultural Studies* 6, no. 3 (2019): 171–84.

132. "Niagara Falls as a Railroad Station," *Niagara Falls Gazette* (New York), May 17, 1854.

133. See Tendai Mutunhu, "John W. Jones: Underground Railroad Station-Master," *Negro History Bulletin* (March–April 1978): 814–18; and Lawrence J. Friedman, "The Gerrit Smith Circle: Abolitionism in the Burned-Over District," *Civil War History* 26 (Mar. 1980): 18–38.

134. The scholarship on Black "responsibility" is immense. The works I have found most helpful include Frederick Cooper, "Elevating the Race: The Social Thought of Black Leaders, 1827–50," *American Quarterly* 24 (Dec. 1972): 604–25; Robert S. Levine, *Martin Delany, Frederick Douglass, and the Politics of Representative Identity* (Chapel Hill: University of North Carolina Press, 1997); Erica L. Ball, *To Live an Antislavery Life: Personal Politics and the Antebellum Black Middle Class* (Athens: University of Georgia Press, 2012).

135. Howe, *Refugees from Slavery,* 40.

136. Drew, *The Refugee,* 25.

137. Drew, *The Refugee,* 209–11.

138. Still, *The Underground Railroad* (London: Benediction Books, 2008), 514.

139. Simpson and Lovejoy, *Under the North Star,* 195.

140. Drew, *The Refugee,* 106–7.

141. *North Star,* March 23, 1849. See Cooper, "Elevating the Race"; and Kevin K. Gaines, *Uplifting the Race: Black Leadership, Politics, and Culture in the Twentieth Century* (Chapel Hill: University of North Carolina Press, 1996).

142. Simpson and Lovejoy, *Under the North Star,* 93–94.

143. Rhodes, *Mary Ann Shadd Cary,* 74–99; and Shirley J. Yee, "Finding a Place: Mary Ann Shadd Clay and the Dilemmas of Black Migration to Canada, 1850–1870," *Frontiers: A Journal of Women Studies* 18, no. 3 (1997): 1–16.

144. Shadd's newspaper colleague was equally active. Samuel Ringgold Ward toured Canada as a speaker for the Canadian Anti-Slavery Society. He was based in Toronto briefly before taking engagements in England and the Caribbean. Ward never returned to Canada. See Kerr-Ritchie, *Freedom's Seekers,* 87–100.

145. John W. Blassingame, ed., *Slave Testimony: Two Centuries of Letters, Speeches, Interviews, and Autobiographies* (Baton Rouge: Louisiana State University Press, 1977), 422–44; Rochester City Directory, 1845 and 1847.

146. In 1851–52, Mr. Morrison was a table waiter who lived at 32 Vine Street in Rochester. He

was listed in the 1850s as a waiter, butler, and barber. During the 1860s (1864, 1865, 1866, 1868, and 1869), he was living at 8 Vine Street in Rochester. The 1865 Rochester Census stated that he was half-Cherokee and born around 1819 in Illinois. Morrison died of paralysis in Rochester on November 21, 1869, and he was laid to rest in Mount Hope Cemetery in the "Flower City" (*Niagara Falls Gazette,* August 5, 1856, and "Obituary" *Niagara Falls Gazette,* November 24, 1869).

147. "Benjamin Pollard Holmes, widower, and Cecelia Jane Reynolds, spinster, both of the city of Toronto," November 19, 1846, Marriage Registers of St. James Anglican Church/Cathedral, York, 1800–1896, reprinted in John Ross Robertson, *Landmarks of Toronto,* vol. 3 (Toronto: John Ross Robertson, 1898), 395; and Frost, *Steal Away Home,* 57–60.

148. These Black families will be thoroughly discussed in chapter 2. See also Frost, *Steal Away Home,* 69, 134.

149. Toronto Tax Assessment Rolls (St. John's Ward) 1854, 1855, and 1856. On the latter two rolls, Cecelia claimed to be a "widow" because she was unsure of the whereabouts of her husband Benjamin. W. C. F. Caverhill, *Caverhill's Toronto City Directory for 1859–60* (Toronto, ON: W. C. F. Caverhill, 1859); "Died," *Toronto Globe,* August 27, 1859; and Frost, *Steal Away Home,* 118–40.

150. Still, *The Underground Railroad* (London: Benediction Books, 2008), 336–37; entry January 10, 1856, Sydney Howard Gay Papers, Rare Books and Manuscripts Library, Columbia University; see also Papson and Calarco, *Secret Lives,* 159; Rochester *Daily Democrat,* April 4, 1862; and Frost, *Steal Away Home,* 160, 164. Note that William Still misspelled or misread William Henry Larrison's last name as "Laminson."

151. Frost, *Steal Away Home,* 188–91.

152. Ward, *Autobiography of a Fugitive Negro,* 138.

2. ROCHESTER, NEW YORK

1. In the past, historical treatments of Rochester, beginning with Whitney R. Cross's classic 1950 publication *The Burned-Over District,* have associated the city with the geographic space west of the Catskill and Adirondack mountains and the religious revivals of the 1820s Second Great Awakening. This American-based treatment does not take into consideration its connections to neighboring British Canada. Milton C. Sernett's 2002 *North Star Country* is by and large a continuum of the scholarship created decades earlier by Cross and does not deal with Rochester as a transnational space.

2. Johnson, *A Shopkeeper's Millennium,* 17–19. See also James W. Darlington, "Peopling the Post-Revolutionary New York Frontier," *New York History* 74 (Oct. 1993): 341–81.

3. Dunbar's farm in Irondequoit was near present-day Winton Road North. See Dorothy S. Truesdale, ed., "American Travel Accounts of Early Rochester," *Rochester History* 16, no. 2 (April 1954): 1–24.

4. Rochester did not become a city until 1834. Prior to that time it was a village.

5. Ena L. Farley, "The African American Presence in the History of Western New York," *Afro-Americans in New York Life and History* 14, no. 1 (Jan. 31, 1990): 10.

6. Robert F. McNamara, "Charles Carroll of Belle Vue Co-Founder of Rochester," *Rochester History* 42, no. 4 (Oct. 1980): 1–28; and Steward, *Twenty-Two Years a Slave,* 126–27.

7. Robert Koch and Henry W. Clune, *The Genesee* (Syracuse, NY: Syracuse University Press, 1988), 38; Herman L. Fairchild, *The Rochester Canyon and the Genesee River Base-Levels* (Rochester, NY: Rochester Academy of Science, 1919), 1–56; Helen I. Cowan, *Charles Williamson: Genesee Promoter, Friend of Anglo-American Rapprochement* (Rochester, NY: Rochester Historical Society, 1941); and Helen I. Cowan, "Charles Williamson and the Southern Entrance to the Genesee Country," *New York History* 31 (1942): 260–74.

8. Lilliam Roemer, "The Genesee River During the War of 1812," *Rochester History* 53, no. 4 (Fall 1991): 1–30; and Ruth Marsh and Dorothy S. Truesdale, "War on Lake Ontario: 1812–1815," *Rochester History* 4, no. 4 (Oct. 1942): 1–24. By 1805, Charlotte was established as a port of entry and was equipped with custom collectors; now it is a neighborhood in Rochester (Joseph W. Barnes, "The Annexation of Charlotte," *Rochester History* 37, no. 1 [Jan. 1975]: 1–28).

9. Nathaniel Rochester Papers, Rochester Public Library, microfilm #5: no. 136, col. 3, Charles Carroll of Belle Vue (Washington, DC) to Nathaniel Rochester, July 25, 1812; and McNamara, "Charles Carroll of Belle Vue Co-Founder of Rochester," 6.

10. McKelvey, *Rochester on the Genesee*, 8–12; Manumission Record, signed by Nathaniel Rochester, freeing Benjamin and Casandra, January 29, 1811, Rochester Family Papers, Department of Rare Books and Special Collections, Rush Rhees Library, University of Rochester (hereafter cited as RFP-UR); Letter from Nathaniel Rochester to Charles Carroll, July 21, 1809, RFP-UR; Letters to Nathaniel Rochester from William B. Rochester, December 18, 1814, and January 5, 1815, RFP-UR.

11. Fannie Rochester Rogers, "Colonel Nathaniel Rochester," *Rochester Historical Society Publication Fund Series,* vol. 3 (Rochester, NY: Rochester Historical Society, 1924), 323; End of life thoughts by Nathaniel Rochester to His Children, October 31, 1830, RFP-UR; Blake McKelvey, "Colonel Nathaniel Rochester," *Rochester History* 24, no. 1 (Jan. 1962): 2; E. Anne Schaetzke, "Slavery in the Genesee Country," *Afro-Americans in New York Life and History* 22, no. 1 (Jan. 1998): 10–11; Farley, "The African American Presence in the History of Western New York," 11; Marilyn S. Nolte, Victoria Sandwick Schmitt, and Christine L. Ridarsky, "'We Called Her Anna': Nathaniel Rochester and Slavery in the Genesee Country," *Rochester History* 71, no. 1 (Spring 2009): 1–24; *Rochester Daily Advertiser,* September 9, 1851; and Ron Netsky, "Portrait of a Slave Trader: Confronting the Real Nathaniel Rochester," *City Newspaper,* February 11, 2004.

12. Steward, *Twenty-Two Years a Slave,* xii–xviii; and Sawallisch, *Fugitive Borders,* 151–97.

13. Steward, *Twenty-Two Years a Slave,* 108–9.

14. Steward, *Twenty-Two Years a Slave,* 128–29.

15. "Leaves from the Past—Rochester Twenty-Eight Years Ago," *Rochester Daily Democrat,* April 19, 1845, col. 2. The conservative *Rochester Union and Advertiser* newspaper took a Democratic stance and was not friendly toward the abolitionist cause. It called itself "the oldest daily newspaper in the country west of the Hudson River." On October 25, 1826, the first edition was published under the name of *the* (Rochester) *Daily Advertiser.* Daily papers were not common outside of large cities. By the Civil War, the *Union and Advertiser* dominated the afternoon newspaper field and benefited from the 1860s wartime era as sales and circulation increased. Alvah Strong's *Rochester Democrat* located on Main Street next door to Frederick Douglass's newspaper office was progressive and supported the ending of Black bondage. In fact, fugitive slaves escaping the American South commonly spent nights in the *Democrat's* composing room sleeping on old papers. William S. Falls, the foreman of the paper, would help the fugitives onward to Canada (Robert Marcotte, *Where They Fell: Stories*

of Rochester Area Soldiers in the Civil War [Franklin, VA: Q Publishing, 2002], 13); Papson and Calarco, *Secret Lives*, 95, 112; quote is from "An Independent Democratic Newspaper," *Rochester Union and Advertiser*, February 15, 1916). For more information on Rochester newspapers, see Paul Benton's "Rochester Journalism" in Edward R. Foreman, ed., *Centennial History of Rochester, New York* (Rochester, NY: Rochester Historical Society, 1932), 2:107–24; and Sharon Palmer, "The Newspapers of the Rochester Area During the Age of Homespun" (Central Library of Rochester and Monroe County, Local History & Genealogy Division, 1966).

16. Steward, *Twenty-Two Years a Slave*, 130–32; and Blake McKelvey, "Light and Shadows in Local Negro History," *Rochester History* 21, no. 4 (Oct. 1959): 2.

17. Steward, *Twenty-Two Years a Slave*, xix–xxi.

18. McKelvey, *Rochester on the Genesee*, 35–42; *Rochester Telegraph*, November 11, 1823; Thomas X. Grasso, "The Erie Canal and Rochester: Past, Present, and Future," *Rochester History* 72, no. 1 (Spring 2010): 1–26; and Blake McKelvey, "Rochester and the Erie Canal," *Rochester History* 11, nos. 3 and 4 (Fall 1949): 1–24.

19. Geneva and Utica, New York, were also rivals (McKelvey, *Rochester on the Genesee*, 22).

20. Steward, *Twenty-Two Years a Slave*, 150–64. The Black community in Rochester postponed the celebration of their emancipation in New York State until July 5 "so as not to interfere with the patriotic displays of our white brethren in commemoration of their freedom" ("130 Years Ago: 1827 Newspaper Gives You Look into City's Past," *Rochester Times-Union*, July 1, 1957; the quote was taken from the *Rochester Advertiser*, a predecessor of the *Times-Union*).

21. *Rochester Daily Telegraph*, June 28, 1828. The signers were all trustees of the local African church: Bosley Baker, Albert Hagerman, J. Green, a barber, Charles Smith, John Tatt, John Patten, William Allen, R. Jones, Isaac Gibbs and James Sharp, cartmen; Robert Wilkin. In 1818, Everard Peck & Co., a firm that also ran a bookstore in the city, founded the *Telegraph*. Derrick and Levi W. Sibley, who were pioneers of early journalism in Rochester, were responsible for running the *Telegraph*'s mechanical department. In 1824, Thurlow Weed (1791–1882), an early Whig "political boss" in Rochester and political advisor to William H. Seward, became the editor of the paper. The following year, he bought the newspaper and ran it with Robert W. Martin as a semiweekly (the *Semi-Weekly Telegraph*) until 1827, when Weed retired and turned over control to Martin. In 1828, the *Telegraph* became a daily, but a year later it merged with the *Rochester Daily Advertiser*, and in 1830 it united with the *Rochester Republican*. Palmer, "The Newspapers of the Rochester Area During the Age of Homespun."

22. United States 1830 Census.

23. See Charles F. Pond, "History of the Third Ward," *Publications of the Rochester Historical Society*, vol. 1, 71–81 (Rochester, NY: Rochester Historical Society, 1922).

24. Winks, *Blacks in Canada*, 162. See also Gabrielle Foreman, Jim Casey, and Sarah Lynn Patterson, eds., *The Colored Conventions Movement: Black Organizing in the Nineteenth Century* (Chapel Hill: University of North Carolina Press, 2021), 113–14, 116, 182, 198.

25. Steward, *Twenty-Two Years a Slave*, 183.

26. Steward, *Twenty-Two Years a Slave*, 184–86.

27. Steward, *Twenty-Two Years a Slave*, 179–80. Steward and his wife added two more children to family while in Canada. Ripley, *Black Abolitionist Papers*, 2:64.

28. Winks, *Blacks in Canada*, 158.

29. Austin Steward quotes are from his narrative and chap. 21: "Roughing in the Wilds of Can-

ada"; Tobin, *From Midnight to Dawn,* 15. See also Austin Steward and Benjamin Paul to John G. Stewart, *Liberator,* September 17, 1831, written in August of 1831; and Susanna Moodie, *Roughing It in the Bush* (1852).

30. James, *Life of Rev. Thomas James,* 6; and Peter Way, *Common Labor: Workers and the Digging of North American Canals* (Baltimore: Johns Hopkins University Press, 1997).

31. Roger E. Carp, "The Limits of Reform: Labor and Discipline on the Erie Canal." *Journal of the Early Republic* 10, no. 2 (Summer, 1990): 191–219.

32. James, *Life of Rev. Thomas James,* 6–9; *The Rights of Man,* April 26, 1834; McKelvey, "Lights and Shadows in the Local Negro History," 3–4; Rochester City Directory, 1841; and "Obituary," *Rochester Union and Advertiser,* April 18, 1891.

33. Austin Steward's quote is from the title of chap. 21 in his narrative *Twenty-Two Years a Slave.* There is an intellectual debate over whether Wilberforce was a "success" or "failure." See the "Introduction" by Jane H. Pease and William H. Pease to Steward's *Twenty-Two Years a Slave,* ix–xv; and Sawallisch, *Fugitive Borders,* 189–97.

34. Everard Peck, George A. Avery, Samuel D. Porter, Levi W. Sibley, Griffith Brothers & Co., and Edwin Scrantom are noted in Howard W. Coles, *The Cradle of Freedom: A History of the Negro in Rochester, Western New York and Canada* (Rochester, NY: 1941), 27.

35. Steward, *Twenty-Two Years a Slave,* quote 292–93; and see 290–99.

36. Musette S. Castle, "A Survey of the History of African Americans in Rochester, New York, 1800–1860," *Afro-Americans in New York Life and History* 13, no. 2 (July 31, 1989): 3. See also Blake McKelvey, "The History of Public Health in Rochester, New York," *Rochester History* 18, no. 3 (July 1956): 1–24.

37. Blake McKelvey, *Rochester, the Water-Power City, 1812–1854* (Cambridge, MA: Harvard University Press, 1945); and Paula Tarnapol Whitacre, *A Civil Life in an Uncivil Time: Julia Wilbur's Struggle for Purpose* (Lincoln, NE: Potomac Books, 2017), 9.

38. The milling center of the United States shifted to places such as Cincinnati, St. Louis, Milwaukee, and Minneapolis, closer to where wheat was being produced in the Midwest.

39. McKelvey, *Rochester on the Genesee,* 43–46; and Blake McKelvey, *Rochester, the Flower City, 1855–1890* (Cambridge, MA: Harvard University Press, 1945).

40. Harriet Jacobs to Amy Post [Rochester, May 1849], in Harriet A. Jacobs, *Incidents in the Life of a Slave Girl. Written by Herself, ed.* Lydia Maria Francis Child (1861; rpr. Cambridge, MA: Harvard University Press, 1987), 230.

41. Ruth Rosenberg-Naparsteack, *Rochester: A Pictorial History* (Virginia Beach, VA: Donning Co., 1989), 62. On a visit to town in 1814, Charles Carroll explained, "It promises to be the garden of the United States and is in fact so" (Nathaniel Rochester Papers, Rochester Public Library, no. 115, col. 4, MS "Journal and Observations of Charles Carroll of B. Vue" on a tour to examine the distilleries and paper mills of the Eastern States, April 1814).

42. US Census, 1840; Rochester City Directory, 1841, 1844, and 1851.

43. Rochester Census, 1840, 1850, and 1860; Rochester City Directory, 1851–52; and Jane H. Pease and William H. Pease, *Bound with Them in Chains: A Biographical History of the Antislavery Movement* (Westport, CT: Greenwood Press, 1972), 121.

44. "Sixth Annual Report," in the *Liberator,* March 17, 1848; Pease and Pease, *Bound with Them in Chains,* 125; and Winks, *Blacks in Canada,* 224–26.

45. For examples of Canada Mission annual reports, see Wilson to Editor, June 24, 1841, in *National Anti-Slavery Standard*, July 8, 1841; *Massachusetts Abolitionist* (Boston, 1839–41), February 11, 1841; *Liberator*, March 17, 1843; *Free American*, July 1, 1841; *American and Foreign Anti-Slavery Reporter*, September 1, 1842, and March 1, 1843; and Canada Mission, *Sixth Annual Report* and *Seventh Annual Report* (Rochester, NY: E. Shepard, 1844).

46. "A paper organization" from Pease and Pease, *Bound with Them in Chains*, 121; "a loose federation" from Simpson and Lovejoy, *Under the North Star*, 31–33; and "lacked any systematic plan" from Winks, *Blacks in Canada*, 224–26.

47. Letter, the Rev. Hiram Wilson, Boston, Massachusetts, to "Dear Brother," October 18, 1850, Archives of the American Missionary Association, Amistad Center, Tulane University, Document 51367. Wilson believed the CMC "never yet yielded up its charge."

48. Pease and Pease, *Bound with Them in Chains*, 132–35; "Rev. Hiram Wilson," *Colored American*, September 29, 1838; "More Practical Measures," *Colored American*, October 27, 1838; and "Bibles for the Refugees in Canada," *Voice of the Fugitive*, August 13, 1851.

49. Letter, Rev. Hiram Wilson, Boston, Massachusetts, to "Dear Brother," October 18, 1850, AMA Archives document 51367, Amistad Research Center, Tulane University, New Orleans.

50. Letter, Lewis Tappan, Corresponding Secretary, American Missionary Association, November 6, 1850, to other members of the Board of the Association (AMA Archives document 79992, Amistad Center, Tulane University); and Letter Rev. Hiram Wilson (St. Catharines) to George Whipple (New York City), December 16, 1850 (AMA Archives document Fl121). These letters discuss the pay offered to Wilson.

51. See Julia Wilbur Large Diary, Haverford College, Quaker and Special Collections, Pennsylvania, Haverford, May 11, 1852.

52. dann j. Broyld, "Rochester, New York: A Transnational Community for Blacks Prior to the Civil War," *Rochester History* 72, no. 2 (Fall 2010): 1–23; and Blight, *Frederick Douglass*, 194–96.

53. Farley, "The African American Presence in the History of Western New York," 13; and Foner, *Frederick Douglass*, 5:83. Du Bois, *The City of Frederick Douglass*, 13. The office was located in the Talman Building.

54. *Rochester Daily Advertiser*, December 18, 1847. Early on, Douglass enlisted Martin Delany and William Cooper Nell to help him with the *North Star*. In 1847, Delany met Douglass in Rochester and signed on as the coeditor. He had experience in the abolitionist newspaper field. His Pittsburgh paper, the *Mystery*, had gone out of business earlier that year. Delany was listed on the *North Star's* masthead as an editor until 1849, despite contributing only occasionally and never moving to Rochester (William S. McFeely, *Frederick Douglass* [New York, NY: W. W. Norton & Co., 1991], 151–55).

55. "Condition of Freed Slaves in Canada," *Douglass' Monthly*, August 1859; "The Elgin Settlement at Buxton, Canada West," *Frederick Douglass' Paper*, August 25, 1854; "Statement in Regard to the Colored Population of Canada," *Frederick Douglass' Paper*, August 6, 1852; "Canada Postage," *North Star*, August 21, 1848; and Blight, *Frederick Douglass*, 297, 306–10.

56. *North Star*, June 30, 1848.

57. "The Bridge at the Falls," *North Star*, January 28, 1848.

58. Stuart, *Report of Charles B. Stuart*, 5.

59. "The First of August," *North Star*, July 21, 1848.

60. *North Star*, August 4, 1848.

61. Nancy Hewitt, *Women's Activism and Social Change: Rochester, New York, 1822–1872* (Lanham, MD: Lexington Brooks, 2001), 130–35.

62. "First of August Celebration," *North Star,* August 11, 1848; "The First of August," *North Star,* July 21, 1848; "Celebration by the Colored People," *Rochester Democrat,* August 1, 1848; and "First of August Celebration in Rochester, N.Y.," *Liberator,* August 18, 1848.

63. dann j. Broyld, "'A Success in Every Particular": British August First Commemorations in North America and the Black Quest for Unblemished Celebrations, 1834–1861," *American Review of Canadian Studies* 47, no. 4 (Dec. 2017): 335–56.

64. "The Colored Celebration Yesterday," *Rochester Daily Advertiser,* August 2, 1848; "Celebration by the Colored People," *Rochester Democrat,* August 1, 1848. See Silverman, "Monarchial Liberty and Republican Slavery," 7–18. See also *North Star,* March 9, 1849.

65. "The Underground Railroad," *Rochester Daily Union,* May 17, 1856; "A Valuable Fugitive," *Rochester Union and Advertiser,* November 20, 1860.

66. *Frederick Douglass' Paper,* June 2, 1854.

67. "Underground Railway," *Rochester Daily Union,* October 15, 1853; *Rochester Daily Democrat,* October 17, 1853.

68. "See How They Run!" *Rochester Daily Democrat,* November 22, 1853.

69. *Rochester Daily Union,* November 30, 1853.

70. "Fugitives from the South," *Rochester Union and Advertiser,* July 9, 1858.

71. "Arrest of Pretended Fugitives," *Rochester Daily Union,* January 22, 1855. Charles Reed was listed as a 35 Mulatto, in Rochester, Ward 1, Monroe County, New York (1860 US Federal Census).

72. "Fugitives from the South," *Rochester Union and Advertiser,* May 22, 1857; US Census, 1860; Rochester City Directory, 1851 and 1857.

73. "Those 'Fugitives from the South,'" and "Mr. Editor," *Rochester Union and Advertiser,* May 23, 1857. A year after the Johnson and Reed incidences, Black laborer James Robinson welcomed "fugitive" Lewis Williams of "destitute circumstances" into his seventh ward home for a few nights. Robinson, "a benevolent, Christian man" was deceived by what the *Union and Advertiser* called "another colored imposter." Williams robbed his host of "six dollars in cash, a pair of pantaloons and a shirt." Robinson contacted the police and Williams was arrested. He served six months in the penitentiary for taking advantage of Robinson's kindness ("Another Colored Imposter," *Union and Advertiser,* August 30, 1858, and August 31, 1858). See also "Fugitive Slaves Among Us!—Caught and Caged!" *Union and Advertiser,* November 12, 1857; Rochester City Directory, 1855 and 1857; *Rochester Daily Union,* December 1, 1856; and *Union and Advertiser,* December 11, 1856.

74. *Rochester Daily Democrat,* July 4, 1837; *Christian Guardian* (Toronto, Upper Canada), July 12, 1837; *Liberator,* August 25, 1837; and *Frederick Douglass' Paper,* September 17, October 12, and November 12, 1852.

75. Williams and Goldie, *Sunshine and Shadow,* 16–18, quotes 75 and 77. From 1855 to 1867, he worked for the railway.

76. Rochester Census, 1850; Toronto Census, 1850. Toronto had a total population of 30,800.

77. Rochester Census, 1850.

78. Samuel Porter to his Grandfather [April 1828], letter appended to Everard Peck to Samuel Porter, April 22, 1828, Samuel D. and Susan Porter Family Papers, University of Rochester; and Sheriff, *Artificial River,* 66.

79. Richard Biddle, *Captain Hall in America* (Philadelphia, PA: Carey and Lea, 1830), 97.

80. McKelvey, *Rochester on the Genesee,* 71.

81. Foner, *Frederick Douglass,* 5:132–33; "The Black-phobia in Rochester," *North Star,* October 3, 1850.

82. "Incivility to Colored Persons in the Street," *North Star,* October 3, 1850.

83. Rosetta Douglass Sprague, "My Mother as I Recall Her," May 10, 1900, rpr. in *Journal of Negro History* 8, no. 1 (January 1923): 97.

84. Rochester Census, 1850.

85. Rochester Census, 1860.

86. Michael Leavy, *Rochester's Corn Hill: The Historic Third Ward* (Charleston, SC: Arcadia Publishing, 2003); Charles Mulford Robinson, *Third Ward Traits* (Rochester, NY: Genesee Press, 1899); and Virginia Jeffery Smith, "Reminiscences of the Third Ward" (Paper given to the Rochester Historical Society, April 1945).

87. Patenaud, "Bound by Pride and Prejudice," 126; Frost, *Steal Away Home,* 142–43. See also Curt Gerling, *Smugtown U.S.A.* (Webster, NY: Plaza Publishers, 1957).

88. Rochester Census, 1850.

89. Rochester City Directory, 1847, 1850, and 1851.

90. Port Hope City (Canada West) Directory, 1856–57; Peterborough (Canada West) Directory, 1859; Frost, *Steal Away Home,* 65, 176–79. See Also dann j. Broyld, "The Power of Proximity: Frederick Douglass and His Transnational Relations with British Canada, 1847–1861." *Afro-Americans in New York Life and History Journal* 41, no. 2 (July 2020): 3–34.

91. East Avenue was then Main Street. The home was owned by abolitionist and jeweler John Kedzie before the Douglass family moved in (Rochester City Directory, 1847). Jane Marsh Parker, "*Reminiscences of Frederick Douglass,*" unpublished typescript in the Howard W. Coles Collection, Rochester Museum and Science Center.

92. On each side of Douglass's residence lived European-American abolitionists and wood-workers William (or Henry) Billinghurt, a carpenter, and Nelson Bostwick, a joiner. The neighbors on the street openly protested the collection of antislavery houses. Around 1849, Joseph Marsh purchased the home of Billinghurt at 2 Alexander Street. Marsh's daughter Jenny (who was also known as Jane; she became Jenny Marsh Parker when she married) noted that Douglass softened the opposition on the block by being "a gentleman and a good neighbor." She explained that the neighborhood children took a liking to Douglass and the feeling was reciprocal. He played the violin and sang for the kids who congregated before his window on warm summer nights. Knowing their favorite songs, "Nelly was a Lady" and "Old Kentucky Home," he was sure to please the crowd. After entertaining the children, he came to the door to bow and receive a "hearty applause." Douglass captured the youngsters' attention, despite the disposition of their parents. As Jenny explained, "Every one of note who came to the city was pretty sure to call upon Frederick Douglass; we had only to watch his front door to see many famous men and women." Douglass "added much to a locality," Jenny asserted, "which before had been rather dull" (Rochester City Directory, 1847; Parker, "*Reminiscences of Frederick Douglass*").

93. See Mark Anthony Cooper, ed., *Dear Father, A Collection of Letters to Frederick Douglass from His Children, 1859–1894* (Philadelphia, PA: Fulmore Press, 1997).

94. Charlotte Murray was believed to be the younger sister of Anna Murray Douglass. See 1850 US Census for members living in the household.

95. William S. McFeely, *Frederick Douglass* (New York, NY: W. W. Norton & Co., 1991), 172; Rose O'Keefe, *Frederick and Anna Douglass in Rochester, New York: Their Home Was Open to All* (Charleston, SC: History Press, 2013).

96. Charles Remond Douglass, "Some Incidents of the Home Life of Frederick Douglass," in Bernier and Taylor, *If I Survive,* 673; *Rochester Express,* June 3, 1872; and *Democrat and Chronicle,* June 3, 1872, on called it a "beautiful grove."

97. The Monroe County records provide no details on the original purchase.

98. Blight, *Frederick Douglass,* xix.

99. Benjamin Quarles, *Frederick Douglass* (New York, NY: Da Capo Press, 1997), 119.

100. Douglass, *Life and Times* (Hartford, CT: Park Publishing Co., 1881), 265, 286.

101. Douglass, *Life and Times* (Park, 1881), 269.

102. Webster had thirty-seven Blacks in a population of 2,446; Sweden had thirty-four among 3,623; Brighton had twenty-one of 3,117; and Greece had eighteen of 4, 219. Counts per the 1850 US Census.

103. Reed and Smith, *The Life and the Adventures of a Haunted Convict,* xxiv–xxv, 6, 8.

104. Charles Remond Douglass, "Some Incidents of the Home Life of Frederick Douglass," in Bernier and Taylor, *If I Survive,* 671; and US Census, 1860.

105. Reed and Smith, *The Life and the Adventures of a Haunted Convict,* 9. Austin always capitalized "Home" when referring to Rochester, which was a clear sign of the affection he held for the city. Also, it is likely that Burrell and Maria Reed named their son Austin after their close friend Austin Steward (xx–xxi).

106. James K. Bryant II, "African-Americans and Domestic Servants in Rochester's Third Ward Community," Rochester, NY: Landmark Society of Western New York, 4. See also Peggy Pascoe, *What Comes Naturally: Miscegenation Law and the Making of Race in America* (New York: Oxford University, 2009).

107. Julia Griffiths to Gerrit Smith, August 26, 1851, Gerrit Smith Papers, George Arents Research Library, Syracuse University; Leigh Fought, *Women in the World of Frederick Douglass* (New York, NY: Oxford University Press, 2017).

108. By late 1853, William Lloyd Garrison, now a political rival, proclaimed in the *Liberator* that Julia was "facile and mischievous" and was destructively swaying the judgment of Douglass. Garrison also asserted that Julia "had caused much unhappiness" within the household of the leading abolitionist. After these denunciations, a letter allegedly written by Mrs. Douglass was sent to Garrison refuting the indictments of Douglass's domestic life as untrue. It read: "Sir,—It is not true, that the presence of a certain person [Julia Griffiths] in the office of Frederick Douglass causes unhappiness in his family. Please insert this in your next paper." Garrison's reaction was mixed. He contended that he "could bring a score of unimpeachable witnesses in Rochester to prove it," but in the same breath expressed regret for the remarks. Harriet Beecher Stowe called Garrison's allegations "unfortunate" ("Frederick Douglass in Chicago," *Liberator,* November 18, 1853, "Letter from Mrs. Douglass," *Liberator,* November 23, 1853, *Liberator,* December 2 and 16, 1853; Harriet Beecher Stowe to William Lloyd Garrison, December 19, 1853, Garrison Collection, Boston Public Library).

109. Waldo E. Martin Jr., *The Mind of Frederick Douglass* (Chapel Hill: University of North Carolina Press, 1984), 43. See also "Frederick Douglass," *National Anti-Slavery Standard,* September 24, 1853; "The Liberator," *Frederick Douglass' Paper,* December 9, 1853; and "The Mask Entirely Removed," *Liberator,* December 16, 1853.

110. Ultimately, Julia Griffiths married Henry O. Crofts, a minister and former Canadian missionary, and Eliza Griffiths married John Dick, a onetime printer in the *North Star* office who boarded with the Douglasses; they emigrated in June 1850 to Canada. It is clear that these women felt a level of comfort in Rochester because it was near to British North America. Blight, *Frederick Douglass*, 204, 312–13.

111. Western New York Anti-Slavery Society, Fair Report [1850], and Amy Post to Frederick Douglass, 2 February 1850, in Isaac and Amy Post Family Papers (cited hereafter as IAPFP), University of Rochester; Amy Post to Frederick Douglass, February 2, 1850, and William C. Nell to Amy Post, 3 July 1850, in IAPFP.

112. *Rochester Republican*, June 8, 1830.

113. Or corner of Spring and Havor Streets (Blight, *Frederick Douglass*, 342).

114. Reed and Smith, *The Life and the Adventures of a Haunted Convict*, xxi–xxii. See also *Report of the Trustees of the African Church in the Village of Rochester* (Rochester, NY: Marshall & Dean, 1828).

115. *Rochester Observer*, October 3, 1828.

116. C. Peter Ripley, ed., *The Black Abolitionist Papers, Vol. 4: The United States, 1847–1858 (Chapel Hill: University of North Carolina Press, 1991)*, 100.

117. James, *Life of Rev. Thomas James*, 16–17.

118. *Rochester Union and Advertiser*, July 26, 1858; and Whitacre, *A Civil Life in an Uncivil Time*, 22.

119. "Disturbing Religious Worship," *Rochester Union and Advertiser*, March 11, 1857. Two youngsters (Jasper Thompson and Thomas Clark County) were arrested for disturbing a church service. Several times during the singing of a hymn they excited the congregation into laughter. The boys pled not guilty and claimed that they were provoked to laugh by a silly joke told by elderly Mr. Taylor, a second-hand clothes dealer.

120. Rochester City Directory, 1844 and 1851.

121. *Rochester Daily Democrat*, September 24, 1835; Second Annual Meeting of the WNYASS, reported in *National Anti-Slavery Standard*, March 6, 1845; and Fifth Annual Meeting of the WNYASS, reported in *North Star*, December 29, 1848. See also Dorn, "A History of the Antislavery Movement in Rochester and Vicinity." The RLASS was initially called the Rochester Ladies' Anti-Slavery and Sewing Society, but the women later dropped the "Sewing" part of their official name by 1855.

122. Fourth Annual Report of the Rochester Ladies Anti-Slavery Society, 1855, William L. Clements Library, University of Michigan.

123. Fifth Annual Report of the Rochester Ladies Anti-Slavery Society, 1856.

124. Seventh Annual Report of the Rochester Ladies Anti-Slavery Society, 1858; and Eighth Annual Report of the Rochester Ladies Anti-Slavery Society, 1859. For example, in 1859: January 7, three fugitives, $8; and January 14, four fugitives, $7.

125. "Rochester Ladies Anti-Slavery Sewing Society," *Frederick Douglass' Paper*, January 1, 1852.

126. Fourth Annual Report of Rochester Ladies Anti-Slavery Society, 2; and Whitacre, *A Civil Life in an Uncivil Time* 34, 224–26.

127. Charles Remond Douglass, "Some Incidents of the Home Life of Frederick Douglass," in Bernier and Taylor, *If I Survive*, 670.

128. *Rochester Daily Democrat*, August 29, 1843.

129. McFeely, *Frederick Douglass*, 164.

130. The mechanically gifted Sibley consolidated the telegraph industry, and in 1856 became the

first president of the Western Union. He later owned a seed supply company and gave money to area groups as a philanthropist. In 1853, German-American Bausch opened a retail optical shop, which sold spectacles and magnifiers. A year later, after suffering from a lack of capital to underwrite the business, he teamed up with German immigrant Henry Lomb to form the Bausch & Lomb Company.

131. Post Office Arcade, Exchange Hall, North end.

132. Athenaeum Building, Exchange Place, "Arcade Exchange Hall, 28 Buffalo Street. The Corinthian's owner, William Reynolds, was not an abolitionist (Amy Hammer-Croughton, "Anti-Slavery Days in Rochester," *Rochester Historical Society Publications* 14 [1936], 139); "Independence Day," *Frederick Douglass' Paper,* July 1, 1852; *Frederick Douglass' Paper,* July 9 and 16, 1852; Colaiaco, *Frederick Douglass and the Fourth of July,* 9–40.

133. "To the Friends and Readers of the North Star," *North Star,* May 5, 1848. In this article, Douglass and Delany explained that "All donations in aid of the paper will be most thankfully received and promptly acknowledged through the columns of the *North Star.*"

134. Douglass, *Life and Times* (Park, 1881), 262.

135. James Miller McKim to Sydney Howard Gay, November 12, 1847, Sydney Howard Gay Papers, Rare Book and Manuscript Library, Columbia University. McKim (1810–1874) was a founding member of the American Anti-Slavery Society and worked for the Pennsylvania Anti-Slavery Society in Philadelphia. He became an abolitionist after reading the work of Garrison. McKim gave support to the family of John Brown after Harpers Ferry, and he recruited African American regiments during the Civil War.

136. Charles Remond Douglass, "Some Incidents of the Home Life of Frederick Douglass," in Bernier and Taylor, *If I Survive,* 669.

137. Blight, *Frederick Douglass,* 190, and chap. 12.

138. "New Publications," *Rochester Daily Union,* December 14, 1853; "New Publications," *Rochester Daily Democrat,* December 23, 1853; "The Autographs for Freedom," *Frederick Douglass' Paper,* April 28, 1854.

139. Frederick Douglass, *Life and Times* (Park, 1881), 262. Abby Kelley Foster of the American Anti-Slavery Society, who worked closely with William Lloyd Garrison and was married to abolitionist lecturer Stephen S. Foster, explained that "those two English girls" Julia and sister Eliza Griffiths "brought him unexpected aid, which enabled him to go on" (Abby Kelley Foster to Sydney Howard Gay, March 19, 1850, Sydney Howard Gay Papers, Rare Book and Manuscript Library, Columbia University). See also Frank E. Fee Jr., "To No One More Indebted: Frederick Douglass and Julia Griffiths, 1849–63," *Journalism History* 37 no. 1 (2011): 12–26.

140. "Prospectus for an Anti-Slavery Paper, North Star," *National Anti-Slavery Standard,* September 30, 1847.

141. *Provincial Freeman,* June 3, 10, 24, and July 1, 1854.

142. Shirley J. Yee, *Black Women Abolitionists: A Study in Activism, 1828–1860* (Knoxville, TN: University of Tennessee Press, 1992), 127.

143. David Ruggles explained the *North Star* was "a beacon light of liberty, to illuminate the pathway of the bleeding, hunted fugitive of the South." *North Star,* December 3, 1847, and January 20, 1848.

144. *Voice of the Fugitive,* April 8, 1852; quote: "Frederick Douglass' Paper," *Voice of the Fugitive,* July 2, 1851. The *Voice of the Fugitive* stated on February 12, 1852, that the *Frederick Douglass' Paper*

"is recommended." Henry Bibb's wife Mary Elizabeth Bibb is now considered by many to be the first female Black journalist in Canada, before Mary Ann Shadd. See Frost and Tucker, *A Fluid Frontier,* chap. 7, "The *Voice of the Fugitive:* A Transnational Abolitionist Organ," by Afua Cooper.

145. Donald G. Simpson explained: "The last issue extant of the *Freeman* is September 6, 1857, and one might have expected that the *Freeman* would have fallen victim, as many other papers did, to the depression of the late fifties. It is not clear when the paper was discontinued. The paper was still being quoted in other journals in the late 1858 and Hurray guessed that it ceased publication by 1859. New evidence proves that the paper was still active at least as late as August 1859" (Simpson and Lovejoy, *Under the North Star,* 95). It could have been 1860: see Rhodes, *Mary Ann Shadd Cary.*

146. Quarles, *Frederick Douglass,* 89–90. Whites bought the papers of Douglass more than Blacks did; the rate was five to one. This was quite typical of all abolitionist newspapers.

147. Rochester City Directory, 1851; *Frederick Douglass' Paper,* May 20 and 27, September 9, 1853; *Liberator,* August 26, 1853; Patrick T. J. Browne, "'To Defend Mr. Garrison': William Cooper Nell and the Personal Politics of Antislavery," *New England Quarterly* 70, no. 3 (Sept. 1997): 428; and McFeely, *Frederick Douglass,* 176.

148. *Frederick Douglass' Paper,* April 18, 1854.

149. "The North Star," *National Anti-Slavery Standard,* December 16, 1847.

150. In 1865, in the town of Ogden, west of the city, Douglass allegedly purchased allotments for some $2,500. He also sold in-law Lewis Sprague an allotment in the Twelfth Ward for $1,200 in September of 1869 (McFeely, *Frederick Douglass,* 172; and *Rochester Union and Advertiser,* September 4, 1869). See also Tianna Mañón and Jake Clapp, "Douglass's Rochester: Rochester Likes to Claim Frederick Douglass as Its Own. Is the Community Living Up to His Legacy?" *City Paper* 47, no. 24, February 14, 2018.

151. *Rochester Gazette,* October 14, 1817; and Reed and Smith, *The Life and the Adventures of a Haunted Convict,* xxi.

152. "Awful Conflagration: Blossom Hotel in Ruins!" *Rochester Daily Union,* January 21, 1854. See also Rochester City Directory, 1847, 1849, 1851, 1861, and 1863.

153. *Rochester Daily Union,* February 16, 1854.

154. "Local Affair," *Rochester Daily Democrat,* March 17, 1854; "City Items," *Rochester Daily Union,* March 16, 1854; "A Word of Parting" *Frederick Douglass' Paper,* March 24, 1854.

155. US Census, 1860; and *Rochester Union and Advertiser,* September 5, 1866. J. P. Morris died from a "lingering illness" at his home on Bowery Street; he was reported as being "a little over 57" years old. He is buried in Mount Hope Cemetery.

156. James K. Bryant II, "Biographical Sketches of Selected African-American Residents of Rochester, New York Third Ward, 1830–1860," Rochester, NY: Landmark Society of Western New York, 69; US 1840 Census; and Rochester City Directory, 1841.

157. Rochester Census, 1850; and Rochester City Directory, 1844 and 1847.

158. Rochester City Directory, 1851; and Frost, *Steal Away Home,* 65, 84, 146–49, 176–79.

159. Rochester City Directory, 1844, 1847, 1851.

160. Du Bois, *The City of Frederick Douglass,* 15.

161. Rochester Census, 1850; and Rochester City Directory, 1849–50.

162. Rochester City Directory, 1849–50; she is not listed in 1847–48 or 1850–51. Her brother John S. Jacobs is not listed at all.

163. "The Bazaar," *North Star*, September 1, 1848; and *North Star*, December 29, 1848. The Anti-slavery Reading Room was advertised in the *North Star* from March 23 to July 27, 1849, as well. See Sinha, *The Slave's Cause.*

164. Harriet Jacobs to Amy Post, Rochester, May 1849, in Jacobs, *Incidents,* 230.

165. Fifth Annual Meeting of the Western New York Anti-Slavery Society; reported in the *North Star*, December 29, 1848.

166. Jacobs, *Incidents,* 189.

167. "Oysters! Oysters!" *North Star*, November 2, 1849. See Jacobs, *A True Tale of Slavery,* 85–87, 108–10, 125–27.

168. US Census, 1850.

169. Rochester City Directory, 1841, 1844, 1845, 1847, 1849.

170. Rochester City Directory, 1845, 1849.

171. US Census, 1860.

172. Loguen, *The Rev. J. W. Loguen as a Slave and a Freeman,* 342–43.

173. Rochester City Directory, 1851.

174. Castle, "A Survey of the History of African Americans in Rochester, New York, 1800–1860," 3–4.

175. Rochester Census, 1860.

176. Rochester Census, 1850.

177. Rochester Census, 1850.

178. See Graham Russell Gao Hodges, *New York City Cartmen, 1667–1850, rev. ed.* (New York, NY: New York University Press, 1986); and Rochester Census, 1860.

179. Rochester City Directory, 1851.

180. Hammer-Croughton, "Anti-Slavery Days in Rochester," 142. This is the same Shields Green that was involved in Harpers Ferry revolt.

181. *Pine and Palm*, July 6, 1861. See also "Rochester at Harpers Ferry," *New York Daily Tribune*, October 22, 1859.

182. Rochester Census, 1860.

183. Reed and Smith, *The Life and the Adventures of a Haunted Convict,* xx–xxi. Maria died "lifeless and frozen stiff" in her home, while her adult children were "scattered over the world." "Suffering Among the Poor," *Rochester Daily Union and Advertiser*, February 13, 1865.

184. Charles Remond Douglass, "Some Incidents of the Home Life of Frederick Douglass," in Bernier and Taylor, *If I Survive,* 670.

185. Castle, "A Survey of the History of African Americans in Rochester, New York, 1800–1860," 4.

186. References to the Fugitive Slave Law: *Rochester Daily Democrat*, November 9, 1850; *Rochester Daily Advertiser*, September 21, 1853; *Rochester Daily Union*, September 3, 1853; and *Rochester Daily Union*, July 6, 1854.

187. For an example, see "Attempted Arrest of Fugitive Slaves," "The Negro Riot in Pennsylvania," *Syracuse Daily Standard*, September 16, 1851.

188. Douglass, *Life and Times* (Park, 1881), 288.

189. Douglass, *Life and Times* (Park, 1881), 288–89.

190. Blackett, *Captive's Quest for Freedom,* 359.

191. William Parker gave Douglass the revolver that slipped from the hands of slaveholder Gorsuch when he fell to his death. It was a token of appreciation and a souvenir of the resistance at

Christiana. Douglass, *Life and Times* (Park, 1881), 289; William Parker, "The Freeman's Story" (1866), in Yuval Taylor, ed., *I Was Born a Slave, Vol. 2: An Anthology of Classic Narratives: 1849–1866* (Chicago, IL: Chicago Review Press, 1999).

192. "The Christiana Hero is in Canada," *Frederick Douglass' Paper*, February 7, 1853; *Frederick Douglass' Paper*, September 25, 1851.

193. *Voice of the Fugitive*, July 15, 1852; and Hepburn, *Crossing the Border*, 95.

194. C. Peter Ripley, ed., *The Black Abolitionist Papers, Vol. 1: The British Isles, 1830–1865* (Chapel Hill: University of North Carolina Press, 1987), 493.

195. John Jacobs had the opportunity to engage audiences in Henrietta, Madison, East Mendon, Avon, and West Bloomfield. The reception to the abolitionists varied, depending on the location. In Canandigua and Hopewell they enjoyed respectable and large crowds. However, at Penn Yan, John had his speech interrupted by a Black heckler; despite the distraction, Douglass explained that he left a "deep impression" on the hundreds of listeners. Even worse, in Bath the doors to all the churches were closed to the touring abolitionists (Jean Fagan Yellin, *Harriet Jacobs: A Life* [New York, NY: Basic Civitas Books, 2004], 99; "Editorial Correspondence," *North Star*, March 9, 1849). In February 1849, the rising leader accompanied Douglass on a two-week speaking tour throughout Western New York. John was disheartened on the 1849 tour by his experiences in the villages surrounding Rochester. He wrote Douglass in April of 1849 explaining that "At no time during my laboring in the cause as a lecturer, have I found so few friends" (John S. Jacobs to Frederick Douglass, *North Star*, April 20, 1849). Also see Harriet Jacobs to Amy Post, 1852, IAPFP, Letter 4; and Jacobs, *Incidents*.

196. *Frederick Douglass' Paper*, August 20, 1852; Philip S. Foner, ed., *Frederick Douglass: Selected Speeches and Writings, abridged and adapted by Taylor Yuval* (Chicago, IL: Lawrence Hill Books, 1999), 207–8. "The Fugitive Slave Law," speech to the National Free Soil Convention at Pittsburgh, August 11, 1852.

197. *Frederick Douglass' Paper*, June 2, 1854; and Jackson, *Force and Freedom*, 73.

198. Jean Fagan Yellin, "Through Her Brother's Eyes: Incidents and 'A True Tale,'" in *Harriet Jacobs and Incidents in the Life of a Slave Girl: New Critical Essays*, ed. Deborah M. Garfield and Rafia Zafar (Cambridge: Cambridge University Press, 1996), 47.

199. Jacobs, *Incidents*, 191.

200. *Buffalo Commercial Advertiser*, August 27, 1851. The *Buffalo Express* explained: "The fugitive slave bill never took a slave out of its limits, though several attempts were made to do so . . . man was always protected in Rochester" (August 10, 1869).

201. Rochester City Directory, 1851.

202. Post Family Papers Non-Correspondence: Minutes of an "Anti-Fugitive Slave Law Meeting of the Colored Citizens of Rochester," William C. Nell, Secretary, Oct. 13, 1851, folder 15.

203. Douglass, *Life and Times* (Park, 1881), 280.

204. Drew, *The Refugee*, 108–12.

205. Rochester City Directory, 1844, 1845, 1849, 1851; also the 1861 (Toronto) Canada Census.

206. "Receipts for the North Star," *North Star*, November 26, 1846, and March 15, 1850; Frederick Douglass to Sydney Howard Gay, June 12, 1852, Sydney Howard Gay Papers, Rare Book and Manuscript Library, Columbia University; and "The Third Baptist Church," *North Star*, March 9, 1849.

207. National Anti-Slavery Standard, August 6, 1853.

208. "A Fugitive in England," *Rochester Democrat* January 29, 1855; and "Summary," *National Anti-Slavery Standard*, February 17, 1855.

209. "Obituary: Death of Grandison Boyd," *Chatham Tri-Weekly Plant,* July 17, 1878; *New York Times,* February 5, 1854; and *National Anti-Slavery Standard,* June 12, 1852. See also Frost, *Steal Away Home,* 40, 45, 64–65, 149.

210. Horace McQuire, "A Reminiscence of Anti-Slavery Days," paper read before the Rochester Historical Society, October 27, 1916, 6–7, Central Library of Rochester and Monroe County Historic Monographs Collection.

211. Quarles, *Frederick Douglass,* 119.

212. Charles Remond Douglass, "Some Incidents of the Home Life of Frederick Douglass," in Bernier and Taylor, *If I Survive,* 672.

213. Still, *The Underground Railroad* (London: Benediction Books, 2008), 598; Letter from Frederick Douglass to Mrs. Anna H. Richardson of Newcastle, England (ca. 1860).

214. Foner, *Gateway to Freedom,* 181. See also Papson and Calarco, *Secret Lives,* 102.

215. Douglass, *Life and Times* (Park, 1881), 280.

216. Note from Frederick Douglass to Amy Post. No Date, IAPFP.

217. *Rochester/Monroe County Freedom Trail Commission: Guidebook to the Underground Railroad and the Abolitionist Movement* (Rochester, NY: Division of the Department of Communications and Special Events of Monroe County, 2003), 86–89. Mrs. Amy Post wrote this account for the Semi-Centennial History of Rochester, 1884.

218. South Fitzhugh Street at Spring Street; this is now the site of the Civic Center.

219. The address was 10 South Sophia Street. Rochester Census, 1850 and 1860.

220. Letter from Frederick Douglass to Miss Poster, October 18, 1857, William L. Clements Library, University of Michigan.

221. See *British Whig* (Kingston, Ontario), October 20, 1847.

222. Examples of fugitives going to Canada from Rochester: *Rochester Union and Advertiser,* May 23, 1857; *Rochester Daily Union,* November 30, 1853; *Rochester Daily Democrat,* October 17, 1853.

223. Larson, *Bound for the Promised Land,* 94.

224. Foner, *Frederick Douglass: Selected Speeches and Writings,* 601.

225. Larson, *Bound for the Promised Land,* 154.

226. Broyld, "Harriet Tubman," 78–98; quote in *Rochester Union and Advertiser,* December 14, 1896.

227. It was also called the Colored National Convention. Foreman, Casey, and Patterson, *The Colored Conventions Movement,* 111, 113–15.

228. Ripley, *Black Abolitionist Papers,* 2:372. Also see Jane H. Pease and William H. Pease, *They Who Would Be Free: Blacks Search for Freedom, 1830–1861* (Champaign: University of Illinois Press, 1990), 123, 139–140, 150, 253–60. In *Provincial Freeman,* April 4, 1857, Isaac D Shadd reacts to the 1853 convention's stance on settlement outside the United States.

229. *Rochester Daily Democrat,* August 13, 1853.

230. Blacks held a total of twelve national conventions in thirty years. A number of them were held in the state of New York. Some have regarded the Rochester Convention as the "most outstanding assemblage of the entire era" despite its clear problems (Berlin and Harris, *Slavery in New York,* 260; Howard H. Bell, "A Survey of the Negro Convention Movement, 1830–1861," PhD diss., Northwestern University, 1953, 166; and Foreman, Casey, and Patterson, *The Colored Conventions Movement*).

231. Jane H. Pease and William H. Pease, "Negro Conventions and the Problem of Black Leadership," *Journal of Black Studies* 2, no. 1 (Sept. 1971): 29–44; "Call for a National Emigration Convention of Colored Men," *Frederick Douglass' Paper,* January 13, 1854.

232. Originally from Maryland, Lloyd Scott, a local clothing merchant, lent a hand in preparing to host the 1853 Convention. He was active in community matters such as education and vigilance but grew disenchanted with his financial progress in Western New York. In the late 1850s, Scott began to entertain the idea of Haitian immigration. After deliberation, he decided to move his wife and six children to Haiti in October of 1861. Canadian-born Barbara Ann Steward, like her relative Austin in the 1830s, was faced with the decision to emigrate. Barbara had resided most of her days in the Rochester area working as a teacher and occasional abolitionist lecturer. Aggravated by the limited employment opportunities open to qualified Black women, Steward began thinking about leaving the United States. She was offered a teaching position in Liberia but declined it and taught at a public school in Wilkes-Barre, Pennsylvania, for a time. In the spring of 1861, Steward announced plans to visit Haiti to evaluate the prospect of a permanent settlement. The trip never occurred because Steward died later that year. Even Douglass, just prior to the Civil War, had his questions about remaining in America. After responding to a letter from a subscriber stating, "No; I do not expect to emigrate to Haiti under any circumstances," suddenly he too suggested that a Black settlement in Haiti might be a plausible objective (Ripley, *Black Abolitionist Papers,* 4:101; *Frederick Douglass' Paper,* June 1, 1855; "Haytian Emigration," *Douglass' Monthly,* March 1861; *Rochester Union and Advertiser,* March 5, 1861; and Blight, *Frederick Douglass,* 335–45.)

233. Lucy N. Coleman, *Reminiscences* (1891; London: Forgotten Books, 2012), 16.

234. McKelvey, "Lights and Shadows in the Local Negro History," 5. See Laura A. McGregor, "The Early History of Rochester Public Schools, 1813–1850," *Rochester Historical Society Publications* 13 (1939): 37–73; and Blake McKelvey, "On the Educational Frontier," *Rochester Historical Society Publications* 17 (1939): 1–36.

235. The site is now the location of the Genesee Hospital.

236. Douglass, *Life and Times* (Park, 1881), 274–75.

237. Frederick Douglass to H. G. Warner, *North Star,* March 30, 1849. It was also reprinted by the *Rochester Courier.* Horatio Gates Warner (1801–1876) was a prominent local attorney and a strong proslavery and anti-Black advocate. He also was a newspaper editor of the *Rochester Courier,* which ran during the 1848 presidential election and later published the *Daily Advertiser* before it consolidated with the *Union.* After the Civil War, Warner purchased a home in Georgia, where he lived until his death (*University of Rochester Library Bulletin* 18, no. 1 [Autumn 1962]; Hammer-Croughton, "Anti-Slavery Days in Rochester," 130; and University of Rochester, Manuscript and Special Collections, Horatio Gates Warner Family Papers).

238. Julia Wilbur Large Diary (Haverford College), June 25, 1849. See also May 19, 1849; June 17, 1849; and July 20, 1849.

239. Hammer-Croughton, "Anti-Slavery Days in Rochester," 130.

240. Douglass, *Life and Times* (Park, 1881), 275.

241. "Colored School Meeting," *North Star,* December 21, 1849; and "Colored School Meeting," *Rochester Daily Democrat,* December 14, 1849.

242. "Schools for Colored Children," *Rochester Daily Democrat,* December 14, 1849.

243. "Colored School Meeting," *Rochester Daily Democrat,* December 14, 1849.

244. "Colored School Meeting," *Rochester Daily Democrat,* December 14, 1849; and "Exhibition of the Colored School," *North Star,* April 27, 1849.

245. Coleman, *Reminiscences,* 16.

246. McKelvey, "Lights and Shadows in the Local Negro History," 6; and *Frederick Douglass' Paper*, July 30, 1852.

247. Charles Remond Douglass, "Some Incidents of the Home Life of Frederick Douglass," in Bernier and Taylor, *If I Survive*, 671.

248. Coleman, *Reminiscences*, 16–17.

249. Douglass, *Life and Times* (Park, 1881), 275–76; Castle, "A Survey of the History of African Americans in Rochester, New York, 1800–1860," 6–9; and S. A. Ellis, "A Brief History of the Public Schools of the City of Rochester," *Rochester Historical Society Publications* 1 (1892): 71–89.

250. Castle, "A Survey of the History of African Americans in Rochester, New York, 1800–1860," 10–11.

251. Castle, "A Survey of the History of African Americans in Rochester, New York, 1800–1860," 11.

252. Farley, "The African American Presence in the History of Western New York," 14. In Monroe County the vote for suffrage was 6,748 to 6,327 in favor of Black enfranchisement. See also Leslie M. Harris, *In the Shadow of Slavery: African Americans in New York City, 1628–1863* (Chicago: University of Chicago Press, 2003), 270.

253. Rochester Union and Advertiser, January 14 and 21, 1861.

254. "The Meeting of Thursday Night," *Rochester Union and Advertiser*, October 11, 1858; and *Rochester Union and Advertiser*, January 12, 1861.

255. "The Meeting of Thursday Night," *Rochester Union and Advertiser*, October 11, 1858; and *Rochester Union and Advertiser*, January 12, 1861. In 1858 as well, Anthony attended an antislavery meeting in Albany, New York, on March 8, 1858, and her remarks were published in the *National Anti-Slavery Standard* on March 20, 1858. She explained, "it is not because of their incapacity, or their satisfaction with their lot, that they are enslaved . . . there is a power outside of them which keeps this mighty nation in chains." And expounded, "Let that power, vested in the United States Government, and endorsed by the popular religious sentiment of the country, be withdrawn, and slavery will speedily come to an end." See also *Rochester Daily Advertiser*, April 16, 1852; *Frederick Douglass' Paper*, April 22, 1852, and June 2, 1853; *Rochester Daily Democrat*, June 5, 1853; *Rochester Daily Union*, June 2, 1853; McFeely, *Frederick Douglass*, 268–69; Benjamin Quarles, "Frederick Douglass and the Woman's Rights Movement," *Journal of Negro History* 25, no. 1 (Jan. 1940): 35–44; Ann D. Gordon, ed., *The Selected Papers of Elizabeth Cady Stanton and Susan B. Anthony: In the School of Anti-Slavery, 1840 to 1866* (New Brunswick, NJ: Rutgers University Press, 1997); and Whitacre, *A Civil Life in an Uncivil Time*, 17–21.

256. See Alma Lutz, "Susan B. Anthony and John Brown," *Rochester History* 15, no. 3 (July 1953): 3–15.

257. Reynolds, *John Brown, Abolitionist*, 138–78, 268–87; and Jackson, *Force and Freedom*, 117–26.

258. Charles Remond Douglass, "Some Incidents of the Home Life of Frederick Douglass," in Bernier and Taylor, *If I Survive*, 670.

259. *Rochester Union and Advertiser*, April 9, 1859.

260. *St. Catharines Journal*, November 3, 1859; John Brown to John Brown Jr., April 8, 1858, Boyd B. Stutler Collection, West Virginia State Archives, Charleston, West Virginia; Fred Landon, "Canadian Negroes and the John Brown Raid," *Journal of Negro History* 6, no. 2 (April 1921): 174–82.

261. Colaiaco, *Frederick Douglass and the Fourth of July*, 124.

262. He was the son of an African King, hence the endearing term: "Emperor." Green was also a product of the illegal slave trade occurring in the United States; he was sold into bondage in South Carolina (Douglass, *Life and Times* [Park, 1881], 317–19, and Coles, *Cradle of Freedom*, 144).

263. "The Black Emperor," *Rochester Union and Advertiser,* October 21, 1859; "Rochester at Harpers Ferry," *New York Daily Tribune,* October 22, 1859; and Louis A. DeCaro Jr., *The Untold Story of Shields Green: The Life and Death of a Harpers Ferry Raider* (New York, NY: New York University Press, 2020), 14–15 and 134–57.

264. Franklin Sanborn called Green "a perfect rattlebrain in talk"; see Franklin Sanborn, *Recollections of Seventy Years, Vol. I* (Boston: Richard C. Badger, 1909), 179.

265. J. T. "Old Brown and His Fellow Prisoners," *Spirit of the Times* (New York), December 3, 1859; and Nicholas Spicer [Alban S. Payne], "John Brown and His Coadjutors," *Spirit of the Times* (New York), February 2, 1860.

266. Coleman, *Reminiscences,* 57–58.

267. Osborne P. Anderson, *A Voice from Harpers Ferry* (1854; rpr. New York, NY: World View Forum, 2000), 23.

268. Douglass, *Life and Times* (Park, 1881), 317–19.

269. Douglass, *Life and Times* (Park, 1881), 320.

270. Douglass, *Life and Times* (Park, 1881), 320.

271. "Owen Brown's Story of His Journey from Hagerstown to Kennedy Farm, with Shields Green, a Colored Man," in Horatio N. Rust Collection, Henry Huntington Library, San Marino, California. See also "Letter from Mr. Owen Brown," *Atlantic Monthly,* July 1874; and Ralph Keeler, "Owen Brown's Escape from Harpers Ferry," *Atlantic Monthly,* March 1874.

272. "Arrival of Men," Kennedy Farm folder, Box 11, in John Brown–Oswald Garrison Villard Collection, Columbia University Rare Book and Manuscript Collection, New York, NY.

273. Janet Kemper Beck, *Creating the John Brown Legend: Emerson, Thoreau, Douglass, Child and Higginson in Defense of the Raid on Harpers Ferry* (Jefferson, NC: McFarland, 2009), 12; and Hannah Geffert, "Regional Black Involvement in John Brown's Raid on Harpers Ferry," in Timothy Patrick McCarthy and John Stauffer, eds., *Prophets of Protest: Reconsidering the History of American Abolitionism* (New York, NY: New Press, 2006), 165–82.

274. *Weekly Anglo-African* (New York, NY), April 28, 1860.

275. Du Bois, *John Brown,* 310–12; and Anderson, *A Voice from Harpers Ferry,* 106. See also Eugene L. Meyer, *Five for Freedom: The African American Soldiers in John Brown's Army.* (Lawrence Hill Books, 2018); and Hannah N. Geffert, "John Brown and His Black Allies: An Ignored Alliance," *Pennsylvania Magazine of History and Biography* 126, no. 4 (Oct. 2002): 591–610.

276. As well as Gerritt Smith, Joshua R. Giddings, Samuel G. Howe, and Frank P. Sanborn.

277. John Stauffer, *Giants: The Parallel Lives of Frederick Douglass and Abraham Lincoln* (New York, NY: Twelve, 2008), 165.

278. Douglass, *Life and Times,* chap. 9, "Increasing Demands of the Slave Power"; Rochester City Directory, 1859; US Census, 1870; Coles, *Cradle of Freedom,* 150.

279. Charles Remond Douglass, "Some Incidents of the Home Life of Frederick Douglass," in Bernier and Taylor, *If I Survive,* 671.

280. *Rochester Union and Advertiser,* October 25, 1859.

281. Charles Remond Douglass, "Some Incidents of the Home Life of Frederick Douglass," in Bernier and Taylor, *If I Survive,* 671.

282. *Rochester Union and Advertiser,* October 25, 1859.

283. Douglass to Amy Post, October 27, 1859, IAPFP.

284. "The Black Emperor," *Rochester Union and Advertiser,* October 21, 1859. See also "Sympathy for John Brown in the North. Brown's Interview with His Follow-Prisoners," *New York Herald,* December 3, 1859; "The Burial of John Brown," *New York Daily Tribune,* December 12, 1859; "The Bodies of Green and Copeland," *New York Daily Tribune,* December 16, 1859; "Execution of the Harpers Ferry Traitors To-Day," *New York Herald,* December 16, 1859; *Toronto Weekly Globe,* November 25, 1859; and *Toronto Weekly Globe,* December 12, 1859.

285. Coleman, *Reminiscences,* 58; and Louis A. DeCaro Jr., *Freedom's Dawn: The Last Days of John Brown in Virginia* (New York, NY: Rowman & Littlefield Publishers, 2015).

286. *Pine and Palm,* July 6, 1861, letter to the editor.

287. "Frederick Douglass," *Rochester Union and Advertiser,* October 27, 1859.

288. "In Pursuit of Fred Douglass," *Toronto Globe,* November 2, 1859. He passed through Toronto on November 7, 1859, en route to Quebec ("Frederick Douglass," *Toronto Globe,* November 8, 1859). The *Frank Leslie's Illustrated Newspaper* in "The Way in Which Fred. Douglass Fights Wise of Virginia" showed how the esteemed abolitionist utilized the signpost "TO CANADA" (November 12, 1859).

289. *Douglass' Monthly,* November 1859.

290. Douglass to Amy Post, October 27, 1859, IAPFP.

291. *Toronto Globe,* November 12, 1859. In *Life and Times,* Douglass said of his trip to England it turned "what I had intended a pleasure a necessity," (Park, 1881), 326.

292. *Toronto Globe,* November 2, November 8, 1859.

293. "Death of Little Annie Douglass," *Douglass' Monthly,* April 1860, 243–44. The article also asserted that the quick departure of Douglass and the family's anxiety did not help the situation.

294. Charles Remond Douglass, "Some Incidents of the Home Life of Frederick Douglass," in Bernier and Taylor, *If I Survive,* 673.

295. *Douglass' Monthly,* June 1860; and Blight, *Frederick Douglass,* 318–20.

296. Despite the immediate grief John Brown caused the Rochester community once he was captured, they still attempted to raise money to rescue him from federal imprisonment. Nonetheless the plan ultimately came to a halt because he was so heavily guarded by troops. The community found alternative ways to honor the beloved Brown. While on a business trip to Harpers Ferry in November of 1859, H. C. Frost obtained two weapons used in the raid and sent them back to Rochester where they were exhibited at the telegraph office. People stood vigil at the Rochester City Hall when Brown was executed on December 2, 1859. Susan B. Anthony and Parker Pillsbury were among those gathered. To many locals, Brown had become a legend, and memorials continued to be held for several years to pay tribute to the slain leader. In 1861, for instance, "John Brown's Body" was sung by three Black chimney sweeps from the roof of City Hall. Afterward they vanished down the chimneys. ("This Afternoon's Report from Harpers Ferry," *Rochester Union and Advertiser,* October 21, 1859; "John Brown's Weapons," *Rochester Union and Advertiser,* November 18, 1859; "John Brown's Execution," *Rochester Union and Advertiser,* December 1, 1859.)

297. Julia Wilbur, Journal Briefs (1844–62), Haverford College, Quaker and Special Collections, Pennsylvania, Haverford, 34; and Julia Wilbur Large Diary, April 7, 1861.

298. *Rochester Evening Express,* October 25, 1859.

299. *Douglass' Monthly,* June 1860.

300. Quarles, *Frederick Douglass*, 119.

301. "An Underground Party," *Rochester Union and Advertiser*, July 31, 1860.

302. "The Depot Removed," *Rochester Union and Advertiser*, October 16, 1860. Also see "Underground Passengers," *Rochester Union and Advertiser*, March 30, 1860; "A Valuable Fugitive," *Rochester Union and Advertiser*, November 20, 1860.

303. Charles Remond Douglass, "Some Incidents of the Home Life of Frederick Douglass," in Bernier and Taylor, *If I Survive*, 673.

304. "Underground Passengers," *Rochester Union and Advertiser*, March 30, 1860; and "A Valuable Fugitive," *Rochester Union and Advertiser*, November 20, 1860.

305. His last name has also been spelled Dungee or Dunjee.

306. Still, *The Underground Railroad* (London: Benediction Books, 2008), 539–44.

3. ST. CATHARINES, CANADA WEST

1. Jackson and Wilson, *St. Catharines: Canada's Canal City*, 35.

2. Alan Hughes, "The Evolution of the Municipality of St. Catharines," *Newsletter of the Historical Society of St. Catharines* (Sept. 2008): 1–7.

3. Gillard and Tooke, *Niagara Escarpment*.

4. See Michael A. Gomez, *Pragmatism in the Age of Jihad: The Precolonial State of Bundu* (Cambridge, MA: Cambridge University Press, 1992).

5. *Pennsylvania Packet and Daily Advertiser*, March 13 and 23, 1779; and *Pennsylvania Gazette*, January 19, 1780.

6. Bill G. Smith and Richard Wojtowicz, *Blacks Who Stole Themselves: Advertisements for Runaways in the Pennsylvania Gazette, 1728–1790* (Philadelphia: University of Pennsylvania Press, 1989), 136.

7. See Pulis, *Moving On*; Cahill, "The Black Loyalist Myth in Atlantic Canada," 76–87; and Alan Gilbert, *Black Patriots and Loyalists: Fighting for Emancipation in the War for Independence* (Chicago: University of Chicago Press, 2012).

8. *Upper Canada Gazette*, July 3, 1793.

9. The signers were: Robert Spranklin, John Gerof, Peter Ling, Jack Baker, Pompadour, Jack Becker, John Cesar, John Jackson, Tom Frey, Jack Wurmwood, John Smith, Peter Green, Michael Grote, Adam Lewis, John Dimon, Simon Speck, Thomas Walker and Saison Sepyed. (Meyler and Meyler, *Stolen Life*, 73–74; see Horne, *Negro Comrades of the Crown*, 45).

10. Meyler and Meyler, *Stolen Life*, 60–74.

11. Dick's Creek is a body of water that ultimately flows into Twelve Mile Creek, a tributary that empties into Lake Ontario. Dick's Creek is named after Richard Pierpoint who was referred to as "Captain Dick." Pierpoint owned land in lots (north to south) 13 and 14 in the sixth concession (east to west) of Grantham Township.

12. In Grantham, James and Humphrey Waters were Pierpoint's closest Black neighbors. Yeoman farmers James and Humphrey Waters both lived in the town of Niagara. In 1795, James had a Crown grant to lot 368, while Humphrey was granted lot 325. In 1818, Humphrey bought lot 363 and later bought lot 330 in 1824. The land stayed in his family until 1913 (Power and Butler, *Slavery and Freedom in Niagara*, 78–85.)

13. Meyler and Meyler, *Stolen Life,* 75–76.

14. Steve Pitt, *To Stand and Fight Together: Richard Pierpoint and the Coloured Corps of Upper Canada* (Toronto: Dundurn Press, 2008); Steve Pitt, "To Stand and Fight Together," *Rotunda* 29, no. 3 (Spring 1997): 11.

15. Meyler and Meyler, *Stolen Life,* 81–84.

16. Jackson and Wilson, *St. Catharines: Canada's Canal City,* 35–36. Jackson explained: "Local history is sometimes difficult to authenticate and can be elusive and subject to varied interpretations. An example is the name and spelling of our [St. Catharines] community" (35).

17. "The Hon. William H. Merritt," *Niagara Mail* (Niagara Falls, Ontario), July 31, 1850.

18. Hughes, "The Evolution of the Municipality of St. Catharines," 2–3.

19. *Colonial Advocate* (Queenston, Ontario), January 1, 1829.

20. Headley Tulloch, *Black Canadians: A Long Line of Fighters* (Toronto, ON: NC Press, 1975), 98. *Black Canadians* provides a copy of Pierpoint's petition. The original is in the National Archives of Canada RG 5. A1. Upper Canada vol. 53 ff. 26440–44. Also see Esmeralda M. A. Thornhill, "So Seldom for Us, So Often Against Us: Blacks and Law in Canada," *Blacks in Canada: Retrospects, Introspects, Prospects* 38, no. 3 (Jan. 2008): 327.

21. Meyler and Meyler, *Stolen Life,* 104–12.

22. *St. Catharines Journal,* October 15, 1835.

23. *British American Journal,* September 24, 1835; *St. Catharines Journal,* October 15, 1835; and *St. Catharines Journal,* November 12, 1835.

24. *St. Catharines Journal,* November 12, 1835. See also Kerr-Ritchie, *Rites of August First;* Henry, *Emancipation Day;* Ikuko Asaka, "'Our Brethren in the West Indies': Self-Emancipated People in Canada and the Antebellum Politics of Diaspora and Empire," *Journal of African History* 97, no. 3 (Summer 2012): 219–39; and Broyld, "'A Success in Every Particular.'" William IV (1765–1837) reigned over the United Kingdom of Great Britain from June 1830 to his death on June 20, 1837. Known as the "Sailor King" due to his time in the British Navy, which allowed him to travel to North America and the Caribbean, he sat on the Throne when slavery was abolished in the British Empire. William's successor was Queen Victoria (Philip Ziegler, *King William IV* New York, NY: Harper & Row, 1973).

25. *St. Catharines Journal,* August 2, 1838. The twelve toasts were as follows: (1) The Queen; (2) The Earl of Durham-the Lieutenant-Governor and their families; (3) The Army and Navy—defenders of our rights and privileges; (4) May peace and prosperity reign throughout the Canadas and never again be disturbed by internal commotions or foreign policy; (5) Our coloured Brethren and Sisters all over the world; (6) May those who are now cruelly detained in slavery soon enjoy the same freedoms as ourselves; (7) Honour, honesty, humanity, humility, health, and happiness; (8) Prosperity to the plough and axe; (9) May unity, concord, and friendship always exist amongst us; (10) When the devil comes into our ranks, may we all help to kick him out; (11) Prosperity to civilization in African and the free settlements of Liberia; and (12) Success to Great Britain and all other countries interested in the cause of freedom (Henry, *Emancipation Day,* 147).

26. Brown, *Narrative,* 117.

27. *Daily Commercial Advertiser* (Buffalo, NY), July 13, 1835; *British American Journal* (St. Catharines), July 23, 1835.

28. Brown, *Narrative,* 123; and Farrisson, "William Wells Brown in Buffalo," 298–314.

29. Meyler and Meyler, *Stolen Life,* 116.

30. See Jackson, *The Welland Canals;* Styran and Taylor, *The Great National Object;* Aitken, *The Welland Canal Company.*

31. Militia Papers, Upper Canadian Military Dispatches 45, as cited by Ernest Green, "Upper Canada's Black Defenders," *Ontario Historical Society Papers and Records* 27 (1931): 379.

32. Winks, *Blacks in Canada,* 152; and "More Canal Riots," *St. Catharines Journal,* December 14, 1843.

33. Kerr-Ritchie, *Rites of August First,* 129; *Provincial Freeman,* June 3, 1854.

34. *St. Catharines Journal,* July 31, 1856.

35. People like Charles Hall, Elizabeth Harris, and Daniel Johns (Davis Cornish), and others who landed in Grantham, Canada West, like Thomas Henry Matthews (Lewis Lee) all are listed in Gay's New York City *Record of Fugitives* and they most likely used Rochester on their venture to Canada. See Sydney Howard Gay, *Record of Fugitives,* Rare Book and Manuscript Library, Columbia University; Foner, *Gateway to Freedom;* and Papson and Calarco, *Secret Lives.* Blackett explained in *The Captive's Quest for Freedom:* "The *Record of Fugitives* is made up of two books covering the period from January 1855 to November 1856. It contains 226 entries, 135 of them sent on by William Still" (392). See also William C. Kashatus, *William Still: The Underground Railroad and the Angel at Philadelphia* (Notre Dame, IN: University of Notre Dame Press, 2021), 131–42.

36. Wayne, "The Black Population of Canada West on the Eve of the American Civil War," 465–81, and David P. Gagan, "Enumerator's Instruction for the Census of Canada 1852 and 1861," *Histoire Sociale/Social History* 8 no. 14 (Nov. 1974): 333–65.

37. Local genealogist Maggie Parnell estimated that in 1851 out of a city population of 2,500, there were fewer than 300 Blacks in St. Catharines. In 1852, the first annual report of the Anti-Slavery Society of Canada estimated that the population of Blacks in St. Catharines and Niagara was 1,500. However, the 1852 St. Catharines Census shows this as an exaggeration, as it indicates that of a total town population of 4,368 only 457 were colored. A few years later in 1855, abolitionist Benjamin Drew estimated that of the approximately 6,000 St. Catharines residents, 800 were Black. However, the *St. Catharines Constitutional* reported on November 7, 1855, that of 7,060 people only 500 were Black. The inconsistencies continued. By 1860 Reverend William M. Mitchell estimated that there were 200 to 250 Blacks in the entire town, which is well short of comparable projections. See Maggie Parnell, *Black History in the Niagara Peninsula* (self-published, 1996), 1; *Anti-Slavery Society of Canada, First Annual Report* (1852); St. Catharines Census, 1852; *St. Catharines Journal,* February 19, 1852; Drew, *The Refugee,* 11; Daniel G. Hill, *The Freedom-Seekers: Blacks in Early Canada* (Agincourt: Book Society of Canada Limited, 1981), 56; and Frederick H. Armstrong, Bryan Walls, Hilary Bates Neary, and Karolyn Smardz Frost, *Ontario's African-Canadian Heritage: Collected Writings by Fred Landon, 1919–1974* (Toronto, ON: Natural Heritage Books, 2009), 172.

38. Siebert, *The Underground Railroad from Slavery to Freedom,* 220.

39. St. Catharines is just nineteen kilometers (twelve miles) from the United States international border.

40. Drew, *The Refugee,* 11.

41. St. Catharines Census, 1871.

42. Concession Street is now Welland Avenue. Hill, *The Freedom-Seekers,* 56.

43. *St. Catharines Journal,* January 28, 1847, and December 12, 1850.

44. *Evening Journal* (St. Catharines), November 2, 1865; *Evening Journal* (St. Catharines), December 20, 1866. *St. Catharines Journal,* September 10, 1857; *St. Catharines Constitutional,* March

29, 1860; and *Evening Journal,* July 13, 1863. "Africa" was used interchangeably as both a neutral and negative statement to describe the settlement. It was used more often as a derogatory statement or with bigoted undertones, yet the context must be checked. Fred Parnell explained: "I would say that the little village was known all over the Township of Grantham under the vulgar name of 'Coontown'" (Letter from Fred Parnell to Mrs. Margaret Gander, *Reminiscences of Fred Parnell,* December 23, 1944, St. Catharines Museum).

45. Welland Railroad Station opened in 1856 on a triangle of land bounded by Welland Avenue, Geneva Street, and Balfour Street (on the corner of Geneva and Welland). The station served the Welland Railroad, which was essentially a north-south line running from Lake Ontario (Port Dalhousie) to Lake Erie (Port Colborne). The other station was located on Great Western Railroad Street at Ridley Road, and it served the Great Western Railway, which ran fundamentally east-west from Windsor to Hamilton and to the border at Niagara Falls.

46. Jackson and Wilson, *St. Catharines: Canada's Canal City,* 48. Individuals such as laborers David Butler and William Hutchinson both had large families and owned frame homes on North, while waiter Robert White and carpenter John Jackson spent time there as well. St. Catharines Census, 1861; and *Toronto: Mitchell & Co.'s General Directory for the Town of St. Catharines and Gazetteer of the Counties of Lincoln and Welland* (Toronto, ON: Mitchell & Co., Publishers, 1865), 68, 41.

47. St. Catharines Census, 1851; Barbara Jeanne Fields, *Slavery and Freedom on the Middle Ground: Maryland During the Nineteenth Century* (New Haven, CT: Yale University Press, 1985); Kay Najiyyah McKelvey, "Early Black Dorchester, 1776–1870: A History of the Struggle of African-Americans in Dorchester County, Maryland, to Be Free to Make Their Own Choices," PhD diss., University of Maryland, 1991.

48. Larson, *Bound for the Promised Land,* 155.

49. William Wells Brown, quoted in Ripley, *Black Abolitionist Papers,* 2:464–66.

50. *Mitchell & Co.'s General Directory,* 49, 27, 60.

51. *St. Catharines Constitutional,* May 2, 1855; and *Provincial Freeman,* May 25, 1855.

52. Jackson and Wilson, *St. Catharines: Canada's Canal City,* 48.

53. Nancy Butler, "Black History in St. Catharines—What the Numbers Say," *Historical Society of St. Catharines Newsletter* (Feb. 1996): 6; and William Wells Brown, quoted in Ripley, *Black Abolitionist Papers,* 2:464–66.

54. Ripley, *Black Abolitionist Papers,* 2:465.

55. Drew, *The Refugee,* 12.

56. St. Catharines 1855 Assessment Roll; St. Catharines Census, 1861; Butler, "What the Numbers Say," 8.

57. *Daily Standard* (St. Catharines), November 19, 1912.

58. William Wells Brown, quoted in Ripley, *Black Abolitionist Papers,* 2:464–66.

59. Grantham Township Census, 1861 and 1871; Larson, *Bound for the Promised Land,* 145, 155.

60. Jackson and Wilson, *St. Catharines: Canada's Canal City,* 19–20; Fred Parnell, "The Colored Village," 39.

61. Grantham Township Census, 1861 and 1871; John Gregory Miller, *Black Heritage in Grantham Township, Lincoln County* (St. Catharines, ON: The Ontario Genealogical Society, Niagara Peninsula Branch, 1993); Larson, *Bound for the Promised Land,* 145, 155, 347.

62. Grantham Township Census, 1861 and 1871. Generations of Nicholsons lived on the land Adam purchased and in the house he constructed.

63. Fred Parnell, "The Colored Village," 39; Batavia Census, 1850; Buffalo Census, 1860; and Grantham Township Census, 1871.

64. Sarah Nicholson died January 24, 1892, at age 14, and Liddia Nicholson died June 12, 1893, at age 12. Adam Nicholson died on January 13, 1911, and was laid to rest at the McNab Church Cemetery; his wife Mary died on May 9, 1918.

65. *North Star,* December 22, 1848; Hiram Wilson to William L. Garrison, March 25, 1848, in the *Liberator,* April 7, 1848; Hiram Wilson to Edmund Quincy, September 27, 1848, in the *Liberator,* October 27, 1848; Jane H. Pease and William H. Pease, *Black Utopia: Negro Communal Experiments in America* (Madison: State Historical Society of Wisconsin, 1963), 71; J. Brent Morris, *Oberlin, Hotbed of Abolitionism: College, Community, and the Fight for Freedom and Equality in Antebellum America* (Chapel Hill: University of North Carolina Press, 2014), 83–87.

66. "The Flight into Canada," *The Liberator,* October 25, 1850.

67. Pease and Pease, *Bound with Them in Chains,* 21 and 132. Chapter 6 in the book is titled, "The Clerical Do-Gooder: Hiram Wilson."

68. Williams and Goldie, *Sunshine and Shadow of Slave Life,* 47–49.

69. *Voice of the Fugitive,* May 21, 1851.

70. This is a message from Wilson to the AMA when he first came to St. Catharines, "Since we came to St. Catharines we have been a good deal perplexed, having to board for a fortnight or more while waiting the arrival of our effects & then we found it difficult to obtain a suitable house to live in as almost every place was occupied except houses for small families. The change has reduced us to emptiness." Letter, Rev. Hiram Wilson (St. Catharines) to George Whipple (New York City), December 16, 1850, A.M.A. Archives Document F1121.

71. *Provincial Freeman,* November 3, 1855.

72. *Provincial Freeman,* November 3, 1855 (rpr. October 23, 1856). See also April 5, May 10, and May 17, 1856.

73. Amelia Shadd Williamson wrote under a pseudonym of "Q," explaining: "the colored people . . . for years have been content to have a Missionary [Wilson] to think for them instead of thinking for themselves and to provide clothing for them, instead of providing it for themselves." *Provincial Freeman,* April 5, 1856; and Rhodes, *Mary Ann Shadd Cary,* 120–21.

74. *Provincial Freeman,* May 10, 1856.

75. "The People of Canada," *Pine and Palm* (Boston, MA), September 7, 14, 21, 28, October 19, November 30, and December 7, 1861; and Drew, *The Refugee,* 11.

76. *St. Catharines Journal,* June 5, 1856.

77. Hiram Wilson (St. Catharines, Canada West) to Hamilton Hill (Oberlin, Ohio), May 24, 1853, Oberlin College Archives, Oberlin, Ohio.

78. Mary A. H. Wilson was Hiram's second wife. His first wife was Miss Hannah Maria Hubbard, whom he married on September 17, 1838, at the Bethel Free Church in Troy, New York. She died at the Dawn Settlement in the home of Mrs. Stowe's "Uncle Tom"—Josiah Henson. Hiram Wilson lived in St. Catharines with Mary and his five children: Lydia M. Wilson (b.1843), Mary E. Wilson (b.1845), George S. Wilson (b.1847), and John J. Wilson (b.1841). He also applied to be the guardian of former slave Alavana Dicken in 1852. Bishop Daniel Alexander Payne explained that Hannah "was of great aid to her self-sacrificing husband, and for many years made her personal influence felt as a blessing to our unfortunate brethren in Canada." See "Married," *Colored American,* September

22, 1838; Bishop Daniel Alexander Payne, *Recollections of Seventy Years* (Nashville, TN: Publishing House of the A. M. E. Sunday School Union, 1888), 66, 319–20; Drew, *The Refugee,* 11.

79. For an example of Wilson's transnational travels in Rochester and elsewise, see this letter: Hiram Wilson (Rochester, New York) to Hamilton Hill (Oberlin, Ohio), February 29, 1848, Oberlin College Archives, Oberlin, Ohio.

80. "The Flight into Canada," *The Liberator,* October 25, 1850.

81. Rev. Hiram Wilson to Rev. Dr. Lothrop, "Canada Mission: Semi Annual Report," May 9, 1857, 1–4, Peabody Essex Museum, Salem, Massachusetts; *St. Catharines Journal,* June 5, 1856; and Rev. Hiram Wilson to Rev. S. K. Lothrop, "New England Society for Propagating the Gospel among North American Indians & Others Records," Oct. 16, 1855, 1–3, Peabody Essex Museum, Salem, Massachusetts. See http://pem-voyager.hosted.exlibrisgroup.com/vwebv/.

82. Rev. Hiram Wilson to William Still, July 2, 1855, in Still, *The Underground Railroad* (Philadelphia, PA: Porter and Coates, 1872), 42; and Letter, Rev. Hiram Wilson (St. Catharines) to George Whipple (New York City), December 16, 1850, AMA Archives document Fl121.

83. Rev. Robert Ker, ed., *Marriage Records: St. George's Parish Church, 1841–1891* (St. Catharines, Ontario: Historic & Centenary Review, 1998).

84. St. Catharines Assessment Records, 1857.

85. "St Paul Street East" was a term that showed up on old maps for a while, but it did not catch on. *St. Catharines Journal,* February 24, 1859; St. Catharines Census, 1861; and *Mitchell & Co.'s General Directory, 1865.*

86. *St. Catharines Constitutional,* August 3, 1865. Also note that some whites entered the community out of sheer curiosity. A visitor to St. Catharines from England was surprised to see that the congregation of a predominantly Black church had "a white face here and there." The tourists came to observe the peculiar race and noticed that they were a "happy," "bright eyes" and "white teeth" people who worshiped in a ridiculous manner. For outsiders to witness whites in the Black section of town could have been extraordinary, but for locals it gradually became quite normal. A St. Catharines resident writing to his sister in England explained, "I may mention as illustration of the state of society, that every one is called, it matters not in what position or occupation they stand, as Mr. or Mrs., or this Gentleman, or that Lady, even the Niggars . . . all becoming citizens and equals." While the writer was supposedly well-meaning, the irony of using a derogatory term to describe Blacks clearly rendered them unequal in the eyes of the writer and demonstrated the larger issue of race in this "important" place (*Evening Journal,* July 13, 1865; *St. Catharines Journal,* January 28, 1847; and *St. Catharines Constitutional,* September 11, 1856).

87. *St. Catharines Journal,* July 1, 1852.

88. *St. Catharines Journal,* July 1, 1852; and "Fight Between Negroes and Whites," *Frederick Douglass' Paper,* July 16, 1852.

89. *Hamilton Gazette,* July 1, 1852; *Hamilton Gazette,* July 8, 1852; "The St. Catharines Riot," *Toronto Globe,* July 31, 1852; and "Fight Between Negroes and Whites," *Frederick Douglass' Paper,* July 16, 1852.

90. *St. Catharines Journal,* July 8, 1852, Editorial Comment.

91. Howe, *Refugees from Slavery,* 45–46.

92. "Canada," *Frederick Douglass' Paper,* September 3, 1852, 2. Douglass announced his visit to St. Catharines in *Frederick Douglass' Paper,* August 13, 1852.

93. St. Catharine Municipal Council Minutes, March 14, 1853.

94. *Toronto Globe,* July 31, 1852; *Provincial Freeman,* March 24, 1853.

95. Chippawa is now a community within the city of Niagara Falls, Ontario.

96. "Good News from Slavery," *Voice of the Fugitive,* September 23, 1852. Reprinted from the *Toronto Examiner.*

97. *Hamilton Gazette,* July 31, 1852. Reprint of July 6, 1852, letter from Hiram Wilson to the editor of the *New York Tribune.*

98. *St. Catharines Journal,* August 5, 1852.

99. "Attempted case of Kidnapping—Riot, &c.," *St. Catharines Constitutional,* August 26, 1855; and *Provincial Freeman,* September 15, 1855.

100. *St. Catharines Journal,* August 30, 1855; *St. Catharines Constitutional,* September 5, 1855; Murray, "Hands across the Border," 186–209.

101. Alvany, A Free Woman of Color, against Joseph J. W. Powell, Executor of Benjamin Dicken and Others, 7–8, East Carolina University, Greenville, NC, Joseph J. W. Powell Papers.

102. *St. Catharines Journal,* August 5, 1852. See also "Good News from Slavery," *Voice of the Fugitive,* September 23, 1852. Reprint from the *Toronto Examiner.*

103. Letter, The Rev. Hiram Wilson, St. Catharines, to George Whipple (New York City). September 1, 1852 [A.M.A. Archives Document Fl-271], page 3.

104. Letter, The Rev. Hiram Wilson, St. Catharines, to Brother Harned (New York City) July 30, 1852 [A.M.A. Archives Document Fl-264].

105. "Take Notice," *St. Catharines Journal,* November 4, 1852 (ad dated October 20, 1852; first printed in issue of October 21, 1852).

106. Alvany, A Free Woman of Color, against Joseph J. W. Powell, Executor of Benjamin Dicken and Others, Joseph J. W. Powell Papers, 8.

107. Crime seemed to increase in the area after 1863. Examples: "The Infanticide Case," *Evening Journal (St. Catharines),* February 25, 1864; *Evening Journal (St. Catharines),* April 23, 1864, James Parker was charged with fighting in the street; *Evening Journal (St. Catharines),* July 28, 1864, six Black boys broke into a building. Of course, some lifelong criminals like Willis Stark, who made the local headlines for several different misdeeds, including assault and slander, existed but nothing extensive. See *St. Catharines Journal,* December 18, 1856; *St. Catharines Constitutional,* February 2, 1860; *St. Catharines Semi-Weekly Post,* September 17, 1861; *St. Catharines Evening Journal,* May 26, 1866; *St. Catharines Evening,* January 7, 1869; and *St. Catharines Evening Journal,* May 4, 1870.

108. Or "hundred yards."

109. *Provincial Freeman,* March 24, 1853.

110. William Wells Brown, quoted in Ripley, *Black Abolitionist Papers,* 2:465.

111. Hill, *The Freedom-Seekers,* 56.

112. Nancy Butler, "Three Black Businessmen in St. Catharines: Thomas Douglas, Aaron Young, and John W. Lindsay," St. Catharines Historical Society, St. Catharines, Ontario, February 6, 1997, 9.

113. Drew, *The Refugee,* 53.

114. American Freedmen's Inquiry Commission Interview, 1863, in Blassingame, *Slave Testimony,* 398; and dann j. Broyld, "'Justice was Refused Me, I Resolved to Free Myself': John W. Lindsay Finding Elements of American Freedom's in British Canada, 1805–1876," *Ontario History* 109, no. 1. (Spring 2017): 27–59.

115. See, for example, St. Catharines Assessment Rolls, 1854, 1855, 1860, 1862, 1863, 1866, 1867, 1871, 1872, 1873, and 1876. Lindsay permitted two fellow blacksmiths, twenty-four-year-old Adam Anderson in 1854 and fifty-year old Joseph Cornish in 1866, to dwell in the edifices he managed. Years later, spinster Louisa Decater lived on Centre Street and, at the time of Lindsay's death, merchant John B. Gwinner inhibited St. Paul Street. As a lifelong dog owner, Lindsay allowed his tenants to possess canines as well (St. Catharines Assessment Rolls, 1854, 1866, 1872, 1876. See Prince, *My Brother's Keeper,* 225, which highlights the 1862 dog situation in St. Catharines.

116. Hogle, "a hardened old sinner," in the mid-1850s was brought before the mayor for keeping a house of "ill-fame." The *Constitutional* reported: "after the charge being fully established, she was mulcted in the sum of $20 . . . which was paid at once." Luckily the house of prostitution did not directly reflect badly on Lindsay, as most of his renters were considered persons of high character. Another one of his houses was destroyed after a big fire broke out in 1862 on the corner of Geneva and St. Paul Streets ("Police Office," *St. Catharines Constitutional,* June 27, 1855; St. Catharines Census, 1861; and *Evening Journal* (St. Catharines), September 16, 1862).

117. Rt. Rev. Dr. Daniel D. Rupwate, "A Historical Significance of the 'Salem Chapel' with Reference to the Underground Railroad Movement and A Tribute to Harriet Tubman" (St. Catharines, ON: Self-published, 2006), 11.

118. The old Methodist church stood in the back of the present-day church on North Street.

119. Rupwate, "Salem Chapel," 11.

120. Owen A. Thomas, *Niagara's Freedom Trail: A Guide to African-Canadian History on the Niagara Peninsula* (Thorold, ON: Assistance of the Ontario Heritage Foundation, 1995), 39.

121. See Broyld, "The 'Dark Sheep' of the Atlantic World: Following the Transnational Trail of Blacks to Canada," in Talton and Mills, *Black Subjects,* 104–5.

122. *St. Catharines Constitutional,* November 7, 1855.

123. Even today the Black Methodist Church is considered architecturally significant to the city of St. Catharines, and it holds a historical designation. The original uneven wooden planking is still visible and stands as a testament to the quality of the structure.

124. *St. Catharines Constitutional,* October 31, 1855. In 1852, Payne was elected and consecrated the sixth bishop of the AME denomination, and he held the position until his death in 1893. Bishop Payne became one of the most influential religious leaders in North America and in 1863 he became the first African American president of a college, Wilberforce University, in the United States. See Bishop Daniel Alexander Payne, *Recollections of Seventy Years,* originally printed in 1888. In 1891, he wrote the first history of his denomination titled: *The History of the A.M.E. Church* (Nashville, TN: Publishing House of the A.M.E. Sunday School Union, 1891).

125. *St. Catharines Constitutional,* October 31, 1855.

126. W. M. Willis, "Origin of the British Methodist Episcopal Church of Canada in St. Catharines," St. Catharines Museum, British Methodist Episcopal Church File (no page numbers); and *St. Catharines Journal,* October 22, 1857.

127. *St. Catharines Journal,* October 22, 1857.

128. See S. J. Celestine Edwards, *From Slavery to a Bishopric, or, The Life of Bishop Walter Hawkins of the British Methodist Episcopal Church Canada* (London: John Kensit, 1891). It stated: "By a convention held in 1856 the Canadian portion separated from the mother church, and called itself the British Methodist Episcopal Church of Canada, under which name it confined its operations

mainly among the coloured population . . . They had had enough of Yankee bounce, intolerance, and hardship in the past, and abundant experience of caste prejudice to hand over their congregation and all their property to the Yankee Eagle. Besides, the white people were too well disposed to them, and they had much more liberty than they could ever hope for from the Negro-hating Yankees to forsake the government of their choice. Indeed, such is the Canadian Negroes' love for their Queen and country that it will ever be impossible for them to act in any way that would show a sign of un-gratefulness or ingratitude. This was the spirit which prompted the members of the British Methodist Episcopal Church to cling to Canada and despise the temptation of joining hands with the American Episcopalians" (151–53).

129. Rupwate, "Salem Chapel," 20–24.

130. Salem Chapel is typical of other African American churches built in Amherstburg and Buxton, Ontario. Everything from festivals to funerals took place at the BME Church. It held a host of public meetings, including antislavery, missionary, and, of course, in British fashion, tea-meetings. The BME Church also had "Camp meetings," outside of town, in which they attempted to convert individuals to Christianity. At an 1860 "monster" assembly of some 8,000 people, the Methodists were able to win souls over to Christ (*St. Catharines Journal*, June 3, 1858; *Provincial Freeman*, October 23, 1854; *St. Catharines Journal*, September 6, 1860; and *St. Catharines Constitutional*, August 22, 1861).

131. Born in 1776, Elder Washington Christian was a native of Virginia who was ordained at New York's Abyssinia Baptist Church and worked as a missionary in New England before arriving in Canada to aid refugee slaves in 1825. A year later, Christian organized the first Baptist church in Toronto, Black or white. He formed other Baptist congregations in St. Catharines, Niagara, Hamilton, and made an extensive tour of Black settlements from Chatham to Sandwich (Windsor) in 1847. Christian continued to preside over his church in the provincial capital until his death in 1850. Karolyn Smardz Frost explained that Christian seemingly founded "new churches wherever he went" (*Dictionary of Canadian Biography, 1836–1850, Vol. VII* [Toronto, ON: University of Toronto Press, 2000], 181–82; and Frost, *Steal Away Home*, 52).

132. *St. Catharines Journal*, March 11, 1841.

133. *St. Catharines Journal*, March 11, 1841.

134. Rev. Hiram Wilson to Rev. S. K. Lothrop, "Semi Annual Report of Canada Mission," October 16, 1855, Peabody Essex Museum, Salem, Massachusetts.

135. *St. Catharines Journal*, July 5 and September 20, 1844.

136. Oral interviews with Marjorie Dawson, February 17 and April 25, 1994; and oral interviews with Mary Flowers, April 18, 1994, St. Catharines Museum, Black Miscellaneous File.

137. *St. Catharines Journal*, September 20, 1844.

138. *Lockport Daily Advertiser and Journal*, June 21, 1859; and *St. Catharines Journal*, June 23, 1859.

139. *St. Catharines Journal*, February 10, 1859.

140. *St. Catharines Journal*, June 26, 1856.

141. "A Preaching Bigamist," *St. Catharines Journal*, June 23, 1859.

142. Stevens, *Anthony Burns*; Frank, *Trials of Anthony Burns*; Maltz, *Fugitive Slave on Trial*.

143. William Wells Brown, quoted in Ripley, *Black Abolitionist Papers*, 2:465.

144. Nancy Butler, "Speech to Thorold and Beaver Dams Historical Society on Anthony Burns," St. Catharines, Ontario, January 29, 1996, 10.

145. *St. Catharines Evening Journal,* May 9, 1862; and *Detroit Free Press,* August 6, 1862.

146. Thomas, *Niagara's Freedom Trail,* 56.

147. Today the St. Catharines Cemetery is Victoria Lawn Cemetery in St. Catharines. Butler, "Speech to Thorold and Beaver Dams Historical Society on Anthony Burns," 10.

148. *St. Catharines Journal* aided liberal causes and took a moderate stance on all issues, while *St. Catharines Constitutional* was staunchly conservative and maintained a wider circulation. The two early editors of the *Journal,* Hiram Leavenworth (1826–43) and Thorpe Holmes (1843–57), took a fairly progressive approach, but in 1857 the tone of the paper changed after William Grant (1857–64) took it over. Under the leadership of Grant, the coverage of Blacks became more racially prejudiced (Joanne M. Corbett, "*St. Catharines Newspapers History,*" St. Catharines Public Library Special Collections, 1994, 1–13). For example, the BME financial woes captured the attention of local newspapers, especially when Reverend Harper accused trustee John W. Lindsay of stealing $200 of the church's money in 1857. Lindsay was surprised by these accusations. Since 1851, he had been entrusted with the Building Fund for Salem Chapel and managed to keep an honorable reputation. On several occasions, Lindsay lent his own horses to haul lumber to the construction site for Salem and advanced his own funds to prevent work stoppages. In a letter to the editor of the *Journal,* Lindsay sought to clear his name. He explained that soon after Reverend Harper became pastor in 1855, some suspicious dealings started to occur. Harper lied about the balance remaining on the church's mortgage, and once he found out that Lindsay was wealthy, he figured he would attempt to swindle him out of a couple hundred dollars. The BME Church was already in financial straits, and Harper's dishonesty only added a layer to their existing problems. The story reached its peak when Lindsay charged Harper with threatening to take his life. The Church's monetary despair seemed to be a favored topic of the press instead of the great outreach they did for American fugitive Blacks (*St. Catharines Journal,* September 3, 1857; "B.M.E. Colored Church," *St. Catharines Journal,* October 22, 1857; "Police Report," *St. Catharines Journal,* July 9, 1857).

149. Letters of Hiram Wilson (St. Catharines, West Canada) to Miss Hannah Gray (New Haven, Connecticut), *Journal of Negro History* 14, no. 3 (July 1929): 344–45. The letter was written on March 22, 1853.

150. *St. Catharines Journal,* April 22, 1852.

151. "Letter from Hiram Wilson," *Voice of the Fugitive,* May 6, 1852.

152. "Letter from Hiram Wilson," *Voice of the Fugitive,* May 6, 1852; and Simpson and Lovejoy, *Under the North Star,* 106.

153. *St. Catharines Journal,* April 15, 1852.

154. *St. Catharines Constitutional,* April 21, 1852.

155. Ripley, *Black Abolitionist Papers,* 2:465; and "Relief of Fugitives in Canada," *The Liberator,* December 20, 1861.

156. There are only limited resources on the Fugitive Aid Society of St. Catharines. This is partly the result of the lack of salvageable 1861 local newspapers. This society, established by Tubman, is discussed more later in this chapter.

157. *The Liberator,* October 25, 1850.

158. Power and Butler, *Slavery and Freedom in Niagara,* 66.

159. St. Catharines Assessment Records, 1854 and 1855; *Daily Standard* (St. Catharines) November 19, 1912.

160. Letter, Rev. Hiram Wilson, St. Catharines, C. W., January 11, 1854, to William Lloyd Garrison, published in the *Liberator,* February 10, 1854.

161. St. Catharines Assessment Roll, 1856.

162. *St. Catharines Constitutional,* July 29, 1853.

163. The Welland House is still on the corner of King and Ontario Streets.

164. "The Canada (monthly) General Railway and Steam Navigation Guide," no. 2, July 1, 1856 (Toronto: Pub. for the Proprietor by MacLear), 9; Jon Sterngass, "African American Workers and Southern Visitors at Antebellum Saratoga Springs," *American Nineteenth Century History* 2, no. 2 (2001): 35–59; and "Saratoga Waters in the Shade," *St. Catharines Journal,* July 28, 1853.

165. *St. Catharines Journal,* August 11, 1859; quote from *St. Catharines Journal,* June 23, 1859.

166. "A Hint from the Spa at St. Catharines," *Toronto Globe,* August 5, 1856.

167. St. Catharines *Constitutional,* September 19, 1855.

168. Agnes Eleanor Lee, Letter, Aug. 6, 1860, St. Catharines to Annie Lee (St. Catharines Museum, 1983).

169. *The Medical Properties of the St. Catharines Mineral Water. E. W. Stephenson, Proprietor* (St. Catharines: H. F. Leavenworth's "Herald" Power Press, 1864), 4.

170. "Concentrated Mineral Water, from the St. Catharines Mineral Well," *Welland Advocate and Review* (Port Robinson), April 10, 1852. See also Colin K. Duquemin, *The Spas at St. Catharines* (Fonthill: Niagara South Board of Education, St. Johns Outdoor Studies Centre, 1982. Outdoor Studies Pamphlet, no. 113), 31 and 95; and Ernest Green, "The Search for Salt in Upper Canada," Ontario Historical Society *Papers and Records* 26 (1930): 406–31.

171. Thomas, *Niagara's Freedom Trail,* 46–47.

172. *St. Catharines Journal,* August 11, 1859.

173. Addresses: St. Catharines' House was on King at the corner of James, and the American Hotel was on James between St. Paul and King.

174. *St. Catharines Journal,* April 29, 1858. Today Port Dalhousie is part of St. Catharines.

175. *St. Catharines Journal,* August 19, 1858.

176. "The St. Catharine's Meeting" and "Disgraceful Outrages," *Provincial Freeman,* August 12, 1854.

177. *Provincial Freeman,* August 12, 1854.

178. *Provincial Freeman,* August 12, 1854, and September 2, 1854; and *The Liberator,* August 25, 1854.

179. *North Star,* August 25, 1854.

180. "The St. Catharine's Meeting," *Provincial Freeman,* August 12, 1854.

181. *St. Catharines Journal,* August 19, 1858; and St. Catharines Assessment Roll 1860.

182. *St. Catharines Journal,* September 18, 1851; and St. Catharines Assessment Roll 1857.

183. Catherine Slaney, *Family Secrets: Crossing the Colour Line* (Toronto, ON: Natural Heritage Books, 2003), 88.

184. *St. Catharines Constitutional,* August 1, 1867. It was announced that he died (Nov. 3, 1883) in *The Globe* (Toronto) November 6, 1883.

185. *St. Catharines Journal,* October 22, 1857.

186. *St. Catharines Journal,* February 21, 1861; Douglas W. Bristol Jr., "Regional Identity, Barbers and the African American Tradition of Entrepreneurialism," *Southern Quarterly* 43, no. 2 (Winter 2006): 337–59.

187. *St. Catharines Evening Journal,* August 17, 1865.

188. Butler, "What the Numbers Say," 7.

189. *Provincial Freeman,* May 25, 1855.

190. *St. Catharines Journal,* September 27, 1855; *Provincial Freeman,* September 29, 1855; and *Provincial Freeman,* October 6, 1855. The September *Freeman* gives a "Description of the articles stolen."

191. *Provincial Freeman,* September 29, 1855; and *St. Catharines Constitutional,* January 2, 1856.

192. Rhodes, *Mary Ann Shadd Cary,* 101–2, 112–14, 117, 159, 173.

193. *Provincial Freeman* (Chatham, Canada West), July 5, 1856, explained: "Births. In St. Catharines, June 22nd, Mrs. D. T. Williamson of a daughter"; and *St. Catharines Constitutional,* October 8, 1856.

194. *St. Catharines Constitutional,* January 14, 1857; and Kent, Canada West Census, 1861. David was listed as a thirty-six-year-old farmer and Amelia was thirty; they had four children all no more than five years of age in 1861.

195. Butler, "What the Numbers Say," 7.

196. St. Catharines Census, 1861.

197. Drew, *The Refugee,* 27; and St. Catharines Census, 1861. Hemsley highlighted, "I have never prayed for wealth nor honor, but only to guide His church and do His will" (Drew, 27).

198. *Mitchell & Co.'s General Directory,* 54.

199. *Evening Journal* (St. Catharines), September 16, 1862; Shirley J. Yee, "Gender Ideology and Black Women as Community-Builders in Ontario, 1850–70," *Canadian Historical Review* 75 (1995): 53–73; Elizabeth Jane Errington, *Wives and Mothers, Schoolmistresses and Scullery Maids: Working Women in Upper Canada, 1790–1840* (Montreal: McGill-Queen's University Press, 1995); and Elizabeth Jane Errington, "Women and Their Work in Upper Canada," *Canadian Historical Association,* no. 64 (2006): 1–43.

200. *Voice of the Fugitive,* September 24, 1851; "Celebration of the First of August," *St. Catharines Journal,* August 14, 1851; and "Anti-Slavery Meeting," *St. Catharines Journal,* December 11, 1851.

201. St. Catharines City Directory, 1879. Elizabeth was listed, "Dunlop, Mrs. Elizabeth (wid Elijah) seamstress, h St. Paul, nr Geneva."

202. Elijah B. Dunlop, Madison Passenger List, December 1852, Inward Shipping Records, Public Record Office of Victoria, Melbourne PROV, VPRS 7667; 1865 St. Catharines Directory; *The Argus* (Ballarat), March 21, 1863, and April 19, 1897. On September 20, 1898, Dunlop died. He was buried at White Hills Cemetery, Bendigo (grave 13615, section unknown). See also *St. Catharines Journal,* September 8, 1853.

203. *Provincial Freeman,* May 6, 1854.

204. *St. Catharines Constitutional,* July 3, 1862.

205. "Canada," *Frederick Douglass' Paper,* September 3, 1852.

206. "Awake thou that Sleepest, and Arise to Union: In this Land of Happiness & Freedom," *St. Catharines Semi-Weekly Post,* January 3, 1854.

207. An industrial school was also proposed at the 1853 National Negro Convention in Rochester.

208. Lindsay explained, "I have taught two colored boys to be blacksmiths since I have been here and they both turned out well. They got into shops, after they had worked with me" (American Freedmen's Inquiry Commission Interview, 1863, in Blassingame, *Slave Testimony,* 404).

209. Also see Reverend Richard Warren, *Narrative of the Life and Sufferings of Rev. Richard Warren (a fugitive slave) Written by Herself* (Hamilton, Canada West, 1850), 19. He wrote of "prosperity" in St. Catharines.

210. "A Recent Tour," *Provincial Freeman,* March 24, 1853.

211. "Canada," *Frederick Douglass' Paper,* September 3, 1852.

212. "More Canal Riots," *St. Catharines Journal,* December 14, 1843.

213. See Howe, *Refugees from Slavery,* 60–64.

214. Drew, *The Refugee,* 20.

215. Freedmen's Inquiry Commission, in Blassingame, *Slave Testimony,* 397.

216. *St. Catharines Journal,* February 27, 1840.

217. Girard, Phillips, and Brown, *A History in Law in Canada, Vol. 1,* 669–70.

218. Winks, *Blacks in Canada,* 374.

219. "School Teacher Wanted," *St. Catharines Journal,* July 1, 1852.

220. *Evening Journal* (St. Catharines), August 15, 1863.

221. 1863 American Freedmen's Inquiry Commission Interview, in Blassingame, *Slave Testimony,* 369–444.

222. Mr. Oscar F. Wilkins was white, and he lived on Welland Avenue, corner of Catherine. *St. Catharines Constitutional,* December 3, 1863.

223. *St. Catharines Journal,* June 5, 1856.

224. *Provincial Freeman,* May 6, 1854.

225. Attorney (Barrister) Mr. James F. Saxon was white. His office was on Queen, at the corner of St. Paul Street.

226. *The Liberator,* December 6, 1839.

227. St. Catharines Census, 1861. Two of their children must have died so young that they were never listed on the census; the others included Elizabeth, Irwin (Irvin), Harriet, Susan, John W., Perish (Paris), and Alfred. See also Carol Lasser, "Enacting Emancipation: African American Women Abolitionists at Oberlin and the Quest for Empowerment, Equality and Respectability," in *Women's Rights and Transatlantic Antislavery in the Era of Emancipation,* ed. Kathryn Kish Sklar and James Brewer Stewart (New Haven: Yale University Press, 2007). It should also be noted that Wilson sent talented Canadian students to Oberlin, demonstrating a two-way exchange of people across the international border. For an example, see Hiram Wilson (St. Catharines, Canada West) to Hamilton Hill (Oberlin, Ohio), February 7, 1853, Oberlin College Archives, Oberlin, Ohio. Wilson writes of sending thirteen-year-old "dark Mulatto" Patsey Ann Wadden to Oberlin for education and improvement. See also Roland M. Baumann, *Constructing Black Education at Oberlin College: A Documentary History* (Athens, OH: Ohio University Press, 2010), and Gray Kornblith and Carol Lasser, *The Struggle for Racial Equality in Oberlin, Ohio* (Baton Rouge: Louisiana State University Press, 2018).

228. Hiram Wilson (St. Catharines, Canada West) to Hamilton Hill (Oberlin, Ohio), April 13, 1852, Oberlin College Archives, Oberlin, Ohio.

229. American Freedmen's Inquiry Commission Interview, 1863, in Blassingame, *Slave Testimony,* 396–408.

230. *Evening Journal* (St. Catharines), February 3, 1871; *St. Catharines Constitutional,* April 13, 1871.

231. Report of Cases Decided in the Court of Queen's Bench, Vol. 31 (Toronto: Rowsell & Hutchi-

son, 1872), 274–79; and John C. Bacher, *Mirror and Catalyst: A History of the St. Catharines Institute and Vocational School 1827–1975* (St. Catharines, ON: The Author, 1975), 15.

232. Butler, "What the Numbers Say," 6.

233. Edward Taper and Moses Young were exceptions to the rule. Edward's father Joseph Taper, who fled to St. Catharines with his family after reading his own runaway ad in a Pennsylvania newspaper, explained, "We have good schools . . . my boy Edward who will be six years next January, is now reading & I intend keeping him at school until he becomes a good scholar." Moses was a top scholar at the Colored School. Young was the son of well-known Black barber Aaron Young. See Joseph Taper to Joseph Long, November 11, 1840, Joseph Long Papers, Special Collections Library, Duke University, Durham, North Carolina; and *St. Catharines Constitutional,* June 28, 1860.

234. "To My Colored Brethren," *St. Catharines Journal, Welland Canal* (Niagara District) *General Advertiser,* March 11, 1841.

235. "Mayor of St. Catharines," *Niagara Mail* (Niagara Falls, ON), January 26, 1853.

236. Drew, *The Refugee,* 59.

237. Parnell, "The Colored Village," 39.

238. "A Dark Affair Cleared Up," *St. Catharines Constitutional,* October 19, 1859.

239. *St. Catharines Journal,* October 6, 1859.

240. St. Catharines Census, 1861; and *Evening Journal* (St. Catharines), November 16, 1865. Instead of calling Mr. Champ, Black or colored, the newspaper proclaimed his Blackness via the Hamitic myth. See also *St. Catharines Constitutional,* June 10, 1857, which highlights a case in which Black barber Thomas P. Casey filed a police report accusing Elizabeth Saunders, a white woman, of using "abusive language" toward his wife. In an effort to keep his wife's name from being smeared and perhaps to make an example of Elizabeth, Casey charged her with slander.

241. See Lynne Marks, "Railing, Tattling and General Humour," *Canadian Historical Review* 81, no. 3 (Sept. 2000): 380–473.

242. In St. Catharines the border was just as powerful a tool as political rights—for better or worse. See the case of Irwin Lindsay, George Myers, and Henry Starks, who were accused of raping Mrs. Catherine Moore, a white woman. "Horrible Outrage upon a Female!" *St. Catharines Constitutional,* June 18, 1863; "Arrest and Escape of an Outlaw," *St. Catharines Constitutional,* July 2, 1863; "Out on Bail," *St. Catharines Constitutional,* July 16, 1863; "Rape," *Evening Journal,* November 5, 1863; and "Lincoln Assizes," *St. Catharines Constitutional,* November 5, 1863.

243. Butler, "What the Numbers Say," 6.

244. Perhaps more Blacks applied for citizenship; the names of fourteen people are missing from the naturalization records available.

245. *Naturalization Entries Records, 1842–49,* Niagara Peninsula Branch, Ontario Genealogical Society, 3. "Naturalization Entries From 1842 to 1849" appears to have been a copy retained by the Land Registry Office, since the second page contains the remark "Memorandum: Mailed the Duplicate original of this Book of Registry, the 23rd February 1843, addressed to the Honorable Richard A. Tucker, Provincial Registrar,—Enclosed also at the same time an Original List of persons who appeared before me for naturalization under the old Law during the year 1841." The volume forms part of the papers and records of the Niagara North Land Registry Office #30. The "author" could be cited as the Land Registrar: John Lyons, who signed and certified the naturalization entries up to Feb. 22, 1843; subsequent naturalizations were certified by the Land Registrar John Powell until November

28, 1849. See also the work of genealogist Guylaine Petrin, who has unpublished research on dozens of naturalizations in Lincoln County.

246. *Naturalization Records 1842–1849 for the Counties of Lincoln and Welland* (St. Catharines, ON: Ontario Genealogical Society, 1993), 3–4. Note that the naturalization records are not complete, by any means, and just because a specific person could not be found in a specific register does not mean that they did not apply for naturalization.

247. See St. Catharines Assessment Roll (St. Paul Ward), 1858; Broyld, "Harriet Tubman"; and the historiography on Tubman in the "Introduction." The most noted treatment is Kate Clifford Larson's *Bound for the Promised Land*. See also Erica Armstrong Dunbar, *She Came to Slay: The Life and Times of Harriet Tubman* (New York, NY: Simon & Schuster, 2019).

248. Sadlier, *Harriet Tubman: Freedom Seeker, Freedom Leader,* 92–93; Larson, *Bound for the Promised Land,* 159, 151–52.

249. Larson, *Bound for the Promised Land,* 162.

250. Milton C. Sernett, *Harriet Tubman: Myth, Memory, and History* (Chapel Hill, NC: Duke University Press, 2007), 77–82.

251. John Brown to John Brown Jr., April 8, 1858, Boyd B. Stutler Collection, West Virginia State Archives, Charleston, West Virginia; and Larson, *Bound for the Promised Land,* 160.

252. William H. Day learned the printer trade working for the *Gazette* of North Hampton, Ohio. He later moved to Cleveland where he got involved in the abolitionist movement and edited the *Cleveland True Democrat* (1851–52) and the *Aliened American* (1853–54). In his short time in St. Catharines, he spoke a couple of times at the BME Church and received praise from Samuel R. Ward and Frederick Douglass for his lectures. In 1858, Day went on a European speaking and fundraising tour. He returned after the Civil War to work for the Freedmen's Bureau. See Quarles, *Black Abolitionists,* 217, 234–35; *St. Catharines Evening Journal,* August 4, 1864; and Todd Mealy, *Aliened American: A Biography of William Howard Day: 1825 to 1865, Vol. 1* (Baltimore, MD: America Star Books, 2010). See *St. Catharines Journal,* November 3, 1859; and Mealy, *Aliened American,* 275–76, regarding Tubman's introduction of Brown to Day.

253. Blackett, *Beating against the Barriers,* 304–10; *Semi-Weekly Post* (St. Catharines), October 29, 1857; *St. Catharines Journal,* October 29, 1857; and *Evening Journal* (St. Catharines), August 4, 1864.

254. *Provincial Freeman,* November 25, 1856.

255. William Howard Day to Gerrit Smith, June 21, 1858, Gerrit Smith Papers, George Arents Research Library, Syracuse University; Rhodes, *Mary Ann Shadd Cary,* 131–32; Simpson and Lovejoy, *Under the North Star,* 94–96; and Blackett, *Beating against the Barriers,* 312–13.

256. *St. Catharines Journal,* November 3, 1859.

257. Stanley Smith, "Old John Brown in Ingersoll," *Ingersoll Tribune Centennial Issue,* 1967; and Simpson and Lovejoy, *Under the North Star,* 373–74. Tubman left St. Catharines late to go to Ingersoll, and Brown waited at the train station for her, but she never came. William H. Day attempted to solve the travel mix-up, yet his attempts were in vain. Day wrote to Brown to connect him with local Ingersoll Blacks that could aid his agenda. Jackson, *Force and Freedom,* 177–26.

258. Jackson, *Force and Freedom,* 111–20, quote on 116.

259. St. Catharines Municipal Council Minutes, December 20, 1858, and December 30, 1858. See also "Christmas," *St. Catharines Journal,* December 23, 1858.

260. St. Catharines Municipal Council Minutes, March 15, 1859, and April 11, 1859.

261. Sernett, *Harriet Tubman: Myth, Memory, and History,* 81–82.

262. Sernett, *Harriet Tubman: Myth, Memory, and History*, 79–81; and Jackson, *Force and Freedom*, 120–26.

263. Blackett, *Beating against the Barriers*, 313–23.

264. Douglass, *Life and Times* (Park, 1881), 327.

265. *St. Catharines Journal*, November 3, 1859. Although the next issue of this newspaper, dated November 10, 1859, contains Part II of a long open letter to the editor of the *Rochester Democrat*, datelined "Upper Canada" and dated October 30, no Part I could be found in this issue of the paper.

266. Martha Coffin Wright to William Lloyd Garrison II, January 10, 1869, Garrison Family Papers, Sophia Smith Collection, Smith College, Northampton, Massachusetts.

267. Larson, *Bound for the Promised Land*, 163.

268. Larson, *Bound for the Promised Land*, 152, 163–65.

269. Larson, *Bound for the Promised Land*, 178.

270. Larson notes: "Tubman probably packed up her family and moved back to the relative safety of St. Catharines" (Larson, *Bound for the Promised Land*, 178).

271. "A Fugitive Slave from Harpers Ferry at Auburn—Narrow Escape from United States Marshall," *New York Herald*, January 21, 1860. Months after coconspirator Osborne P. Anderson had partaken in John Brown's insurrection, he was in Auburn for unknown reasons but was able to successfully elude authorities.

272. *Evening Journal* (St. Catharines), December 1, 1864.

273. Ripley, *Black Abolitionist Papers*, 2:465.

274. Still, *The Underground Railroad* (Philadelphia, PA: Porter and Coates, 1872), 279–80; Bradford, *Scenes in the Life of Harriet Tubman*, 27–35; Kashatus, *William Still*, 139; Larson, *Bound for the Promised Land*, 133–36, 159.

275. For Shadd's complaints on Wilson, see *Provincial Freeman*, November 3, 1855 (rpr. October 23, 1856). Also see April 5, May 10, and May 17, 1856.

276. Hiram Wilson (St. Catharines, Canada West) to Hamilton Hill (Oberlin, Ohio), November 22, 1850, Oberlin College Archives, Oberlin, Ohio.

277. Larson, *Bound for the Promised Land*, 192–93; Sadlier, *Harriet Tubman: Freedom Seeker, Freedom Leader*, 103.

278. Broyld, "Harriet Tubman," 78–98. There are only limited resources on the Fugitive Aid Society of St. Catharines, partly because many local newspapers from 1861 are not salvageable. Quote: *Auburn Citizen*, March 11, 1913, written in a June 16, 1868, letter by Wendell Phillips; and Jeff W. Grigg, *The Combahee River Raid: Harriet Tubman & Lowcountry Liberation* (Charleston, SC: History Press, 2014), chap. 1.

279. *Frederick Douglass' Paper*, December 18, 1857; Rev. Hiram Wilson, St. Catharines, C. W., October 30, 1857, to *The Congregationalist*; rpr. in *National Anti-Slavery Standard*, November 21, 1857.

280. Still, *The Underground Railroad* (London: Benediction Books, 2008), 514.

281. Frost, *I've Got a Home in Glory Land*, 300–302.

282. "Emancipation Day," *St. Catharines Journal*, August 5, 1858.

283. "West India Emancipation," *St. Catharines Journal*, August 4, 1859.

284. "First of August," *St. Catharines Journal*, August 16, 1860. See full poem in Appendix. Also *St. Catharines Journal*, July 26, 1860; and *St. Catharines Constitutional*, July 26, 1860, which highlight the coming celebration.

4. A BORDER THAT DIVIDES BUT ALSO UNITES

1. See Jason Kaufman, *The Origins of Canadian and American Political Differences* (Cambridge, MA: Harvard University Press, 2009); and Guadalupe Correa-Cabrera and Victor Konrad, eds., *North American Borders in Comparative Perspective* (Tucson, AZ: University of Arizona Press, 2020).

2. Baud and Van Schendel, "Toward a Comparative History of Borderlands," 242.

3. Stuart, *Report of Charles B. Stuart*, 3. See also *Provincial Freeman*, November 3, 1855; and *New York Times*, January 5, 1881.

4. Austin Steward initially thought "if they [Blacks] would but retire to the country and purchase a piece of land, cultivate and improve it, they would be far richer and happier than they can be in the crowded city. But he returned from Wilberforce to Rochester." Steward, *Twenty-Two Years a Slave*, 167, and see chap. 2 regarding Rochester as well.

5. Dagenais and Mauduit, *Revolutions across Borders*, 97.

6. Miller, *Borderline Crime*, 19–39.

7. Steward, *Twenty-Two Years a Slave*, 311–15, Coles, *Cradle of Freedom*, 83; and *Frederick Douglass' Paper*, July 27, 1855.

8. Silverman, "Monarchial Liberty and Republican Slavery," 10; see also Asaka, "'Our Brethren in the West Indies'"; Broyld, "'A Success in Every Particular.'"

9. *North Star*, August 10, 1849; Steward, *Twenty-Two Years a Slave*, 311–15; and *New York Daily Tribune*, August 2, 1855.

10. Ward, *Autobiography*, 139.

11. Floyd John Miller, *The Search for Black Nationality: Black Emigration and Colonization, 1787–1863* (Champaign: University of Illinois Press, 1975); Wilson Jeremiah Moses, *The Golden Age of Black Nationalism, 1850–1925* (Hamden, CT: Archon Books, 1978); and Neil Robert, *Freedom as Marronage* (Chicago: University of Chicago Press, 2015); Sylviane A. Diouf, *Slavery's Exiles: The Story of the American Maroons* (New York, NY: New York University Press, 2014); Richard Price, ed., *Maroon Societies: Rebel Slave Communities in the Americas, 3rd ed* (Baltimore, MD: Johns Hopkins University Press, 1996).

12. *Provincial Freeman*, March 24, 1853.

13. *St. Catharines Post*, October 28, 1856; and *St. Catharines Journal*, October 29, 1856.

14. See Raymond L. Hall, *Black Separatism in the United States* (Hanover, NH: University Press of New England, 1987); Pease and Pease, *Black Utopia*; Benedict Anderson, *Imagined Communities: Reflections on the Origin and Spread of Nationalism* (London: Verso, 2006); Elizabeth Rauh Bethel, *The Roots of African-American Identity: Memory and History in Antebellum Free Communities* (New York, NY: St. Martin's, 1999).

15. *Provincial Freeman*, May 6, 1854; *Provincial Freeman*, April 15, 1854; and Girard, Phillips, and Brown, *A History in Law in Canada, Vol. 1*, 669–70.

16. "Colored People of Canada," *Douglass' Monthly*, May 1859.

17. *Antislavery Bugle*, January 14, 1854. See also "A Home for Fugitives," *Syracuse Daily Journal*, August 15, 1856; and Rev. Hiram Wilson to Rev. S. K. Lothrop, "New England Society for Propagating the Gospel among North American Indians & Others," October 16, 1855, Peabody Essex Museum, Salem, Massachusetts.

18. "Colored People of Canada," *Douglass' Monthly*, May 1859.

19. *Syracuse Daily Standard,* June 5, 1856. See also *Syracuse Journal,* April 4, 1853; *Syracuse Reveille,* August 27, 1849.

20. *Provincial Freeman,* March 23, 1853.

21. Robert, *Freedom as Marronage;* Diouf, *Slavery's Exiles;* and Price, *Maroon Societies.*

22. *St. Catharines Journal,* September 10, 1857.

23. Howe, *Refugees from Slavery,* 104. See also Matthew Furrow, "Samuel Gridley Howe, the Black Population of Canada West, and the Racial Ideology of the 'Blueprint for Radical Reconstruction,'" *Journal of American History* 97, no. 2 (Sept. 2010): 344–70.

24. Drew, *The Refugee,* 20–27.

25. Drew, *The Refugee,* 49.

26. Still, *The Underground Railroad* (London: Benediction Books, 2008), 332–34. See also "Condition of Fugitives in Canada," *Provincial Freedom,* October 13, 1855.

27. Freedmen's Inquiry Commission, in Blassingame, *Slave Testimony,* 437–38; and Ripley, *Black Abolitionist Papers,* 2:39; and Parker Smith to Jacob C. White Jr., July 1861, Jacob C. White Papers, Moorland-Spingarn Research Center, Howard University.

28. Still, *The Underground Railroad* (London: Benediction Books, 2008), 539–45. Dungy stayed under the paw of the British Lion for four years before returning to the United States. He traveled back to Richmond, Virginia, to visit his old home after the Civil War. There, he met with the governor's two daughters, who were part of the family that held him in bondage. The younger one told Dungy that she "prayed for him," while the older one commented that she believed he was too "good a Christian to run away." She also thought that the letter Dungy sent from Rochester back to her "papa" was rather "naughty" (Still, *The Underground Railroad,* 541–45).

29. Joseph Taper to Joseph Long, November 11, 1840, Joseph Long Papers, Special Collections Library, Duke University, Durham, North Carolina.

30. Drew, *The Refugee,* 134.

31. Drew, *The Refugee,* 46.

32. Howe, *Refugees from Slavery,* 102.

33. *Weekly Anglo-African,* August 31, 1861.

34. American Freedmen's Inquiry Commission Interview, 1863, in Blassingame, *Slave Testimony,* 398; and Fought, *Women in the World of Frederick Douglass,* 185.

35. Hiram Wilson letter to Rev. Dr. Lothrop, October 4, 1860, from the Peabody Essex Museum, Salem, Massachusetts. See also "Mr. Lincoln's Reception in Rochester—The Trip to Albany," *Rochester Democrat,* February 19, 1861; "The President Elect," *Douglass' Monthly,* March 1861.

36. *Advocate of Freedom,* October 29, 1840.

37. *Montreal Witness,* April 20, 1846. Wilson wrote the letter from Rochester, New York, on February 9, 1846.

38. Semi Annual Report, Rev. Hiram Wilson, St. Catharines, Canada West, to Rev. Dr. Lothrop, Secretary of the Society for the Propagation of the Gospel, May 10, 1861, from the Peabody Essex Museum, Salem, Massachusetts.

39. Loguen, *The Rev. J. W. Loguen as a Slave and a Freeman,* 344.

40. Farley, "The African American Presence in the History of Western New York," 10; Rochester Census, 1860.

41. St. Catharines Census, 1861. The 1861 population of St. Catharines was 6,384. See also "Black

History in the Niagara Peninsula" by Maggie Parnall for detailed numbers on the Black population in St. Catharines.

42. "Reverse migration" is discussed in the Introduction and in subsequent chapters, sometimes by name but mostly via examples.

43. See Arenson, "Experience Rather than Imagination," 73–77; and Harold Holzer, Edna Greene Medford, and Frank J. Williams, *The Emancipation Proclamation: Three Views* (Baton Rouge: Louisiana State University Press, 2006).

44. *Rochester Union and Advertiser,* April 19, 1861; *Democrat and American,* April 19, 1861; and *Douglass' Monthly,* May 1861.

45. Edwin D. Morgan held office between 1858 and 1862. Ruth Rosenberg-Naparsteck, "A Growing Agitation: Rochester Before, During, and After the Civil War," *Rochester History* 46, nos. 1 & 2 (Jan. & April 1984): 27.

46. Frederick Douglass to Samuel J. May, August 30, 1861; and "Fighting Rebels with Only One Hand," *Douglass' Monthly,* September 1861.

47. "What About a Colored Regiment?" *Rochester Union and Advertiser,* February 9, 1863.

48. Julia G. Crofts to Douglass, Leeds, England, December 6, 1861, Frederick Douglass Papers, Library of Congress; and "War with England," *Douglass' Monthly,* January 1862.

49. Blight, *Frederick Douglass,* 334.

50. "Men of Color to Arms!" *Union and Advertiser,* March 3, 1863; see also Benjamin Quarles, *The Negro in the Civil War* (Boston: Little, Brown, 1969); Ira Berlin, Barbara J. Fields, Steven F. Miller, Joseph P. Reidy, and Leslie S. Rowland, eds., *Slaves No More: Three Essays on Emancipation and the Civil War* (Cambridge, Eng.: Cambridge University Press, 1992); and Leonard L. Richards, *Who Freed the Slaves? The Fight over the Thirteenth Amendment* (Chicago: University of Chicago Press, 2015).

51. "Men of Color to Arms!" *Union and Advertiser,* March 3, 1863; and Frederick Douglass to Gerrit Smith, Rochester, NY, March 6, 1863, Gerrit Smith Papers, Syracuse University.

52. "Going South," *Union and Advertiser,* August 20, 1863.

53. Samuel May to John B. Estlin, Boston, MA, September 30, 1847, Anti-Slavery Collection, Boston Public Library.

54. Though Martin Delany made an unfounded claim that "The *Freeman* in fact, has a much larger circulation among the colored people than the *Frederick Douglass Paper,*" it's clear that Douglass's periodicals definitely fared better than their contemporaries. See "What Does It Mean," *Provincial Freeman,* July 12, 1856.

55. Charles Remond Douglass, "Some Incidents of the Home Life of Frederick Douglass," in Bernier and Taylor, *If I Survive,* 670.

56. *Evening Journal* (St. Catharines), August 26, 1863.

57. "Men of Color to Arms!" *Union and Advertiser,* March 3, 1863; and David W. Blight, *Frederick Douglass' Civil War: Keeping Faith in Jubilee* (Baton Rouge: Louisiana State University Press, 1991), 161–72. Douglass also explained, "If speech alone could have abolished slavery, the work would have been done long ago." "Free Speech Outrage. An Anti-Slavery Meeting Broken Up by a Mob in Boston," *Douglass' Monthly,* January 1861.

58. Larson, *Bound for the Promised Land,* 212; and Grigg, *The Combahee River Raid.*

59. Gumbs, "Prophecy in the Present Tense," 142–44.

60. Larson, *Bound for the Promised Land,* 201–21; and *National Anti-Slavery Standard,* August 8, 1863.

61. Larson, *Bound for the Promised Land,* 221–28. See also *Toronto Globe,* April 2, 1913. See also the Tenth Annual Reports of the Rochester Ladies Anti-Slavery Society, 1861. The RLASS was sending aid to Tubman.

62. *Douglass' Monthly,* August 1861.

63. *New York Herald,* December 27, 1861. There was even a secret police force established to protect against Confederate agents. See Jeff Keshen, "Cloak and Dagger: Canada West's Secret Police, 1864–1867," *Ontario History* 79, no. 4 (Dec. 1987): 356, 358.

64. "The Colored Company," *St. Catharines Constitutional,* January 9, 1862, and February 6, 1862.

65. *Provincial Freeman,* August 5, 1854.

66. Steward, *Twenty-Two Years a Slave,* 321.

67. William Wells Brown, quoted in Ripley, *Black Abolitionist Papers,* 2:465.

68. *Evening Journal* (St. Catharines), July 23, 1863.

69. *Evening Journal* (St. Catharines), July 9, 1863; July 11, 1863; "A Big Scare," *Evening Journal* (St. Catharines), July 13, 1863; and July 15, 1863.

70. *Evening Journal* (St. Catharines), July 9, 1863.

71. "Worth Attention," *Evening Journal* (St. Catharines), March 13, 1866.

72. Some of the businessmen in St. Catharines believed that the war could perhaps make them more money. The *Evening Journal* remarked, "The troubles on 'the other side,' we imagine, will cause large numbers to seek recreation or health in Canada much earlier this season than in previous years." See "Local and Miscellaneous," *Evening Journal* (St. Catharines), May 3, 1862.

73. The fife has its origins in medieval Europe and was employed in military settings and in marching bands. It is a small high-pitched flute that is normally constructed with six finger holes (some have ten or eleven holes). *Consolidated Lists of Civil War Draft Registrations from 1863–1865.* NM-65, Entry 172, 620 Volumes. NAI: 4213514. Records of the Provost Marshal General's Bureau (Civil War), Record Group 110. The United States National Archives at Washington, DC. Also, Reid, *African Canadians in Union Blue,* 95; Winks, *The Civil War Years;* Boyko, *Blood and Daring;* Prince, *My Brother's Keeper.*

74. Mason's Island was also known as Analostan Island, and later it was named Theodore Roosevelt Island. See "Negroes Invading the Sacred Soil," *Washington National Republican,* May 22, 1863 and July 26, 1865; William B. Dobak, *Freedom by the Sword: The U.S. Colored Troops, 1862–67* (Washington, DC: GPO, 2011); Elizabeth Clark-Lewis, *First Freed: Washington, DC, in the Emancipation Era* (Washington, DC: Howard University Press, 2002); Mary E. Curry, "Theodore Roosevelt Island: A Broken Link to Early Washington, DC, History," *Records of the Colombian Historical Society* 71/72: 14–33; Willard Webb, "John Mason of Analostan Island," *Arlington Historical Magazine* 5 (Oct. 1976): 33–35.

75. Grant LaFleche, "Bringing Life to the 'Niagara Nine,'" *St. Catharines Journal,* February 22, 2003.

76. *Evening Journal* (St. Catharines), April 29, 1864.

77. *St. Catharines Constitutional,* May 11, 1865.

78. "The Mob in New York," *New York Times,* July 14, 1863; "The New York Riot: The Killing of Negroes," *Buffalo Morning Express,* July 18, 1863; *New York Daily News,* July 13, 1863; and *New York Daily Tribune,* July 14, 15, 16, 17, 18, 1863. See also Iver Bernstein, *The New York City Draft Riots: Their Significance for American Society and Politics in the Age of the Civil War* (New York, NY: Oxford University Press, 1991); and Barnet Schecter, *The Devil's Own Work: The Civil War Draft Riots and the Fight to Reconstruct America* (New York, NY: Walker Books, 2005).

79. *Evening Journal* (St. Catharines), July 23, 1863.

80. *Evening Journal* (St. Catharines), July 27, 1863; and Kevin Quashie, *The Sovereignty of Quiet: Beyond Resistance in Black Culture* (New Brunswick, NJ: Rutgers University Press, 2012).

81. Rochester City Directory, 1864.

82. Rochester City Directory, 1864. Francis was known as Frank.

83. Civil War Substitutes from the Rochester Area Index. Rochester, NY: Rochester Public Library, Local History Collection (unpublished); Rochester City Directory, 1861; and US Census, 1860.

84. Julia Wilbur Large Diary (Haverford College), December 22, 1860; and Whitacre, *A Civil Life in an Uncivil Time*, 70–77.

85. Secretary's Report, Twelfth Annual Report, Rochester Ladies' Anti-Slavery Society Records, William L. Clements Library, University of Michigan, Ann Arbor.

86. Julia Wilbur Journal Briefs (1844–62), Haverford College, Quaker and Special Collections, Pennsylvania, Haverford, 34; and Whitacre, *A Civil Life in an Uncivil Time*, 78–81.

87. Julia Wilbur Large Diary, March 15, 1864, May 21, 1864, and May 19, 1849 (Jacobs quote). See also the Tenth, Twelfth, Thirteenth, Fifteenth, and Sixteenth Annual Reports of the Rochester Ladies Anti-Slavery Society, 1861, 1863, 1864, 1865, 1866, and 1867. They have long passages about the work of Wilbur.

88. Amy Post to Isaac Post, n.d., Post Family Papers Project, University of Rochester; and Whitacre, *A Civil Life in an Uncivil Time*, 144. Post used "their" instead of "there."

89. *Evening Journal* (St. Catharines), April 16, 1864; and "Worth Attention," *Evening Journal* (St. Catharines), March 13, 1866.

90. *Evening Journal,* April 23, 1864; "Death of Hiram Wilson," *Liberator,* May 13, 1864; Pease and Pease, *Bound with Them in Chains,* 115–39.

91. *Evening Journal,* April 23, 1864, and April 30, 1864.

92. *St. Catharines Constitutional,* November 30, 1865.

93. John Joel Wilson (b. 1841; d. October 27, 1919); Lydia Maria Wilson (b. 1842; d. 1865); Mary Ellen Wilson (b. 1844; d. 1865); George Sturges Wilson (b. 1847; d. 1868).

94. On leave in August 1863, after being wounded, Wilson returned to St. Catharines, the *Evening Journal* reported. "He looks well, and seems determined to give the Confeds. another chance to shoot him," and the periodical noted his "preferment for meritorious conduct in the field." A year later, the *Constitutional* was informed that Wilson "was wounded in the face" during a Union strike on Petersburg "whether dangerously or not we are not informed." Miraculously, Wilson survived other injuries at the Battle of the Crater and the Battle at Fair Oaks. He managed to return to St. Catharines after the war but not without health difficulties. Wilson had a saber cut to his left hand, yielding his fingers partially useless, and missing teeth due to his being shot to the face. He also suffered from bad hearing as well as from back, nerve, and joint pains. The veteran went into business as a grocer on St. Paul Street and wedded Mary Alice Smith; the couple had four children. See *Evening Journal* (St. Catharines), August 6, 1863; *St. Catharines Constitutional,* August 11, 1864; *Evening Journal* (St. Catharines), August 4, 1864; US Pension Records, National Archives, Washington, DC, Application 1,075,534, Certificate 826, 998 (November 4, 1891) and Application 1,034,670, Certificate 788,132, (September 26, 1914).

95. Capt. Harper Wilson, "History of the 23d U.S.C.T., or 2d D.C.: Courage Tested, Endurance Tried, Efficiency in Every Phase of the Soldier's Life at the Front Exhibited," *The National Tribune* (Washington, DC), February 25, 1904; and Dobak, *Freedom by the Sword,* 338, 343, 362–65. Wilson

later relocated to Winnipeg, Manitoba, where he ran a retail fruit business and later got involved in city government as an inspector; he died on August 28, 1914. The *St. Catharines Standard* on April 29, 1913, explained that: "Still able to get around, is the Captain Harper Wilson is a Civil War Veteran." "Winnipeg Loses a Valued Citizen in Harper Wilson," *Winnipeg Telegram,* August 29, 1914; and "Death of Captain Harper Wilson," *Manitoba Free Press,* August 29, 1914. Harper Wilson died at his Winnipeg home on 219 Spence Street and was laid to rest in Elmwood Cemetery.

96. Mary Alice Smith from Glenmorris, Ontario, married Wilson on May 2, 1871. The couple had son William Harper Wilson on August 3, 1873; Perry Hoover Wilson on September 18, 1874, in St. Catharines; Grant Howard Wilson followed on August 27, 1883; and Sherman Wilson on June 10, 1891, in Winnipeg, Manitoba.

97. *Evening Journal* (St. Catharines), December 30, 1864; and *Evening Journal* (St. Catharines), January 3, 1864.

98. American Freedmen's Inquiry Commission Interview, 1863, in Blassingame, *Slave Testimony,* 398.

99. *Evening Journal* (St. Catharines), April 17, 1865, and April 20, 1865. The "Union Jack" is the flag of the United Kingdom; in Canada, it was known as the Royal Union Flag. See also *Union and Advertiser,* April 17, 1865 April 18, 1865, April 20, 1865, April 24, 1865, April 26, 1865, April 27, 1865, and April 29, 1865, as well as Edna Greene Medford, *Lincoln and Emancipation* (Carbondale, IL: Southern Illinois University Press, 2015), 103–8, and Quarles, *Lincoln and the Negro.*

100. *St. Catharines Constitutional,* August 17, 1865; and *Evening Journal* (St. Catharines), August 24, 1864.

101. *St. Catharines Constitutional,* August 24, 1865. It should be noted that supporters of the Southern cause resided in St. Catharines during and after the Civil War. In fact, when the former President of the Confederate States Jefferson Davis visited St. Catharine in October of 1867, he worshipped at the St. George's Anglican Church and was met by well-wishers at the Welland House ("Jeff Davis," *St. Catharines Constitutional,* October 10, 1867).

102. *Evening Journal* (St. Catharines), October 7, 1867.

103. The *Evening Journal* (St. Catharines) reported on April 16, 1864, that Hiram Wilson was "very ill" and only "slight hopes are entertained of his recovery." He died later that day. A casket and hearse were sent for Wilson, and his funeral took place at the American Presbyterian Church on April 24, 1864 (Date is unclear). See also "Death of Hiram Wilson," *Liberator,* May 13, 1864. Wilson's "cottage," which Mary Ann Shadd had criticized for the high cost of construction, was put on sale in short order for "very reasonable terms." (*Evening Journal,* April 23, 1864, and April 30, 1864.)

104. John J. Wilson to Douglass, August 8, 1888, Frederick Douglass Papers, "General Correspondence, 1841–1912," Reel 5, Frame 16, Library of Congress. John Joel Wilson was born in Canada in 1840. A graduate of Oberlin, he spent time in London, went on to be a business manager at a New York City manufacturing business, and a proprietor of a summer hotel at Lake George, NY. In 1870, Wilson married Annie Taylor in Manhattan; they had two children. At the time he wrote Douglass to reflect on his past in St. Catharines, he also requested a lecture from him on John Brown for a YMCA in Harlem. Wilson later spent time at the Hampton Institute working as a Superintendent of Mechanical Work but resigned in January of 1899. In 1919, he died in Warren County, New York (Library of Congress, microfilm of The Southern Workman and Hampton School Record, #01585).

105. Blight, *Frederick Douglass,* 660.

106. Charles Remond Douglass, "Some Incidents of the Home Life of Frederick Douglass," in Bernier and Taylor, *If I Survive*, 673.

107. Rosetta Douglass Sprague, "My Mother as I Recall Her," rpr. *Journal of Negro History* 8, no. 1 (January 1923): 101. She also highlighted: "Being herself [Frederick] one of the first agents of the Underground Railroad she [Anna] was an untiring worker along that line. To be able to accommodate in a comfortable manner the fugitives that passed our way, father enlarged his home where a suite of rooms could be made ready for those fleeing to Canada" (97–98).

EPILOGUE

1. Rayford W. Logan, *The Negro in American Life and Thought: The Nadir, 1877–1901* (New York, NY: Dial Press, 1954); and Winks, *Blacks in Canada*, 288–336. Logan and Winks give different time frames for the nadir in North America. In the United States, Logan concluded that the nadir ended in 1901 as a result of improved race relations, but historian John Hope Franklin extended the period to encompass the Progressive Era (1920s). In Canada, Winks stated that the nadir lasted from 1865 to 1930. See Carter G. Woodson, *A Century of Negro Migration* (Washington, DC: Association for the Study of Negro Life and History, 1918), chap. 2.

2. The Ku Klux Klan and Jim Crow laws happened in Canada as well. See, for example, Allan Bartley, *The Ku Klux Klan in Canada: A Century of Promoting Racism and Hate in the Peaceable Kingdom* (Halifax, NS: Formac Publishing, 2020); and Leonard Albert Paris, *Jim Crow Also Lived Here: Structural Racism and Generational Poverty-Growing Up Black in New Glasgow, Nova Scotia* (Altona, MB: Friesen Press, 2020).

3. On June 2, 1872, the home of Frederick Douglass on South Avenue burnt down after a fire broke out in a barn near the house. Rosetta and Nathan Sprague, fire company men, and neighbors all attempted to save it. *Rochester Democrat and Chronicle,* June 3, 1872; *Rochester Express,* June 3, 1872; *New York Times,* June 6, 1872; *New National Era,* June 13, 1872; *Rochester Union and Advertiser,* June 17, 1872; and Douglass to Amy Post, July 18, 1872, IAPFP.

4. Broyld, "The Power of Proximity," 3–34.

5. McFeely, *Frederick Douglass,* 305–23; Blight, *Frederick Douglass,* 651–52; *Washington Grit* cited in *New York Globe,* February 9, 1884; Kami Fletcher, *The Niagara Movement: The Black Protest Reborn* (South Carolina: VDM Verlag, 2008); Angela Jones, "The Niagara Movement 1905–1910: A Revisionist Approach to the Social History of the Civil Rights Movement," *Journal of Historical Sociology* 23, no. 3 (2010): 453–500.

6. Mia Bay, *To Tell the Truth Freely: The Life of Ida B. Wells* (New York, NY: Hill & Wang, 2010), 3–14. Bay pondered in the Introduction—"If Iola Were a Man?"

7. Robert Smalls to Helen Pitts Douglass, February 21, 1895, Frederick Douglass Papers, Yale University, New Haven, CT; John W. Hutchinson to Helen Pitts Douglass, February 22, 1895, Frederick Douglass Papers, Yale University; *New York Times,* February 20, 1895.

8. W. E. B. Du Bois, *The Souls of Black Folks: Essays and Sketches* (Chicago, IL: A. C. McClurg, 1903). See the chapter "Of Mr. Booker T. Washington and Others."

9. Louis R. Harlan, ed., *The Booker T. Washington Papers* (Champaign: University of Illinois Press, 1974), 3:583–87; and James Olney, "The Founding Fathers—Frederick Douglass and Booker T.

Washington; or, The Idea of Democracy and a Tradition of African-American Autobiography," *Amerikastudies/American Studies* 35 (1990): 281–96.

10. Jacqueline M. Moore, *Booker T. Washington, W. E. B. Du Bois, and the Struggle for Racial Uplift* (New York, NY: Rowman & Littlefield Publishers, 2003), 12–13.

11. Elliott M. Rudwick, "The Niagara Movement," *Journal of Negro History* 42, no. 3 (July 1957): 177.

12. Kerri K. Greenidge, *Black Radical: The Life and Times of William Monroe Trotter* (New York, NY: Liveright, 2019).

13. See Foreman, Casey, and Patterson, *The Colored Conventions Movement.*

14. *Washington Bee,* August 12, 1905; "Niagara Movement for Black Race Began," *Buffalo Enquirer,* July 13, 1905; "Niagara Movement: Colored Men Assembled at Fort Erie," *Niagara Gazette,* July 14, 1905; "For Welfare of Colored Race," *Buffalo Courier,* July 15, 1905; and Angela Jones, *African American Civil Rights: Early Activism and the Niagara Movement* (New York, NY: Praeger, 2011), 21–23.

15. *New York Age,* February 8, 1906.

16. Jones, *African American Civil Rights,* 23–24; and Brands, *The Zealot and the Emancipator,* 398–99.

17. Rudwick, "The Niagara Movement," 186; and *Cleveland Gazette,* March 19, 1904.

18. *Cleveland Gazette,* September 7, 1907.

19. *Washington Bee,* September 14, 1907. In times past, Boston was linked to Rochester via fugitives and Blacks from Toronto and Halifax settled in the chief New England city; Oberlin College sent teachers and missionaries, such as Harriet E. Lindsay, Anthony Burns, Elijah Barnett Dunlop, and Hiram Wilson, to St. Catharines (see Morris, *Oberlin, Hotbed of Abolitionism;* and Greenidge, *Black Radical,* x and 42–55).

20. Jones, *African American Civil Rights,* 22 and 71–72. They also ran a newspaper the *Moon,* before the *Horizon.*

21. Du Bois, "Niagara Movement," *Horizon* (Nov. 1909); Du Bois, "Subscribers" *Horizon* (May 1910); Jones, *African American Civil Rights,* 70–73.

22. *Washington Bee,* June 30, July 14, August 30, 1906, and September 23, 1905.

23. Trotter, deemed a "maverick," "loose cannon," and "a burden to the Niagara Movement" by some, asserted that Du Bois was not "radical enough," their clashes led to disengagement, and ultimately to Trotter's resignation (Greenidge, *Black Radical,* 132; *New York Age,* November 14, 1907; Greenidge, *Black Radical,* 128; and Jones, *African American Civil Rights,* 72 and 120).

24. Gilbert Jonas, *Freedom's Sword: The NAACP and the Struggle against Racism in America, 1909-1969* (New York: NY: Routledge, 2004).

25. Eric Foner, *Reconstruction: America's Unfinished Revolution, 1863-1877, Undated Edition* (New York: NY: Harper Perennial, 2014).

26. Susan D. Carle, "Race, Class, and Legal Ethics in the Early NAACP (1910-1920)," *Law and History Review* 20, no. 1 (Spring 2002): 103.

27. Winks, *Blacks in Canada,* 448 and 473–74.

28. Ryan J. Kirkby, "The Revolution Will Not Be Televised: Community Activism and the Black Panther Party, 1966–1971," *Canadian Review of American Studies* 41, no. 1 (2011): 25–62; Dawn Rae Flood, "A Black Panther in the Great White North: Fred Hampton Visits Saskatchewan, 1969," *Journal for the Study of Radicalism* 8, no. 2 (Fall 2014): 21–50; Ian Lumsden, ed., *Close the 49th Parallel,*

Etc.: The Americanization of Canada (Toronto, ON: University of Toronto Press, 1970), especially the essay by James Laxer, "The Americanization of the Canadian Student Movement," 278–86.

29. Joseph Mensah, *Black Canadians: History, Experience, Social Conditions* (New York, NY: Fernwood Publishing Company, 2004),71–86. See Funké Aladejebi, *Schooling the System: A History of Black Women Teachers* (Montreal: McGill-Queen's University Press, 2021).

30. *North Star,* July 6, 1849.

31. Papers of Margaret H. Hall, MMC 618, Manuscript Reading Room, Letter no. 5, Library of Congress, Washington, DC.

32. See Jennifer Lemak, "Advancement Comes Slowly: African American Employment in Rochester, New York, During the Great Migration," *New York History* 92, no. 1/2 (Winter/Spring 2011): 78–98.

33. Broyld, "The 'Dark Sheep' of the Atlantic World: Following the Transnational Trail of Blacks to Canada," in Talton and Mills, *Black Subjects,* 98.

34. Jane Helleiner, "Whiteness and Narratives of a Racialized Canada-US Border at Niagara," *Canadian Journal of Sociology/Cahiers canadiens de sociologie* 37, no. 2 (2012): 109–35; Emmanuel Brunet-Jailly, "A New Border? A Canadian Perspective of the Canada-US Border Post-9/11," *International Journal* 67, no. 4 (Autumn 2012): 963–74. See *International Journal*'s entire special issue, "Canada after 9/11," which includes Sandrine Tolazzi, "Living Together: Canada, 10 Years after 9/11"; Earl Fry, "The Canada-US Relationship One Decade After 9/11." See also Matthew Longo, *The Politics of Borders: Sovereignty, Security, and the Citizen after 9/11* (New York, NY: Cambridge University Press, 2017), as well as Reece Jones, *Open Borders: In Defense of Free Movement* (Athens: University of Georgia Press, 2019), and David Newman, "The Lines that Continue to Separate Us: Borders in Our 'Borderless' World," *Progress in Human Geography* 30, no. 2 (2006): 143–61.

35. *North Star,* July 6, 1849.

36. Broyld, "The 'Dark Sheep' of the Atlantic World: Following the Transnational Trail of Blacks to Canada," in Talton and Mills, *Black Subjects,* 95–108; and Jane Helleiner, "'As Much American as a Canadian Can Be': Cross-Border Experience and Regional Identity Among Young Borderlanders in Canadian Niagara," *Anthropologica* 51, no. 1 (2009): 225–38.

37. dann j. Broyld and Matthew Warshauer, "Harriet Tubman and Andrew Jackson: A Match Made in the U.S. Treasury Department," blog post to *Borealia* and *The Republic* (June 2016), https://earlycanadianhistory.ca/2016/06/13/harriet-tubman-and-andrew-jackson-a-match-made-in-the-u-s-treasury-department/; and *Toronto Globe,* April 2, 1913.

38. Larson, *Bound for the Promised Land,* 225–26, 252, 279.

39. Broyld, "Harriet Tubman," 90–91.

40. "This Is British Soil," *Toronto Globe,* April 2, 1913.

41. Sean Lahman, "Rochester Airport to be Renamed for Frederick Douglass," *Rochester Democrat and Chronicle,* August 12, 2020; and Justin Murphy, "Rochester Airport Renamed to Honor Frederick Douglass," February 14, 2021.

42. Michelle York, "A Fast Boat to Rochester?" *New York Times,* December 14, 2003; Michelle York, "After a Ferry Venture Fails, Criticism and Questions," *New York Times,* August 21, 2006; Jan Wong, "Ferry Bad Place," *Toronto Globe & Mail,* November 29, 2003; Steve Orr, "The Full Monty: A Timeline of Our Fast Ferry's Checkered Past," *Rochester Democrat and Chronicle,* March 29, 2019.

Bibliography

PRIMARY SOURCES

Manuscripts

American Missionary Association Archives, Dillard University, New Orleans
    Mary Ann Shadd Cary Papers
    Hiram Wilson Letters
Boston Public Library
    Anti-Slavery Collection
    William Lloyd Garrison Papers
    Thomas Wentworth Higginson Papers
Brock University, St. Catharines, ON
    Rick Bell Collection
    St. Catharines Tax Assessment Roll
Columbia University, New York
    Black Abolitionist Papers
    John Brown Papers
    John Brown–Oswald Garrison Villard Collection
    Record of Fugitives
    Sydney Howard Gay Papers
Cornell University, Kroch Library, Rare Books and Manuscripts Room, Ithaca, NY
    Anti-Slavery and Civil War Collection
    Samuel J. May Anti-Slavery Collection
Detroit Public Library, Burton Collection, Detroit, MI
    Amherstburg History Files
    Blacks in Canada Files
Duke University, Durham, North Carolina
    Joseph Long Papers
East Carolina University
    Joseph J. W. Powell Papers

Fort Malden National Historic Park Museum, Amherstburg, Ontario
    Fugitive Slave Files and Black Assessment Rolls
Hamilton Public Library, Hamilton, Ontario
    Black History Files
Hiram Walker Historical Museum, Windsor, Ontario
Harvard University (Houghton Library)
    Samuel Gridley Howe Papers
Haverford College, Quaker and Special Collections
    Julia Wilbur Papers
        Journal Briefs, 1844–62
        Large Diaries, 1844–73
        Pocket Diaries, 1856–95
Henry Huntington Library, San Marino, California
    Horatio N. Rust Collection
Library of Congress, National Archives, Washington, DC
    American Colonization Society Papers
    American Freedmen's Inquiry Commission Interviews
    Department of the Interior's Records Pertaining to Slave Trade and Negro
        Colonization
    Frederick Douglass Papers
    Papers of Margaret H. Hall
Massachusetts Historical Society, Boston, MA
    William Lloyd Garrison Papers
Moorland-Spingarn Research Center, Howard University, Washington, DC
    Mary Ann Shadd Cary Papers
    Frederick Douglass Collection
    James T. Rapier Papers
    Gerrit Smith Papers
    Jacob C. White Papers
National Library and Archives of Canada, Ottawa
    George Brown Papers, 1851–67
    Canada Original Correspondence
    Canadian Sessional Papers
    M. M. Dillion Papers, vol. 59 of Civil Secretary's Correspondence, 1840–63
    Dispatches from the Colonial Office, 1794–1865
    Dispatches from the Lieutenant Governors to the Governor General, 1839–41
    Letter Book of Dispatches from the Colonial Office, 1842–55
    William King Papers
    Minute Books of the Executive Council, 1841–67

Upper Canada Land Petitions
Upper Canada States Paper, 1791–1841
New Jersey Historical Society
Benjamin Drew Letters
New York Historical Society, New York, NY
The Slavery Collection
North Buxton Museum, North Buxton, Ontario
British Methodist Episcopal Church Records
Shadd Family Records
Oberlin College Archives
Hiram Wilson Papers
Ohio Historical Society
Wilbur H. Siebert Papers
Ontario Provincial Archives, Toronto
Mary Ann Shadd Cary Papers
Crown Land Papers, Upper Canada, 1830–41
Mackenzie-Lindsey Fonds
Alvin D. McCurdy Papers
Provincial Statutes, 1841–66
Toronto City Council Paper, 1834–68
Wesleyan Methodist Church (Black) of Toronto, Minutes
Western District Court Minutes, 1821–70
Peabody Essex Museum, Salem, Massachusetts
New England Society for Propagating the Gospel among North American Indians
and Others Records
Semi Annual Report of Canada Mission
Pennsylvania Historical Society/The Library Company of Philadelphia
Pennsylvania Anti-Slavery Society Collection
William Still Papers
Rochester Historical Society
Central Library of Rochester and Monroe County Historic Monographs Collection
Rochester Public Library
Nathaniel Rochester Papers
Schomburg Center for Black Culture, New York Public Library, New York City
Robin W. Winks Collection on Blacks in Canada
Smith College, Northampton, Massachusetts
Garrison Family Papers, Sophia Smith Collection
St. Catharines Museum
British Methodist Episcopal Church File

Reminiscences of Fred Parnell
St. Catharines Public Library Special Collections
    Joanne M. Corbett, "*St. Catharines Newspapers History*"
    Name Index—St. Catharines Black Community, 1854–81
    St. Catharine Municipal Council Minutes
St. John Fisher College
    The Frederick Douglass Papers Collection
State University of New York at Buffalo
    Dr. Monroe Fordham Papers
Syracuse University
    Gerrit Smith Papers
Toronto Public Library
    Anderson Ruffin Abbott Papers
    Elgin Association Annual Reports, 1852–55
    Toronto Tax Assessment Rolls
Tulane University
    American Missionary Association Archives
University of Detroit Mercy, Detroit, MI
    Black Abolitionist Archive
University of Michigan, William L. Clements Library
    Rochester Ladies Anti-Slavery Society Papers
University of Pennsylvania Library, Philadelphia
    Original run of the *Provincial Freeman*
University of Rochester
    Frederick Douglass Letters Collection
    Fish Family Papers
    Samuel D. and Susan Porter Family Papers
    Isaac and Amy Post Family Papers
    Rochester Family Papers
    Rochester Ladies' Anti-Slavery Society Papers
    William Henry Seward Papers
    Horatio Gates Warner Family Collection
University of Western Ontario Library, London
    Black Canadian Research Project Papers, 1972–76
    Black History Files
    Regional History—Country Records Collections with accompanying petitions from
        black citizens
    Donald Simpson Papers
West Virginia State Archives
    Boyd B. Stutler Collection

Yale University
    Frederick Douglass Papers

Newspapers and Periodicals

UNITED STATES

Advocate of Freedom, published in several locations, including Augusta, Hallowell, Cumberland, and Bowdoin, Maine, 1838–41

African Repository and Colonial Journal, Washington, DC, 1825–64

Anglo-African Newspaper, New York, 1859

Anti-Slavery Examiner, New York, 1836–45

Atlantic Monthly, 1857–

Brooklyn Daily Eagle, New York, 1850, 1858, 1859

Buffalo Courier, 1828–1982

Buffalo Daily Republic, 1848–57

Buffalo Daily Republic and Times, 1857–59

Buffalo Enquirer, 1891–1925

Buffalo Evening Post, 1852–77

Christian Recorder, Philadelphia, 1862–66

Colored American, New York, 1837–41

Daily Democrat, Rochester

Daily Union, Washington, DC

Douglass' Monthly, Rochester, 1859–63

Emancipator (New York City, then Boston), 1833–50

Frank Leslie's Illustrated Newspaper, 1855–1922

Frederick Douglass' Paper, Rochester, 1851–60

Horizon, 1907–10

Liberator, Boston, 1836–61

National Anti-Slavery Standard, New York, 1849–51

National Tribune, Washington, DC

New National Era, Washington, DC, 1870–74

New York Age, 1887–1953

New York Globe, 1880–84

New York Times, 1851–

New-York Tribune, 1841–1924

Niagara Falls Gazette, 1854–96

North Star, Rochester, 1847–51

Pennsylvania Gazette, 1728–1800

Pennsylvania Packet and Daily Advertiser, 1771–1840

Pine and Palm, Boston, 1861–62

Rights of Man, Rochester, 1833–18??
Rochester Daily Advertiser, 1827–1953
Rochester Daily Democrat, 1834–70
Rochester Daily Telegraph, 1827–29
Rochester Daily Union, 1852–56
Rochester Democrat
Rochester Democrat and Chronicle, 1870–
Rochester Express
Rochester Telegraph, 1818–30
Rochester Union and Advertiser, 1856–1918
Syracuse Daily Journal, 1845–99
Syracuse Standard, 1828–99
Tory Daily Times, 1851–1903
Tory Whig, 1834–73
Washington Bee, 1882–1922 (gaps in publication in 1893 and 1895)
Washington Post, 1877–
Weekly Anglo-African, 1859–65

CANADA
British American Journal, 1834
Christian Recorder, 1854–1902
Chronicle, Chatham, 1849–50
Colonial Advocate, Toronto, 1824–34
Constitution, St. Catharines, 1859–69
Evening Journal, St. Catharines
Farmers' Journal, 1826–33
Farmers' Journal & Welland Canal Intelligencer (St. Catharines)
Globe, Toronto, 1844–
Hamilton Gazette, 1852–55
Journal of Education for Upper Canada, Toronto, 1848–77
Manitoba Free Press, Winnipeg, 1872–2001
Montreal Witness, 1845–1938
Niagara Chronicle, 1837
Niagara Mail, 1840–70
Niagara Reporter, 1833–42
Ontario Messenger, 1810–56
Patriot, Toronto, 1851–52
Planet, Chatham, 1857–68
Provincial Freeman, Chatham, Toronto, Windsor, 1852–60

St. Catharines Constitutional, 1850–71
St. Catharines Daily Times, 1870–75
St. Catharines Journal, 1835–61
St. Catharines News Times, 1872–75
St. Catharines Semi-Weekly Post, 1854–61
St. Catharines Standard, 1891–
Upper Canada Gazette, 1793–1813
Voice of the Bondsman, Stratford, 1856–57
Voice of the Fugitive, Sandwich, Windsor, 1851–53
Western Planet, Chatham, 1853–57
Winnipeg Telegram, 1898–1920

ENGLAND
British and Foreign Anti-Slavery Reporter, London, 1840–60
The (London) Times, 1785–

Reports of Societies

American Anti-Slavery Society
    Annual Reports, 1834–40, 1855–60
American and Foreign Anti-Slavery Society
    Annual Reports, 1847–53
Anti-Slavery Society of Canada
    Annual Reports, 1852, 1853, 1857
British and Foreign Anti-Slavery Society
    Annual Reports, London, 1840–51, 1855–63

Pamphlets

Brown, George. *The American War and Slavery: Speech of the Honourable George Brown at the Anniversary Meeting of the Anti-Slavery Society of Canada.* Toronto, February 3, 1863. Manchester, 1863.
King, William, and Robert Burns. *Fugitive Slaves in Canada, Elgin Settlement.* 1860.
The Medical Properties of the St. Catharines Mineral Water. E. W. Stephenson, Proprietor. St. Catharines: H. F. Leavenworth's "Herald" Power Press, 1864.
Naturalization Entries Records, 1842–49. Niagara Peninsula Branch, Special Collections, Ontario Genealogical Society, 1–28.
Niagara Falls International Bridge Company. Rochester, NY: Jerome & Brother, 1847.
Public Prayer for Civil Rules and the Slavery Question Being a Contrast Between the Apolo-

gists for Slavery in the United States and the Ministers of Religion in Great Britain and Her Colonies. By an anonymous correspondent of the *Ecclesiastical and Missionary Record* [n.p., 1851].

Report of Cases Decided in the Court of Queen's Bench, Vol. 31. Toronto: Rowsell & Hutchison, 1872.

Report of the Trustees of the African Church in the Village of Rochester. Rochester, NY: Marshall & Dean, 1828.

Rochester Ladies Anti-Slavery Society. *Autographs for Freedom.* Boston, 1853.

Scoble, John. *Fugitive Settlement in Canada.* Uncle Tom's Cabin Almanac or Abolitionist Memento. London, 1853.

Shadd, Mary Ann. *A Plea for Emigration or Notes of Canada West in Its Moral, Social, and Political Aspect: Suggestions Respecting Mexico, W. Indies and Vancouver's Island, For the Information of Colored Emigrants.* Detroit, MI: George W. Pattison, 1852.

Stuart, Charles B. *Report of Charles B. Stuart, Chief Engineer of the Lockport and Niagara Falls Rail-Road Company: to the Directors: Showing the Estimated Cost, and Probable Income of the Road, If Extended from Lockport to Rochester.* Rochester, NY: J. M. Patterson & Co., January 1, 1846.

Books

Adam, Nehemiah, D. D. *A South-Side View of Slavery.* 1854. London: Forgotten Books, 2012.

Anderson, Osborne. *A Voice from Harpers Ferry.* 1861. New York, NY: World View Forum, 2000.

Anti-Slavery Society of Canada. *Constitution and Bye-Laws of the Anti-Slavery Society of Canada.* Toronto, ON: G. Brown, 1851.

Barham, William. *Descriptions of Niagara.* Gravesend, England: Compiler, 1847.

Barrett, Philip. *Gilbert Hunt, the City Blacksmith.* Richmond, VA: James Woodhouse, 1859.

Bibb, Henry. *Narrative of the Life and Adventures of Henry Bibb, an American Slave, Written by Himself.* New York: Author, 1849.

Biddle, Richard. *Captain Hall in America.* Philadelphia, PA: Carey and Lea, 1830.

Black, Leonard. *The Life and Sufferings of Leonard Black, a Fugitive from Slavery. Written by Himself.* New Bedford: Benjamin Lindsey, 1847.

Bradford, Sarah. *Harriet Tubman, the Moses of Her People.* New York: Geo. R. Lockwood & Son, 1886.

———. *Scenes in the Life of Harriet Tubman.* Auburn, NY: W. J. Moses, 1869 and 1926.

Brown, William Wells. *Narrative of William W. Brown, A Fugitive Slave.* Boston, 1847.

Caverhill, W. C. F. *Caverhill's Toronto City Directory for 1859–60.* Toronto, ON: W. C. F. Caverhill, 1859.

Chesnutt, Charles Waddell. *Frederick Douglass.* Boston: Small, Maynard & Company, 1899.

Clarke, Lewis Garrard. *Narrative of the Sufferings of Lewis Clarke, During a Captivity of More than Twenty-Five Years, Among the Algerines of Kentucky, One of the So Called Christian States of North America.* Boston: David H. Ela, Printer, 1845.

Coleman, Lucy N. *Reminiscences.* 1891. London: Forgotten Books, 2012.

Craft, William. *Running a Thousand Miles for Freedom; or the Escape of William and Ellen Craft from Slavery.* London: William Tweedie, Strand, 1860.

Douglass, Frederick. *The Life and Times of Frederick Douglass.* Mineola, NY: Dover Publications, Inc., 2003. Reprint, 1881; revised in 1892.

———. *Life and Times of Frederick Douglass: His Early Life as a Slave, His Escape from Bondage, and His Complete History to the Present Time.* Hartford, CT: Park Publishing Co., 1881. Available on "Documenting the American South" website: https://docsouth.unc.edu/neh/texts.html#D.

———. *My Bondage and My Freedom.* New York: Miller, Orton and Mulligan, 1855. Available on "Documenting the American South" website: https://docsouth.unc.edu/neh/texts.html#D.

———. *Narrative of the Life of Frederick Douglass, an American Slave, Written by Himself.* Boston: Anti-Slavery Office, 1845. Available on "Documenting the American South" website: https://docsouth.unc.edu/neh/texts.html#D.

Drayton, Daniel. *Personal Memoir of Daniel Drayton, for Four Years and Four Months a Prisoner (for Charity's Sake) in Washington Jail, Including a Narrative of the Voyage and Capture of the Schooner Pearl.* Boston: B. Marsh, 1854.

Drew, Benjamin. *The Refugee: Or the Narratives of Fugitive Slaves in Canada.* New York, NY: John P. Jewett and Company, 1856.

Du Bois, W. E. B. *The Souls of Black Folks: Essays and Sketches.* Chicago, IL: A. C. McClurg, 1903.

Edwards, Celestine, S. J. *From Slavery to a Bishopric or, The Life of Bishop Walter Hawkins of the British Methodist Episcopal Canada.* London: John Kensit, 1891.

Fisher & Taylor St. Catharines Directory, 1875–76. Fisher & Taylor Publishers: Toronto, ON, 1875.

Frederick, Francis. *Autobiography of Rev. Francis Frederick, of Virginia.* Baltimore: J. W. Woods, Printer, 1869.

Goings, Henry, Calvin Schermerhorn, Michael Plunkett, and Edward Gaynor, eds. *Rambles of a Runaway from Southern Slavery.* ca. 1860s. Charlottesville: University of Virginia Press, 2012.

Hall, Captain Basil. *Travels in North America in the Years 1827 and 1828.* Edinburgh: Cadell and Co., 1829.

Henson, Josiah. *Truth Stranger Than Fiction: Father Henson's Story of His Own Life.* Boston: John P. Jewett, 1858.

Hinks, Peter P., ed. *David Walker's Appeal to the Coloured Citizens of the World.* 1829; rpr. University Park: Pennsylvania State University Press, 2000.

Howe, Samuel Gridley. *The Refugees from Slavery in Canada West: Report to the Freedmen's Inquiry Commission.* Boston: Wright and Potter, 1864.

Jackson, Andrew. *Narrative and Writings of Andrew Jackson, of Kentucky; Containing an Account of His Birth, and Twenty-Six Years of His Life While a Slave; His Escape. . . .* Syracuse, NY: Daily and Weekly Star Office, 1847.

Jackson, Mattie J. *The Story of Mattie J. Jackson: Her Parentage, Experience of Eighteen Years in Slavery, Incidents During the War, Her Escape from Slavery: A True Story.* Lawrence, MA: Sentinel Office, 1866.

Jacobs, Harriet A., *Incidents in the Life of a Slave Girl. Written by Herself,* ed. Lydia Maria Francis Child. 1861. Reprint, Cambridge, MA: Harvard University Press, 1987.

Jacobs, John S. *A True Tale of Slavery. From The Leisure Hour: A Family Journal of Instruction and Recreation.* London: Stevens and Co., 1861.

James, Thomas. *Life of Rev. Thomas James, by Himself.* Rochester, NY: Post Express Printing Company, 1886.

Jennings, Paul. *A Colored Man's Reminiscences of James Madison.* Brooklyn: G. C. Beadle, 1865.

Johnson, Isaac. *Slavery Days in Old Kentucky. A True Story of a Father Who Sold His Wife and Four Children. By One of the Children.* Ogdensburg, NY: Republican & Journal Print, 1901.

Kirk, Highland Clare. *A History of the New York State Teachers' Association.* New York: E. L. Kellogg, 1883.

Loguen, Jermain Wesley. *The Rev. J. W. Loguen, as a Slave and as a Freeman. A Narrative of Real Life.* Syracuse, NY: J. G. K. Truair & Co., 1859.

Mason, Isaac. *Life of Isaac Mason as a Slave.* Worcester, MA: s.n. 1893.

Mitchell & Co's General Directory for the Town of St. Catharines and Gazetteer of the Counties of Lincoln and Welland for 1865. Toronto: Mitchell & Co., 1865.

Moodie, Susanna. *Roughing It in the Bush.* London, 1852.

Murray, Henry A. *Lands of Slave and the Free, or, Cuba, the United States, and Canada,* 2 vols. London: J. W. Parker, 1855.

Northup, Solomon. *Twelve Years a Slave: Narrative of Solomon Northup, a Citizen of New-York, Kidnapped in Washington City in 1841, and Rescued in 1853.* Auburn, NY: Derby and Miller, 1853.

Payne, Bishop Daniel Alexander. *The History of the A. M. E. Church.* Nashville, TN: Publishing House of the A. M. E. Sunday School Union, 1891.

———. *Recollections of Seventy Years.* Nashville, TN: Publishing House of the A. M. E. Sunday School Union, 1888. Rpr.: New York, NY: Arno Press, 1968.

Pennington, James W. C. *The Fugitive Blacksmith or Events in the History of James W. C. Pennington.* 3rd ed. London: Charles Gilpin, 1850.

Reed, Austin, and Caleb Smith, eds. *The Life and the Adventures of a Haunted Convict.* New York, NY: Random House, 2016.

Report of the Trustees of the African Church in the Village of Rochester. Rochester, NY: Marshall & Dean, 1828.

Robertson, John Ross. *Landmarks of Toronto,* vol. 3. Toronto: John Ross Robertson, 1898.

Robinson, Charles Mulford. *Third Ward Traits.* Rochester, NY: Genesee Press, 1899.

Rogers, Fannie Rochester. "Colonel Nathaniel Rochester," *Rochester Historical Society Publication Fund Series,* vol. 3. Rochester, NY: Rochester Historical Society, 1924.

Ross, Alexander Milton. *Recollections and Experience of An Abolitionist; From 1855 to 1865.* Toronto: Rowsell & Hutchison, 1876.

Sanborn, Franklin. *Recollections of Seventy Years, Vol. I.* Boston: Richard C. Badger, 1909.

Smallwood, Thomas. *A Narrative of Thomas Smallwood, (Coloured Man:) Giving an Account of His Birth—The Period He Was Held in Slavery—His Release—and Removal to Canada, etc. . . . .* Toronto: Smallwood; James Stephens, 1851.

Stevens, Charles Emery. *Anthony Burns: A History.* Boston: John P. Jewett and Company, 1856.

Steward, Austin. *Twenty-Two Years a Slave, and Forty Years a Freeman.* Rochester, NY: William Alling, 1857.

Still, William. *The Underground Railroad: A Record of Facts, Authentic Narrative, Letters, & C, Narrating Hardships, Hairbreadth Escapes and Death Struggles of the Slaves in Their Efforts of Freedom, As Related by Themselves and Others, or Witnessed by the Author Together with Sketches of Some of the Largest Stockholders, and Most Liberal Aiders and Advisers of the Road.* London: Benediction Books, 2008.

Still, William. *The Underground Railroad.* Philadelphia, PA: Porter and Coates, 1872.

Thompson, John. *The Life of John Thompson, a Fugitive Slave; Containing His History of 25 Years in Bondage, and His Providential Escape. Written by Himself.* Worcester: John Thompson, 1856.

Thoreau, Henry David. *A Yankee on Canada.* 1866; rpr. Portland, OR: WestWinds Press, 2016.

Turner, Frederick Jackson, and John Mack Faragher, eds. *Rereading Frederick Jackson Turner: "The Significance of the Frontier in American History" and Other Essays.* New Haven, CT: Yale University Press, 1999.

Ward, Samuel Ringgold. *Autobiography of a Fugitive Negro: His Anti-Slavery Labours in the United States, Canada, and England.* London: John Snow, 1855.

Warren, Reverend Richard. *Narrative of the Life and Sufferings of Rev. Richard Warren (a fugitive slave) Written by Herself.* Hamilton, Canada West, 1850.

Washington, Booker T. *Up from Slavery: An Autobiography.* Garden City, NJ: Doubleday, 1901.

Watkins, James. *Struggles for Freedom; or The Life of James Watkins, Formerly a Slave in Maryland, U.S. . . .* Manchester, [Eng.]: Printed for James Watkins by A. Heywood, Oldham Street, 1860.

Williams, Isaac D., and William F. Goldie. *Sunshine and Shadow of Slave Life, Reminis-*

cences as told by Isaac D. Williams to "Tege." East Saginaw, MI: Evening News Printing and Binding House, 1885.

Woodson, Carter G. *A Century of Negro Migration.* Washington, DC: Association for the Study of Negro Life and History, 1918.

SECONDARY SOURCES

Books

Adams, Michael, David Jamieson, and Amy Langstaff. *Fire and Ice: The United States, Canada and the Myth of Converging Values.* New York, NY: Penguin Group, 2005.

Aitken, Hugh G. J. *The Welland Canal Company: A Study in Canadian Enterprise.* Cambridge, MA: Harvard University Press, 1954.

Ajzenstat, Janet. *The Political Thought of Lord Durham.* Montreal: McGill-Queen's University Press, 1988.

Aladejebi, Funké. *Schooling the System: A History of Black Women Teachers.* Montreal: McGill-Queen's University Press, 2021.

Alexander, De Alva Stanwood. *A Political History of the State of New York: Volume 2: 1833–1861.* Elibron Classics Series. New York: Biblio Bazaar, 2008.

Alcxander, William H., Cassandra L. Newby-Alexander, and Charles H. Ford. *Voices from within the Veil: African Americans and the Experience of Democracy.* Newcastle, UK: Cambridge Scholars Publishing, 2008.

Anderson, Benedict. *Imagined Communities: Reflections on the Origin and Spread of Nationalism.* London: Verso, 2006.

Anderson, John Jacob, and Alexander Clarence Flick. *A Short History of the State of New York.* 1902. New York, NY: Kessinger Publishing Company, 2008.

Andrews, William L. *Slavery and Class in the American South: A Generation of Slave Narrative Testimony, 1840–1865.* New York, NY: Oxford University Press, 2019.

Archer, Richard. *Jim Crow North: The Struggle for Equal Rights in Antebellum New England.* New York, NY: Oxford University Press, 2020.

Armstrong, Frederick H., Bryan Walls, Hilary Bates Neary, and Karolyn Smardz Frost. *Ontario's African-Canadian Heritage: Collected Writings by Fred Landon, 1919–1974.* Toronto, ON: Natural Heritage Books, 2009.

Arnstin, Walter L. *Queen Victoria.* New York, NY: Palgrave Macmillan, 2005.

Aron, Stephen. *American Confluence: The Missouri Frontier from Borderland to Border State.* Bloomington, IN: Indiana University Press, 2009.

Bacher, John C. *Mirror and Catalyst: A History of the St. Catharines Institute and Vocational School, 1827–1975.* St. Catharines, ON: The Author, 1975.

Baker, Gordon S. *Imperfect Revolution: Anthony Burns and the Landscape of Race in Antebellum America.* Kent, OH: Kent State University Press, 2011.

Baker, H. Robert. *Prigg v. Pennsylvania: Slavery, the Supreme Court, and the Ambivalent Constitution.* Lawrence: University Press of Kansas, 2012.

Bald, F. Clever. *Detroit's First American Decade, 1796–1805.* Ann Arbor: University of Michigan Press, 1948.

Ball, Erica L. *To Live an Antislavery Life: Personal Politics and the Antebellum Black Middle Class.* Athens: University of Georgia Press, 2012.

Barbour, Hugh, ed. *Quaker Crosscurrents: Three Hundred Years of Friends in the New York Yearly Meetings.* Syracuse, NY: Syracuse University Press, 1995.

Barry, Kathleen. *Susan B. Anthony: A Biography.* New York, NY: New York University Press, 1988.

Bartley, Allan. *The Ku Klux Klan in Canada: A Century of Promoting Racism and Hate in the Peaceable Kingdom.* Halifax, NS: Formac Publishing, 2020.

Baumann, Roland M. *Constructing Black Education at Oberlin College: A Documentary History.* Athens: Ohio University Press, 2010.

Bay, Mia. *To Tell the Truth Freely: The Life of Ida B. Wells.* New York, NY: Hill & Wang, 2010.

Beck, Janet Kemper. *Creating the John Brown Legend: Emerson, Thoreau, Douglass, Child and Higginson in Defense of the Raid on Harpers Ferry.* Jefferson, NC: McFarland, 2009.

Behiels, Michael D., and Reginald C. Stuart. *Transnationalism: Canada–United States History into the Twenty-First Century.* Montreal: McGill-Queen's University Press, 2010.

Bender, Thomas. *A Nation Among Nations: America's Place in World History.* New York, NY: Hill & Wang, 2006.

———, ed. *Rethinking American History in a Global Age.* Berkeley: University of California Press, 2002.

Bell, Richard. *Stolen: Five Free Boys Kidnapped into Slavery and Their Astonishing Odyssey Home.* New York, NY: Simon & Schuster, 2019.

Berlin, Ira. *The Making of African America: The Four Great Migrations.* New York, NY: Penguin Books, 2010.

———. *Many Thousands Gone: The First Two Centuries of Slavery in North America.* Cambridge, MA: Harvard University Press, 1998.

———. *Slaves without Masters: The Free Negro in the Antebellum South.* New York: Vintage, 1976.

Berlin, Ira, and Leslie M. Harris, eds. *Slavery in New York.* New York, NY: New Press, 2005.

Berlin, Ira, Barbara J. Fields, Steven F. Miller, Joseph P. Reidy, and Leslie S. Rowland, eds. *Slaves No More: Three Essays on Emancipation and the Civil War.* Cambridge, Eng.: Cambridge University Press, 1992.

Bernier, Celeste-Marie, and Andrew Taylor, eds. *If I Survive: Frederick Douglass and Family in the Walter O. Evans Collection.* Edinburgh, Scotland: Edinburgh University Press, 2018.

Bernstein, Iver. *The New York City Draft Riots: Their Significance for American Society and Politics in the Age of the Civil War.* New York, NY: Oxford University Press, 1991.

Bernstein, Peter L. *Wedding of the Waters: The Erie Canal and the Making of a Great Nation.* New York, NY: W. W. Norton & Company, 2006.

Bertley, Leo W. *Canada and Its People of African Descent.* Pierrefonds, QC: Bilongo, 1977.

Bethel, Elizabeth Rauh. *The Roots of African-American Identity: Memory and History in Antebellum Free Communities.* New York, NY: St. Martin's, 1999.

Blackett, R. J. M. *Beating against the Barriers: The Lives of Six Nineteenth-Century Afro-Americans.* Ithaca, NY: Cornell University Press, 1989.

———. *Building an Antislavery Wall: Black Americans in the Atlantic Abolitionist Movement, 1830–1860.* Baton Rouge: Louisiana State University Press, 1983.

———. *The Captive's Quest for Freedom: Fugitive Slaves, the 1850 Fugitive Slave Law, and the Politics of Slavery.* New York, NY: Cambridge University Press, 2018.

———. *Divided Hearts: Britain and the American Civil War.* Baton Rouge: Louisiana State University Press, 2001.

———. *Making Freedom: The Underground Railroad and the Politics of Slavery.* Chapel Hill: University of North Carolina Press, 2013.

Blassingame, John W., ed. *The Frederick Douglass Papers, 5 volumes.* New Haven, CT: Yale University Press, 1979–92.

———. *The Slave Community: Plantation Life in the Antebellum South.* New York, NY: Oxford University Press, 1979.

———, ed. *Slave Testimony: Two Centuries of Letters, Speeches, Interviews, and Autobiographies.* Baton Rouge: Louisiana State University Press, 1977.

Blight, David W., ed. *Frederick Douglass: Prophet of Freedom.* New York, NY: Simon & Schuster, 2018.

———. *Frederick Douglass' Civil War: Keeping Faith in Jubilee.* Baton Rouge: Louisiana State University Press, 1991.

———. *Passages of Freedom: The Underground Railroad in History and Memory.* Washington, DC: Smithsonian Books, 2004.

———. *Race and Reunion: The Civil War in American Memory.* Cambridge, MA: Harvard University Press, 2001.

Blue, Frederick J. *The Free Soilers: Third Party Politics, 1848–54.* Champaign: University of Illinois Press, 1973.

Bogdanor, Vernon. *The Monarchy and the Constitution.* New York, NY: Oxford University Press, 1995.

Boggs, Samuel W. *International Boundaries: A Study of Boundary Functions and Problems.* New York, NY: Columbia University Press, 1940.

Bolster, W. Jeffrey. *Black Jacks: African American Seamen in the Age of Sail.* Cambridge, MA: Harvard University Press, 1997.

Bolton, S. Charles. *Fugitives from Injustice: Freedom-Seeking Slaves in Arkansas: Historic Resource Study.* Scotts Valley, CA: CreateSpace Independent Publishing Platform, 2013.

Bordewich, Fergus M. *Bound for Canaan: The Epic Story of the Underground Railroad, American's First Civil Rights Movement.* New York, NY: Amistad, 2006.

Botting, Gary. *Extradition Between Canada and the United States.* Ardsley, NY: Transnational Publishers, Inc., 2005.

Boyd, Herb. *Black Detroit: A People's History of Self-Determination.* New York, NY: HarperCollins, 2017.

Boyko, John. *Blood and Daring: How Canada Fought the American Civil War and Forged a Nation.* Toronto, ON: Vintage Canada, 2013.

Bracey, John H., August Meier, Elliot Rudwick, et al. *Blacks in the Abolitionist Movement.* Balmont, CA: Wadsworth Publishing Company, 1971.

Bramble, Linda. *Black Fugitive Slaves in Early Canada.* Vanwell History Project Series. St. Catharines, ON: Vanwell, 1988.

Brands, H. W. *The Zealot and the Emancipator: John Brown, Abraham Lincoln, and the Struggle for American Freedom.* New York, NY: Doubleday, 2020.

Brebner, Bartlet. *Canada: A Modern History.* Ann Arbor: University of Michigan Press, 1960.

Bristow, Peggy, ed. *We're Rooted Here and They Can't Pull Us Up: Essays in African Canadian Women's History.* Toronto, ON: University of Toronto Press, 1994.

Brock, Lisa, Robin D. G. Kelley, and Karen Sotiropoulos. *Transnational Black Studies.* Durham, NC: Duke University Press, 2003.

Brode, Patrick. *Odyssey of John Anderson.* Toronto, ON: University of Toronto Press, 1989.

Bromell, Nick. "A 'Voice from the Enslaved': The Origins of Frederick Douglass's Political Philosophy of Democracy." *American Literary History* 23, no. 4 (Winter 2011): 697–723.

Brown, Christopher Leslie. *Moral Capital: Foundations of British Abolitionism.* Chapel Hill: University of North Carolina Press, 2006.

Brown, Gordon. *Incidental Architect: William Thornton and the Cultural Elite of Early Washington, DC, 1794–1828.* Athens: Ohio University Press, 2009.

Brown-Kubisch, Linda. *The Queen's Bush Settlement: Black Pioneers 1839–1865.* Toronto, ON: Natural Heritage, 2004.

Brunet-Jailly, Emmanuel. *Borderlands: Comparing Border Security in North America and Europe.* Ottawa, QC: University of Ottawa Press, 2007.

Buchanan, Allen, and Margaret Moore, eds. *States, Nations, and Borders: The Ethics of Making Boundaries.* Cambridge, MA: Cambridge University Press, 2003.

Buckmaster, Henrietta. *Let My People Go: The Story of the Underground Railroad and the Growth of the Abolition Movement.* New York, NY: Harper & Brothers Publishers, 1941.

Buckner, Phillip, ed. *Canada and The British Empire*. New York, NY: Oxford University Press, 2008.

———. *The Transition to Responsible Government: British Policy in British North America*. Westport, CT: Greenwood Press, 1985.

Bukowczyk, John J., Nora Faires, David R. Smith, Randy William Widdis. *Permeable Border: The Great Lakes Basin as Transnational Region, 1650–1990*. Pittsburgh, PA: University of Pittsburgh Press, 2005.

Burin, Eric. *Slavery and the Peculiar Solution: A History of the American Colonization Society*. Gainesville, FL: University Press of Florida, 2008.

Burke, Ronald K. *Samuel Ringgold Ward, Christian Abolitionist*. New York, NY: Garland, 1995.

Caffrey, Kate. *The Twilight's Last Gleaming: Britain vs. America 1812–1815*. New York, NY: Stein and Day, 1977.

Calarco, Tom. *The Underground Railroad in the Adirondack Region*. Jefferson, NC: McFarland, 2004.

Calhoon, Robert M., Timothy M. Barnes, and George A. Rawlyk, eds. *Loyalists and Community in North America*. Westport, CT: Greenwood Press, 1994.

Camp, Stephanie M. H. *Closer to Freedom: Enslaved Women and Everyday Resistance in the Plantation South*. Chapel Hill: University of North Carolina Press, 2004.

Campbell, Randolph B. *An Empire for Slavery: The Peculiar Institution in Texas, 1821–1865*. Baton Rouge: Louisiana State University Press, 1989.

Campbell, Stanley W. *The Slave Catchers: Enforcement of the Fugitive Slave Law, 1850–1860*. Chapel Hill: The University of North Carolina Press, 1970.

Canniff, William. *History of the Province of Ontario*. Toronto, ON: A. H. Hovey, 1872.

Carol, Wilson. *Freedom at Risk: The Kidnapping of Free Blacks in America, 1780–1865*. University Press of Kentucky, 1994.

Carroll, Francis. *A Good and Wise Measure: The Struggle for the Canadian-American Border, 1783–1842*. Toronto, ON: University of Toronto Press, 2001.

Carson, Clayborne, Emma J. Lapsansky-Werner, and Gary B. Nash. *African American Lives: The Struggle for Freedom*. New York, NY: Peason, 2005.

Carton, Evan. *John Brown and the Soul of America*. New York, NY: Free Press, 2006.

———. *Patriotic Treason: John Brown and the Soul of America*. New York, NY: Free Press, 2006.

Christianson, Scott. *Freeing Charles: The Struggle to Free a Slave on the Eve of the Civil War*. Champaign: University of Illinois Press, 2010.

Clark-Lewis, Elizabeth. *First Freed: Washington, DC, in the Emancipation Era*. Washington, DC: Howard University Press, 2002.

Clinton, Catherine Clinton. *Harriet Tubman: The Road to Freedom*. New York, NY: Little, Brown and Company, 2004.

Close, Stacey K. *Elderly Slaves of the Plantation South*. New York, NY: Routledge, 1996.

Cohen, Lara Langer. *Early African American Print Culture*. Philadelphia: University of Pennsylvania Press, 2014.

Colaiaco, James A. *Frederick Douglass and the Fourth of July*. New York, NY: Palgrave Macmillan, 2006.

Coles, Howard W. *The Cradle of Freedom: A History of the Negro in Rochester, Western New York and Canada*. Rochester, NY: Oxford Press, 1941.

Collison, Gary. *Shadrach Minkins: From Fugitive to Citizen*. Cambridge: Harvard University Press, 1997.

Conrad, Earl. *General Harriet Tubman*. Washington, DC: Associated Publishers, 1943.

Cooper, Afua. *The Handing of Angelique: The Untold Story of Canadian Slavery and the Burning of Old Montreal*. Toronto, ON: Harper Collins Publishers, 2006.

Cooper, Mark Anthony, ed. *Dear Father, A Collection of Letters to Frederick Douglass from His Children, 1859–1894*. Philadelphia, PA: Fulmore Press, 1997.

Correa-Cabrera, Guadalupe, and Victor Konrad, eds. *North American Borders in Comparative Perspective*. Tucson: University of Arizona Press, 2020.

Cowan, Helen I. *Charles Williamson: Genesee Promoter, Friend of Anglo-American Rapprochement*. Rochester, NY: Rochester Historical Society, 1941.

Craig, Gerald M., and Jeffrey L. McNairn. *Upper Canada: The Formative Years, 1784–1841*. New York, NY: Oxford University Press, 2014.

Cross, Whitney R. *The Burned-Over District: The Social and Intellectual History of Enthusiastic Religion in Western New York, 1800–1850*. Ithaca, NY: Cornell University Press, 2006.

Curry, Leonard P. *The Free Black in Urban America, 1800–1850: The Shadow of the Dream*. Chicago: University of Chicago Press, 1981.

Dagenais, Maxime, and Julien Mauduit, eds. *Revolutions across Borders: Jacksonian American and the Canadian Rebellion*. Montreal: McGill-Queen's University Press, 2019.

David, James Corbett. *Dunmore's New World: The Extraordinary Life of a Royal Governor in Revolutionary America—with Jacobites, Counterfeiters, Land Schemes, Shipwrecks, Scalping, Indian Politics, Runaway Slaves, and Two Illegal Royal Weddings*. Charlottesville: University of Virginia Press, 2013.

Davis, David Brion. *Challenging the Boundaries of Slavery*. Cambridge, MA: Harvard University Press, 2003.

———. *Inhuman Bondage: The Rise and Fall of Slavery in the New World*. New York, NY: Oxford University Press, 2006.

Davis, Irene Moore. *Our Own Two Hands: A History of Black Lives in Windsor*. Windsor, ON: Biblioasis, 2019.

Davis, Rodney O., and Douglas L. Wilson, eds. *The Lincoln-Douglas Debates*. Champaign: University of Illinois Press, 2008.

de B'béri, Boulou Ebanda, Nina Reid-Maroney, and Handel Kashope Wright, eds. *The Promised Land: History and Historiography of the Black Experience in Chatham-Kent's Settlements and Beyond*. Toronto, ON: University of Toronto Press, 2014.

DeCaro, Louis A., Jr. *Freedom's Dawn: The Last Days of John Brown in Virginia*. New York, NY: Rowman & Littlefield Publishers, 2015.

———. *The Untold Story of Shields Green: The Life and Death of a Harpers Ferry Raider*. New York, NY: New York University Press, 2020.

Delbanco, Andrew. *The War Before the War: Fugitive Slaves and the Struggle for America's Soul from the Revolution to the Civil War*. New York, NY: Penguin Press, 2018.

Dennison, Matthew. *Queen Victoria: A Life of Contradictions*. New York, NY: St. Martin's Press, 2014.

DeRamus, Betty. *Freedom by Any Means: Con Games, Voodoo Schemes, True Love and Lawsuits on the Underground Railroad*. New York, NY: Atria Books, 2009.

Dickerson, Vanessa D. *Dark Victorians*. Champaign: University of Illinois Press, 2008.

Dictionary of Canadian Biography, 1836–1850, Volume VII. Toronto, ON: University of Toronto Press, 2000.

Diedrich, Maria. *Love Across Color Lines: Outtilie Assing and Frederick Douglass*. New York: NY: Farrar, Straus and Giroux, 1999.

Diener, Alexander C., and Joshua Hagen, eds. *Borderlines and Borderlands: Political Oddities at the Edge of the Nation-State*. New York, NY: Rowman & Littlefield Publishers, 2010.

———. *Borders: A Very Short Introduction*. New York, NY: Oxford University Press, 2012.

Dilbeck, D. H. *Frederick Douglass: America's Prophet*. Chapel Hill: University of North Carolina Press, 2018.

Diouf, Sylviane A. *Slavery's Exiles: The Story of the American Maroons*. New York, NY: New York University Press, 2014.

Dobak, William B. *Freedom by the Sword: The U.S. Colored Troops, 1862–67*. Washington, DC: GPO, 2011.

Donnan, Hastings, and Thomas M. Wilson, eds. *Borderlands: Ethnographic Approaches to Security, Power, and Identity*. Lanham, MD: University Press of America, 2010.

———. *Borders: Frontiers of Identity, Nation and State*. New York, NY: Routledge, 1999.

Douglas, R. Alan. *Uppermost Canada: The Western District and the Detroit Frontier, 1800–1850*. Detroit, MI: Wayne State University Press, 2001.

Douglass, Frederick. *Douglass: Autobiographies*. New York: Library of America, 1994.

Drache, Daniel. *Border Matters: Homeland Security and the Search for North America*. Halifax, NS: Fernwood, 2004.

Dray, Philip. *Capitol Man: The Epic of Reconstruction through the Lives of the First Black Congressman*. Boston: Houghton Mifflin Company, 2008.

Drescher, Seymour. *The Mighty Experiment: Free Labor versus Slavery in British Emancipation*. New York, NY: Oxford University Press, 2004.

Du Bois, Eugene E. *The City of Frederick Douglass: Rochester's African-American People and Place.* Rochester, NY: The Landmark Society of Western New York, 1994.

Du Bois, W. E. B. *John Brown.* Philadelphia, PA: George W. Jacobs & Co., 1909.

Ducharme, Michel. *Le concept de liberté au Canada à l'époque des Révolutions atlantiques (1776–1838).* Montreal: McGill-Queen's University Press, 2010. English edition: *The Idea during the Age of Atlantic Revolutions.* Montreal: McGill-Queen's University Press, 2014.

Dunaway, Wilma A. *The African-American Family in Slavery and Emancipation.* New York, NY: Cambridge University Press, 2003.

Dunbar, Erica Armstrong. *She Came to Slay: The Life and Times of Harriet Tubman.* New York, NY: Simon & Schuster, 2019.

Earle, Jonathan H. *Jacksonian Antislavery and the Politics of Free Soil, 1824–1854.* Chapel Hill: University of North Carolina Press, 2004.

Elgersman, Maureen G. *Unyielding Spirits: Black Women and Slavery in Early Canada and Jamaica.* New York, NY: Routledge, 1999.

Ericson, David F. *Slavery and the American Republic: Developing the Federal Government, 1791–1861.* Lawrence: University of Kansas Press, 2011.

Errington, Elizabeth Jane. *Wives and Mothers, Schoolmistresses and Scullery Maids: Working Women in Upper Canada, 1790–1840.* Montreal: McGill-Queen's University Press, 1995.

Essah, Patience. *A House Divided: Slavery and Emancipation in Delaware, 1638–1865.* Charlottesville: University Press of Virginia, 1996.

Etcheson, Nicole. *Bleeding Kansas: Contested Liberty in the Civil War Era.* Lawrence: University Press of Kansas, 2004.

Fairchild, Herman L. *The Rochester Canyon and the Genesee River Base-Levels.* Rochester, NY: Rochester Academy of Science, 1919.

Fehrenbacher, Don E., and Ward M. McAfee, eds. *Slaveholding Republic: An Account of the United States Government's Relations to Slavery.* New York, NY: Oxford University Press, 2002.

Feldberg, Michael. *The Turbulent Era: Riot and Disorder in Jacksonian America.* New York, NY: Oxford University Press, 1980.

Fields, Barbara Jeanne. *Slavery and Freedom on the Middle Ground: Maryland During the Nineteenth Century.* New Haven, CT: Yale University Press, 1985.

Finkelman, Paul. *Dred Scott v. Sandford: A Brief History with Documents.* Boston: Bedford Books, 1997.

———. *Millard Fillmore: The American Presidents Series: The 13th President, 1850–1853.* New York, NY: Times Books, 2011.

Fiske, David A., Clifford W. Brown, and Rachel Seligman. *Solomon Northup: The Complete Story of the Author of Twelve Years a Slave.* New York, NY: Praeger, 2013.

Fitzgerald, Keith. *The Face of the Nation: Immigration, the State, and the National Identity.* Stanford, CA: Stanford University Press, 1996.

Fletcher, Kami. *The Niagara Movement: The Black Protest Reborn.* South Carolina: VDM Verlag, 2008.

Flick, Alexander Clarence. *Loyalism in New York during the American Revolution.* New York, NY: Columbia University Press, 1901.

Foner, Eric. *Free Soil, Free Labor, Free Men: The Ideology of the Republican Party before the Civil War with a New Introductory Essay.* New York, NY: Oxford University Press, 1995.

———. *Gateway to Freedom: The Hidden History of the Underground Railroad.* New York, NY: W. W. Norton & Company, 2015.

———. *Reconstruction: America's Unfinished Revolution, 1863–1877, Undated Edition.* New York: NY: Harper Perennial, 2014.

Foner, Philip S., ed. *Frederick Douglass: Selected Speeches and Writings.* Abridged and adapted by Taylor Yuval. Chicago, IL: Lawrence Hill Books, 1999.

———, ed. *The Life and Writings of Frederick Douglass.* 5 vols. (New York, NY: International Publishers, 1950–75).

Foote, Thelma. *Black and White Manhattan: The History of Racial Formation in Colonial New York City.* New York, NY: Oxford University Press, 2004.

Forbes, Robert Pierce. *The Missouri Compromise and Its Aftermath: Slavery and the Meaning of America.* Chapel Hill: University of North Carolina Press, 2007.

Fordham, Monroe, ed. *The African American Presence in New York State History: Four Regional History Surveys.* Albany, NY: SUNY New York African American Institute, 1989.

Foreman, Edward R., ed. *Centennial History of Rochester, New York,* 4 vols. Rochester, NY: Rochester Historical Society, 1932.

Foreman, Gabrielle, Jim Casey, and Sarah Lynn Patterson, eds. T*he Colored Conventions Movement: Black Organizing in the Nineteenth Century.* Chapel Hill: University of North Carolina Press, 2021.

Foster, Frances Smith. *'Til Death or Distance Do Us Part: Love and Marriage in African America.* New York, NY: Oxford University Press, 2009.

Fought, Leigh. *Women in the World of Frederick Douglass.* New York, NY: Oxford University Press, 2017.

Frank, Albert J. von. *The Trials of Anthony Burns: Freedom and Slavery in Emerson's Boston.* Cambridge, MA: Harvard University Press, 1998.

Franklin, John Hope, and Loren Schweninger. *Runaway Slaves: Rebels on the Plantation.* New York, NY: Oxford University Press, 1999.

Frey, Sylvia R. *Water from the Rock: Black Resistance in a Revolutionary Age.* Princeton, NJ: Princeton University Press, 1992.

Freyer, Tony, and Lyndsay Campbell. *Freedom's Conditions in the U.S., Canadian Borderlands in the Age of Emancipation.* Durham, NC: Carolina Academic Press, 2011.

Frost, Karolyn Smardz. *Steal Away Home: One Woman's Epic Flight to Freedom and Her Long Road Back to the South.* Toronto, ON: HarperCollins Publishers, 2017.

———. *I've Got a Home in Glory Land: A Lost Tale of the Underground Railroad.* New York, NY: Farrar, Straus and Giroux, 2007.

Frost, Karolyn Smardz, and Veta Smith Tucker, eds. *A Fluid Frontier: Slavery, Resistance, and the Underground Railroad in the Detroit River Borderland.* Detroit, MI: Wayne State University Press, 2016.

Frost, Karolyn Smardz, Bryan Walls, Hilary Bates Neary, and Frederick H. Armstrong. *Ontario's African-Canadian Heritage: Collected Writings by Fred Landon, 1918–1967.* Toronto, ON: Dundurn Press, 2009.

Fryer, Mary Beacock, and Christopher Dracott. *John Graves Simcoe, 1752–1806: A Biography.* Toronto, ON: Dundurn Press, 1998.

Furnas, J. C. *The Road to Harpers Ferry.* New York: William Sloane Associates, 1959.

Gaines, Kevin K. *Uplifting the Race: Black Leadership, Politics, and Culture in the Twentieth Century.* Chapel Hill: University of North Carolina Press, 1996.

Gara, Larry. *The Liberty Line: The Legend of the Underground Railroad.* Lexington: University of Kentucky Press, 1961.

Garfield, Deborah M., and Rafia Zafar, eds. *Harriet Jacobs and Incidents in the Life of a Slave Girl: New Critical Essays.* Cambridge: Cambridge University Press, 1996.

Gates, Lillan F. *After the Rebellion: The Later Years of William Lyon Mackenzie.* Toronto, ON: Dundurn Press, 1996.

Gayler, Hugh J. *Niagara's Changing Landscapes.* Ottawa, ON: Carleton University Press, 1994.

Gellman, David N. *Emancipating New York: The Politics of Slavery and Freedom, 1777–1827.* Baton Rouge: Louisiana State University Press, 2006.

Genovese, Eugene. *Roll, Jordan, Roll: The World the Slaves Made.* New York, NY: Random House, 1974.

Gerling, Curt. *Smugtown U.S.A.* Webster, NY: Plaza Publishers, 1957.

Gerzina, Gretchen Holbrook, ed. *Black Victorians, Black Victoriana.* New Brunswick, NJ: Rutgers University Press, 2003.

Gibbins, Roger. *Canada as Borderlands Society.* Orono, ME: Canadian-American Center, 1989.

Gilbert, Alan. *Black Patriots and Loyalists; Fighting for Emancipation in the War for Independence.* Chicago: University of Chicago Press, 2012.

Gillard, William, and Thomas Tooke. *Niagara Escarpment.* Toronto, ON: University of Toronto Press, 1975.

Gillian, Gill. *We Two: Victoria and Albert: Rulers, Partners, Rivals.* New York, NY: Ballantine Books, 2009.

Gilpin, R. Blakeslee. *John Brown Still Lives! America's Long Reckoning with Violence, Equality and Change.* Chapel Hill: University of North Carolina Press, 2011.

Gilroy, Paul. *The Black Atlantic: Modernity and Double Consciousness*. Cambridge, MA: Harvard University Press, 1993.

Girard, Philip, Jim Phillips, and Blake Brown. *A History in Law in Canada, Vol. 1: Beginnings to 1866*. Toronto, ON: University of Toronto Press, 2018.

Glaude, Eddie S. *Exodus: Religion, Race and Nation in Early 19th Century Black America*. Chicago: University of Chicago Press, 2000.

Glazebrook, G. P. De T. *A History of Transportation in Canada*. New Haven, CT: Yale University Press, 1938.

Gleeson, David T., and Simon Lewis. *Ambiguous Anniversary: The Bicentennial of the International Slave Trade Bans*. Columbia: University of South Carolina Press, 2012.

Goldman, Mark. *High Hopes: The Rise and Decline of Buffalo, New York*. Albany: State University of New York Press, 1983.

Gomez, Michael A. *Pragmatism in the Age of Jihad: The Precolonial State of Bundu*. Cambridge, MA: Cambridge University Press, 1992.

Gordon, Ann D., ed. *The Selected Papers of Elizabeth Cady Stanton and Susan B. Anthony: In the School of Anti-Slavery, 1840 to 1866*. New Brunswick, NJ: Rutgers University Press, 1997.

Gorrell, Gena K. *North Star to Freedom: The Story of the Underground Railroad*. Don Mills, ON: Stoddart Publishing, 1996.

Goyal, Yogita. *Runaway Genres: The Global Afterlives of Slavery*. New York: NY: New York University Press, 2019.

Graber, Mark A. *Dred Scott and the Problem of Constitutional Evil*. Cambridge: Cambridge University Press, 2006.

Graybill, Andrew, and Benjamin Johnson, eds. *Bridging National Borders in North America: Transnational and Comparative Histories*. Durham, NC: Duke University, 2010.

Gerber, David A. *The Making of an American Pluralism: Buffalo, New York, 1825–1860*. Champaign: University of Illinois Press, 1989.

Greenidge, Kerri K. *Black Radical: The Life and Times of William Monroe Trotter*. New York, NY: Liveright, 2019.

Greenspan, Ezra. *William Wells Brown: An African American Life*. New York, NY: W. W. Norton, 2014.

Greenwood, Frank Murray, and Barry Wright. *Canadian State Trials: Rebellion and Invasion in the Canadas, 1837–1839, Vol. 2*. Toronto, ON: University of Toronto Press, 1990.

Greer, Allan. *The Patriots and the People: The Rebellion of 1837 in Rural Lower Canada*. Toronto, ON: University of Toronto Press, 1993.

Griffler, Keith P. *Front Line of Freedom: Africans and the Forging of the Underground Railroad in the Ohio Valley*. Lexington: University of Kentucky Press, 2004.

Grigg, Jeff W. *The Combahee River Raid: Harriet Tubman & Lowcountry Liberation*. Charleston, SC: History Press, 2014.

Guay, David R. P. *Great Western Railway of Canada: Southern Ontario's Pioneer Railway.* Toronto, ON: Dundurn Press, 2015.

Gueizo, Allen C. *Lincoln and Douglas: The Debates that Defined America.* New York, NY: Simon & Schuster, 2009.

Guyatt, Nicholas. *Bind Us Apart: How Enlightened Americans Invented Racial Segregation.* New York, NY: Basic Books, 2016.

Hahn, Steven. *A Nation without Borders: The United States and Its World in an Age of Civil Wars, 1830–1910.* New York, NY: Viking, 2016.

———. *The Political Worlds of Slavery and Freedom.* Cambridge, MA: Harvard University Press, 2009.

Hall, Raymond L. *Black Separatism in the United States.* Hanover, NH: University Press of New England, 1978.

Hall, Ryan. *Beneath the Backbone of the Work: Blackfoot People and the North American Borderlands, 1720–1877.* Chapel Hill: University of North Carolina Press, 2020.

Hämäläinen, Pekka, and Benjamin Johnson. *Major Problems in the History of North American Borderlands.* Belmont, CA: Wadsworth, 2011.

Hamilton, Holman. *Prologue to Conflict: The Crisis and Compromise of 1850.* New York, NY: W. W. Norton & Company, Inc., 2008.

Harlan, Louis R., ed. *The Booker T. Washington Papers, Vol. 3 1889–95.* Champaign: University of Illinois Press, 1974.

Harris, Leslie M. *In the Shadow of Slavery: African Americans in New York City, 1628–1863.* Chicago: University of Chicago Press, 2003.

Harrold, Stanley. *The Rise of Aggressive Abolitionism: Addresses to the Slaves.* Lexington: University of Kentucky Press, 2004.

Harvey, David. *The Condition of Postmodernity: An Enquiry into the Origins of Cultural Change.* Oxford: Blackwell, 1989.

Henrick, George and Willene, eds. *Fleeing for Freedom: Stories of the Underground Railroad as Told by Levi Coffin and William Still.* Chicago, IL: Ivan R. Dee, 2004.

Henry, Natasha L. *Emancipation Day: Celebrating Freedom in Canada.* Toronto, ON: Dundurn Press, 2010.

Hepburn, Sharon. *Crossing the Border: A Free Black Community in Canada.* Champaign: University of Illinois Press, 2007.

Herzog, Lawrence A. *Where North Meets South: Cities, Space, and Politics on the U.S.–Mexico Border.* Austin: University of Texas Press, 1990.

Hesslink, George K. *Black Neighbors: Negroes in a Northern Rural Community.* Indianapolis: Bobbs- Merrill, 1968.

Hewitt, Nancy. *Women's Activism and Social Change: Rochester, New York, 1822–1872.* Lanham, MD: Lexington Brooks, 2001.

Highsmith, Carol M., and Ted Landphair. *Pennsylvania Avenue: America's Main Street.* Washington, DC: American Institute of Architects Press, 1996.

Hill, Daniel G. *The Freedom-Seekers: Blacks in Early Canada*. Agincourt: The Book Society of Canada Limited, 1981.

Hill, Lawrence. *Trials and Triumphs: The Story of African-Canadians*. Toronto, ON: Umbrella Press, 1993.

Hine, Darlene Clark, and Jacqueline A. McLeod, eds. *Crossing Boundaries: Comparative History of Black People in Diaspora*. Bloomington: Indiana University Press, 1999.

A History of the Vote in Canada. Ottawa, ON: Office of the Chief of the Chief Electoral of Canada, 2007.

Hodges, Graham Russell. *New York City Cartmen, 1667–1850*. Rev. ed. New York, NY: New York University Press, 1986.

———. *Root and Branch: African Americans in New York and East Jersey, 1613–1863*. New York: Oxford University Press, 2004.

Hoerder, Dirk. *Creating Societies: Immigrant Lives in Canada*. Montreal: McGill-Queen's University Press, 2000.

Holt, Michael F. *The Political Crisis of the 1850s*. New York, NY: W. W. Norton & Co., 1983.

Holzer, Harold, Edna Greene Medford, and Frank J. Williams. *The Emancipation Proclamation: Three Views*. Baton Rouge: Louisiana State University Press, 2006.

Horne, Gerald. *Negro Comrades of the Crown: African Americans and the British Empire Fight the U.S. Before Emancipation*. New York, NY: New York University Press, 2012.

Horton, James Oliver. *Free People of Color: Inside the African American Community*. Washington, DC: Smithsonian Institution Press, 1993.

Horton, James Oliver, and Lois E. Horton. *In Hope of Liberty: Culture, Community, and Protest Among Northern Free Blacks, 1700–1860*. New York, NY: Oxford University Press, 1997.

Horwitz, Tony. *Midnight Rising: John Brown and the Raid That Sparked the Civil War*. New York, NY: Picador, 2011.

Howe, Daniel Walker. *The Political Culture of American Whigs*. Chicago: University of Chicago Press, 1979.

Hudson, J. Blaine. *Fugitive Slaves and the Underground Railroad in the Kentucky Borderland*. Jefferson, NC: McFarland, 2002.

Humez, Jean M. *Harriet Tubman: The Life and the Life Stories*. Madison: University of Wisconsin Press, 2003.

Hunter, Carol. *To Set the Captives Free: Reverend Jermain Wesley Loguen and the Struggle for Freedom in Central New York, 1835–1872*. New York: Garland, 1993.

Hutchinson, Paul. *An Index to the Map of the Town of St. Catharines, Canada West: Surveyed, Drawn and Published by Marcus Smith, 1852*. St. Catharines, ON: Slabtown Press, ca. 1996.

Jackson, John N. *St. Catharines Ontario: Its Early Years*. Belleville, ON: Mika Publishing Co., 1976.

———. *The Welland Canals and their Communities: Engineering, Industrial, and Urban Transformation.* Toronto, ON: University of Toronto Press, 1997.

Jackson, John N., and Sheila M. Wilson. *St. Catharines Canada's Canal City.* St. Catharines, ON: The St. Catharines Standard Limited, 1992.

Jackson, John N., John Burtniak, and Gregory P. Stein. *The Mighty Niagara: One River—Two Frontiers.* Amherst, NY: Prometheus Books, 2003.

Jackson, Kellie Carter. *Force and Freedom: Black Abolitionists and the Politics of Violence.* Philadelphia: University of Pennsylvania Press, 2019.

Johnson, Ludwell H. *Division and Reunion: America, 1848–1877.* New York, NY: John Wiley & Sons, 1978.

Johnson, Paul E. *A Shopkeeper's Millennium: Society and Revivals in Rochester, New York, 1815–1837.* New York, NY: Hill & Wang, 2004.

Johnson, Walter. *River of Dark Dreams: Slavery and Empire in the Cotton Kingdom.* Cambridge, MA: Harvard University Press, 2013.

———. *Soul by Soul: Life Inside the Antebellum Slave Market.* Cambridge, MA: Harvard University Press, 2001.

Jonas, Gilbert. *Freedom's Sword: The NAACP and the Struggle against Racism in America, 1909–1969.* New York: NY: Routledge, 2004.

Jones, Angela. *African American Civil Rights: Early Activism and the Niagara Movement.* New York, NY: Praeger, 2011.

Jones, Howard. *To the Webster-Ashburton Treaty: A Study in Anglo-American Relations, 1783–1843.* Chapel Hill: University of North Carolina Press, 1977.

Jones, Reece. *Open Borders: In Defense of Free Movement.* Athens: University of Georgia Press. 2019.

Jones, Stephen B. *Boundary Making: A Handbook for Statesmen, Treaty Editors and Boundary Commissioners.* Washington, DC: Carnegie Endowment for International Peace, 1945.

Kashatus, William C. *Just Over the Line: Chester County and the Underground Railroad.* West Chester, PA: Chester Country Historical Society, 2002.

———. *William Still: The Underground Railroad and the Angel at Philadelphia.* Notre Dame, IN: University of Notre Dame Press, 2021.

Kaufman, Jason. *The Origins of Canadian and America Political Differences.* Cambridge, MA: Harvard University Press, 2009.

Kenny, Kevin, ed. *Ireland and the British Empire.* New York, NY: Oxford University Press, 2004.

Kerr-Ritchie, Jeffrey R. *Freedom's Seekers: Essays on the Comparative Emancipation.* Baton Rouge: Louisiana State University Press, 2013.

———. *Rebellious Passage: The Creole Revolt and America's Coastal Slave Trade.* New York, NY: Cambridge University Press, 2019.

————. *Rites of August First: Emancipation in the Black Atlantic World.* Baton Rouge: Louisiana State University Press, 2007.

Kilbourn, William. *The Firebrand: William Lyon Mackenzie and the Rebellion in Upper Canada.* Toronto, ON: Dundurn Press, 2008.

Kilgore, De Witt Douglas. *Astrofuturism: Science, Race, and Visions of Utopia in Space.* Philadelphia: University of Pennsylvania Press, 2003.

Kilson, Martin L., and Robert I. Rotberg, eds. *The African Diaspora: Interpretive Essays.* Cambridge, MA: Harvard University Press, 1976.

Koch, Robert, and Henry W. Clune. *The Genesee.* Syracuse, NY: Syracuse University Press, 1988.

Kornblith, Gary, and Carol Lasser. *The Struggle for Racial Equality in Oberlin, Ohio.* Baton Rouge: Louisiana State University Press, 2018.

Kratts, Michelle Ann. *Melting Pot: Niagara's Rich Ethnic Heritage.* Scotts Valley, CA: CreateSpace Independent Publishing Platform, 2017.

Kyvig, David E., and Myron A. Marty. *Nearby History: Exploring the Past Around You,* 3rd ed. Lanham, MD: AltaMira Press, 2010.

Lampe, Gregory. *Frederick Douglass: Freedom's Voice, 1818–1845.* Lansing: Michigan State University Press, 2004.

Landon, Fred. *Canada's Part in Freeing the Slaves.* Toronto, ON: N.P., 1919.

Larkin, Janet Dorothy. *Overcoming Niagara: Canals, Commerce, and Tourism in the Niagara-Great Lakes Borderland Region, 1792–1837.* Albany: SUNY Press, 2018.

LaRoche, Cheryl Janifer. *Free Black Communities and the Underground Railroad: The Geography of Resistance.* Champaign: University of Illinois Press, 2014.

Larson, Kate Clifford. *Bound for the Promised Land: Harriet Tubman, Portrait of An American Hero.* New York, NY: Ballantine Books, 2004.

Lawson, Bill, and Frank Kirkland, eds. *Frederick Douglass: A Critical Reader.* Malden, MA: Blackwell Publishers, Inc., 1999.

Leavy, Michael. *Rochester's Corn Hill: The Historic Third Ward.* Charleston, SC: Arcadia Publishing, 2003.

Lecker, Robert. *Borderlands: Essays in Canadian-American Relations.* Toronto, ON: ECW Press, 1991.

Levine, Robert S. *Martin Delany, Frederick Douglass, and the Politics of Representative Identity.* Chapel Hill: University of North Carolina Press, 1997.

Lewis, James K. *Religious Life of Fugitive Slaves and the Rise of Coloured Baptist Churches, 1820–1865, In What Is Now Known as Ontario.* New York, NY: Arno Press, 1980.

Lewis, Paul E. *Niagara Gorge Bridges: Marvels of Engineering.* St. Catharines, ON: Looking Back Press, 2008.

Litwack, Leon F. *North of Slavery: The Negro in the Free North, 1790–1860.* Chicago: University of Chicago Press, 1961.

Logan, Rayford W. *The Betrayal of the Negro: From Rutherford B. Hayes to Woodrow Wilson*. New York, NY: Da Capo Press, 1997.

——. *The Negro in American Life and Thought: The Nadir, 1877–1901*. New York, NY: Dial Press, 1954.

Longo, Matthew. *The Politics of Borders: Sovereignty, Security, and the Citizen after 9/11*. New York, NY: Cambridge University Press, 2017.

Lowry, Beverly. *Harriet Tubman: Imagining A Life*. New York, NY: Anchor Books, 2007.

Lubet, Steven. *Fugitive Justice: Runaways, Rescuers, and Slavery on Trial*. Belknap Press, 2010.

Lumsden, Ian, ed. *Close the 49th Parallel, Etc.: The Americanization of Canada*. Toronto, ON: University of Toronto Press, 1970.

Mackey, Frank. *Black Then: Blacks and Montreal, 1780s–1880s*. Montreal: McGill-Queen's University Press, 2004.

——. *Done with Slavery: The Black Fact in Montreal, 1760–1840*. Montreal: McGill-Queen's University Press, 2010.

Maddox, Lucy. *The Parker Sister: A Border Kidnapping*. Philadelphia, PA: Temple University Press, 2016.

Malone, Dumas, and Basil Rauch. *Crisis of the Union, 1841–1877*. New York: Appleton-Century-Crofts, 1960.

Maltz, Earl M. *Fugitive Slave on Trial: The Anthony Burns Case and Abolitionist Outrage*. Lawrence: University Press of Kansas, 2010.

Manning, Patrick. *The African Diaspora: A History Through Culture*. New York, NY: Columbia University Press, 2010.

Marable, Manning, and Vanessa Agard-Jones. *Transnational Blackness: Navigating the Global Color Line*. New York, NY: Palgrave Macmillan, 2008.

Marcotte, Robert. *Where They Fell: Stories of Rochester Area Soldiers in the Civil War*. Franklin, VA: Q Publishing, 2002.

Martin, Waldo E., Jr. *The Mind of Frederick Douglass*. Chapel Hill: University of North Carolina Press, 1984.

Martinez, Oscar J. *Border People: Life and Society in the U.S.-Mexico Borderlands*. Tucson: University of Arizona Press, 1994.

Mathieu, Sarah-Jane, *North of the Color Line: Migration and Black Resistance in Canada, 1870–1955*. Chapel Hill: University of North Carolina Press, 2010.

Mayer, George H. *The Republican Party, 1854–1966*. 2nd ed. New York, NY: Oxford University Press, 1967.

Mayer, Henry. *All on Fire: William Lloyd Garrison and the Abolition of Slavery*. New York, NY: St. Martin's Griffin, 1998.

Mayfield, John. *Rehearsal for Republicanism: Free Soil and the Politics of Antislavery*. Port Washington, NY: Kennikat Press, 1980.

Maynard, Robyn. *Policing Black Lives: State Violence in Canada from Slavery to the Present.* Halifax, NS: Fernwood Books, 2017.

McCarthy, Timothy Patrick, and John Stauffer, eds. *Prophets of Protest: Reconsidering the History of American Abolitionism.* New York, NY: New Press, 2006.

McDaniel, W. Caleb. *The Problem of Democracy in the Age of Slavery: Garrisonian Abolitionists and Transatlantic Reform.* Baton Rouge: Louisiana State University Press, 2015.

McDonough, Daniel, and Kenneth W. Noe, eds. *Politics and Culture of the Civil War Era: Essays in Honor of Robert W. Johannsen.* Selinsgrove, PA: Susquehana University Press, 2006.

McFeely, William S. *Frederick Douglass.* New York, NY: W. W. Norton & Co., 1991.

McGinty, Brian. *John Brown's Trial.* Cambridge, MA: Harvard University Press, 2009.

McGlone, Robert E. *John Brown's War Against Slavery.* Cambridge: Cambridge University Press, 2009.

McGowan, James A. *Station Master on the Underground Railroad: The Life and Letters of Thomas Garrett.* Jefferson, NC: McFarland, 2009.

McGowan, James A., and William C. Kashatus. *Harriet Tubman: A Biography.* Santa Barbara, CA: Greenwood, 2011.

McGreevy, Patrick. *Stairway to Empire: Lockport, the Erie Canal and the Shaping of America.* Albany, NY: State University of New York Press, 2009.

McKelvey, Blake. *A Panoramic History of Rochester and Monroe Country New York.* Woodland Hills, CA: Windsor Publications, Inc., 1979.

——. *Rochester.* 4 vols. Cambridge, MA: Harvard University Press, 1945–61.

——. *Rochester: A Brief History.* Lewiston, NY: Edwin Mellon Press, 1984.

——. *Rochester on the Genesee: The Growth of a City.* Syracuse, NY: Syracuse University Press, 1993.

——. *Rochester, the Flower City, 1855–1890.* Cambridge, MA: Harvard University Press, 1945.

——. *Rochester, the Water-Power City, 1812–1854.* Cambridge, MA: Harvard University Press, 1945.

McManus, Edgar J. *A History of Negro Slavery in New York.* Syracuse, NY: Syracuse University Press, 1966.

McPherson, James M. T*he Negro's Civil War: How American Negroes Felt and Acted during the War for the Union.* New York, NY: Pantheon Books, 1965.

Mealy, Todd. *Aliened American: A Biography of William Howard Day,* 2 vols.; *Vol. 1: 1825 to 1865,* and *Vol. 2: 1866 to 1900.* Baltimore, MD: America Star Books, 2010.

Medford, Edna Greene. *Lincoln and Emancipation.* Carbondale, IL: Southern Illinois University Press, 2015.

Melish, Joanne Pope. *Disowning Slavery: Gradual Emancipation and "Race" in New England, 1780–1860.* Ithaca, NY: Cornell University Press, 2000.

Mensah, Joseph. *Black Canadians: History, Experience, Social Conditions*. New York, NY: Fernwood Publishing Company, 2004.

Metcalfe, William, ed. *Understanding Canada: A Multidisciplinary Introduction to Canadian Studies*. New York, NY: New York University Press, 1982.

Meyer, Eugene L. *Five for Freedom: The African American Soldiers in John Brown's Army*. Chicago, IL: Lawrence Hill Books, 2018.

Meyler, Peter, and David Meyler. *A Stolen Life: Searching for Richard Pierpoint*. Toronto, ON: Natural Heritage Books, 1999.

Migdal, Joel S., ed. *Boundaries and Belonging: States and Societies in the Struggle to Shape Identities and Local Practices*. Cambridge, MA: Cambridge University Press, 2004.

Miles, Tiya. *The Dawn of Detroit: A Chronicle of Slavery and Freedom in the City of the Straits*. New York, NY: New Press, 2017.

Miller, Bradley. *Borderline Crime: Fugitive Criminals and the Challenges of the Border, 1819–1914*. Toronto, ON: University of Toronto Press, 2016.

Miller, Floyd John. *The Search for a Black Nationality: Black Emigration and Colonization, 1863–1878*. Champaign: University of Illinois Press, 1975.

Miller, John Gregory. *Black Heritage in Grantham Township, Lincoln County*. St. Catharines, ON: The Ontario Genealogical Society, Niagara Peninsula Branch, 1993.

Miller, Monica L. *Slaves to Fashion: Black Dandyism and the Styling of Black Diasporic Identity*. Durham, NC: Duke University Press, 2009.

Moore, Jacqueline M. *Booker T. Washington, W. E. B. Du Bois, and the Struggle for Racial Uplift*. New York, NY: Rowman & Littlefield Publishers, 2003.

Moore, Stephen P. *Bootleggers and Borders: The Paradox of Prohibition on a Canada-U.S. Borderland*. Lincoln: University of Nebraska Press, 2014.

Mora, Anthony. *Border Dilemmas: Racial and National Uncertainties in New Mexico, 1848–1912*. Durham, NC: Duke University Press, 2011.

Morgan, Kenneth. *Slavery and the British Empire: From Africa to America*. New York, NY: Oxford University Press, 2008.

Morley, Jefferson. *Snow-Storm in August: Washington City, Francis Scott Key, and the Forgotten Race Riot of 1835*. New York, NY: Doubleday, 2012.

Morris, J. Brent. *Oberlin. Hotbed of Abolitionism: College, Community, and the Fight for Freedom and Equality in Antebellum America*. Chapel Hill: University of North Carolina Press, 2014.

Morris, Thomas D. *Free Men All: The Personal Liberty Laws of the North, 1780–1861*. Baltimore, MD: Johns Hopkins University Press, 1974.

Moses, Wilson Jeremiah. *The Golden Age of Black Nationalism, 1850–1925*. Hamden, CT: Archon Books, 1978.

Moss, Richard Shannon. *Slavery on Long Island: A Study in Local Institutional and Early African-American Communal Life*. New York, NY: Garland Publishing, 1993.

Murphy, Angela F. *The Jerry Rescue: The Fugitive Slave Law, Northern Rights, and the American Sectional Crisis.* New York, NY: Oxford University Press, 2014.

Murray, David. *Colonial Justice: Justice, Morality, and Crime in Niagara District, 1791–1849.* Toronto, ON: University of Toronto Press, 2002.

Murray, Hannah-Rose. *Advocates of Freedom: African American Transatlantic Abolitionism in the British Isles.* Cambridge, UK: Cambridge University Press, 2020.

Naturalization Records 1842–1849 for the Counties of Lincoln and Welland. St. Catharines, ON: Ontario Genealogical Society, 1993.

Newby, M. Dalyce. *Anderson Ruffin Abbott: First Afro-Canadian Doctor.* Markham, ON: Fitzhenry and Whiteside, 1998.

Newman, Richard, Patrick Rael, and Philip Lapsansky, eds. *Pamphlets of Protest: An Anthology of Early African-American Protest Literature, 1790–1860.* New York, NY: Routledge, 2000.

Nwankwo, Ifeoma Kiddoe. *Black Cosmopolitanism: Racial Consciousness and Transnational Identity in the Nineteenth-Century Americas.* Philadelphia: University of Pennsylvania Press, 2005.

Oakes, James B. *The Radical and the Republican: Frederick Douglass, Abraham Lincoln, and the Triumphs of Antislavery.* New York, NY: W. W. Norton & Co., 2007.

Oates, Stephen B. *To Purge this Land with Blood: A Biography of John Brown.* New York: Harper & Row, 1970.

Obadele-Starks, Ernest. *Freebooters and Smugglers: The Foreign Slave Trade in the United States after 1808.* Fayetteville: University of Arkansas Press, 2007.

O'Donnell, Neil. *The Niagara Frontier's Unwritten History.* Kernersville, NC: Argus Enterprises International, 2012.

O'Donovan, Susan E. *Becoming Free in the Cotton South.* Cambridge, MA: Harvard University Press, 2010.

Ohmae, Kenichi. *The Borderless World: Power and Strategy in the Interlinked Economy.* New York, NY: Harper Business, 1990.

Oickle, Alvin F. *The Man with the Branded Hand.* Everett, MA: Lorelli Slater Publisher, 1998.

O'Keefe, Rose. *Frederick and Anna Douglass in Rochester, New York: Their Home Was Open to All.* Charleston, SC: History Press, 2013.

Olaniyan, Tejumola, and James H. Sweet, eds. *The African Diaspora and the Disciplines.* Bloomington: Indiana University Press, 2010.

Oldfield, J. R. *The Ties that Bind: Transatlantic Abolitionism in the Age of Reform, c. 1820–1866.* Liverpool, UK: Liverpool University Press, 2020.

Pacheco, Josephine F. *The Pearl: A Failed Slave Escape on the Potomac.* Chapel Hill: University of North Carolina Press, 2005.

Papson, Don, and Tom Calarco. *Secret Lives of the Underground Railroad in New York*

City: Sydney Howard Gay, Louis Napoleon and the Record of Fugitives. Jefferson, NC: McFarland, 2015.

Pargas, Damian Alan. *Fugitive Slaves and Spaces of Freedom in North America.* Gainesville, FL: University Press of Florida, 2018.

Paris, Leonard Albert. *Jim Crow Also Lived Here: Structural Racism and Generational Poverty—Growing Up Black in New Glasgow, Nova Scotia.* Altona, MB: Friesen Press, 2020.

Parnell, Maggie. *Black History in the Niagara Peninsula.* Self-Published, 1996.

Pascoe, Peggy. *What Comes Naturally: Miscegenation Law and the Making of Race in America.* New York: Oxford University Press, 2009.

Pease, Jane H., and William H. Pease. *Black Utopia: Negro Communal Experiments in America.* Madison: State Historical Society of Wisconsin, 1963.

———. *Bound with Them in Chains: A Biographical History of the Antislavery Movement.* Westport, CT: Greenwood Press, 1972.

———. "Introduction." In *Twenty-Two Years a Slave and Forty Years a Freeman,* by Austin Steward, ix–xv. Mineola, NY: Dover Publications, 2004.

———. *They Who Would Be Free: Blacks Search for Freedom, 1830–1861.* Champaign: University of Illinois Press, 1990.

Pettinger, Alasdair. *Frederick Douglass and Scotland, 1846: Living an Antislavery Life.* Edinburgh, UK: Edinburgh University Press, 2020.

Pitt, Steve. *To Stand and Fight Together: Richard Pierpoint and the Coloured Corps of Upper Canada.* Toronto, ON: Dundurn Press, 2008.

Potter, David M., and Don E. Fehrenbacher, eds. *The Impending Crisis, 1848–1861.* New York, NY: Harper & Row, 1976.

Power, Michael, and Nancy Butler. *Slavery and Freedom in Niagara.* Niagara-on-the-Lake, ON: Niagara Historical Society, 1993.

Pratt, Anna. *Securing Borders.* Vancouver, BC: University of British Columbia Press, 2005.

Price, Richard, ed. *Maroon Societies: Rebel Slave Communities in the Americas.* 3rd ed. Baltimore, MD: Johns Hopkins University Press, 1996.

Prince, Bryan. *I Came as a Stranger: The Underground Railroad.* Toronto, ON: Tundra, 2004.

———. *My Brother's Keeper: African Canadians and the American Civil War.* Toronto, ON: Dundurn Press, 2015.

Pryor, Elizabeth Stordeur. *Colored Travelers: Mobility and the Fight for Citizenship Before the Civil War.* Chapel Hill: University of North Press, 2016.

Pulis, John W., ed. *Moving On: Black Loyalists in the Afro-Atlantic World.* New York, NY: Garland, 1999.

Quarles, Benjamin. *Allies for Freedom: Blacks and John Brown.* New York, NY: Oxford University Press, 1974.

———. *Black Abolitionists.* New York, NY: Oxford University Press, 1969.

———. *Frederick Douglass.* New York, NY: Da Capo Press, 1997.

———. *Lincoln and the Negro.* New York, NY: Da Capo Press, 1990.

———. *The Negro in the Civil War.* Boston: Little, Brown, 1969.

Quashie, Kevin. *The Sovereignty of Quiet: Beyond Resistance in Black Culture.* New Brunswick, NJ: Rutgers University Press, 2012.

Quigley, David, and David Gellman. *Jim Crow New York: A Documentary History of Race and Citizenship, 1777–1877.* New York, NY: New York University Press, 2003.

Rael, Patrick. *Black Identity and Black Protest in the Antebellum North.* Chapel Hill: University of North Carolina Press, 2002.

Ramirez, Bruno, with Yves Otis. *Crossing the 49th Parallel: Migration from Canada to the United States 1900–1930.* Ithaca, NY: Cornell University Press, 2001.

Rasmussen, William M. S., and Robert S. Tilton. *The Portent: John Brown's Raid in American Memory.* Richmond, VA: Virginia Historical Society, 2009.

Rathgeber, Brent, and Andrew Coyne. *Irresponsible Government: The Decline of Parliamentary Democracy in Canada.* Toronto, ON: Dundurn Press, 2014.

Rayback, Joseph G. *Free Soil: The Election of 1848.* Lexington: University Press of Kentucky, 1970.

Redkey, Edwin S., ed. *A Grand Army of Black Men: Letters from African-American Soldiers in the Union Army, 1861–1865.* Cambridge, Eng.: Cambridge University Press, 1992.

Reed, Harry. *Platform for Change: The Foundations of the Northern Free Black Community, 1775–1865.* East Lansing: Michigan State University Press, 1994.

Reed, Ishmael. *Flight to Canada.* New York, NY: Simon & Schuster, 1998.

Reid, Richard M. *African Canadians in Union Blue: Volunteering for the Cause in America's Civil War.* Kent, OH: Kent State University Press, 2014.

Remini, Robert V. *At the Edge of the Precipice: Henry Clay and the Compromise that Saved the Union.* New York, NY: Basic Books, 2010.

Resendez, Andres. *Changing National Identities at the Frontier: Texas and New Mexico, 1800–1850.* New York, NY: Cambridge University Press, 2005.

Reynolds, David S. *John Brown, Abolitionist: The Man Who Killed Slavery, Sparked the Civil War, and Seeded Civil Rights.* New York, NY: Alfred A. Knopf, 2005.

———. *Waking Giant: America in the Age of Jackson.* New York, NY: HarperCollins Publishers, 2008.

Rhodes, Jane. *Mary Ann Shadd Cary: The Black Press and Protest in the Nineteenth Century.* Bloomington: Indiana University Press, 1998.

Rice, Alan J., and Martin Crawford, eds. *Liberating Sojourn: Frederick Douglass and Transatlantic Reform.* Athens: University of Georgia Press, 1999.

Richards, Leonard L. *Who Freed the Slaves? The Fight over the Thirteenth Amendment.* Chicago: University of Chicago Press, 2015.

Richardson, Heather Cox. *West from Appomattox: The Reconstruction of America after the Civil War*. New Haven, CT: Yale University Press, 2007.

Riddell, William Renwick. *The Slave in Upper Canada, 1852–1865*. Lancaster, PA: n.p., 1919.

Riendeau, Roger. *A Brief History of Canada, 2nd ed*. New York, NY: Facts On File, Inc., 2007.

Ripley, C. Peter, ed. *The Black Abolitionist Papers,* 5 vols. Chapel Hill: University of North Carolina Press, 1985–92. See http://silverbox.gmu.edu/dscff/s/aaaw/item/2219.

Rizzo, Dennis. *Parallel Communities: The Underground Railroad in South Jersey*. New York, NY: History Press, 2008.

Roberts, Neil. *Freedom as Marronage*. Chicago: University of Chicago Press, 2015.

Robinson, Gwendolyn, and John W. Robinson. *Seek the Truth: A Story of Chatham's Black Community*. Canada: N.P., 1989, 2004, and 2005.

Robinson, Marsha R. *Purgatory between Kentucky and Canada: African Americans in Ohio*. Newcastle upon Tyne, UK: Cambridge Scholars Publishing, 2013.

Rochester/Monroe County Freedom Trail Commission: Guidebook to the Underground Railroad and the Abolitionist Movement. Rochester, NY: Division of the Department of Communications & Special Events of Monroe County, 2003.

Romney, Paul. *Getting It Wrong: How Canadians Forgot Their Past and Imperiled Confederation*. Toronto, ON: University of Toronto Press, 1999.

Rosenberg-Naparsteack, Ruth. *Rochester: A Pictorial History*. Virginia Beach, VA: The Donning Co., 1989.

Rothman, Adam. *Slave Country: American Expansion and the Origins of the Deep South*. Cambridge, MA: Harvard University Press, 2005.

Ruggles, Jeffrey, *The Unboxing of Henry Brown*. Richmond: Library of Virginia, 2003.

Rusert, Britt. *Fugitive Science: Empiricism and Freedom in Early African American Culture*. New York, NY: New York University Press, 2017.

Sadlier, Rosemary. *Harriet Tubman: Freedom Seeker, Freedom Leader*. Toronto, ON: Dundurn Press, 2012.

———. *Harriet Tubman and the Underground Railroad: Her Life in the United States and Canada*. Toronto: Umbrella Press, 1997.

———. *Mary Ann Shadd: Publisher, Teacher, Suffragette*. Toronto, ON: Umbrella Press, 1995.

Sadowski-Smith, Claudia, ed. *Globalization on the Line: Culture, Capital, and Citizenship at U.S. Borders*. New York, NY: Palgrave, 2002.

Salafia, Matthew. *Slavery's Borderland: Freedom and Bondage along the Ohio River*. Philadelphia: University of Pennsylvania Press, 2019.

Sawallisch, Nele. *Fugitive Borders: Black Canadian Cross-Border Literature at Mid-Nineteenth Century*. New York, NY: Columbia University Press, Transcript Publishing, 2019.

Schama, Simon. *Rough Crossings: The Slaves, and the American Revolution.* New York, NY: HarperCollins Publishers, 2007.

Schecter, Barnet. *The Battle for New York, the City at the Heart of the American Revolution.* New York, NY: Penguin Books, 2003.

———. *The Devil's Own Work: The Civil War Draft Riots and the Fight to Reconstruct America.* New York, NY: Walker Books, 2005.

Schoolman, Martha. *Abolitionist Geographies.* Minneapolis: University of Minnesota Press, 2014.

Scott, James C. *Domination and the Arts of Resistance: Hidden Transcripts.* New Haven, CT: Yale University Press, 1990.

———. *Weapons of the Weak: Everyday Forms of Peasant Resistance.* New Haven, CT: Yale University Press, 1985.

Sernett, Milton C. *Abolition's Axe: Beriah Green, Oneida Institute and the Black Freedom Struggle.* Syracuse, NY: Syracuse University Press, 1986.

———. *Harriet Tubman: Myth, Memory, and History.* Chapel Hill, NC: Duke University Press, 2007.

———. *North Star Country: Upstate New York and the Crusade for African American Freedom.* Syracuse, NY: Syracuse University Press, 2002.

Shadd, Adrienne. *The Journey from Tollgate to Parkway: African Canadians in Hamilton.* Toronto, ON: Dundurn Press, 2010.

Shadd, Adrienne, Afua Cooper, and Karolyn Smardz Frost. *The Underground Railroad: Next Stop, Toronto!* Toronto, ON: Natural Heritage, 2009.

Sheriff, Carol. *The Artificial River: The Erie Canal and the Paradox of Progress, 1817–1862.* New York, NY: Hill & Wang, 1996.

Siebert, Wilbur H. *The Underground Railroad from Slavery to Freedom: A Comprehensive History.* New York, NY: Dover Publications, 2006.

Siepel, Kevin H. *Joseph Bennett of Evans and the Growing of New York's Niagara Frontier.* Angola, NY: Spruce Tree Press, 2011.

Silverman, Jason A. *Unwelcome Guests: Canada West's Response to American Fugitive Slaves.* Millwood, NY: Associated Faculty Press, 1985.

Simpson, Donald G., and Paul E. Lovejoy, eds. *Under the North Star: Black Communities in Upper Canada.* Trenton, NJ: African World Press, 2005.

Sinha, Manisha. *The Slave's Cause: A History of Abolition.* New Haven, CT: Yale University Press, 2016.

Sklar, Kathryn Kish, and James Brewer Stewart, eds. *Women's Rights and Transatlantic Antislavery in the Era of Emancipation.* New Haven, CT: Yale University Press, 2007.

Slaney, Catherine. *Family Secrets: Crossing the Colour Line.* Toronto, ON: Natural Heritage Books, 2003.

Slaughter, Thomas P. *Bloody Dawn: The Christiana Riot and Racial Violence in the Antebellum North.* New York: Oxford University Press, 1991.

Smith, Bill G., and Richard Wojtowicz. *Blacks Who Stole Themselves: Advertisements for Runaways in the Pennsylvania Gazette, 1728–1790.* Philadelphia: University of Pennsylvania Press, 1989.

Smith, Gene Allen. *The Slaves' Gamble: Choosing Sides in the War of 1812.* New York, NY: Palgrave Macmillan, 2013.

Smith, Michael Peter, and Luis Eduardo Guarnizo, eds. *Transnationalism from Below: Comparative Urban & Community Research Vol. 6.* New Brunswick, NJ: Transaction Publishers, 1998.

Smith, Stephen R. I. *Violence, Order, and Unrest: A History of British North America, 1749–1876.* Toronto, ON: University of Toronto Press, 2019.

Smith, T. Watson. *The Slave in Canada.* Halifax, NS: Nova Scotia Historical Society Collection, 1899.

Spanning Niagara: The International Bridges, 1848–1962. Seattle: University of Washington Press, 1984.

Stanford, P. Thomas. *The Plea of the Ex Slaves Now in Canada.* Bradford, ON: Clegg and Tetley, 1885.

Stauffer, John. *Giants: The Parallel Lives of Frederick Douglass and Abraham Lincoln.* New York, NY: Twelve, 2008.

Stauffer, John, and Zoe Trodd. *Picturing Frederick Douglass: An Illustrated Biography of the Nineteenth Century's Most Photographed American.* New York, NY: Liveright, 2015.

———. *The Tribunal: Responses to John Brown and the Harpers Ferry Raid.* Cambridge, MA: Harvard University Press, 2012.

Steinman, D. B. *Spanning Niagara: The Builders of the Bridge.* New York, NY: Arno Press, 1972.

Stevens, Frank Walker. *The Beginnings of the New York Central Railroad: A History.* New York, NY: G. P. Putnam, 1926.

Stevens, William John. *Mayors of (Town and City of) St. Catharines, First Edition.* Self-Published, 2004.

Stewart, James Brewer, and Kathryn Kish, eds. *Women's Rights and Transatlantic Slavery in the Era of Emancipation.* New Haven, CT: Yale University Press, 2007.

Stouffer, Allen P. *Light of Nature and the Law of God: Antislavery in Ontario, 1833–1877.* Baton Rouge: Louisiana State University Press, 1992.

Stuart, Reginald C. *Transnationalism: Canada–United States History into the Twenty-First Century.* Montreal: McGill-Queen's University Press, 2010.

Stuckey, Sterling. *The Ideological Origins of Black Nationalism.* Boston: Beacon Press, 1972.

Styran, Roberta M., and Robert R. Taylor. *The Great National Object: Building the Nineteenth-Century Welland Canals.* Montreal: McGill-Queen's University Press, 2012.

Sweeney, Fionnghuala. *Frederick Douglass and the Atlantic World.* Liverpool: Liverpool University Press, 2007.

Switala, William J. *Underground Railroad in New York and New Jersey*. Mechanicsburg, PA: Stackpole Books, 2006.

Talton, Benjamin, and Quincy T. Mills. *Black Subjects in Africa and Its Diasporas: Race and Gender in Research and Writing*. New York, NY: Palgrave MacMillan, 2011.

Taylor, Alan. *The Divided Ground: Indians, Settlers, and the Northern Borderland of the American Revolution*. New York, NY: Vintage Books, 2006.

Taylor, Amy Murrell. *Embattled Freedom: Journeys through the Civil War's Refugee Camps*. Chapel Hill: University of North Carolina Press, 2020.

Taylor, Elizabeth Dowling. *A Slave in the White House: Paul Jennings and the Madisons*. New York, NY: Palgrave Macmillan, 2012.

Taylor, George Rogers. *The Transportation Revolution, 1815–1860*. New York, NY: Harper & Row, 1951.

Taylor, Yuval, ed. *I Was Born a Slave, Vol. 2: An Anthology of Classic Narratives: 1849–1866*. Foreword by Charles Johnson. Chicago, IL: Chicago Review Press, 1999.

Thomas, Owen A. *Niagara's Freedom Trail: A Guide to African-Canadian History on the Niagara Peninsula*. Thorold, ON: For the Region Niagara Tourist Council, 1995.

Thompson, Dorothy. *Queen Victoria: Gender and Power*. London: Virago Press, 2001.

Thomson, Colin A. *Blacks in Deep Snow: Black Pioneers in Canada*. Don Mills, ON: J. M. Dent and Sons, 1979.

Tobin, Jacqueline L., with Hettie Jones. *From Midnight to Dawn: The Last Tracks of the Underground Railroad*. New York, NY: Anchor Book, 2007.

Trotman, C. James. *Frederick Douglass: A Biography*. Santa Barbara, CA: Greenwood, 2011.

Trudel, Marcel. *Canada's Forgotten Slaves: Two Hundred Years of Bondage*. Translated by George Tombs. Montreal: Véhicule Press, 2013.

Truett, Samuel. *Fugitive Landscapes: The Forgotten History of the U.S.-Mexico Borderlands*. New Haven, CT: Yale University Press, 2006.

Tulloch, Headley. *Black Canadians: A Long Line of Fighters*. Toronto, ON: NC Press, 1975.

Tyler-McGraw, Marie. *An African Republic: Black and White Virginians in the Making of Liberia*. Chapel Hill, NC: University of North Carolina Press, 2014.

Ullman, Victor. *Look to the North Star: A Life of William King*. Toronto, ON: Umbrella Press, 1969.

Ural, Susannah J., ed. *Civil War Citizens: Race, Ethnicity, and Identity in America's Bloodiest Conflict*. New York, NY: New York University Press, 2010.

Varon, Elizabeth R. *Disunion! The Coming of the American Civil War, 1789–1859*. Chapel Hill: University of North Carolina Press, 2008.

Walcott, Rinaldo. *Black Like Who? Writing, Black, Culture*. Toronto, ON: Insomniac Press, 2018.

Walker, Barrington. *The African Canadian Legal Odyssey*. Toronto, ON: University of Toronto Press, 2012.

———. *Race on Trial: Black Defenders in Ontario's Criminal Courts, 1858–1958*. Toronto, ON: University of Toronto Press, 2010.

Walker, James W. St. G. *The Black Loyalists: The Search for a Promised Land in Nova Scotia and Sierra Leone, 1783–1870*. Toronto, ON: University of Toronto, 1992.

Walker, James W. St. G., and Patricia Thorvaldson. *Identity: The Black Experience in Canada*. Toronto: Ontario Educational Communications Authority and Gage Educational Publishing, 1979.

Waller, Maureen. *Sovereign Ladies: Sex, Sacrifice, and Power—The Six Reigning Queens of England*. New York, NY: St. Martin's Press, 2007.

Walther, Eric H. *The Shattering of the Union: America in the 1850s*. Wilmington, DE: Scholarly Resources, Inc., 2003.

Walton, Jonathan William. *Haven or Dream Deferred for American Blacks: Chatham, Ontario, 1830–1860*. Ottawa, ON: Canadian Historical Association, 1978.

Warren, Robert Penn. *John Brown: The Making of a Martyr*. New York: Payson and Clarke, 1929; rpr., St. Clair Shores: Scholarly Press, 1970.

Waugh, John C. *On the Brink of Civil War: The Compromise of 1850 and How It Changed the Course of American History*. Lanham, MD: Rowman & Littlefield, 2003.

Way, Peter. *Common Labor: Workers and the Digging of North American Canals*. Baltimore, MD: Johns Hopkins University Press, 1997.

Weisenburger, Steven. *Modern Medea: A Family Story of Slavery and Child-Murder from the Old South*. New York, NY: Hill & Wang, 1998.

Weiss, John McNish. *On Stony Ground: American Origins of the Black Refugees of the War of 1812 Settled in Nova Scotia and New Brunswick*. London: McNich & Weiss, 2006.

Whitacre, Paula Tarnapol. *A Civil Life in an Uncivil Time: Julia Wilbur's Struggle for Purpose*. Lincoln, NE: Potomac Books, 2017.

White, Shane, and Graham White. *Stylin': African American Expressive Culture, from Its Beginnings to the Zoot Suit*. Ithaca, NY: Cornell University Press, 1999.

Whitfield, Harvey Amani. *Blacks on the Border: The Black Refugees in British North America, 1815–1860*. Hanover, NH: University Press of New England, 2006.

———. *North to Bondage: Loyalist Slavery in the Maritimes*. Toronto, ON: UBC Press, 2016.

———. *The Problem of Slavery in Early Vermont, 1777–1810*. Barre, VT: Vermont Historical Society, 2014.

Williams, Heather Andrea. *Help Me to Find My People: The African American Search for Family Lost in Slavery*. Chapel Hill: University of North Carolina Press, 2016.

Williams, Lillian Serece. *Strangers in the Land of Paradise: Creation of an African-American Community in Buffalo, New York, 1900–1940*. Bloomington: Indiana University Press, 2000.

Wilson, Carol. *Freedom at Risk: The Kidnapping of Free Blacks in America, 1780–1865*. Lexington: University Press of Kentucky, 1994.

Wilson, Sheila M. *Taking the Waters: A History of the Spas of St. Catharines*. St. Catharines, ON: St. Catharines Historical Society, 1999.

Winks, Robin W. *The Blacks in Canada: A History*. Montreal: McGill-Queen's University Press, 1971.

———. *The Civil War Years: Canada and the United States*. Montreal: McGill-Queen's University Press, 1999.

Wolin, Sheldon, and Nicholas Xenos, eds. *Fugitive Democracy and Other Essays*. Princeton, NJ: Princeton University Press, 2016.

Wong, Edlie L. *Neither Fugitive nor Free: Atlantic Slavery, Freedom Suits, and the Legal Culture of Travel*. New York, NY: New York University Press, 2009.

Wyckoff, William. *The Developer's Frontier: The Making of the Western New York Landscape*. New Haven, CT: Yale University Press, 1988.

Yee, Shirley J. *Black Women Abolitionists: A Study in Activism, 1828–1860*. Knoxville, TN: University of Tennessee Press, 1992.

Yellin, Jean Fagan. *Harriet Jacobs: A Life*. New York, NY: Basic Civitas Books, 2004.

Ziegler, Philip. *King William IV*. New York, NY: Harper & Row, 1973.

Zilversmit, Arthur. *The First Emancipation: The Abolition of Slavery in the North*. Chicago: University of Chicago Press, 1967.

Articles

Adams, Tracey Lynn. "Making a Living: African Canadian Workers in London, Ontario, 1861–1901." *Labour/Le Travail* 67, no. 1 (2011): 9–43.

Adelman, Jeremy, and Stephen Aron. "From Borderlands to Borders: Empires, Nation-States, and the Peoples in Between in North American History." *American Historical Review* 104, no. 3 (June 1999): 814–41.

Agnew, John. "The Territorial Trap: The Geographical Assumptions of International Relations Theory." *Review of International Political Economy* 1, no. 1 (1994): 53–80.

Andrucki, Max J., and Jen Dickinson. "Rethinking Centers and Margins in Geography: Bodies, Life Course, and the Performance of Transnational Space." *Annals of the Association of American Geographers* 105, no. 1 (January 2015): 203–18.

Archuleta, Micki. "Life, Liberty, and the Pursuit of Happiness: A Fugitive Slave on Individual Rights and Community Responsibilities." *Nineteenth Century Studies* 19 (2005): 35–45.

Arenson, Adam. "Experience Rather than Imagination: Researching the Return Migration of African North Americans during the American Civil War and Reconstruction." *Journal of American Ethnic History* 32, no. 2 (Winter 2013): 73–77.

Arthurs, H. W. "Civil Liberties-Public Schools-Segregation of Negro Students." *Canadian Bar Review* 41 (Sept. 1963): 453–57.

Asaka, Ikuko. "'Our Brethren in the West Indies': Self-Emancipated People in Canada and the Antebellum Politics of Diaspora and Empire." *Journal of African History* 97, no. 3 (Summer 2012): 219–39.

Baker, H. Robert. "The Fugitive Slave Clause and the Antebellum Constitution." *Law and History Review* 30, no. 4 (Nov. 2012): 1133–74.

Barnes, Joseph W. "The Annexation of Charlotte." *Rochester History* 37, no. 1 (Jan. 1975): 1–28.

Barret, James R., and David Roediger. "Inbetween Peoples: Race, Nationality, and the 'New Immigrant' Working Class." *Journal of American Ethnic History* 16 (Spring 1997): 3–44.

Basinger, Scott J. "Regulating Slavery: Deck-Stacking and Credible Commitment in the Fugitive Slave Act of 1850." *Journal of Law, Economics, & Organization* 19, no. 2 (Oct. 2003): 307–42.

Baud, Michiel, and Willem Van Schendel. "Toward a Comparative History of Borderlands." *Journal of World History* 8 (Fall 1997): 211–42.

Bauer, Raymond A., and Alice H. Bauer. "Day to Day Resistance to Slavery." *Journal of Negro History* 37 (Oct. 1942): 388–419.

Bell, Howard H. "Expressions of Negro Militancy in the North, 1840–1860." *Journal of Negro History* 45, no. 1 (Jan. 1960): 11–20.

Best, Stephen, and Saidiya Hartman. "Fugitive Justice." *Representations* 92, no. 1 (Fall 2005): 1–15.

Black, Frederick R. "Bibliographic Essay; Benjamin Drew's Refuge and the Black Family." *Journal of Negro History* 57 (1972): 284–89.

Bonthius, Andrew. "The Patriot War of 1837–1838: Locofocoism with a Gun?" *Labour/Le Travail* 52 (Fall 2003): 9–43.

Boxill, Bernard R. "Frederick Douglass's Patriotism." *Journal of Ethics* 13, no. 4 (2009): 301–17.

Bristol, Douglas W., Jr. "Regional Identity, Barbers and the African American Tradition of Entrepreneurialism." *Southern Quarterly* 43, no. 2 (Winter 2006): 337–59.

Brooks, Elaine. "Massachusetts Anti-Slavery Society" *Journal of Negro History* 30, no. 3 (July 1945): 311–30.

Brown, Ira V. "Pennsylvania, 'Immediate Emancipation,' and the Birth of the American Anti-Slavery Society." *Pennsylvania History: A Journal of Mid-Atlantic Studies* 54, no. 3 (July 1987): 163–78.

Browne, Patrick T. J. "'To Defend Mr. Garrison': William Cooper Nell and the Personal Politics of Antislavery." *New England Quarterly* 70, no. 3 (Sept. 1997): 415–42.

Broyld, dann j. "The 'Dark Sheep' of the Atlantic World: Following the Transnational Trail of Blacks to Canada." In *Black Subjects: Race and Research in Africa and the Atlantic World,* ed. Benjamin Talton and Quincy T. Mills, 95–108. New York, NY: Palgrave MacMillan, 2011.

———. "Fannin' Flies and Tellin' Lies: Black Runaways and American Tales of Life in

British Canada Before the Civil War." *American Review of Canadian Studies* 44, no. 2 (April 2014): 169–86.

———. "Harriet Tubman: Transnationalism and the Land of a Queen in the Late Antebellum." *The Meridians: Feminism, Race, and Transnationalism,* special issue: "Harriet Tubman: A Legacy of Resistance," 12, no. 2 (Nov. 2014): 78–98.

———. Interview with Donna M. Ford, a descendent of Adam Nicholson, St. Catharines, Ontario, October 5, 2017.

———. "'Justice was Refused Me, I Resolved to Free Myself': John W. Lindsay Finding Elements of American Freedom's in British Canada, 1805–1876." *Ontario History* 99, no. 1 (Spring 2017): 27–59.

———. "The Power of Proximity: Frederick Douglass and His Transnational Relations with British Canada, 1847–1861." *Afro-Americans in New York Life and History Journal* 41, no. 2. (July 2020): 3–34.

———. "Rochester, New York: A Transnational Community for Blacks Prior to the Civil War." *Rochester History* 72, no. 2 (Fall 2010): 1–23.

———. "'A Success in Every Particular": British August First Commemorations in North America and the Black Quest for Unblemished Celebrations, 1834–1861." *American Review of Canadian Studies* 47, no. 4 (Dec. 2017): 335–56.

———. "The Underground Railroad as Afrofuturism: Enslaved Blacks Who Imagined A Future and Used Technology to Reach The 'Outer Spaces of Slavery.'" *Journal of Ethnic and Cultural Studies* 6, no. 3 (2019): 171–84.

Broyld, dann j., and Matthew Warshauer, "Harriet Tubman and Andrew Jackson: A Match Made in the U.S. Treasury Department," blog post to *Borealia* and *The Republic* (June 2016). https://earlycanadianhistory.ca/2016/06/13/harriet-tubman-and-andrew-jackson-a-match-made-in-the-u-s-treasury-department/.

Brunet-Jailly, Emmanuel. "A New Border? A Canadian Perspective of the Canada-US Border Post-9/11." *International Journal* 67, no. 4 (Autumn 2012): 963–74.

Bryant, James K., II. "African-Americans and Domestic Servants in Rochester's Third Ward Community." Rochester, NY: Landmark Society of Western New York.

———. "Biographical Sketches of Selected African-American Residents of Rochester, New York Third Ward, 1830–1860." Rochester, NY: Landmark Society of Western New York.

Brydon, Diana. 2001. "Black Canadas: Rethinking Canadian and Diasporic Cultural Studies." *Revista Canaria De Estudios Ingleses* 43 (Nov.): 101–17.

Butler, Nancy. "Black History in St. Catharines—What the Numbers Say." *Historical Society of St. Catharines Newsletter* (Feb. 1996): 1–8.

———. "Speech to Thorold and Beaver Dams Historical Society on Anthony Burns." St. Catharines, Ontario. January 29, 1996, 1–10.

———. "Three Black Businessmen in St. Catharines: Thomas Douglas, Aaron Young, and John W. Lindsay," St. Catharines Historical Society, St. Catharines, Ontario. February 6, 1997, 1–12. At St. Catharines Public Library Special Collections.

Cahill, Barry. "The Black Loyalist Myth in Atlantic Canada." *Acadiensis* 29, no. 1 (Autumn 1999): 76–87.

Cano, Gustavo. "Organizing Immigrant Communities in American Cities: Is this Transnationalism, or What?" Working Paper 103 Center for Comparative Immigration Studies University of California, San Diego, La Jolla, CA, August 2004.

Careless, J. M. S. "Mid-Victorian Liberalism in Central Canadian Newspapers, 1850–1867." *Canadian Historical Review* 31 (Sept. 1950): 221–36.

Carle, Susan D. "Race, Class, and Legal Ethics in the Early NAACP (1910–1920)." *Law and History Review* 20, no. 1 (Spring 2002): 97–146.

Carnochan, Janet. "Slave Rescue in Niagara Sixty Years Ago." *Niagara Historical Society* 2 (1897): 8–18.

Carp, Roger E. "The Limits of Reform: Labor and Discipline on the Erie Canal." *Journal of the Early Republic* 10, no. 2 (Summer 1990): 191–219.

Cassell, Frank A. "Slaves of the Chesapeake Bay Area and the War of 1812." *Journal of Negro History* 57, no. 2 (April 1972): 144–55.

Castle, Musette S. "A Survey of the History of African Americans in Rochester, New York, 1800–1860." *Afro-Americans in New York Life and History* 13, no. 2 (1989): 7–32.

Castronovo, Russ. "'As to Nation, I Belong to None': Ambivalence, Diaspora, and Frederick Douglass." *American Transcendental Quarterly* 9 (Sept. 1995): 245–55.

Clavin, Matthew. "A Second Haitian Revolution: John Brown, Toussaint Louverture, and the Making of the American Civil War." *Civil War History* 54, no. 2 (2008): 117–45.

Cobb, W. Montague. "A Short History of the Freedmen's Hospital." *Journal of the National Medical Association* 54 (May 1962): 273–89.

Coleman, Beth. "Race as Technology." *Camera Obscura* 24, no. 1 (2009): 177–207.

Collison, Gary. "'Loyal and Dutiful Subjects of her Gracious Majesty, Queen Victoria': Fugitive Slaves in Montreal, 1850–1866." *Quebec Studies* 19 (1994–95): 59–70.

Cooper, Afua. "Acts of Resistance: Black Men and Women Engage Slavery in Upper Canada." *Ontario History* 99 (2007): 5–17.

———. "The Fluid Frontier: Blacks and the Detroit River Region—A Focus on Henry Bibb." *Canadian Review of American Studies* 30, no. 2 (2000): 129–49.

———. "The Search for Mary Bibb, Black Woman Teacher in Nineteenth-Century Canada West." *Ontario History* 83, no. 1 (March 1991): 39–54.

Cooper, Frederick. "Elevating the Race: The Social Thought of Black Leaders, 1827–50." *American Quarterly* 24 (Dec. 1972): 604–25.

Cowan, Helen I. "Charles Williamson and the Southern Entrance to the Genesee Country." *New York History* 31 (1942): 260–74.

Culbertson, Graham. "Frederick Douglass's 'Our National Capital': Updating L'Enfant for an Era of Integration." *Journal of American Studies* 48, no. 4 (2014): 911–35.

Curry, Mary E. "Theodore Roosevelt Island: A Broken Link to Early Washington, DC, History." *Records of the Colombian Historical Society* 71/72: 14–33.

Darlington, James W. "Peopling the Post-Revolutionary New York Frontier." *New York History* 74 (Oct. 1993): 341–81.

Derreck, Tom. "In Bondage: Black Slavery Arrived in Canada in 1628 Aboard a Privateer's Ship. It would not be Abolished for More Than Two Centuries." *The Beaver* (Feb.–March 2003): 14–19.

De Santis, Vincent P. "The Republican Party and the Southern Negro, 1877–1897." *Journal of Negro History* 45, no. 2 (April 1960): 71–87.

Dunlop, R. G., W. L. Mackenzie, John H. Dunn, Adolphus Judah, W. R. Abbot, David Hollin, Malcolm Cameron, and J. Levy. "Records Illustrating the Condition of Refugees from Slavery in Upper Canada before 1860." *Journal of Negro History* 13 no. 2 (April 1928): 199–207.

Dunning, T. P. "The Canadian Rebellions of 1837–38: An Episode in Northern Borderland History." *Australasian Journal of American Studies* 14, no. 2 (Dec. 1995): 31–47.

Ellis, S. A. "A Brief History of the Public Schools of the City of Rochester." *Rochester Historical Society Publications* 1 (1892): 71–89.

Errington, Elizabeth Jane. "Women and Their Work in Upper Canada." *Canadian Historical Association,* no. 64 (2006): 1–43.

Este, David C. "Black Canadian Historical Writing 1970–2006: An Assessment." *Journal of Black Studies* 38, no. 3 (Jan. 2008): 388–406.

Eusebius, Mary Eusebius. "A Modern Moses: Harriet Tubman." *Journal of Negro Education* 19, no. 1 (Winter 1950): 16.

Faires, Nora. "Across the Border to Freedom: The International Underground Railroad Memorial and the Meanings of Migration." *Journal of American Ethnic History* 32, no. 2 (Winter 2013): 38–67.

———. "Going Across the River: Black Canadians and Detroit Before the Great Migration." *Citizenship Studies* 10 (Feb. 2006): 117–34.

Farley, Ena L. "The African American Presence in the History of Western New York." *Afro-Americans in New York Life and History* 14, no. 1 (Jan. 31, 1990): 27–89.

Farrell, John Kevin. "Schemes for the Transplanting of Refugee American Negroes from Upper Canada in the 1840s." *Ontario History* 52 (Dec. 1960): 245–49.

Farrisson, William E. "William Wells Brown in Buffalo." *Journal of Negro History* 39, no. 4 (Oct. 1954): 298–314.

Fee, Frank E., Jr. "To No One More Indebted: Frederick Douglass and Julia Griffiths, 1849–63." *Journalism History* 37, no. 1 (2011): 12–26.

Finkelman, Paul. "Prigg v. Pennsylvania and the Northern State Courts: Anti-Slavery Use of a Pro-Slavery Decision." *Civil War History* 25, no. 1 (1979): 5–35.

Fisch, Audrey A. "'Negrophilism' and British Nationalism: The Spectacle of the Black American Abolitionist." *Victorian Review* 19, no. 2 (Winter 1993): 20– 47.

Flood, Dawn Rae. "A Black Panther in the Great White North: Fred Hampton Visits Saskatchewan, 1969." *Journal for the Study of Radicalism* 8, no. 2 (Fall 2014): 21–50.

Foner, Eric. "Politics and Prejudice: The Free Soil Party and the Negro, 1849–1852." *Journal of Negro History* 50, no. 4 (Oct. 1965): 239–56.

Forbes, Ella. "'By My Own Right Arm': Redemptive Violence and the 1851 Christiana, Pennsylvania, Resistance." *Journal of Negro History* 83 (1998): 159–67.

Fox-Genovese, Elizabeth, and Eugene D. Genovese. "The Political Crisis of Social History: A Marxian Perspective." *Journal of Social History* 10 no. 2 (1976): 205–20.

Freehling, William W. "The Founding Fathers and Slavery." *The American Historical Review* 77, no. 1 (Feb. 1972): 81–93.

Friedman, Lawrence J. "The Gerrit Smith Circle: Abolitionism in the Burned-Over District." *Civil War History* 26 (Mar. 1980): 18–38.

Frost, Karolyn. "Communities of Resistance: African Canadians and African Americans in Antebellum Toronto." *Ontario History* 99 (2007): 44–63.

Furrow, Matthew. "Samuel Gridley Howe, the Black Population of Canada West, and the Racial Ideology of the 'Blueprint for Radical Reconstruction.'" *Journal of American History* 97, no. 2 (Sept. 2010): 344–70.

Gagan, David P. "Enumerator's Instruction for the Census of Canada 1852 and 1861." *Histoire Sociale/Social History* 8, no. 14 (Nov. 1974): 333–65.

Gallant, Sigrid Nicole. "Perspective on the Motives for the Migration of African-American to and from Ontario, Canada: From the Abolition of Slavery in Canada to the Abolition of Slavery in the United States." *Journal of Negro History* 86, no. 3 (Summer 2001): 391–408.

Gara, Larry. "Friends and the Underground Railroad." *Quaker History* 51, no. 1 (Spring 1962): 3–19.

———. "Propaganda Uses of the Underground Railway." *Mid-America* 34 (July 1952): 151–71.

———. "The Underground Railroad: Legend or Reality?" *Proceedings of the American Philosophical Society* 105, no. 3 (June 27, 1961): 334–39.

Geffert, Hannah N. "John Brown and His Black Allies: An Ignored Alliance." *Pennsylvania Magazine of History and Biography* 126, no. 4 (Oct. 2002): 591–610.

Gienapp, William E. "Nativism and the Creation of a Republican Majority in the North before the Civil War." *Journal of American History* 72, no. 3 (Dec. 1985): 529–59.

Gilbert, Emily. "Leaky Borders and Solid Citizens: Governing Security, Prosperity and Quality of Life in a North American Partnership." *Antipode* 39, no. 1 (2007): 77–98.

Goldstein, Leslie Friedman. "Violence as an Instrument for Social Change: The Views of Frederick Douglass, 1817–1895." *Journal of Negro History* 61, no. 1 (1976): 61–72.

Goodheart, Lawrence B. "The Chronicles of Kidnapping in New York: Resistance to the Fugitive Slave Law." *Afro-Americans in New York and History* 8 (Jan. 1984): 7–15.

Gordon, A. H. "The Struggle of the Negro Slaves for Physical Freedom." *Journal of Negro History* 13, no. 1 (Jan. 1928): 22–35.

Gosse, Van. "As a Nation, the English Are Our Friends': The Emergence of African American Politics in the British Atlantic World, 1772–1861." *American Historical Review* (Oct. 2008): 1003–28.

Grasso, Thomas X. "The Erie Canal and Rochester: Past, Present, and Future." *Rochester History* 72, no. 1 (Spring 2010): 1–26.

Gravely, William B. "The Dialectic of Double-Consciousness in Black American Freedom Celebrations, 1808–1863." *Journal of Negro History* 67, no. 4 (Winter 1982): 302–17.

Green, Ernest. "The Search for Salt in Upper Canada." *Ontario Historical Society Papers and Records* 26 (1930): 406–31.

———. "Upper Canada's Black Defenders." *Ontario Historical Society Papers and Records* 27 (1931): 365–91.

Greer, Allan. "1837–38: Rebellion Reconsidered." *Canadian Historical Review* 76, no 1 (1995): 1–18.

Gumbs, Alexis Pauline. "Prophecy in the Present Tense: Harriet Tubman, the Combahee Pilgrimage, and Dreams Coming True." *Meridians* 12, no. 2 (2014): 142–52.

Hall, Stephen G. "To Render the Private Public: William Still and the Selling of 'the Underground Rail Road.'" *Pennsylvania Magazine of History and Biography* 127, no. 1 (Jan. 2003): 35–55.

Hämäläinen, Pekka, and Samuel Truett. "On Borderlands." *Journal of American History* 98, no. 2 (2011): 338–61.

Hamilton, James Cleland. "John Brown in Canada." *Canadian Magazine* (Dec. 1894): 119–40.

Hammer-Croughton, Amy. "Anti-Slavery Days in Rochester." *Rochester Historical Society Publications* 14 (1936): 113–56.

Harris, Marc L. "The Meaning of Patriot: The Canadian Rebellion and American Republicanism, 1837–1839." *Michigan Historical Review* 23, no. 1 (Spring 1997): 33–69.

Hartgrove, W. B. "The Story of Josiah Henson." *Journal of Negro History* 3 (1918): 1–21.

Helleiner, Jane. "As Much American as a Canadian Can Be": Cross-Border Experience and Regional Identity Among Young Borderlanders in Canadian Niagara." *Anthropologica*. 51, no. 1 (2009): 225–38.

———. "Whiteness and Narratives of a Racialized Canada–US Border at Niagara." *Canadian Journal of Sociology / Cahiers canadiens de sociologie* 37, no. 2 (2012): 109–35.

Henbree, Michael F. "The Question of 'Begging': Fugitive Slave Relief in Canada, 1830–1865." *Civil War History* 37, no. 4 (Dec. 1991): 314–27.

Hepburn, Sharon A. Roger. "Following the North Star: Canada as a Haven for Nineteenth-Century American Blacks." *Michigan Historical Review* 25, no. 2 (Fall 1999): 91–126.

Herrendorf, Berthold, James A. Schmitz Jr., and Arilton Teixeira. "The Role of Transportation in U.S. Economic Development: 1840–1860." *International Economic Review* 53, no. 3 (Aug. 2012): 693–715.

Hesse, Barnor. "Escaping Liberty: Western Hegemony, Black Fugitivity." *Political Theory* 42, no. 3 (June 2014): 288–313.

Hickman, Jared. "Douglass Unbound." *Nineteenth-Century Literature* 68, no. 3 (2013): 323–62.

Hill, Daniel G. "Early Black Settlements in the Niagara Peninsula." In John Burtniak and Patricia G. Dirks, eds., *Immigration and Settlement in the Niagara Peninsula: Proceedings of the Third Annual Niagara Peninsula History Conference, Brock University, April 25–26, 1981,* 65–80. St. Catharines, ON: Brock University, 1981.

Hill, Marvin S. "The Rise of Mormonism in the Burned-over District: Another View." *New York History* 61 (Oct. 1931): 411–30.

Hite, Roger W. "Voice of a Fugitive: Henry Bibb and Ante-bellum Black Separatism." *Journal of Black Studies* 4 no. 3 (March 1974): 269–84.

Hughes, Alan. "The Evolution of the Municipality of St. Catharines." *Newsletter of the Historical Society of St. Catharines* (Sept. 2008): 1–7.

Humez, Jean M. "In Search of Harriet Tubman's Spiritual Autobiography." *NWSA Journal* 5, no. 2 (Summer 1993): 162–82.

Hungerford, Edward. "Early Railroads of New York." *New York History* 13, no. 1 (Jan. 1932): 75–89.

Johnson, Walter. "On Agency." *Journal of Social History* 37 (Fall 2003): 113–24.

Jones, Angela. "The Niagara Movement, 1905–1910: A Revisionist Approach to the Social History of the Civil Rights Movement." *Journal of Historical Sociology* 23, no. 3 (2010): 453–500.

Kang, Nancy. "'As If I Had Entered a Paradise': Fugitive Slave Narratives and Cross-Border Literary History." *African American Review* 39, no. 3 (Fall 2005): 431–57.

Kearney, Michael. "Borders and Boundaries of State and Self at the End of Empire." *Journal of Historical Sociology* 4, no. 1 (March 1991): 52–74.

Kelley, Sean. "'Mexico in His Head': Slavery and the Texas-Mexico Border, 1810–1860." *Journal of Social History* 37, no. 3 (Spring 2004): 709–23.

Kelly, Wayne E. "Canada's Black Defenders: Former Slaves Answered the Call to Arms." *Beaver* 77 (April–May 1977): 31–34.

Ker, Rev. Robert, ed. *Marriage Records: St. George's Parish Church, 1841–1891.* St. Catharines, ON: Historic & Centenary Review, 1998.

Kerber, Linda. "Abolitionists and Amalgamators: The New York City Race Riots of 1834." *New York History* 48 (1967): 28–39.

Keshen, Jeff. "Cloak and Dagger: Canada West's Secret Police, 1864–1867." *Ontario History* 79, no. 4 (Dec. 1987): 353–87.

Kimmel, Janice Martz. "Break Your Chains and Fly for Freedom." *Michigan History* 80 (1996): 20–27.

Kirkby, Ryan J. "The Revolution Will Not Be Televised: Community Activism and the Black Panther Party, 1966–1971." *Canadian Review of American Studies* 41, no. 1 (2011): 25–62.

Klingman, Peter D., and David T. Geithman. "Negro Dissidence and the Republican Party, 1864–1872." *Phylon* 40, no. 2 (2nd Qtr. 1979): 173–82.

Landon, Fred. "Abolitionist Interest in Upper Canada." *Ontario History* 44 (Oct. 1952): 165–77.

———. "The Anderson Fugitive Case." *Journal of Negro History* 7, no. 3. (July 1922): 233–42.

———. "Anthony Burns in Canada." *Ontario Historical Society Papers and Reports and Proceedings* (1923): 17–21.

———. "The Anti-Slavery Society of Canada." *Journal of Negro History* 4 (1919): 33–40.

———. "Canada's Part in Freeing the Slaves." *Ontario Historical Society Papers and Records* 17 (1919): 74–78.

———. "The Canadian Anti-Slavery Group Before the Civil War." *University Magazine* (Dec. 1918): 540–47.

———. "Canadian Negroes and the John Brown Raid." *Journal of Negro History* 6, no. 2 (April 1921): 174–82.

———. "Canadian Negroes and the Rebellion of 1837." *Journal of Negro History* 7, no 4 (Oct. 1922): 377–79.

———. "From Chatham to Harpers Ferry." *Canadian Magazine* 13 (1919): 441–48.

———. "Fugitive Slaves in London before 1860." *London and Middlesex Historical Transactions* 10 (1919): 25–38.

———. "Henry Bibb, A Colonizer." *Journal of Negro History* 5, no. 4 (Oct. 1920): 437–47.

———. "The Negro Migration to Canada after the Passing of the Fugitive Slave Act." *Journal of Negro History* 5, no. 1 (Jan. 1920): 22–36.

———. "A Pioneer Abolitionist in Upper Canada." *Ontario History* 52 (June 1960): 77–83.

———. "The Work of the American Missionary Association among the Negro Refugees in Canada West, 1848–64." *Ontario Historical Society Papers and Records* 21 (1924): 198–205.

Larkin, Janet. "The Oswego Canal: A Connecting Link Between the United States and Canada, 1819–1837." *Ontario History* 103, no. 1 (Spring 2011): 23–41.

Larson, Kate C. "Racing for Freedom: Harriet Tubman's Underground Railroad Network through New York." *Afro-Americans in New York Life and History* 36 (Jan. 2012): 7–33.

Law, Howard. "'Self-Reliance Is the True Road to Independence': Ideology and the Ex-slave in Buxton and Chatham." *Ontario History* 77, no. 2 (June 1985): 107–21.

Lemak, Jennifer. "Advancement Comes Slowly: African American Employment in Rochester, New York, During the Great Migration." *New York History* 92, no. 1/2 (Winter/Spring 2011): 78–98.

Lewis, Earl. "To Turn as on a Pivot: Writing African Americans into a History of Overlapping Diasporas." *American Historical Review* 100 (June 1995): 765–87.

Lindsay, Arnett G. "Diplomatic Relations between the United States and Great Britain Bearing on the Return of Negro Slaves." *Journal of Negro History* 5 (Oct. 1920): 391–419.

Lutz, Alma. "Susan B. Anthony and John Brown." *Rochester History* 15, no. 3 (July 1953): 1–16.

MacDonald, Cheryl. "Mary Ann Shadd in Canada: Last Stop on the Underground Railroad." *The Beaver* (Feb./March 1990): 32–38.

MacKay, R. A. "The Political Ideas of William Lyon Mackenzie." *Canadian Journal of Economics and Political Science* 3, no. 1 (Feb. 1937): 1–22.

Maginnes, David R. "The Case of the Court House Rioters in the Rendition of the Fugitive Slave Anthony Burns, 1854." *Journal of Negro History* 56, no.1 (Jan. 1971): 31–42.

Mañón, Tianna, and Jake Clapp. "Douglass's Rochester: Rochester Likes to Claim Frederick Douglass as Its Own: Is the Community Living Up to His Legacy?" *City Paper* 47, no. 24, February 14, 2018.

Marks, Lynne. "Railing, Tattling and General Humour." *Canadian Historical Review* 81, no. 3 (Sept. 2000): 380–473.

Marsh, Ruth, and Dorothy S. Truesdale. "War on Lake Ontario: 1812–1815." *Rochester History* 4, no. 4 (Oct. 1942): 1–24.

Mason, Matthew. "The Battle of the Slaveholding Liberators: Great Britain, the United States, and Slavery in the Early Nineteenth Century." *William and Mary Quarterly*, Third Series 59, no. 3 (July 2002): 665–96.

McDaniel, W. Caleb. "The Fourth and the First: Abolitionist Holidays, Respectability, and Radical Interracial Reform." *American Quarterly* 57, no. 1 (March 2005): 129–51.

McGreevy, Patrick. "The End of America: The Beginning of Canada." *Canadian Geographer* 32, no. 4 (1989): 307–18.

McGregor, Laura A. "The Early History of Rochester Public Schools, 1813–1850." *Rochester Historical Society Publications* 13 (1939): 37–73.

McKelvey, Blake, "Colonel Nathaniel Rochester." *Rochester History* 24, no. 1 (Jan. 1962): 1–26.

———. "On the Educational Frontier." *Rochester Historical Society Publications* 17 (1939): 1–36.

———. "The History of Public Health in Rochester, New York." *Rochester History* 18, no. 3 (July 1956): 1–24.

———. "Lights and Shadows Local Negro History." *Rochester History* 21, no. 4 (Oct. 1959): 1–27.

———. "Railroads in Rochester's History." *Rochester History* 30, no. 4 (Oct. 1968): 1–26.

———. "Rochester and the Erie Canal." *Rochester History* 11, nos. 3 and 4 (Fall 1949): 1–24.

———. "Rochester's Ethnic Transformations." *Rochester History* 25, no. 3 (July 1963): 1–24.

McNamara, Robert F. "Charles Carroll of Belle Vue Co-Founder of Rochester." *Rochester History* 42, no. 4 (Oct. 1980): 1–28.

Middleton, Stephen. "The Fugitive Slave Crisis in Cincinnati, 1850–1860: Resistance, Enforcement, and Black Refugees." *Journal of Negro History* 72, no.1/2 (Winter 1987): 20–32.

Murphy, Angela. "'It Outlaws Me, and I Outlaw It': Resistance to the Fugitive Slave Law in Syracuse, New York." *Afro-Americans in New York Life History* 28, no. 1 (Jan. 2004): 43–72.

Murray, Alexander L. "The Extradition of Fugitive Slaves from Canada: A Revaluation." *Canadian Historical Review* 43, no. 4 (1962): 298–313.

Murray, David. "Hands across the Border: The Abortive Extradition of Solomon Moesby." *Canadian Historical Review of American Studies* 30 (2000): 186–209.

Mutunhu, Tendai. "John W. Jones: Underground Railroad Station-Master." *Negro History Bulletin* (March–April 1978): 814–18.

Myers, John L. "American Antislavery Society Agents and the Free Negro, 1833–1838." *Journal of Negro History* 52, no. 3 (July 1967): 200–219.

———. "The Beginning of Anti-Slavery Agencies in New York State." *New York History* 43, no. 2 (April 1962): 149–81.

———. "The Major Effort of National Anti-Slavery Agents in New York State, 1836–1837." *New York History* 46, no. 2 (April 1965): 162–86.

Newman, David. "The Lines that Continue to Separate Us: Borders in Our 'Borderless' World." *Progress in Human Geography* 30, no. 2 (2006): 143–61.

Nichol, Heather. "Resiliency of Change? The Contemporary Canada–U.S. Border." *Geopolitics* 10 (2005): 767–90.

Nielsen, Cynthia R. "Resistance Is Not Futile: Frederick Douglass on Panoptic Plantations and Un-making of Docile Bodies and Enslaved Souls." *Philosophy and Literature* 35, no. 2 (2011): 251–68.

Nolte, Marilyn S., Victoria Sandwick Schmitt, and Christine L. Ridarsky. "'We Called Her Anna': Nathaniel Rochester and Slavery in the Genesee Country." *Rochester History* 71, no. 1 (Spring 2009): 1–24.

Okur, Nilgun Anadolu. "Underground Railroad in Philadelphia, 1830–1860." *Journal of Black Studies* 25, no. 5 (May 1995): 537–57.

Olney, James. "The Founding Fathers—Frederick Douglass and Booker T. Washington; or, the Idea of Democracy and a Tradition of African-American Autobiography." *Amerikastudies/American Studies* 35 (1990): 281–96.

Osborn, Ronald. "William Lloyd Garrison and the United States Constitution: The Political Evolution of an American Radical." *Journal of Law and Religion* 24, no. 1 (2008/2009): 65–88.

Paquette, Robert L. "Social History Update: Slave Resistance and Social History." *Journal of Social History* 24, no. 3 (Spring 1991): 681–85.

Parker, Bradley. "Toward an Understanding of Borderland Processes." *American Antiquity* 71, no. 1 (Jan. 2006): 77–100.

Pearson, Ralph L. "A Quantitative Approach to Buffalo's Black Population of 1860." *Afro-Americans in New York Life and History* 12 (July 1988): 19–34.

Pease, Jane H., and William H. Pease. "Confrontation and Abolition in the 1850s." *Journal of American History* 58, no. 4 (March 1972): 923–37.

———. "Negro Conventions and the Problem of Black Leadership." *Journal of Black Studies* 2, no. 1 (Sept. 1971): 29–44.

Phillips, Betty S. "Upstate and Downstate in New York." *Names* 31 (1983): 41–50.

Pierce, Preston E. "Liberian Dreams, West African Nightmare: The Life of Henry W. Johnson, Part One." *Rochester History* 67, no. 4 (Fall 2004): 1–24.

Pitt, Steve. "To Stand and Fight Together." *Rotunda* 29, no. 3 (Spring 1997): 11.

Pond, Charles F. "History of the Third Ward." *Publications of the Rochester Historical Society* 1 (1922): 71–81.

Preston, E. Delorus. "The Genesis of the Underground Railroad." *Journal of Negro History* 18, no. 2 (April 1933): 340–58.

Prichard, Linda K. "The Burned-Over District Reconsidered: A Portent of Evolving Religious Pluralism in the United States." *Social Science History* 8 (Summer 1984): 243–65.

Quarles, Benjamin. "The Breach between Douglass and Garrison." *Journal of Negro History* 23, no. 2 (April 1938): 144–54.

———. "Frederick Douglass and the Woman's Rights Movement." *Journal of Negro History* 25, no. 1 (Jan. 1940): 35–44.

Raible, Christopher. "'A Journey Undertaken Under Peculiar Circumstances': The Perilous Escape of William Lyon Mackenzie, December 7 to 11, 1837." *Ontario History* 108, no. 2 (Autumn 2016): 131–55.

Reinders, Robert C. "Anglo-Canadian Abolitionism: The John Anderson Fugitive Case, 1860–61." *Renaissance and Modern Studies* 19 (1975): 72–97.

Rhodes, Jane. "The Contestation over National Identity: Nineteenth-Century Black Americans in Canada." *Canadian Review of American Studies* 30 (2000): 175–86.

Richardson, Jean. "Buffalo's Antebellum African American Community and the Fugitive Slave Law of 1850." *Afro-Americans in New York Life and History* 27, no. 2 (July 2003): 29–45.

Riddell, William Renwick. "Le Code Noir." *Journal of Negro History* 10, no. 3 (1925): 321–29.

———. "The Fugitive Slave in Upper Canada." *Journal of Negro History* 5, no. 3 (July 1920): 340–58.

———. "The Slave in Upper Canada." *Journal of Negro History* 4, no. 4 (Oct. 1919): 372–95.

Roach, Monique Patenaude. "The Rescue of William 'Jerry' Henry: Antislavery and Racism in the Burned-Over District." *New York History* 82, no. 2 (Spring 2001): 135–54.

Roemer, Lillian. "The Genesee River During the War of 1812." *Rochester History* 53, no. 4 (Fall 1991): 1–30.

Rogers, Melvin L. "David Walker and the Political Power of Appeal." *Political Theory* 43, no. 2 (April 2015): 208–33.

Rogers, Richard Lee. "The Urban Threshold and the Second Great Awakening: Revivalism in New York State, 1825–1835." *Journal for the Scientific Study of Religion* 49, no. 4 (Dec. 2010): 694–709.

Rosenberg-Naparsteck, Ruth. "A Growing Agitation: Rochester Before, During, and After the Civil War." *Rochester History* 46, nos. 1 & 2 (Jan. & April 1984): 1–40. https://library web.org/~rochhist/v46_1984/v46i1-2.pdf.

Rowe, David L. "A New Perspective on the Burned-over District: The Millerites in Upstate New York." *Church History* 47 (Dec. 1978): 408–20.

Rudwick, Elliott M. "The Niagara Movement." *Journal of Negro History* 42, no. 3 (July 1957): 177–200.

Rupwate, Rt. Rev. Dr. Daniel D. "A Historical Significance of the 'Salem Chapel' with Reference to the Underground Railroad Movement and A Tribute to Harriet Tubman." St. Catharines, ON: Rt. Rev. Dr. Daniel D. Rupwate, Self-published, 2006.

Russell, Hilary. "Underground Railroad Activists in Washington, DC." *Washington History* 13, no. 2 (Fall/Winter 2001/2002): 28–49.

Sayenga, Donald. "Wired Together." *Wire Journal Internal* 40, no. 10. (Oct. 2007): 72–80.

Schaetzke, E. Anne. "Slavery in the Genesee Country (also known as Ontario County) 1789 to 1827." *Afro-Americans in New York Life and History* 22, no. 1 (Jan. 1998): 7–40.

Scheiber, Harry N., and Stephen Salsbury. "Reflections on George Rogers Taylor's 'The Transportation Revolution, 1815–1860': A Twenty-Five Year Retrospect." *Business History Review* 51, no. 1 (Spring 1977): 79–89.

Schermerhorn, Calvin. "Rambles of a Runaway from Southern Slavery: The Freedom Narrative of Henry Goings." *The Virginia Magazine of History and Biography* 119, no. 4 (2011): 314–49.

Schmitt, Victoria Sandwick. "Rochester's Frederick Douglass—Part One." *Rochester History* 67, no. 3 (Summer 2005): 1–28.

———. "Rochester's Frederick Douglass—Part Two." *Rochester History* 67, no. 4. (Fall 2005): 1–32.

Schwalm, Leslie Ann. "'Overrun with Free Negroes': Emancipation and Wartime Migration in the Upper Midwest." *Civil War History* 50, no. 2 (2004): 145–74.

Schweninger, Loren. "A Fugitive Negro in the Promised Land: James Rapier in Canada, 1856–1864." *Ontario History* 67 (1975): 94–104.

Sernett, Milton C. "'A Citizen of No Mean City': Jermain W. Loguen and the Antislavery Reputation of Syracuse." *Syracuse University Library Associates Courier* 22 (Fall 1987): 33–55.

———. "First Honor: Oneida Institute's Role in the Fight Against American Racism and Slavery." *New York History* 66, no. 2 (April 1985): 101–22.

———. "On Freedom's Threshold: The African American Presence in Central New York, 1760–1940." *Afro-American in New York Life and History* 19 (Jan. 1995): 43–91.

Shadd, Adrienne. "Chloe Cooley and the 1793 Act to Limit Slavery in Upper Canada" (unpublished report to Ontario Heritage Trust, 2007).

Shortridge, William P. "The Canadian-American Frontier during the Rebellions of 1837–1838." *Canadian Historical Review* 7 (March 1926): 13–26.

Silverman, Jason H. "The American Fugitive Slave in Canada: Myth and Realities." *Southern Studies* 19 (Fall 1980): 215–27.

———. "Monarchial Liberty and Republican Slavery: West Indies Emancipation Celebrations in Upstate New York and Canada West." *Afro-Americans in New York Life History* 10 (Jan. 1986): 7–18.

———. "Revisiting Black Canada: Notes on Recent Literature." *Journal of Negro History* 68, no. 1 (Winter 1983): 93–94.

Small, Shirley, and Esmeralda M. A. Thornhill. "Harambec! Quebec Black Women Pulling Together." *Journal of Black Studies* 38, no. 3 (Jan. 2008): 427–42.

Smith, Virginia Jeffery. "Reminiscences of the Third Ward." Paper presented to the Rochester Historical Society, April 1945.

Sokolow, Jayme A. "The Jerry McHenry Rescue and the Growth of Northern Antislavery Sentiment during the 1850s." *Journal of American Studies* 16, no. 3 (Dec. 1982): 427–45.

Sterngass, Jon. "African American Workers and Southern Visitors at Antebellum Saratoga Springs." *American Nineteenth Century History* 2, no. 2 (2001): 35–59.

Struble, Joseph P. "Captured Images: The Daguerreian Years in Rochester, 1840 to 1860." *Rochester History* 62, no. 1 (2000): 1–24.

Strum, Harvey. "To Feed the Hungry: Rochester and Irish Famine Relief." *Rochester History* 68, no. 3 (Summer 2006): 1–22.

Talman, James J. "The Newspaper Press of Canada West, 1850–1860." *Transactions of the Royal Society of Canada,* 2d series, 33 (1939): 117–31.

Tate, Gayle T. "The Jerry McHenry Recuse and the Growth of Northern Antislavery Sentiment During the 1850s." *Journal of Black Studies* 28, no. 6 (July 1998): 764–82.

Thompson, Priscilla. "Harriet Tubman, Thomas Garrett, and the Underground Railroad." *Delaware History* 22 (Spring–Summer 1986): 1–21.

Thornhill, Esmeralda M. A. "So Seldom for Us, So Often Against Us: Blacks and Law in Canada." *Blacks in Canada: Retrospects, Introspects, Prospects* 38, no. 3 (Jan. 2008): 317–37.

Tiffany, Orrin Edward. "The Relations of the United States to the Rebellion of 1837–1838." *Buffalo Historical Society Publication* 8 (1905): 7–147.

Tillery, Tyrone. "The Inevitability of the Douglass-Garrison Conflict." *Phylon* 37, no. 2 (2nd Qtr. 1976): 137–49.

Truesdale, Dorothy S., ed. "American Travel Accounts of Early Rochester." *Rochester History* 16, no. 2 (April 1954): 1–24.

Voss-Hubbard, Mark. "The Political Culture of Emancipation: Morality, Politics, and the State in Garrisonian Abolitionism, 1854–1863." *Journal of American Studies* 29, no. 2 (Aug. 1995): 159–84.

Waldstreicher, David. "Reading the Runaways: Self-Fashioning, Print Culture, and Confidence in Slavery in the Eighteenth-Century Mid-Atlantic. *William and Mary Quarterly* 56, no. 2 (June 2006): 142–60.

Watkins, Ralph. "A Reappraisal of the Role of Voluntary Associations in the African American Community." *Afro-Americans in New York Life and History* 14, no. 2 (July 1990): 51–60.

———. "A Survey of African American Presence in the History of Downstate New York Area." *Afro-Americans in New York Life and History* 15 (Jan. 1991): 53–79.

Wayne, Michael. "The Black Population of Canada West on the Eve of the American Civil War. A Reassessment Based on the Manuscript Census of 1861." *Histoire Sociale/Social History* 28, no. 56 (Nov. 1995): 465–81.

Weber, David J. "The Spanish Borderlands of North America: A Historiography." *OHA Magazine of History* 14, no. 4 (Summer 2000): 5–11.

Wellman, Judith. "Crossing Over Cross: Whitney Cross's *Burned-over District* as Social History." *Reviews in American History* 17 (March 1989): 159–74.

Wesley, Charles. "The Negroes of New York in the Emancipation Movement." *Journal of Negro History* 24, no. 1 (Jan. 1969): 65–103.

White, Arthur O. "The Black Movement Against Jim Crow Education in Buffalo, New York, 1800–1900." *Phylon* 30, no. 4 (4th Qtr. 1969): 375–93.

Whitfield, Harvey Amani. "The Development of Black Refugee Identity in Nova Scotia, 1813–1850." *Left History* 10 (Fall 2005): 9–31.

———. "We Can Do as We Like Here": An Analysis of Self-Assertion and Agency Among Black Refugees in Halifax, Nova Scotia, 1813–1821." *Acadiensis* 32, no. 1 (Autumn 2002): 29–49.

———. "White Archives, Black Fragments: The Study of Enslaved Black People in the Maritimes." *The Canadian Historical Review* 101, no. 3 (Sept. 2020): 323–45.

Widdis, Randy William. "Borders, Borderlands and Canadian Identity: A Canadian Perspective." *International Journal of Canadian Studies* 15 (Spring 1997): 49–66.

Wilson, Hiram, and Wm. H. Bishop. "Letters of Hiram Wilson to Miss Hannah Gray." *Journal of Negro History* 14, no. 3 (1929): 344–50.

Wilson, Ivy G. "On Native Ground: Transnationalism, Frederick Douglass, and 'The Heroic Slave.'" *PMLA: Publications of the Modern Language Association of America* 121, no. 2 (2006): 435–68.

Winks, Robin W. "The Canadian Negro: A Historical Assessment: The Problem of Identity: Part I." *Journal of Negro History* 53, no. 4 (Oct. 1968): 283–300.

———. "The Canadian Negro: A Historical Assessment: The Problem of Identity: Part II." *Journal of Negro History* 54, no. 1 (Jan. 1969): 1–18.

Winsboro, Irwin D. S., and Joe Knetsch. "Florida Slaves, the 'Saltwater Railroad' to the Bahamas, and Anglo-American Diplomacy." *Journal of Southern History* 79 (Feb. 2013): 51–78.

Yanuck, Julius. "The Garner Fugitive Slave Case." *Mississippi Valley Historical Review* 40, no. 1 (1953): 47–66.

Yee, Shirley J. "Finding a Place: Mary Ann Shadd Clay and the Dilemmas of Black Migration to Canada, 1850–1870." *Frontiers: A Journal of Women's Studies* 18, no. 3 (1997): 1–16.

———. "Gender Ideology and Black Women as Community-Builders in Ontario, 1850–70." *Canadian Historical Review* 75 (1995): 53–73.

Yeo, Debra Ann. "Niagara's Freedom Trail." *What's Up Niagara Magazine* (Oct. 1993): 10–16.

Zorn, Roman J. "An Arkansas Fugitive Slave Incident and Its International Repercussions." *The Arkansas Historical Quarterly* 16, no. 2 (Summer 1957): 139–49.

———. "Criminal Extradition Menaces the Canadian Haven for Fugitive Slaves, 1841–1861." *Canadian Historical Review* 38 (Dec. 1957): 284–94.

Master's Theses and Doctoral Dissertations

Baglier, Janet Dorothy. "The Niagara Frontier: Society and Economy in Western New York and Upper Canada." PhD diss., State University of Buffalo, 1993.

Brooks, Catherine L. "Negro Colonization Projects and Settlements in Canada Until 1865." MA thesis, Howard University, 1945.

Broyld, Daniel J. "Borderland Blacks: Rochester, New York, and St. Catharines, Ontario, 1850–1860." PhD diss., Howard University, 2011.

Carlesimo, Peter. "The Refugee Home Society: Its Origin, Operation, and Results, 1851–1876." MA thesis, University of Windsor, 1973.

Cohen, Gretchen W. "Clip Not Her Wings: Female Abolitionists in Rochester, New York, 1838–1868." MA thesis, City College of New York, 1994.

Cooper, Afua Ava Pamela. "Doing Battle in Freedom's Cause: Henry Bibb, Abolitionism, Race Uplift, and Black Manhood, 1842–1854." PhD diss., University of Toronto, 2000.

Dorn, Adelaide Elizabeth. "A History of the Antislavery Movement in Rochester and Vicinity." MA thesis, University of Buffalo, 1932.

Karlsson, Ann-Marie Elisabet. "Signs in Blood: Racial Violence and Antebellum Narratives of Resistance." PhD diss., University of California, Berkeley, 1995.

Krauter, Joseph F. "Civil Liberties and the Canadian Minorities." PhD diss., University of Illinois, 1968.

Jackson, Kellie Carter. "Force and Freedom: Black Abolitionists and the Politics of Violence, 1850–1860." PhD diss., Columbia University, 2010.

Johnson, Lulu Merle. "The Negro in Canada, Slave and Free." MA thesis, University of Iowa, 1930.

Landon, Fred. "The Relation of Canada to the Anti-Slavery and Abolition Movements in the United States." MA thesis, University of Western Ontario, 1919.

———. "Unwelcome Guests: American Fugitive Slaves in Canada, 1830–1860." PhD diss., University of Kentucky, 1981.

McKelvey, Kay Najiyyah. "Early Black Dorchester, 1776–1870: A History of the Struggle of African-Americans in Dorchester County, Maryland, to Be Free to Make Their Own Choices." PhD diss., University of Maryland, 1991.

Murray, Alexander L. "Canada and the Anglo-American Anti-Slavery Movement: A Study in International Philanthropy." PhD diss., University of Pennsylvania, 1960.

Nenno, Beverly Hausser. "The Impact of American Slavery on Black Experience in Raleigh Township, Canada-West From 1850–1872." PhD diss., State University of New York at Buffalo, 1997.

Patenaud, Monique. "Bound by Pride and Prejudice: Black Life in Frederick Douglass' New York." PhD diss., University of Rochester, 2012.

Pemberton, Ian Cleghorn. "The Anti-Slavery Society of Canada." MA thesis, University of Toronto, 1967.

Rhodes, Jane. "Breaking the Editorial Ice: Mary Ann Shadd Cary and the *Provincial Freeman*." PhD diss., University of North Carolina at Chapel Hill, 1992.

Scroggins, Marvin Keith. "Educational Leadership Modalities of Afrocentric Alliance Building: The Political Theory of Henry Highland Garnet." EdD diss., School of Intercultural Studies, Biola University, 1993.

Sheffield, Wilfred. "Background and Development of Negro Baptists in Ontario." Bachelor of Divinity, McMaster University, 1952.

Simpson, Donald G. "Negroes in Ontario from the Early Times to 1870." PhD diss., University of Western Ontario, 1971.

Walton, Jonathan. "Blacks in Buxton and Chatham, 1830–1890: Did the 49th Parallel Make a Difference?" PhD diss., Princeton University, 1979.

Wiggins, William H., Jr. "Free at Last! A Study of Afro-American Emancipation Day Celebrations." PhD diss., Indiana University, 1974.

Wilkins, Joe Bassette, Jr. "Window on Freedom: The South's Response to the Emancipation of the Slaves in the British West Indies, 1833–1861." PhD diss., University of South Carolina, 1977.

Wilson, Ruth Danenhower. "Canadian Colonies of Descendants of American Slaves." MA thesis, New York University, 1948.

Yanuck, Julius. "The Fugitive Slave Law and the Constitution." PhD diss., Columbia University, 1953.

Index